International Technic

**IBM Framework for
and Design Overview**

MW01518894

18-00

>n,

September 2001

First Edition (September 2001)

Comments may be addressed to:
IBM Corporation, International Technical Support Organization
Dept. JLU Building 107-2
3605 Highway 52N
Rochester, Minnesota 55901-7829

8.3.4 Data warehouse modeling and construction. 385
8.3.5 Products provided by other companies 388
8.4 BI solution 391
8.4.1 Solution overview. 391
8.4.2 Static application design 394
8.4.3 Selected components 396

Chapter 9. Performance 397
9.1 Bottlenecks 397
9.1.1 Client and network. 398
9.1.2 Server 398
9.2 Technologies. 398
9.2.1 Network 398
9.2.2 Servers 400
9.2.3 Load balancing 404
9.2.4 Security. 405
9.3 Products 409
9.3.1 WebSphere Edge Server 409
9.3.2 Andrew File System (AFS). 416
9.3.3 Workload management in WebSphere Application Server 418

Appendix A. Test tips 421
A.1 The test format. 421
A.2 The test questions 422
A.3 Sample Test 811: Designing IBM e-business solutions 423
A.4 Sample Test 811: Answers 425
A.5 Sample Test 812: e-business Core Knowledge 426
A.6 Sample Test 812: Answers 429

Appendix B. Competitive information 431
B.1 Microsoft .NET architecture overview 431
B.1.1 Microsoft .NET products and services 432
B.1.2 .NET benefits 433
B.1.3 Architecture comparison 434
B.1.4 Summary 437
B.2 Sun Microsystems e-business overview 438
B.3 Oracle e-business overview. 440
B.4 BEA WebLogic and IBM WebSphere software comparison 442
B.4.1 BEA and IBM e-business product and technology comparison 442
B.4.2 WebSphere software platform summary 444

Appendix C. Special notices 445

Appendix D. Related publications 449
D.1 IBM Redbooks 449
D.2 Referenced Web sites 449
D.3 How to get IBM Redbooks 450
D.4 IBM Redbooks collections 450

How to get IBM Redbooks 451
IBM Redbooks fax order form 452

Index 453

IBM Redbooks review 463

6.1.2 E-commerce operations 31
6.2 Problem space for an e-commerce solution .31
6.3 Technology requirements for an e-commerce solution 31
6.3.1 Personalization 31
6.3.2 Secure payment transactions 31
6.3.3 Customer management 32
6.3.4 Order tracking 32
6.3.5 Catalog management 32
6.3.6 Scalability 32
6.3.7 Availability 32
6.3.8 Performance 32
6.3.9 Searching 32
6.4 Products for the e-commerce solution 32
6.4.1 WebSphere Commerce Suite 32
6.5 Decision blocks for an e-commerce solution 32
6.5.1 Application server 32
6.5.2 Connectors 32
6.5.3 Enterprise application and data 33
6.5.4 Security 33
6.5.5 Performance 33
6.6 E-commerce solution 33
6.6.1 Solution overview 33
6.6.2 Static and dynamic application design .33
6.6.3 Dynamic application security 33
6.6.4 WebSphere Commerce Suite solution strengths and weaknesses . .33

Chapter 7. Business integration 335
7.1 Supplier integration 336
7.1.1 Overview of the problem space 336
7.1.2 Requirements for the new e-business solution 337
7.1.3 Design block decisions 341
7.1.4 Products for the solution 345
7.1.5 Solution 348
7.1.6 Summary 352
7.2 Supplier integration with workflow 352
7.2.1 Overview of the problem space 353
7.2.2 Requirements for the new e-business solution 354
7.2.3 Design block decisions 356
7.2.4 Products overview for the solution 359
7.2.5 Dynamic view of the automated business process 360
7.2.6 Strengths and weaknesses of the solution using IBM products 362

Chapter 8. Business Intelligence 365
8.1 Overview of Business Intelligence 366
8.1.1 What Business Intelligence is 366
8.1.2 Main BI terms 367
8.1.3 Business Intelligence implementations 370
8.2 Business Intelligence solution requirements 374
8.2.1 Business Intelligence solution architecture requirements 375
8.3 Product overview for Business Intelligence solutions 382
8.3.1 Business Intelligence applications 382
8.3.2 Business Intelligence tools 383
8.3.3 Access enablers 385

Preface

In a few short years, e-business has gone from a simple concept to an undeniable reality, and for good reason. It works for everyone: consumers, businesses, and governments. The primary values of e-business, such as cost savings, revenue growth, and customer satisfaction, are proving to be only the tip of the iceberg. Having realized the benefit of Web-enabling individual business processes, many companies now seek further Return On Investment (ROI) by integrating new and existing e-business applications and technologies. The key to their success is to find a way to give customers what they want without the expense of traditional business operations.

This IBM Redbook explains the IBM approach to creating e-business solutions. This book targets I/T specialists who want to learn about proven technologies, products, and solutions to build advanced e-business application. It also targets technical professional who are planning to take IBM Test 811, Designing e-business Solutions, and IBM Test 812, e-business Core Knowledge.

Some of the topics in this book include an overview of IBM Framework for e-business, its technologies, and products; security issues in e-business applications; and solutions for Customer Relationship Management, e-commerce, business integration, and Business Intelligence. The information in this book is designed to help you prepare for IBM Test 811 and IBM Test 812. This self-study certification guide includes helpful tips for taking the test and sample questions.

The team that wrote this redbook

This redbook was produced by a team of specialists from around the world working at the International Technical Support Organization Rochester Center.

Aleksandr V. Nartovich is a Senior I/T Specialist in the IBM International Technical Support Organization (ITSO) Rochester Center. He joined the ITSO in January 2001 after working as a developer in the IBM WebSphere Business Components (WSBC) organization. During the first part of his career, Aleksandr was a developer in AS/400 communications. Later, he shifted his focus to business components development on WebSphere. Aleksandr holds a degree in Computer Science from the University of Missouri-Kansas City, as well as a degree in Electrical Engineering from Minsk Radio Engineering Institute. You can reach Aleksandr at: alekn@us.ibm.com

Peter Teh is an IT Architect at IBM Global Services Australia. After working in a variety of professions and industries, he started his career with IBM GSA in September 1998. In Melbourne, he has been "e-enabling" business processes for a major telecommunications company in a number of projects. In September 2000, he successfully completed his professional certification as an IBM e-business Solution Designer. Peter holds a Bachelor of Science Degree in Computer Science and Accounting from Monash University, Australia. You can reach Peter at: peterteh@au1.ibm.com

Vishal Mathur is a Senior Software Engineer in IBM Global Services, India. He has been with IBM since February, 1998. For the last two years, he has focussed on e-business solutions. He holds a degree in Electronics and Communication from the University of Karnataka, India. His areas of expertise include Internet security and e-business solution architecture. He was part of the team that developed the first payment gateway in India and holds one patent in the field of Internet security. He is a certified IBM e-business Solution Designer. You can reach Vishal at: vmathur@in.ibm.com

Tarek Abou Aly is an Advisory IT Specialist working at the Cairo Technology Development Center, in Egypt. He has worked at IBM for more than five years, but has nine years of experience with AS/400 platform solutions, predominantly in developing, consulting, implementing, and occasionally teaching. He also contributes to the architecture development, consulting services, and development of Arabic support on the IBM @server iSeries server. He holds a Computer and Automatic Control Degree from the Faculty of Engineering, Ain Shams University in Cairo, Egypt. He is currently pursuing an MBA with a focus on International Business at the Maastricht School of Management, Netherlands. His interests include e-business solutions architecture and development. He can be reached by e-mail at: aboualy@eg.ibm.com

Thanks to the following people for their invaluable contributions to this project:

Brian R. Smith
IBM ITSO, Rochester Center

Deborah Cottingham
Sam McAfee
Julie Shore
IBM US

Comments welcome

Your comments are important to us!

We want our Redbooks to be as helpful as possible. Please send us your comments about this or other Redbooks in one of the following ways:

- Fax the evaluation form found in "IBM Redbooks review" on page 463 to the fax number shown on the form.
- Use the online evaluation form found at ibm.com/redbooks
- Send your comments in an Internet note to redbook@us.ibm.com

Chapter 1. Introduction

In its simplest sense, e-business is the use of Internet technologies to improve and expand a business. Most companies understand this and have begun the evolution from traditional business practices to e-business.

Businesses have a requirement for a scalable, reliable, and secure electronic foundation. This includes reliable and available servers, industry-leading software and middleware, and consulting services from experts with industry-specific knowledge.

This redbook is written for people who are interested in delivering solutions for e-business. The following chapters give you a broad understanding of the technologies used in e-business and how to apply them. This book also covers solution areas in Customer Relationship Management, e-commerce, application integration, and business integration.

The material covered in this book gives you a complete overview of the technologies used in e-business. This content is the basis for you to design e-business solutions. If you are interested in gaining IBM professional certification in e-business, this book will serve as a useful tool in preparing you for the test.

1.1 Book overview

The chapters and appendices in this book give you a comprehensive overview on the technologies and products used in the IBM Framework for e-business. The chapters also cover business scenarios where you can apply the IBM Framework for e-business.

Chapter 2, "IBM Framework for e-business" on page 7, introduces an overall view of the IBM Framework for e-business. This chapter discusses the fundamental concepts and technologies used in the Framework. It also discusses how the IBM Framework for e-business can help you develop and deploy new applications to meet your organization's demands. Using the Framework tools and methodologies, you can quickly build e-business applications.

Chapter 3, "IBM Framework for e-business products, technology" on page 65, describes and explains, in brief, the IBM software products and technologies that map into the Framework for e-business. The chapter is organized into two parts. The first part covers the technologies, and the second part covers the products in the IBM Framework for e-business.

Chapter 4, "Security" on page 205, explains the security requirements and solutions for your e-business. The chapter also introduces the products that are used in the IBM Framework for e-business to provide security and management of your e-business. Tivoli security products can provide an integrated security solution that will assure continuity of service for Web and legacy applications with a single centralized management point. WebSphere Application Server can provide authentication and authorization for your applications down to the method level of your servlets.

Chapter 5, "Customer Relationship Management (CRM)" on page 237, discusses the key technologies, products, decisions, and experiences in building solutions for Customer Relationship Management (CRM) e-business problems. CRM is discussed in the context of Web marketing, CRM with data access, and CRM with transactions.

Chapter 6, "E-commerce" on page 311, explains key design elements for e-commerce applications. It focuses on the key technologies, products, and design decisions. This chapter discusses online sales, where users interface with an online store or mall, which typically includes the concepts of a shopping cart and an electronic wallet. A sample solution for online sales e-business problems is presented. The chapter also describes the products WebSphere Commerce Suite (WCS), and IBM Payment Suites. The design emphasis is on key design decisions regarding the client, network, server, application server, security, and performance.

Chapter 7, "Business integration" on page 335, discusses business integration solutions using the IBM Framework for e-business. These solutions are built on the foundation of Enterprise Application Integration (EAI) technologies to provide a complete business-centric solution. EAI integrates internal applications, and business integration uses the same technology to extend the enterprise to the suppliers, distributors and partners.

Chapter 8, "Business Intelligence" on page 365, discusses the key design elements for Business Intelligence applications. It focuses on the key technologies, products, and design decisions. It includes a sample solution for Business Intelligence e-business problems. The chapter explains how to make better business decisions through the intelligent use of data assets. It covers how to give access to the right data, analyze the data for insights, and use this analysis to make better decisions. It describes the products Visual Warehouse, OLAP Server, and Intelligent Miner for Data. The design emphasis is on key design decisions regarding the client, network, server, application server, security, and performance.

Chapter 9, "Performance" on page 397, explains the problem areas or the bottlenecks that hinder the performance of an applications, the technologies that are used to make performance friendly applications, and the products provided by the Framework that are used to enhance performance.

Appendix A, "Test tips" on page 421, provides some insight to IBM Tests 811 and 812. The appendix is designed to give you an idea of what to expect before you enter the examination and to remove as many elements of surprise as possible.

Appendix B, "Competitive information" on page 431, discusses competitive e-business solutions. Where applicable, the IBM Framework for e-business or components of the Framework are compared to what IBM competitors have or intend to have in the marketplace. It includes an overview on the Microsoft, Sun Microsystems, Oracle, and BEA e-business offerings, and how they compare to the IBM Framework for e-business and products.

1.2 IBM Certified for e-business

The IBM Framework for e-business certification program combines both business and technical training to give you the solid background necessary to build successful e-businesses. This redbook will assist you in completing the training and prepare you for testing. By fulfilling the requirements for the certification, you can:

- Further grow your educational level on broad e-business concepts
- Acquire proven skills to differentiate yourself in a competitive environment
- Enhance your earning potential and the possibilities of career advancement

You will also contribute to your company's success. The e-business professional certification for individuals creates a solid foundation for:

- Differentiating your company among its competitors
- Strengthening business ties to IBM and opening new marketing opportunities
- Receiving better access to technology
- Sharing the valuable experience of implementing e-business solutions
- Helps your company advance toward IBM Certified for e-business – Business Partner Status

1.2.1 IBM Certified for e-business: Solution Designer

This certification validates the ability to translate customer business requirements into an implementable e-business solution. It takes into consideration security, networking, and existing customer environments to design a secure scalable solution using the IBM Framework for e-business methodologies and best practices. It applies to those who want to demonstrate expertise in e-business solution design.

To attain the IBM Certified for e-business - Solution Designer certification, you must pass Test 811. To take this test, you must first fulfill these prerequisites:

- Have a minimum of six months solution design experience specifically with e-business solutions

- Have approximately two years general IT consulting or architecting experience

- Maintain a working knowledge of the Internet, security, networking, and Java as a platform

- Complete training in IBM Framework for e-business

Test 811 is designed to assess your ability to design an implementable e-business solution. It tests your skills in the following areas:

- Gathering customer requirements:

  - Identify the solution objectives and goals.

  - Identify possible business solution scenarios (e-commerce, Internet applications, messaging, and integration).

  - Propose and justify potential products.

  - Given current transaction rates and growth projections, identify future scaling requirements.

  - Design a plan that addresses current requirements, allows future scaling, and integrates with existing infrastructure.

- Evaluating customer security requirements:
  - Given a customer network topology and security requirements, determine firewall requirements.
  - Determine how to identify a client (customer) throughout the network.
  - Given a network topology, determine how to move protocols through the network.
- Creating a functional level e-business solution design:
  - Identify the critical design issues and devise trade-offs.
  - Choose the proper IS platform and Framework for e-business components.
  - Devise trade-offs to solve hardware and technology limitations.
  - Estimate CPU size, workload, and performance needs. Evaluate the customer client/server issues.
  - Evaluate the command model object versus the remote call model.
  - Given a customer's requirement to send commands, determine the most appropriate method for messages to be sent.
  - Given a client/server environment, determine the protocols to be used.
  - Given a client/server environment, identify the interface design issues.
  - Evaluate issues with the thin client model.
- Validating the functional e-business solution design:
  - Determine the impact the solution has on other business processes and units.
  - Define the customer business processes.
  - Define long term business process strategies.
  - Align vendor strategies with long-term business process strategies.
  - Map an immediate solution to long term business/technology plan.
  - Evaluate products and platforms and determine proof of concept design.
  - Build and test proof of concept.
- Integrating the solution with existing systems:
  - Document the existing infrastructure.
  - Given a functional design specification, identify integration points and points of entry to the network.
  - Identify technologies to exploit integration points and points of entry.
  - Determine the impact of integration on existing infrastructure and business processes.
  - Design, develop, test, and implement the integration solution.
- Creating an e-business design document and project plan:
  - Identify deliverables (customer and consulting).
  - Establish rough estimates of the time and resources (people and technology) resources that are required.
  - Determine the availability of resources and the impact of other commitments.

- Highlight the project risk.

- Define the terms and technology.

- Specify the project timeline.

- Determine discrete tasks required to develop and implement the design and identify project milestones.

- Determine the skill sets needed for the individual tasks.

- Identify candidate resources and skill sets available.

- Identify the effort required for individual tasks.

- Define parameters, working times, and resource utilization.

- Allocate resources to individual tasks.

- Establish acceptance criteria and project end point.

- Transitioning to the project management team:
  - Hand-off the project to the project managers.
  - Hold a pre-development meeting with the project team.
  - Ensure the project meets the technical specifications.
  - Provide technical guidance on an "on-call" basis.
  - Verify that the solution meets the customer's objectives.
  - Review the acceptance test results.

For more information, visit the Web site at:
`http://www.ibm.com/certify/certs/ebcpsdes.shtml`

1.2.2 IBM Certified for e-business: Solution Technologist

This certification validates your ability to understand and articulate e-business, issues, strategies, and methodologies. It focuses on a well-rounded perspective of e-business. It tests the value, vision, and deep technical skills required to implement at least one key IBM or qualifying e-business product (hardware or software) or to develop a solution using one of key IBM or qualifying e-business development tools.

To attain the IBM Certified for e-business – Solution Technologist certification, you must have approved technical certification and pass one exam. You can find the list of approved technical certifications at:
`http://www.ibm.com/certify/certs/eb_tcert.shtml`

To take this test, you must fulfill these prerequisites:

- Have a minimum of six months e-business experience
- Have approximately two years of general IT experience
- Maintain a general knowledge of the Internet, security, networking, and open standards

The objectives of Test 812 focus on:

- Defining and describing e-business:

  - Definition
  - e-business cycle
  - Critical elements of a successful e-business

- Describing the main e-business solutions, their characteristics, and elements:
    - Customer Relationship Management
    - Supply Chain Management
    - Commerce

- Identifying and describing the significance (element, use, and value) of the main technologies used in e-business:
    - Java
    - XML

- Describing and articulating the elements and benefits of IBM Framework for e-business:
    - Structure
    - Elements

For more information, see: http://www.ibm.com/certify/certs/ebcpstec.shtml

Chapter 2. IBM Framework for e-business

An e-business is an organization that interacts with its customers, suppliers, business partners, and employees by using Web technologies to reach new markets and build lasting relationships. IBM Framework for e-business is a proven approach for building and integrating successful e-business applications. It includes products from IBM and other leading software vendors that are:

- Industry standards-based for maximum flexibility in a multi-vendor environment. The examples of such standards are Linux, CORBA, Java, Hypertext Markup Language (HTML) and eXtensible Markup Language (XML). It includes the client, application server, data, and infrastructure standards that make it possible for a client to access data and services anywhere in the network.

- Implemented on servers for rapid deployment and update.

- Scalable as offerings and volumes grow.

Figure 1 shows how e-business applications that are implemented on servers tie customers to different e-business activities.

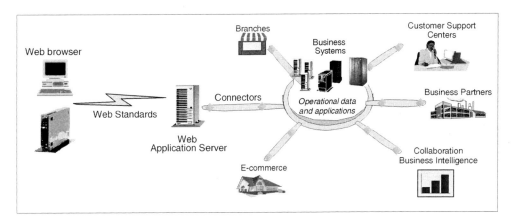

Figure 1. Server-based e-business applications

The Framework environment allows for:

- Building on the *existing IT investment* to use the current information system deployed in the enterprise and to promote fast growth

- *Reusing elements* for quick action to capture opportunities and respond to challenges

- Designing *management capabilities* into the application for maximum performance and availability

You can find the latest e-business information on the Web at:
`http://www.ibm.com/ebusiness`

This chapter introduces an overall view of the Framework for e-business. The following chapters explain the technology details of each component and how they apply to different domains.

e-business applications requirements

An e-business connects critical business systems directly to customers, employees, suppliers, and distributors via the Web to:

- Improve time to market
- Access a broader base of customers and suppliers
- Improve efficiency
- Reduce costs

To achieve these benefits, existing businesses must transform their traditional business processes with e-business applications. New businesses, sometimes called "NetGens", can adopt e-business applications from the beginning to achieve the same benefits. To allow e-businesses to reap the desired benefits, e-business applications must meet some fundamental requirements. They must be:

- **Standards-based**: To ensure portability of e-business applications across multiple client and server platforms and to improve flexibility and time to market.

- **Server-centric**: To allow e-business applications to be developed and deployed quickly, to expand access to a broad range of client types, and to offer improved management and deployment capabilities that are characteristic of modern e-business applications.

- **Scalable**: To allow e-business applications to handle highly variable and unpredictable loads in today's Web environment.

- **Available**: To address the global nature of the Web, which requires e-business applications to run 24-hours a day, seven-days a week, with guaranteed quality of service.

- **Secure**: To address customers', suppliers', and other constituents' demands for secure Web interactions, in recognition of the potential risks of doing business on the Web.

- **Easy to develop and deploy**: To achieve lower costs and faster time to market.

- **Manageable**: To achieve lower maintenance costs and contribute to higher availability.

- **Able to leverage and extend existing assets**: To improve time to market and reduce cost of development and deployment, while improving security, reliability, and scalability.

2.1 Framework overview

IBM Framework for e-business is at the core of the IBM e-business software strategy. IBM developed Framework for e-business to help customers build, run, and manage successful e-business applications. It is a set of recommendations and products to develop an e-business application.

Framework for e-business consists of:

- A standards-based foundation that enables multiplatform and multivendor solutions. The IBM deliverable here is commitment to embrace and advance industry standards.

- An easy-to-understand approach in developing applications that are specially tuned to run in this environment. IBM offers a design, development, and deployment model based on industry-specific patterns that guide you through the process.

- State-of-the-art software and scalable servers that allow you to build and run e-business applications.

Framework for e-business helps you develop and deploy the new applications your organization demands. Using the Framework tools and methodologies, you can quickly build e-business applications.

2.1.1 What can the Framework do for you?

When customers adopt the Framework, they're adopting a proven methodology, products, and tools. They gain the benefits of an entire approach rather than a single product or point solution. Using the tools and methodologies that Framework for e-business offers, you can substantially reduce the development time of an e-business application.

Since the Framework is based on open, multiplatform, and multivendor standards, it can support multiple clients and servers, as well as multiple standards for development and deployment. The most important features of the Framework are:

- IBM is committed to support and enhance open industry standards.

- The Framework supports heterogeneous client environments. This means that customers can build e-business applications that can access any client including PCs, vending machines, personal digital assistants (PDAs), and cell phones. The Framework also supports integration standards, such as XML and CORBA/Internet Inter-ORB Protocol (IIOP), that integrate the heterogeneous exchange of data between applications and systems.

- Because the Framework supports the Java programming language, customers can develop Java applications that can run on any Web application server and deliver content to any client. Customers can use the Java language to write their applications on their platform of choice and then run them on any platform. They can use Java transcoding capability to deliver customized content to any client.

- The Framework supports application protocols, such as SMTP and POP/IMAP, that enable chat, e-mail, and management applications. In addition, the Framework supports communication standards, such as SSL and TCP/IP, that enable security-rich applications and smart cards.

2.1.2 Development and deployment patterns methodology

The Framework includes information on e-business patterns, which are a group of assets that can be used as an aid in designing, developing, and deploying e-business solutions. The patterns include:

- Application designs for e-business
- Application topology
- Runtime topology
- Technology options and guidelines

Using this defined, repeatable methodology helps developers reduce the time to develop and deploy e-business solutions.

2.2 The e-business cycle

e-business is more than a technology discussion. The move requires a clear vision of what needs to be done and an equally clear picture of how to make that vision a reality. The e-business cycle is the IBM transitioning model for guiding customers from their legacy businesses into e-businesses.

The Internet is driving a new networked economy. This opens a door to new business models and classes of applications that enable companies to conduct business in a fundamentally different way. IBM calls this *e-business*. The IBM approach is to work with customers to take e-business from a concept to a working reality via a concrete set of actions. These actions form the *e-business life cycle* that you can follow in developing your solution. The steps include:

1. Transforming the business processes
2. Building new applications
3. Running them in a scalable, available, secure environment
4. Leveraging knowledge and information

Each of the steps represents a concrete set of actions. An organization may be active in more than one phase at any one time. This is also an iterative process.

Each step in the transformation of a traditional business to an e-business is an iteration through the cycle. The e-business cycle is shown in Figure 2.

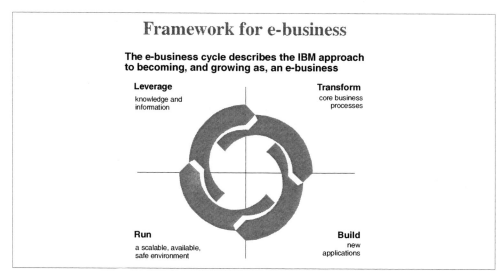

Figure 2. The e-business cycle

IBM works side by side with customers to help them transition from a traditional business model to the e-business model.

2.2.1 Transforming business processes

This stage focuses on transforming core business processes (as shown in Figure 2). It involves extending an existing business model into the networked world to create an e-business model. Businesses are defined in new ways by applying Internet technologies to create maximum value for them.

When transforming business processes, it is imperative that you view each process in its overall context. Streamlining individual processes without regard for their overall context merely results in a better individual process. It may not necessarily have the effect you desired, which is to improve your e-business value and service to customers.

To become an e-business, you should change some of the current business processes. This means doing business in a new way by taking advantage of Web technologies to create maximum value for your business. It's about business, not just technology. e-business opens up dramatic new options for managing customer and employee relations, unifying the supply chain, and conducting commerce. The key differentiator in the networked world is to provide business value with solutions that will help customers to achieve maximum value as they make the transition from traditional business to an e-business.

Here are some hints for transforming the existing processes:

- Focus on priority processes
- Exploit the reach of the Web
- Extend existing applications

2.2.2 Building new applications

The next logical step is to create a new Web-enabled application around transformed business processes (as shown in Figure 2). Transforming core business processes requires a new generation of applications. Building also encompasses migrating existing applications to the Web using an open standards-based approach.

The attributes of e-business applications are:

- Standards-based
- Server-centric
- Leveraging core systems
- Scalable
- Quick to deploy and easy to use
- Manageable

The standards-based approach is an integral part of enabling your e-business. By definition, it allows your customers, business partners, and suppliers to connect to your business using standards-based software.

Applications built today must satisfy two competing requirements: an increase in functionality and a decrease in time to market. The only solution is to build applications that are made from components that are quick to develop and deploy.

A new generation of innovative applications to develop Web sites, integrate systems and data, serve Web-based users, and secure assets and user privacy is required to expand and integrate business processes. e-business applications run on servers that leverage existing applications and data and grow to meet user demands. IBM can design, develop, and integrate these applications or provide the framework for you to develop them yourself. IBM Framework for e-business is designed to help you build and deploy a new generation of applications that are standards-based, flexible, and easy to change. e-business continues to be about starting simple and growing fast.

Follow these hints to help you build new applications:

- Integrate new and existing applications
- Create reusable business assets
- Use an open standards-based approach

2.2.3 Running applications in a scalable, available, secure environment

The "Run" stage shown in Figure 2 on page 10 refers to the ability of an organization to deploy and run a scalable, available, and safe environment. Usually, the infrastructure is built around the business and applications. Users want systems that are easy to use, yet always responsive. The infrastructure services need to have:

- Availability
- Scalability
- Manageability
- Security

e-business systems are considered mission critical. They must be accessible; secure; available 24-hours a day, 7-days a week (24 x 7); easy to manage and support; and compatible with the existing IT infrastructure. IBM provides a managed environment with scalable servers, flexible clients, and advanced networking and storage systems.

To run an e-business solution, consider these hints:

- Maximize deployment flexibility
- Secure the network platform
- Employ single-action management

2.2.4 Leveraging knowledge and information

The "Leverage" stage shown in Figure 2 on page 10 is about using existing knowledge and information. A responsive organization will make intelligent use of all types of data and organizational knowledge.

To attract and retain your best customers, you need a precise portrait of what their needs and buying patterns are. Business Intelligence paints that picture by analyzing and interpreting vast quantities of data, such as customer demographics, product purchase histories, cross-sales, service calls, Internet experiences, and online transactions. Then it turns this analysis into insight and develops conclusive fact-based strategies to gain a competitive edge.

Using the latest e-business technologies, this intelligence can then be distributed around your company or around the world to help make crucial and profitable decisions, such as:

- Which markets to enter
- Which customers to pursue
- Which products to promote

This step uses lessons learned from previous experience to enhance the business processes that take advantage of the other steps in the e-business life cycle. e-business is a knowledge multiplier. You can create a competitive advantage by capturing information and turning it into wisdom, extend and solidify your brand image, and develop profitable and loyal customers. IBM Business

Intelligence and knowledge management solutions and services can help you to anticipate your consumers' needs, assess customer and product profitability, identify product line extensions, model risk scenarios, and detect fraud.

Consider these hints for leveraging knowledge and information:

- Use data to sharpen decision making
- Increase responsiveness through knowledge management

2.3 Framework elements

IBM Framework for e-business consists of guidelines to help develop e-business applications. It is focused on a Web-oriented style of network computing that has evolved from traditional client/server computing. It incorporates the 3-tier application architecture including:

- Presentation services
- Web-centered business logic
- Data storage and legacy systems

A prototypical three-tier architecture consists of:

- A client tier that contains logic related to the presentation of information (including the graphical user interface (GUI)) and requests to applications through a browser or Java applet.

- Web application servers containing the business logic and processes that control the reading and writing of data.

- Servers that provide the data storage and transactional applications used by the Web application server processes.

The application elements that reside in these three logical tiers are connected through a set of industry-standard protocols, services, and software connectors.

The high-level architecture elements of the Framework include:

- The *system model*, which presents an overview of the system elements and interconnection between them.

- The *application programming model*, which highlights the software tools and products used to build, run, and manage e-business applications.

2.3.1 System model

IBM Framework for e-business provides a model for designing e-business solutions. The Framework is based on an n-tier distributed environment where any number of tiers of application logic and business services are separated into components that communicate with each other across a network. In its most basic form, the Framework can be depicted as a "logical" three-tier computing model. This means that there is a logical, but not necessarily physical, separation of processes. This model is designed to support clients with high-function Web application and servers for small and large enterprises.

The characteristics imposed by the Framework system model help designers to meet the requirements of e-business applications. Figure 3 shows a high-level system model for running an e-business application.

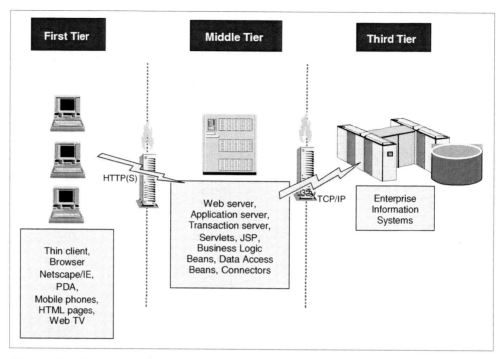

Figure 3. The Framework system model

2.3.1.1 First tier

The main function of the client in this model is to present information and results produced by an application to the user. In this system model, the clients are sometimes referred to as "thin" clients. This means that little or no application logic is executed on the client and, therefore, relatively little software is required to be installed on the client.

Clients are implemented with industry-standard technologies, interact with the user, communicate with a middle tier via standard protocols, and send and receive standard data formats. The Framework features the "thin client" to improve manageability, flexibility, and time to market. This is contrary to the "fat client", which provides higher computing power and storage capacity at the expense of increased management requirements.

Clients supported in the Framework can range from pervasive devices, such as PDAs, smartcards, and digital wireless telephones, to network computers and PCs. The first tier supports a wide range of technology such as:

- **Internet browsers**: Many browsers are available such as Netscape Navigator or Internet Explorer.

- **Personal digital assistants**: They are small devices that give you access to a wide range of Web applications and services. Many PDAs are developed and exist on the market today, such as Palm Pilot by 3Com or iPAQ by Compaq.

- **Mobile phones**: These are efficient data access devices for a wide range of information.

- **Web TV and Internet-connected appliances**

The common thread that ties these clients to the Web application server is their implementation of a set of widely supported, Internet-based technologies and protocols, along with Java which, enables them to provide interaction between users and applications.

The current trend is to simplify the access to the Internet with smaller devices. These devices could be moved or carried easily, while giving the ability to access data or applications, such as stock purchase or inquiry, banking operation access, and online shopping.

2.3.1.2 Middle tier

Middle-tier servers include a standards-based Web server, to interact with the client tier and define user interaction, and a Web application server, to execute business logic independently of the client type and user interface style. The Web application server is the platform that provides the runtime environment for the application's business logic. It is implemented using various Internet and Java technologies, including the HTTP server and the Enterprise Java services that enable rapid development and deployment of applications in a distributed network environment.

Java servlets, JavaServer Pages, and Enterprise JavaBeans are examples of the components deployed in the Web application server. These server-side components communicate with their clients and other application components via Hypertext Transfer Protocol (HTTP) or IIOP, and use the directory and security services provided by the network infrastructure. They can also leverage database, transaction, and groupware facilities.

The middle-tier servers incorporate several application integration technologies for communicating with applications, data, and services in other tiers. The middle tier is the core tier in Web enabling an application. The middle tier hosts many servers and services, including:

- Web servers
- Web application servers
- Transaction servers
- Servlets
- JavaBeans
- Connectors

You'll find more information about these servers and services throughout the book.

2.3.1.3 Third tier

The Enterprise Information System (EIS) tier includes new and existing internal applications, services, data, and external applications. A significant amount of data resides on the Enterprise Information System. Examples of EIS include:

- Customer Information Control System (CICS) server
- Legacy applications developed on mainframes or legacy systems
- Relational databases such as DB2

Different technologies are developed to unleash the data in EIS to the Internet and e-business solutions.

For this model to work, you need to interconnect and manage three tiers using:

- Network infrastructure
- System management products
- Connectors

Network infrastructure

The network infrastructure ties the tiers together and connects them to the Internet and extranets using standard protocols and data formats. It also provides such functions as service location, security-related capabilities, and technologies to improve scalability. The network infrastructure uses industry state-of-the-art technology.

System management

The Framework's systems management component defines the services and tools to manage e-business applications and the underlying infrastructure as a single entity. For intranet environments, Enterprise Systems Management (ESM) integrates the management aspects of e-business applications to provide a consolidated view of an enterprise's business solutions and the underlying IT resources. For the Internet environment, the Framework introduces Cross-Enterprise Systems Management that supports a collaborative management approach to extend management functions to environments that span company boundaries.

The management functions allow you to:

- Efficiently deploy software to the right users, on the right platform, at the right time

- Monitor the availability and performance of the hardware and software

- Control access to and usage of e-business applications and their resources

- Support management operations for e-business applications and their resources

The connectors to external services

External services are fundamental to the emergence of the Web application model because they are the result of years of corporate investment in information technology. They are the applications and data. They are the business assets that need to be made available to the Web in a secure, controlled way to enable companies to leverage their value to customers, employees, and suppliers in intranets and extranets.

The components that make it feasible are called *connectors*. They connect the new business logic in the middle tier to the vast accumulated assets in a company's existing applications and data systems. Connectors are part of the application integration layer of the Framework.

2.3.2 Application programming model

The application programming model highlights the software tools and products used to build, run, and manage e-business applications. The Framework design promotes:

- Field-tested methodology that simplifies the development and deployment of the new applications

- Rich product portfolio to support a broad range of applications

- Cross-platform standards, including Java
- Building complete solutions for an enterprise

Framework for e-business, as shown in Figure 4, provides:

- Development tools and components to build e-business applications.
- Application server software to run the e-business application. WebSphere Application Server and Domino provide transaction capabilities that range from simple Web publishing to enterprise transaction processing.
- Secure network and management software to secure the operations of an e-business application and enable the effective management of the operations.
- A wide range of platforms to run e-business applications, including AIX, HP-UX, Linux, OS/390, OS/400, Solaris, and Windows.

Note: Linux is a very strategic element for IBM. The company is enabling all its servers to support Linux.

The Framework is constantly evolving to support more industry standards, expand the product offerings, and make the methodologies stronger.

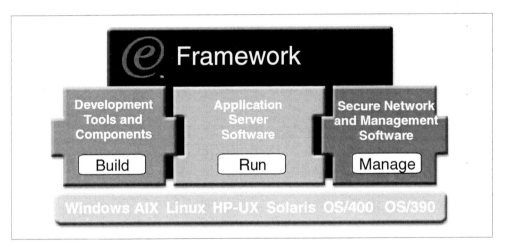

Figure 4. The IBM Framework for e-business

2.3.2.1 Development tools and components: Build
IBM offers a large set of development tools to build e-business solutions. Figure 5 shows a list of the development tools and components.

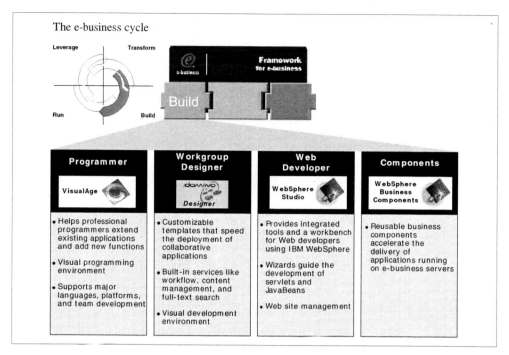

Figure 5. Framework for e-business: Development tools and components

The development tools portfolio contains powerful application development software, including:

- **VisualAge for Java**: This is a tool that supports a visual construction and visual programming environment. This means that it allows developers to create both the GUI and the logic behind the interface. Visual programming improves developer productivity and shortens development time. For more product information, refer to the Web site:
  http://www.ibm.com/software/ad/vajava/

- **Domino Designer**: This is an integrated development environment. It enables developers to rapidly build secure Web applications that incorporate enterprise data and streamline business processes. For more product information, refer to the Web site:
  http://www.lotus.com/home.nsf/welcome/dominodesigner

- **WebSphere Studio**: This provides an easy-to-use tool set that helps reduce the time and effort when creating, managing, and debugging multiplatform Web applications. It is used to develop the visual layout of dynamic Web pages. WebSphere Studio supports JSPs, full HTML, JavaScript, and Dynamic HTML (DHTML). It uses wizards (for generating database-driven pages) and updates and corrects links automatically when content changes. WebSphere Studio allows developers to integrate their favorite content-creation tools and provides local and remote debugging with the industry's first JSP debugger. It promotes a team development environment where multiple team members can share the same code base. For more product information, refer to the Web site:
  http://www.ibm.com/software/webservers/studio/

- **IBM WebSphere Business Components (WSBC)**: These are reusable software implementation packages. The components provide a coherent set of functions. WSBC can be independently developed, delivered, and assembled

with other components. IBM has developed WebSphere Business Components to help you reduce development time, create applications that operate across diverse infrastructures, and deliver value to your company. WSBC builds on the business components that IBM developed in the San Francisco project. For more product information, refer to the Web site:
http://www.ibm.com/software/webservers/components/

HotMedia software is a recent addition to development tools. It lets customers enrich the information on their Web sites with such effects as panoramas, sound, and animation, without a plug-in.

2.3.2.2 Application server software: Run
The application servers include runtime environments that are available on all major platforms. Customers want to choose where to run their applications. The Framework gives customers complete deployment flexibility. They can run their applications on the platform that makes the most business sense. Figure 6 shows a highlight of the application server software.

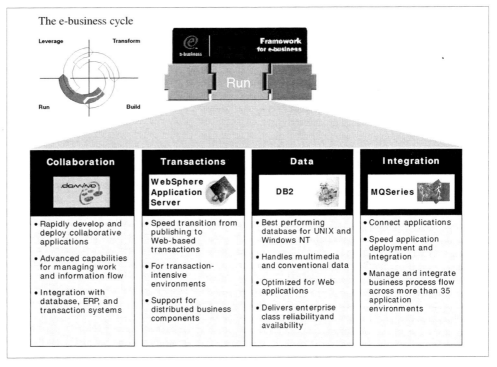

Figure 6. Framework for e-business: Application server software

The application server software includes:

- **Collaboration**: Domino provides a multi-platform foundation for collaboration and e-business, which drives solutions ranging from corporate messaging to Web-based transactions. Domino's integrated application services, such as security, workflow, and content management, optimize the platform for rapid delivery of the collaborative Web applications you need to initiate and strengthen key business relationships. Built-in connection services provide access to leading relational databases, transaction systems, and Enterprise Resource Planning (ERP) applications. For more information, visit the Web site at: http://www.lotus.com/home.nsf/welcome/domino

- **Transaction**: IBM WebSphere Application Server is an e-business application deployment environment built on open standards-based technology. It is available in three editions:
    - The Standard Edition lets you use Java servlets, JavaServer Pages, and XML to quickly transform static Web sites into vital sources of dynamic Web content.
    - The Advanced Edition is a high-performance EJB server for implementing EJB components that incorporate business logic.
    - The Enterprise Edition integrates Enterprise JavaBeans (EJB) and Common Object Request Broker Architecture (CORBA) components to build high-transaction, high-volume e-business applications. For more information, go to: `http://www.ibm.com/software/webservers/appserv/`

- **Database**: DB2 helps customers leverage their information by delivering the performance, scalability, reliability, and availability needed for e-business applications. DB2 integrates these core strengths with differentiated features for the targeted applications in offerings that are easy to deploy, use, and manage. For more product information, refer to the Web site: `http://www-4.ibm.com/software/data/db2/`

- **Integration**: MQSeries provides an open, scalable, industrial-strength messaging and information infrastructure, which enables enterprises and beyond to integrate business processes. For more product information, refer to the Web site at: `http://www-4.ibm.com/software/ts/mqseries/`

Build/run synergy

The Framework application development tools and server software work together synergistically. For example, VisualAge for Java includes a runtime environment for WebSphere. This allows programmers to deliver applications more quickly because they can test applications on the fly.

2.3.2.3 Secure network and management software: Manage

The Framework includes a complete portfolio of security and management products and services. Figure 7 highlights the management products.

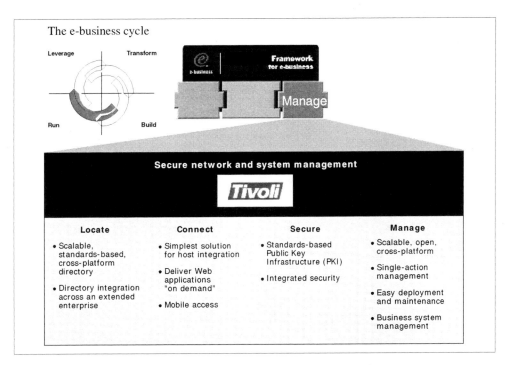

Figure 7. Framework for e-business: Secure network and management software

Tivoli security products are a family of flexible products that allow customers to protect their business data and secure their network operations and systems. Tivoli offers a broad portfolio of security software and services that can run on multiple platforms. The offerings let customers choose the degree of security they want. Tivoli products provide the security and management framework that customers need to protect business-critical applications and information assets. Tivoli offers complete control of user accounts and system security services.

In the systems management arena, the family of Tivoli products provide system management tools and services for the entire enterprise. It simplifies the software distribution, by monitoring the systems operations and providing high availability. Tivoli management software can distribute a software upgrade to thousands of computers on a single network, check each one for viruses and security breaches, and track hundreds of other critical applications. Every day companies all over the world, including 96% of Fortune 500 companies, use Tivoli products and services. These companies recognize that in order to grow their businesses in today's market, simple, seamless IT management is essential.

For the latest information on Tivoli products and services, go to the Web site at: http://www.tivoli.com/

To help meet the market demand for access control, authorization and administration, IBM acquired DASCOM, Inc., an industry leader in Web-based and enterprise security technology.

2.4 e-business solution spaces

To create a systematic approach for building a successful e-business application, IBM has developed the *e-business solution space* (Figure 8). With this approach, the process of developing an e-business application is divided into three main categories:

- **Problem space**: Represents IBM's classification of the main e-business problem areas

- **Technology and product space**: Highlights the technology and products used to develop a solution for each problem area

- **Design space**: Resolves the design issues related to developing an e-business solution

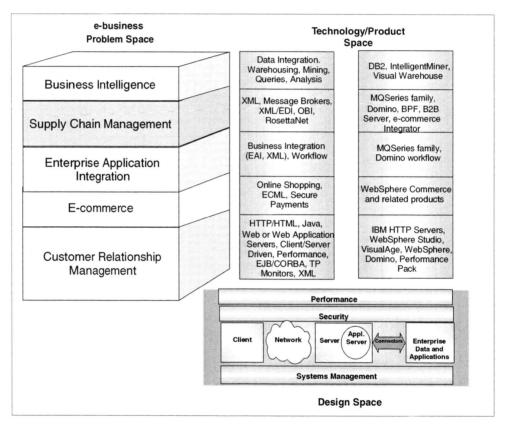

Figure 8. The e-business solution space

The following sections present more details about each e-business solution space.

2.4.1 Problem space

IBM worked with many customers to build e-business solutions. The main problem areas as identified by IBM are shown in Figure 9.

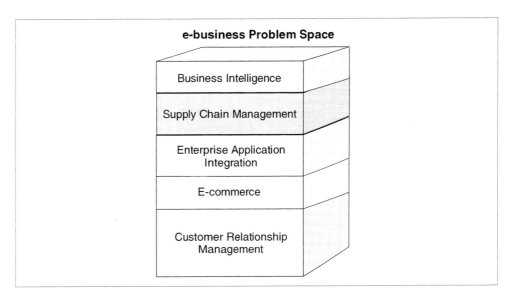

Figure 9. The e-business problem space

Customer Relationship Management (CRM)

Businesses spend a significant amount of effort to improve customer service. They need tools that focus on managing the customer "holistically," so they can:

- Provide consistent, value-add experiences through a single, long-running dialog

- Deal with each customer as an individual

- Recall and reference all previous interactions

- Accommodate each customer's needs and preferences

- Effectively reach a larger number of customers, and provide quality and effective customers service

Customers can directly access their information in a secure manner or even perform business transactions remotely.

E-commerce

E-commerce is expanding to include all the activities related to buying, selling, and marketing over the Internet. Many businesses need to perform commerce operations over the Internet to allow people to securely buy goods and services electronically. This effort is in addition to advertising, marketing, shopping, purchasing, and paying. Businesses are striving for a solution to allow:

- Enterprises to extend their reach to new customers and manage transactions electronically

- Consumers to purchase, in confidence, knowing their transactions are secure and their privacy is protected

E-commerce has evolved from consumers conducting basic transactions on the Web, to a complete retooling of the way partners, suppliers, and customers transact. Now you can link dealers and suppliers online, reducing lag time and paperwork. You can move procurement online by setting up an extranet that links directly to vendors, cutting inventory carrying costs and becoming more responsive to your customers. You can streamline your financial relationships with customers and suppliers by Web-enabling billing and payment systems.

Enterprise Application Integration (EAI)
Enterprises rely on line of business applications to perform their core activities, like Enterprise Resource Planning (ERP). Businesses need to extend the access to the applications over the Internet in an efficient, reliable, and secure manner.

Most enterprises have multiple applications responsible for a part of the business process. EAI solutions integrate all these applications to provide a uniform user interface to these applications.

Supply Chain Management (SCM)
A supply chain is the way an enterprise ties together internally and externally the people, processes, and related information associated with its flow of goods. Supply Chain Management is a strategic approach that unites all steps in the cycle, from initial product design and the procurement of raw materials through production, shipping, distribution, and warehousing, until a finished product is delivered to a customer.

Businesses need to manage the supplier orders efficiently and enable the use of the just-in-time (JIT) production model, by sustaining continuous production stream with the minimum stock on hand.

Business Intelligence (BI)
Customers need to gather, manage, and analyze vast amounts of data to gain insights to drive strategic business decisions and to support operational processes with new functions. Customers need to understand the hidden relationships in the data that accumulated over time and across different operations.

2.4.1.1 IBM Patterns for e-business
To help customers with the problems identified in the problem space, IBM developed Patterns for e-business as a group of reusable assets that can help speed the process of developing applications. The reusable assets consist of:

- The patterns that identify the interaction between users and businesses.

- Application and runtime topologies that are driven by the customer's requirements and describe the shape of applications and the supporting runtime needed to build the e-business application.

- Product mappings to populate the solution. The product mappings are based on previous walkthroughs and testing.

- Guidelines for the design, development, deployment, and management of e-business applications.

Using an approach based on the Framework for e-business, you leverage the experience of others to create solutions quickly either for a small local business or a large multinational enterprise.

To simplify the e-business solution design, select the business pattern that best meets your customer's needs. The list of available patterns includes:

- The business patterns:

    - Self-service
    - Information Aggregation
    - Collaboration
    - Extended Enterprise

- The integration patterns:

    - Access Integration
    - Application Integration

- The composite patterns:

    - Electronic Commerce
    - e-Marketplace
    - Portals
    - Account Access

Self-service

The Self-Service business pattern, also known as the User-to-Business (U2B) pattern, captures the essence of direct interactions between interested parties and a business. Interested parties include customers, business partners, stakeholders, employees, and all other individuals with whom the business intends to interact. For simplicity, these interested parties are referred to as users. In this definition business represents various types of organizations including large enterprises, small and medium businesses, government agencies, and so on.

Examples of the Self-service pattern include:

- Convenience banking:

    - View account balances
    - View recent transactions
    - Pay bills/transfer funds
    - Stop payments
    - Manage bank card

- Discount brokerage:

    - Portfolio summary
    - Detailed holdings
    - Transaction history
    - Quotes and news
    - Buy and sell stocks

Electronic commerce

Electronic commerce is the set of products and processes facilitating the secure purchase of goods and services over the Web, including such functions as:

- Advertising
- Marketing
- Shopping
- Purchasing
- Paying
- Shipping/delivery

E-commerce is a special case of online interaction between users and businesses where products are sold through a catalog using such components as a shopping cart or wallet. The pattern can also include links to back-end systems that provide inventory updates, order processing, delivery systems, and credit checking.

E-commerce solutions allow enterprises to reach new customers and manage transactions electronically. Consumers can purchase with confidence, knowing their transactions are secure and their privacy is protected.

Extended Enterprise

The Extended Enterprise business pattern, which is also known as the Business-to-Business pattern (B2B) pattern, addresses the interactions and collaborations between business processes in separate enterprises. This pattern can be observed in solutions that implement programmatic interfaces to connect inter-enterprise applications. In other words, it does not cover applications that are directly invoked using a user interface by business partners across organizational boundaries.

Note: Extended Enterprise, where both parties belong to the same company, is covered under "Application integration" on page 27.

Information Aggregation

The Information Aggregation business pattern, which is also known as the User-to-Data (U2D) pattern, can be observed in e-business solutions that allow users to access and manipulate data that is aggregated from multiple sources. This business pattern captures the process of taking large volumes of data, text, images, video, and so on, and using tools to extract useful information from them. These tools may personalize data to suit user preferences, distill summary information from large volumes of data, use algorithms to identify trends hidden in the data, or answer users' hypothetical "what-if" questions about potential business scenarios. Information Aggregation is often referred to in these terms:

- Management information systems (MIS)
- Decision support systems (DSS)
- Data warehousing
- Business Intelligence

The Information Aggregation pattern, therefore, addresses a set of requirements and system environments known as the *informational environment*, which supports the management and control of business activities over time. The informational environment depends on an operational environment where the business activities are recorded on a minute-to-minute basis, as the original source of much of the information needed to manage and control the business.

The distinguishing characteristics of the informational environment include:

- The user does not connect to a traditional transaction system to perform an operational business process.

- The user perceives an interaction with the data directly, not with a system.

- The user has significant freedom and flexibility in accessing the data, which is often specially prepared to suit the user or the end-user tool being used.

The data accessed by a user of the informational environment has these characteristics:

- The data is not the company's prime operational data.
- The data includes a copy of relevant operational data and other data as necessary.
- The data includes a historical set of data.

Information Aggregation addresses two distinct, but related, areas of functionality. First, it addresses users' needs for access to, and use of, the informational environment to manage business activities. Second, it defines how the informational environment is populated from the operational environment.

Collaboration

The Collaboration business pattern, which is also known as the User-to-User (U2U) pattern, enables interaction and collaboration between users. This pattern can be observed in solutions that support small or extended teams who need to work together in order to achieve a joint goal.

Collaboration examples include:

- e-mail
- Bulletin boards
- Newsgroups
- Instant messaging
- Team rooms
- Online meetings
- Ad hoc workflow

Application integration

This solution links together applications within a business. Application integration can be used within a business pattern or between business patterns. An example is ERP integration.

Access Integration

The Access Integration pattern describes those recurring designs that enable access to one or more business patterns. In particular, this pattern enables access from multiple channels (devices) and integrates the common services required to support a consistent user interface.

e-Marketplace

e-Marketplaces are trading exchanges that facilitate and promote buying, selling and business communities among trading partners within certain industries. These solutions represent some of the most comprehensive and complex e-business applications that exist today. There are three types of e-Marketplaces:

- Trading Exchange
- Sell-Side Hub
- Buy-Side Hub

A Trading Exchange allows buyers and sellers to trade goods and services on a public site. The Composite pattern for a Trading Exchange consists of:

- The *Self-Service business pattern* that facilitates the interaction between the buyer and the e-Marketplace. Activities such as purchasing from an aggregated catalog, participating in auctions or making exchanges are performed using this pattern.

The Self-Service business pattern also helps the non-commerce seller perform functions such as updating the catalog, checking orders, checking Request for Quotations and accessing orders.

- The *Information Aggregation business pattern* is used to create the e-Marketplace catalog from the multiple sources of suppliers' product files, pricing files and advertising literature and so on.

- The *Application Integration pattern* is used to integrate these two business patterns seamlessly and also to integrate with existing e-Marketplace support systems like billing.

- The *Access Integration pattern* is used to provide a Portal interface, single sign-on functions and personalization functions for the e-Marketplace.

In addition to these basic functions there could be many additional functions that can be added to an e-Marketplace as it evolves. Consider these examples:

- The Collaboration business pattern can be used to enable the purchasing approval process

- The Extended Enterprise business pattern can be used on both the buyer and seller side of the e-Marketplace. On the buyer side, the pattern defines the interaction between the buyer's procurement system and the commerce functions of the e-Marketplace. On the seller side, this pattern defines the interaction between the procurement functions of the e-Marketplace and its suppliers.

In a Sell-Side Hub, the seller owns the e-Marketplace and uses it as a vehicle to sell goods and services to prospective buyers across the Web. The Composite pattern for the Sell-Side Hub includes the following patterns:

- Access Integration pattern that helps provide a unified customer interface

- Self-Service business pattern that allows users to browse through a catalog, create an order and place an order with the hub

- Information Aggregation business pattern that is used to create the e-Marketplace catalog from the multiple sources of suppliers' product files, pricing files and advertising literature and so on

- Application Integration patterns that integrate the Business Patterns that are a part of the Sell-side hub

In addition to these basic functions, there can be several variations on this pattern. These include:

- Adding a Collaboration business pattern that allows for and enables auctions, reverse auctions and other collaborative buying functions

- Adding an Information Aggregation business pattern that will help integrate and present a unified catalog that combines raw catalog data with expert advice, product comparisons and recommendations that can be pulled off public internet sites

- Adding an Extended Enterprise business pattern that will integrate the Sell-Side hub with external service providers such as a financial institution to handle credit processing or shipping company to handle the physical delivery of goods

In a Buy-Side Hub the buyer of goods owns the e-Marketplace and uses it as a vehicle to leverage the buying or procurement budget to solicit the best deals for goods and services from prospective sellers across the Web. The Composite pattern for the Buy-Side Hub includes:

- Access Integration pattern that helps provide a unified customer sign-on capability and a personalized user interface

- Collaboration business pattern that will allow users to post bids, participate in auctions and respond to Requests for Proposals (RFP) and Requests For Quotations (RFQ)

- Self-Service business pattern that allows buyers to create RFQs and RFPs

- Application Integration patterns that integrate the Buy-Side Hub with procurement systems and other core business applications

In addition to these basic functions, there can be several variations on this pattern. These include:

- Adding an Information Aggregation business pattern that will help integrate content sources across the Web

- Adding an Extended Enterprise business pattern that will integrate the buy-side hub with external service providers such as financial institutions

Portals

A Portal solution is typically designed to aggregate multiple information sources and applications to provide a single, seamless and personalized access for its users. There are many variations of Portal applications. The Composite pattern for Portal applications is made up of an Access Integration pattern that facilitates functions such as single sign-on, multiple device support and personalization plus at least one other business pattern.

Many variants of portal applications exist. But, two of the most commonly seen implementations include:

- An Enterprise Intranet Portal
- A Collaboration Application Service Provider (ASP)

Account Access

Account Access solutions provide customers around-the-clock access to their account information. They also allow users to inquire, update and delete information on their individual accounts. There are many applications that fall under this category of solutions, ranging from trading applications provided by online brokerages to account manager functions provided by utilities such as telephone companies. This category of solutions also includes account access applications provided by banks, credit card companies and insurance companies.

The Composite pattern for an Account Access solution consists of:

- An Access Integration pattern that provides a unified mechanism to implement single sign-on capabilities. This pattern is also used to provide a personalized experience to the account holder.

- A Self-Service business pattern which provides access to information stored in core business systems and databases

- The solution may optionally include an Information Aggregation pattern in cases where information from multiple accounts is summarized to provide a single unified portfolio view to the customer.

- The solution can also include the Collaboration business pattern as functions such as online chat with a customer service representative and help desk support are added to it.

- If the solution has any one of the optional Business patterns the solution may optionally include an Application Integration pattern to seamlessly combine multiple Business patterns.

You must carefully select the pattern that best suits your customer requirements case to take advantage of the pattern solution provided. Table 1 suggests a mapping between the problem space and the IBM Patterns for e-business.

Table 1. Business patterns corresponding to different solution areas

e-business problem space	Business pattern
Customer Relationship Management	Self-service
E-commerce	Electronic Commerce, e-Marketplace
Supply Chain Management	Extended Enterprise
Business Intelligence	Information Aggregation
Business application integration	Mixture of the patterns

For the latest information on IBM Patterns for e-business, go to:
http://www.ibm.com/developerworks/patterns/

Once you select the pattern that corresponds to the e-business solution you are designing, the Web site presents a step-by-step approach to suggest a design for your solution.

2.4.2 Design space

To develop an e-business solution, the Framework for e-business highlights the decision blocks shown in Figure 10.

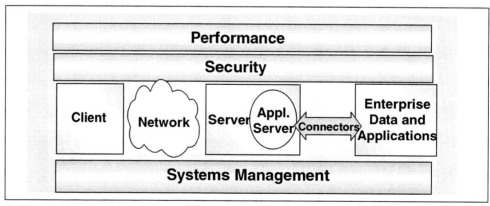

Figure 10. Design space

To achieve an optimal solution, a designer should perform two fundamental tasks for each block:

1. Describe the key decisions that need to be made, the impact of the decision on the solution, and suggestions on how to make the decision
2. Identify known options or products for each logical block

This section discusses the key decisions in the following decision blocks:

- Client
- Network
- Application server
  - Application logic
  - Application development tools

- Enterprise applications and data
- Connectors
- System management
- Security
- Performance

2.4.2.1 Clients

The clients (as shown in Figure 10) supported by the Framework are "thin clients". This means that little or no application logic is executed on the client and, therefore, relatively little software is required to be installed on the client. In this model, applications are managed on the server and dynamically downloaded "on-demand" to requesting clients. As such, the client portions of new applications should be implemented in HTML, Dynamic HTML, XML, and Java applets. The clients can range from pervasive devices, such as PDAs, screen phones, and smartcards, to network computers and PCs.

Table 2 shows the key decision factors, their impact on the client design, and some suggestions.

Table 2. Client logical block: Decisions, impact, and suggestions

Decisions	Impact	Suggestions
Who is the customer (Internet or intranet)?	On an intranet, you may have some control over the hardware and software specifications of the clients. You may even choose to use some client types other than, or in addition to, a standard browser.	If your application is to be made available over the Internet, your design point may be the two leading browsers.
What is the user's skill level?	This will impact the screen design.	You may want to plan for human factors studies of the dialogs. Other related factors include possible requirements to support the text-only mode of operations for sight-impaired people or for scientific professionals, who have been reported to prefer the speed of text-only mode when reading academic papers online.

Decisions	Impact	Suggestions
What languages should the site support?	You clearly need to support the language of the country of your e-business customer set. If you need to support more than one language, you should think carefully about the implications of maintaining versions of your pages in different languages.	Use site translation management tools to help in translating the site content.
Is normal HTML presentation adequate, or should the user interface be enhanced through the use of Java applets?	Applets take time to download and may be a concern over dial-up connections.	Java applets can be used to make the presentation more flexible and user friendly.
How will the choice of client affect end-to-end response?	- If an HTML page has many complex objects, the number of connections required by HTTP may be large, download time may be impacted, and rendering time in the browser may suffer. - The use of Java applets will slow down initial response while the applet loads, but may allow subsequent interactions to be faster.	You should consider key Internet technologies and how they might affect the response time. Compare response times of HTML with Java applets.
Will the client control the interaction?	A client-driven interaction will require synchronous connection to the server. Carefully consider authentication and authorization issues, who is in charge, and how to ensure integrity throughout the session.	An applet is a reasonable choice to interface directly (usually through a gateway in the Web server) to back end applications and data. This can be a straightforward way to Web-enable back-end systems with a minimum of modification.
Will the state or session be managed by the client?	If the client manages a state/session, then consider the appropriate technologies (see the options in Table 3), along with the security concerns of maintaining information on the client.	You can use cookies, a hidden field or URL component, or applet to manage the session state. See 3.1, "Technology" on page 65, for details. Table 3 shows the state management options on the client.

Decisions	Impact	Suggestions
Will a pervasive computer, such as a PDA or mobile phone, be presented by the same content as the normal browser?	If the same page is presented to both browsers and PDAs with limited display area, then you should significantly reduce the size of the data presented to PDAs without sacrificing the content.	Use transcoders to dynamically extract the important data from the Web pages and present it in a compact form to PDAs.
Will the site use proprietary scripts, tags, or plug-ins?	The use of proprietary features limits the application's portability.	Only use proprietary scripts, tags, and plug-ins when you can control the type of clients (for example, in intranet solutions) and when their use is mandated.

Table 3 shows the session and state management options to assist you in the selection of the state management for the clients

Table 3. Session and state management options

Type	Uses	Comments
Cookies	Maintain session state	See the note below for a description of cookies. Also note that a user may set their browser to refuse cookies because of (unfounded) fears that they introduce privacy exposures. For that reason, your application should be designed to work when cookies are unavailable.
Hidden fields or URL component	Maintain session state	Hidden fields or strings appended as options to a URL can be used to contain an encoded field that defines the session state. Note that because these are visible to users either directly or via the browser View Source command, they should not contain passwords in clear text, for example. The server should also take care to destroy the session variable at the completion of a transaction because the information could persist in the browser's cache. This would allow a subsequent user of the workstation to attempt to continue the previous user's transaction.
Applets	Manage session	An entire transaction consisting of several interactions with a server can be performed by a single Java applet, which therefore maintains the state. This is more complex to implement because it involves selecting and implementing a protocol for communicating between the applet and its partner on the host.

Note: The cookie is a mechanism introduced by Netscape, but is now standard across most browsers. The server can request a piece of information to be stored on the client computer, which can then be retrieved on a subsequent transaction. Expiration time can be associated with cookies. For a shopping card application, the expiration time might be in the order of minutes, where for tracking browsing patterns, the expiry period might be months or years. The server matches a returned cookie, which is typically a large random-looking number, against previously issued cookies to determine whether this is a new or known user.

2.4.2.2 Network

The network infrastructure (as shown in Figure 10 on page 30) provides a platform for the entire architecture. It includes the following services, all based on open standards:

- **TCP/IP and network services**: Dynamically assign IP addresses as devices enter and leave the network, such as DHCP.

- **Security services**: Based on public key technology that supports user identification and authentication, access control, confidentiality, data integrity, and non-repudiation of transactions.

- **Directory services**: Locate users, services, and resources in the network

- **File and print services**: Are accessed and managed via a standard Web browser interface

Table 4 shows the key decision factors, their impact on the network design, and some suggestions.

Table 4. Network logical block: Decisions, impact, and suggestions

Decisions	Impact	Suggestions
What protocol will you use?	HTTP is the standard protocol used by browsers. Other protocols that you might find are file transfer protocol (FTP) and HTTP over Secure Sockets Layer (HTTPS). Application protocols might include IIOP, remote method invocation (RMI), Messaging, or remote procedure call (RPCs).	Try to use standard protocols as much as possible and ensure that the firewalls will support the selected protocols. Determine which parts of the interaction necessitate HTTPS, since HTTPS will affect performance.
Are there more than one protocols being used?	If yes, then the new application being developed will have to handle communicating over different network protocols.	Think about a standard communications mechanism between applications that can hide the network protocols from the application being developed.
Is the network reliable?	If not, then you may lose messages between applications across the network.	Use a reliable messaging software to avoid losing messages over a unreliable network. Alternatively, consider replication technologies.

Decisions	Impact	Suggestions
Will the network traffic be a major bottleneck for performance?	To understand the impact of the e-business application on your network, you need to know the data and application placement. An analysis of the projected transaction volumes, the amount of data that is typically requested, and the amount of interaction are required to help with decisions on network options.	Lack of attention to this area could cause severe performance problems. Think of using HTTP sprayers to help ease the network traffic by distributing it across a set of Web servers.
What about data, object and application placement?	In order to understand the impact of the e-business application on your network, you need to know the data and application placement.	An analysis of the projected transaction volumes, the amount of data that is typically requested, and the amount of object interaction are required to help with decisions about your architectural alternatives.
What security functions are required or provided by this building block?	Protocols can affect security design.	You need to check whether the IIOP, RMI, Messaging, or RPCs that you may be considering can flow across your network. The level of encryption that you are considering will affect your network requirements and have performance implications.
Will your existing network function as required?	While your current network infrastructure may function with the introduction of a new e-business solution, additional work may be needed in network design.	The network may need to be expanded with additional function or capacity. This activity would typically be a separate effort, perhaps conducted in parallel with the development of the new e-business solution.
How does the network affect your end-to-end response time?	Compare estimated traffic against available bandwidth to come up with initial estimates of network responses.	Take into account peaks and average loadings.

2.4.2.3 Web application server

The Web application server (as shown in Figure 10 on page 30) is the platform that provides the runtime environment for the application's business logic. It is implemented using various Internet and Java technologies, including the HTTP server and the Enterprise Java services that enable rapid development and deployment of applications in a distributed network environment.

Web application server consists of two main decision blocks:

- Application logic
- Application development tools

Application logic

Application logic is built from the following components:

- Enterprise JavaBeans (EJB)
- Servlets
- JavaServer Pages (JSP)
- Common Gateway Interface (CGI) programs

Table 5 shows the key decision factors, their impact on the application logic design, and some suggestions.

Table 5. Application server logical block: Decisions, impact, and suggestions

Decisions	Impact	Suggestions
Is this a logical two-, three-, or n-tier solution?	The main impact is the placement of logic (presentation, business, and data access) on the tiers. In particular, you should answer the question of whether the application server is in charge of managing transactions, security, and access to back-end applications.	To directly access back-end applications, use the middle tier as a gateway. The client should be thin (HTML based), the server should manage interaction, and the application server should have business logic and data access logic. Even in a physical 2-tier, client/server approach, ensure that the client is thin, and the server separates the management of interaction (Web server) from the application/-business logic and data access (Web application server). A two-tier solution is only suitable for providing direct access to existing applications. Most likely, you will use an n-tier solution, with a separate Web server from the application server to handle security, manage transactions, and access back-end applications.
Has it been determined whether to use component-based development, traditional programming development, or integrated packages?	Existing packages, if they meet requirements, are usually faster to implement. Component-based development, with its built-in reuse capability, also offers implementation benefits in conjunction with appropriate development tools.	A component-based solution (for example, EJB) provides the best choice if the application will change and needs to interoperate with other systems. Procedural programming can be used to extend existing applications.

Decisions	Impact	Suggestions
Is the server primarily used as a gateway to connect to back-end applications?	A gateway runs on the server and interfaces between a client and the back-end system. This can be a straightforward way to Web-enable back-end systems with a minimum of modification.	Usually this is a good approach if there are hard time constraints since usually no modifications are required to the back-end application code. Try to use existing gateways, for example, Net.Data to access back-end databases, CICS Transaction Gateway to access CICS applications, and MQSeries Internet Gateway to access MQ-based applications.
How will the application be split between client-side logic and server-side logic?	The key decision is who is in charge of the transactional context (for example, begin-commit in a 2-phase commit), it can be the client, the server, or the back-end tier.	Use server-driven interaction, with a clear separation of interaction logic from business logic. Let the business logic handle transactions and access to back-end applications.
How will the presentation logic be separated from the business logic?	Most applications will need to support multiple client types. The user interface logic and the business logic will evolve independently.	Wrap the business logic with a simple task-based interface, for example, by using a Command Bean. Don't expose the details of the business logic object model.
Should the server provide indexing and searching or other site navigation aids?	Some servers, or server packages, provide these capabilities as standard, but depending on your requirements, you may need a special purpose indexing/search engine.	Do not try writing your own search engine. It is a good idea to use the standard capabilities provided by the server. List the searching capabilities that you need: - Do you need to be able to search a single server or many? - What should be indexed: HTML files, word processor files, PDF files, other formats, or databases?
Will the site use Java applets? What are their connectivity requirements?	As part of the standard security built in to Java, an applet can only communicate with the server from which it was downloaded.	If the applet needs to communicate with another server, this has to be done indirectly via its own server or through the use of digitally signed applets.

Decisions	Impact	Suggestions
How can you estimate the server component of end-to-end response time?	This is usually not straight forward. In practice, the results that you will achieve will depend, in large measure, on your application design. You should include some performance testing in your project plan.	The Standard Performance Evaluation Corporation at http://www.specbench.org now includes SPECweb and SPECJVM among its published results. At best, these results can be used to gain a general feel for the relative speeds of various processors and allow a very rough estimate of transaction throughput.

Application development tools

The Framework provides a broad range of tools to enable creation, deployment, and management of e-business applications for Internet, extranet, and intranet environments. It also supports integrating third-party tools into the development process. The Framework supports the different skill sets involved in developing Web applications, providing tools that target specific skill sets, and facilitates collaboration among members of the development team.

Table 6 shows the key decision factors, their impact on the selection of the application development tools, and some suggestions.

Table 6. Application development tools: Decisions, impact, and suggestions

Decisions	Impact	Suggestions
Will the application development tools facilitate different parts of the application to be built by personnel with appropriate skills?	Developing the presentation, business, and data access logic requires different skill sets. It is difficult to have one person or one team build the entire e-business application.	Make sure that the different tools (for example, for Web page creation, Web site management, UI building, application development, and connecting to the back-end systems) all work well together.
How much integration is provided by the application development tool set?	The degree to which the type of e-business application development is integrated into a single development environment can help provide productivity for the development team.	Ensure that all tools can interoperate, for example, the parts produced in one tool are usable in another using round trip engineering. Ensure that the parts that make up the entire project can be managed and controlled in a consistent manner.
How will a team development environment be supported?	The development tools should support a team environment providing integrity for application code.	The development environment should facilitate building an application from many parts developed by different teams. Also, debugging in such an integrated environment should allow all the parts in the application to be executed together.

Decisions	Impact	Suggestions
Will the code be developed on one platform and deployed on another? How is the application deployed across n-tiers?	The development tools should allow for the development of code on the platform that is most productive for developers, and then assist in deployment to other platforms. The deployment must facilitate spreading the application appropriately across n-tiers.	The development tools should include the ability to package modules for deployment on different servers. This functionality can be provided by the development environment or by allowing development tools to interoperate with system management tools.
How does the tool assist the developer in ensuring all parts of complex components have been completed?	Components have very complex interfaces that need to be implemented correctly and completely to allow them to function correctly. For example, a server component may need to define a client-side proxy, a copy helper, a key to find the component, an interface to store/restore the component, etc., to allow it to function properly in an n-tier solution.	Tools should provide smart guides that assist the developer in a step-by-step process to ensure that all the necessary parts of the components are properly defined.

2.4.2.4 Enterprise data and application

The enterprise data and application (as shown in Figure 10 on page 30) are fundamental to the emergence of the Web application model because they are the result of years of corporate investment in information technology. These are the applications and data that everyone depends on daily, and they are the business assets that need to be made available to the Web in a secure, controlled way to enable companies to leverage their value for customers, employees, and suppliers in intranets and extranets. They are implemented by different software and platforms from various suppliers and manufacturers.

A carefully detailed description of the existing data and application will impact the design and selection of the e-business connectors and the method of integration with the Web application server, for example:

- If the enterprise application is residing on a mainframe, the CICS client needs to be used for data interchange.

- If the enterprise application runs on a non-IBM modern platform, you may consider using MQSeries to exchange message with the Web application server.

Table 9 shows the key decision factors, their impact on the Enterprise data access design, and some suggestions.

Table 7. Enterprise data access building block: Decisions, impact, and suggestions

Decisions	Impact	Suggestions
Do the service hours for the enterprise data repository match the e-business application targets?	You may have to make some policy decisions about how to treat requests that cannot be handled immediately.	Options include asking the user to resubmit or placing the request on a queue for later handling, with possible confirmation by e-mail.
How will you map the access authorization rules for the corporate database to your e-business user identification?	This will be an important question if you intend to enable a controlled ability for certain Web users to update corporate database records.	We recommend you define the access rights and control them by one server.
Is your e-business application using the corporate data for reference (that is, read-only access)?	There may be performance or other advantages to working with a local extract of the database if the requirement for data currency permits.	Use an efficient connector to link to the reference data in the enterprise application server.
Is the data in a format that is easily accessed by distributed systems?	Enterprise Data may be held in extended binary coded decimal interchange code (EBCDIC) and require translation to ASCII for presentation on the browser. Implications that may (or may not) affect your design include different sorting sequences and number formats.	Consider careful data format conversion because there may be some incompatibilities in the character representation across platforms.
If additional code is needed to gain access to data (for example, non-relational data), how will this code be developed?	If your enterprise data is located on a mainframe, you may need to develop additional CICS transactions or MQSeries triggered transactions to interface to existing data or application logic.	You need to decide how this code will be developed and if there are resources available to develop this additional interface code.

Decisions	Impact	Suggestions
If access is to relational databases, can the SQL be structured to minimize network traffic?	When enterprise data can be accessed with SQL calls, you should review the number of calls needed to satisfy a request. Since issuing SQL calls can be simple, it is sometimes tempting to rely on this when designing the architectural alternatives.	Be careful that your architecture does not force you into issuing too many SQL calls, therefore, reducing performance because of network traffic. Consolidating SQL calls with the appropriate use of joins can reduce network traffic. Using stored procedures to consolidate SQL calls can also reduce network traffic. Using a transaction monitor can also provide a way to reduce server-to-enterprise server interactions. Also, resist the temptation to design business logic into the stored procedure because you will loose flexibility in your design.
What are the commit and rollback requirements of the application?	For Web applications, you need to pay particular attention to incomplete or cancelled transactions. At times of slow network response, the user is very likely to click the Stop button on the browser and immediately retry the transaction.	Your application design must allow for this.

Table 10 gives brief general comments about ways to access back-end systems.

Table 8. Enterprise data and applications

Type	Uses	Comments
Relational database management system (RDBMS)	Enterprise data	RDBMSs are now the standard data repository. Most products offer one or more options for Web-enablement.
Transactional systems monitor	High-volume transactional access to enterprise data	Special-purpose transaction monitors, such as CICS and Encina, can often handle larger volumes of transactions than Web servers.
Packaged solutions	Standard applications	Your client may have standard packages that you need to include in your solution. Examples include ERP packages from various vendors or business software from companies, such as SAP.

2.4.2.5 Connectors

Connectors (as shown in Figure 10 on page 30) play a key role in linking and extending the Framework's Web application programming environment to other programming environments. This means that existing, reliable business applications can be extended to the Web with minimal changes. Specifically, connectors enable Web access to:

- Relational and hierarchical data as stored in IBM and other vendors' databases

- Application programs that run in transactional environments such as CICS, IMS, and Encina

- Applications written for object-oriented programming environments such as OMG's CORBA

- Industry applications from vendors such as SAP, Baan, and PeopleSoft

- Services outside the enterprise such as payment system clearinghouses and security key registry services

By protecting investments in proven, reliable applications and systems, connectors allow businesses to realize the competitive advantages of the Web more quickly and less expensively.

Table 9 shows the key decision factors, their impact on the connectors design, and some suggestions.

Table 9. Connectors building block: Decisions, impact, and suggestions

Decisions	Impact	Suggestions
What enterprise systems, applications, and data do the e-business application need to access?	The type of data, application, platform, and network may influence the technologies that you may need to consider in different architectural alternatives.	Use standard connectors (for example, JDBC or ODBC to access relational data) wherever possible. The only time that you should use non-standard connectors is when you access existing applications without modification or when performance is a major issue.
How should data be transferred between different systems?	Data needs to be transferred in a format that is compatible to the systems that are using it. If the systems do not agree on the data format they interchange, data will be lost across the systems.	Relational database systems provide ways to access distributed data that handle the data types and data conversion requirements. For other transfer mechanisms, you should determine the complexity level of the data. From this, you should determine whether a self-describing message format, such as that provided by the XML technology, is needed.
How current does the information have to be?	If the information does not have to be updated in real-time, you may be able to use local extracts or caches to improve performance.	Use local extracts or caches for information, state, and personalization.

Decisions	Impact	Suggestions
Will the application require synchronous or asynchronous access to the enterprise applications and data?	The use of an asynchronous messaging with assured message delivery allows the application to continue operation even if the network connection or remote application is unavailable. Synchronous technology requires a connection to be available whenever the application is available.	Asynchronous messaging does not preclude using it in a synchronous mode. Access resources involved in a 2-phase commit transaction via a synchronous mode.
Will you require access to different operating system, network protocols, and application environments?	Although TCP/IP is the standard network protocol of the Web, your back-end systems may be using other protocols. Also, applications may be using standard or non-standard APIs. If protocol conversation is needed, you have to decide where is the best place to do the conversion.	Use protocol converters provided by the tool or product that is used for development. For example, most application servers provide connectors to communicate with CICS or IMS applications.
Is a new user interface (UI) required? If so, what kind?	If you are accessing enterprise data or application logic that currently has a defined user interface, you may need a redesign of that interface allowing program access. Alternatively, you may need to employ the use of technologies that allow access to the logic and data.	Try not to change any of the enterprise application logic because there may be other interfaces to it already in place. Use wrappers and the appropriate call interface (for example, External Presentation Interface (EPI) versus External Call Interface (ECI) versus External CICS Interface (EXCI) to access CICS applications). Performance may dictate the best call interface (for example, ECI over EPI for CICS.)
Will you require additional security policies?	Enterprise data and applications may have their own access security policies controlled and administered separately from those in place for the Internet environment. If access to enterprise data and applications is needed, how will security policies be enforced?	If the application server is a trusted node, then it can act as a proxy to the enterprise data and applications. If not, the user IDs and passwords must be mapped from the application or Web server to the enterprise servers. Ensure that the connector technology that you are using can support the security needs.

Decisions	Impact	Suggestions
Can you predict what scalability and performance you will require?	Failing to properly size the connectors speed and throughput could cause severe system performance degradation.	Give careful consideration to performance when designing the application. If you choose to go with a prototype, you should allow time to review the design for performance before going into production.

As part of the connectors building block, you should try to decide which attributes to look for when interfacing into enterprise data and applications as shown in Table 10.

Table 10. Connector types

Type	Uses	Comments
Messaging	Asynchronous access to enterprise servers	Messaging middleware can simplify the application programming task by handling queueing, time-out, and recovery/restart conditions. You can also use messaging middleware in a pseudo-synchronous mode. Typically, messaging technology can support large message sizes. Some RPC approaches may be limited in message size requiring additional programming to handle large messages.
JDBC/ODBC	Database calls	These are database-independent interfaces for Java servlets or application programs to make calls to databases that may be on the same or another server.
Native interfaces	Database calls	Many database vendors have implemented native application program interfaces to their own databases that offer a performance advantage over ODBC at the expense of application portability.
Remote Procedure Call	To call programs on remote servers	You may not need to program at the RPC level if you have an application builder that takes care of this for you.
Conversational	Little used in e-business applications	This is typically low-level program-to-program communication using protocols, such as advanced program-to-program communication (APPC) or sockets.

2.4.2.6 Systems management

Within an enterprise, systems management services (as shown in Figure 10 on page 30) provide the core functionality that supports end-to-end management across networks, systems, middleware, and applications. The Framework provides:

- The tools and services that support management of the complete life cycle of an application from installation and configuration, to the monitoring of its operational characteristics.

- A collaborative management approach for establishing and following procedures to share information and coordinate problem resolution with business partners. This collaborative approach includes:

- Policy management
- Data repository
- Scheduling
- Report generation

System management is a broad term that encompasses many disciplines, such as performance measurement, availability reporting, reactive problem reporting, software distribution. It also includes updates, proactive monitoring to anticipate problems, and other problem determination tools. Many of these system management disciplines can be applied, to some degree, even when the network is the Internet (an environment over which you have no control).

However, you should note that some things, such as end-to-end performance management or problem determination of network outages, cannot be done for the Internet. Other things, such as the distribution of software updates, are quite applicable to the Internet.

It is tempting to create a pilot site as a proof of concept and then put the site live on the Internet without considering system management issues. However, it is usually harder to add system management tools and techniques after your site has gone live.

Table 11 shows some of the system management policy decisions concerning the management and operation of the system that you should resolve during the architecture development phase and describes the impact of those decisions on the design.

Table 11. System management decision points

Decision	Impact
Does the company have the infrastructure to install and run its own e-business server?	If not, you may need to factor into your design ways of developing the appropriate infrastructure. This may lead to recommendations for personnel, technologies, and support products, or the customer may want to have a third party host the service.
What hours should the service be available?	Keep in mind that the company's site may be accessed from different time zones and that typical Internet users expect 100 percent availability.
Is it acceptable to have any scheduled downtime for maintenance?	If not, make a provision in the design for how maintenance and upgrades are to be made. Availability issues such as these will affect the cost of the solution. If back-end systems are subject to interruption for backup or maintenance, the customer may still want their home page to be available to give details of service status.
How important is it that the service never be interrupted, even for unscheduled component failures?	Avoiding all single points of failure may be costly. Investigate for redundancy in all components.
If interruptions occur, what should the target time for restoring service be?	This implies that service-level agreements should be established. Knowing the requirements for the service-level agreements will impact the decision points for availability of your e-business solution.

Decision	Impact
How should partial or total service failures be monitored and handled?	Think about how the application will handle failures. Technologies, such as Simple Network Management Protocol (SNMP), assist in monitoring the application environment by making use of Management Information Base (MIB) standards. You should investigate how well the management tools you select support these management standards.
What are the response time targets?	Response time targets may vary by transaction type. Establishing an end-to-end budget for response time provides a way to checkpoint each component within the building blocks during the design phase, as well as later during implementation and testing.
Do you need a recovery plan for this e-business system, or will it be covered by your organization's existing processes?	This should cover the loss of individual components, such as hard drives or processors, as well as a disaster that involves the entire site.
How should the architecture support the process of problem reporting, tracking, and fixing?	Who should be alerted, and how, if there is a hardware or software problem that affects the site?
What statistics do you need to keep about the site, and how will they be analyzed?	One essential measure of the effectiveness of a site is the number of visitors. It is important to understand how easy it is to find information by tracking their navigation patterns.
What instrumentation should you include in the design to measure performance, response times, and availability?	You need these details to make informed decisions about capacity plans. Also, your application can provide event information so that operations can take proactive steps to recover in case of an application failure.
Should the architecture include a repository for statistical data?	Can you make an estimate of the storage space required by the repository? Does the design need to include off-loading historic statistical data to archival storage?

2.4.2.7 Security

Security services (as shown in Figure 10 on page 30) include:

- The check for user authentication using the information stored in the directory

- Encryption services needed to provide privacy and non-repudiation capabilities, and, where needed, a certificate authority

- Proxy servers and firewalls that provide managed isolation between public and private networks using packet filtering, content filtering, address filtering, caching, and "address hiding" techniques

- Virtual private network (VPN) services that effectively provide secure paths for private data through the public Internet

Key security requirements for e-business include:

- **Authorization**: How do you ensure that users are who they claim to be? How do different elements in the system locate and determine whether to trust one another? How do you enable new customers or business partners to access existing systems without major changes to existing security infrastructure? Whose identity should be used to determine authorization: the end user, the server, or some other entity?

- **Asset protection**: Can you keep data confidential and private when it's stored and when it's traveling across untrusted networks? How can you be sure that the data doesn't change while it's stored or in transit?

- **Accountability**: How can you tell who did what and when? How can you ensure, and prove, that requests and results are not altered, inadvertently or maliciously?

- **Administration**: Can you define the security policy? Can you ensure that policies are consistent across all elements of applications, systems, platforms, and networks?

- **Assurance**: Can you convince yourself that the system keeps its security promises? How can you ensure that the infrastructure and application resources, including systems, networks, and data, are not presently under attack?

- **Availability**: How do you prevent attacks on elements of the system that cause disruptions in service? How do you design for fault tolerance and ensure that applications and data are restored in the event of a serious failure? How can you keep the system up and running 7 X 24 and make necessary modifications to the application, the systems, and the enterprise network?

The services provided by the Framework for e-business allow you to deal effectively with these requirements.

Table 12 lists the questions you need to consider when deciding on the security policy, procedures, and practices for your company's site.

Table 12. Security building block: Decisions, impact, and suggestions

Decisions	Impact	Suggestions
Do transactions need to be encrypted?	Encryption is an expensive operation and will impact your end-to-end budget. Deciding such things as which transactions or which parts of a message need encryption, and the levels of encryption needed inside the firewall versus outside the firewall, may impact the design and, certainly, the technologies. Analyze technologies, such as Secure Socket Layer (SSL) and SET, for applicability.	Use a minimum acceptable security level. To apply SET, the country has to approve and support it, or you must find a Certification Authority and a bank supporting SET to perform the transactions.

Decisions	Impact	Suggestions
If servers or clients will be located outside the USA, is 40-bit encryption acceptable?	The U.S. is relaxing some controls over the export of cryptographic products. Financial institutions in many countries can now obtain export licenses. If this does not apply, your customer may need to seek strong cryptography from non-US sources.	Find out what is the minimum acceptable encryption level. If a high encryption level is required, then obtain the necessary approval to supply the allowed encryption level.
How will users be identified?	Decide what information will be open to all visitors and at what point users need to be identified. Table 13 summarizes the technologies used to identify users. Cookies can also be used to recognize repeat visitors to the site without needing to know any of their personal details. Evaluate the use of digital signatures for applicability.	See comments on Table 13.
Is there an existing customer database that should be used to identify online visitors to the site?	User profiling can help collect information about visitors to your customer's site providing capabilities to dynamically control interactions with users. Investigating technologies to enable these possibilities should be pursued.	Try to minimize the replication of the user profiles databases to ease the management and maintenance of the security definition. Ideally it is better to have the user profiles defined once.
Does your customer need to restrict access to parts of the site?	The number and placement of firewalls is important to restrict unwarranted access to sensitive data and applications. Reviewing existing IBM Intellectual Assets can help understand proven techniques for using firewalls and designing solutions that properly position components around firewalls for asset protection.	Try to minimize the use of firewalls to enhance performance, without sacrificing network security.
What privacy rules should be applied to information provided by users?	Policies should be in place for the use of collected user data. Many countries now have legislation governing the holding of personal data on computer files.	Define the policies that comply to the countries and customers security regulations.
What are the legal requirements and company policies for auditing content, changes, and transactions?	Companies have been held legally liable for the contents of their Web site.	Review the legislative restriction and abide to it.

Decisions	Impact	Suggestions
Does the company already have a secure demilitarized zone (DMZ) into which the Web server could be placed?	If so, you must ensure that the current Web architecture will support requirements of the new e-business solution or decide on compromises to allow your e-business solution to operate within established guidelines.	Use best practices, and review the security requirements.

Table 13 lists various methods of user authentication on the Web with explanatory notes. Table 3 on page 33 offers guidance on state management and its security implications. Revisit these security considerations when dealing with each building block.

Table 13. User identification

Identification method	Uses	Comments
Basic authentication	Simple user ID and password authentication	*Basic authentication* has a specific meaning within the Web protocol. It is supported by most servers, including Domino, and allows simple control over access to files and directories based on a user ID. There are two main shortcomings to this method: - The password is masked, rather than encrypted for transmission; so, this mechanism is not recommended for high-value transactions without some other form of authentication. - The browser caches the password and resubmits it on demand for later transactions. There is no explicit logoff mechanism. This makes it unsuitable for walk up-and-use kiosk applications. Unless a user remembers to close the browser, their identity can be assumed by the next user of the workstation. Basic authentication is, in most cases, used in conjunction with SSL 2. Here, the password is actually encrypted as the data traffic generally is.
Client certificates	Strong authentication	This method authenticates a user with public/private key technology. The technique is used by Notes/Domino and by the standard X.509 certificates of the Web SSL3 protocol. Because of the infrastructure required to issue and manage certificates, this technology is not yet widespread on the Web, although it is well-handled by Notes and Domino. IBM and Lotus are leading industry initiatives to enhance the interoperability of digital certificates.
Application-specific	General user authentication	In this method, user identification is handled completely within the application. The application controls password verification and maintenance. This is the most common way of authenticating visitors to a protected or e-business site. Frequently, the application includes a facility for a forgotten password to be mailed to the e-mail address associated with a user's account.

Identification method	Uses	Comments
Cookies	Not for authentication, but to associate a visitor to your site with previous transactions	Although it is reasonable to use a cookie to maintain state during a shopping transaction, application designers should not rely on cookies for recognition of users across visits separated by days or more. If the user accesses your site from a different workstation or has reinstalled their software, the cookie will not be available to the server.

For the latest security information, consult the Web site at:

http://www.ibm.com/security

2.4.2.8 Performance

The e-business solution performance (as shown in Figure 10 on page 30) is an important factor of successful solution. The response time must consistently meet the required targets regardless of the number of users accessing the system. Reaching higher performance requires extra costs in the system and applications used in the solution. Accurate sizing of the deployed equipment depends on:

- The number of users accessing the solution
- The processing load they will generate on the system
- The storage capacity and processing power each user needs
- The predicted growth of the company

2.4.3 Technology and product space

We have identified different types of problems in developing an e-business solution and looked at the decision-making considerations for each element of the solution. Now we discuss the technology that IBM offers for each problem space.

IBM provides a wide range of solutions to the problem space. An e-business solution is developed using the e-business tools and components shown in Figure 8 on page 22.

To develop an e-business solution for a certain problem, use the proper technology provided by the Framework technology space such as HTTP, HTTPS, XML, EJB, and CORBA. IBM offers products that implement the state of the art technologies, provides them in an easy to use manner, and customizes them to fit each problem space. The technology column in Figure 8 on page 22 lists the technologies used to solve a particular problem and product column lists corresponding IBM products. Consider these examples:

- For Business Intelligence solutions, data integration products provide many features such as data warehousing, mining queries, and analysis. These features are integrated into such products as DB2, Intelligent Miner, or Visual Warehouse.

- For Supply Chain Management solutions, such technologies as XML and Message brokers are key to a successful solution. The products used to develop SCM solutions, such as the MQSeries family, Domino, or E-commerce Integrator, support the necessary technology to develop an SCM solution.

Each product that is provided for a specific solution supports the necessary technology for successful implementation. Technology and product details are outlined in Chapter 3, "IBM Framework for e-business products, technology" on page 65.

2.5 Designing e-business solutions

Designing an e-business solution is not an exact science, meaning no step-by-step checklists are provided. This section does not attempt to be a comprehensive source of technical and product information. However, it presents a broadly-defined approach that, when coupled with business information, helps you design e-business solutions. This chapter focuses on the importance of keeping your solution architecture-centric.

The major steps (as suggested in Figure 11) needed to design an e-business solution are:

1. Gather the customer's requirements.
2. Develop a set of architectural alternatives.
3. Choose one of the architectural alternatives.
4. Select components that address the chosen alternative.

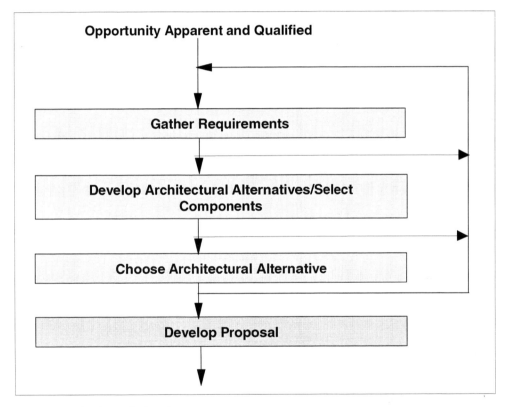

Figure 11. e-business design steps

This is an iterative process. If a significant new requirement surfaces after you have developed the architectural alternatives, you may need to go back and redevelop the alternatives. Similarly, if during the choice of the architecture alternative, you find that the customer indicates none of the alternatives really meets their requirements, you need to go back and gather the requirements again.

Each of these phases is described in more detail in the following sections.

2.5.1 Step 1: Gathering the requirements

Focus on the importance of understanding the requirements, not on techniques, methods, or notations. Remember, the business requirements drive the e-business solution. Do not allow technology to drive the solution.

There are multiple techniques that can be used to gather the business requirements. If a company has identified an opportunity, some of the requirements may already be known. The challenge is to bring these requirements forward, analyze them, and prioritize them so that the process of identifying architectural alternatives can begin.

In addition to business requirements, there is another set of requirements to gather. These could include obstacles, existing conditions, and functional or technical requirements that you or your company have already decided on and must adhere to in the solution (for example, Oracle is the relational database that must be used, or Windows is the client platform). You may need to deal with these because your company may have already decided on them as a company standard.

Organize workshops, interviews, and meetings to gather the customer requirements for the solution you are designing. Agree with the customer on the actual requirements, and describe the outcome details including:

- Business drivers
- Functional requirements
- Nonfunctional requirements
- Existing customer environment

The requirements depend on the e-business solution and the customer needs.

2.5.1.1 Business drivers

It is important to understand the forces that drive the business when designing a solution. They form the basis from which other requirements derive and provide the justification for the eventual solution.

The objective of this step is to gather sufficient requirements to develop several architectural alternatives for consideration. Business requirements themselves do not usually equate directly to technological solutions. However, questions about the business drivers offer a valuable tool to uncover requirements that can be used in the solution design.

Remember that we started with the assumption that an e-business opportunity had been identified and qualified. Although a design is not yet available, some early notion of a solution is typically in the mind of the architects or decision makers, such as "Make our customer order information available from the Internet." To further refine the company requirements, ask the following questions:

- Increase the number of customers?
- Lower operating costs?
- Enhance the image of the company?
- Get our products to market faster?
- Make our business more competitive?
- Reduce our development cycle?
- Increase revenue or decrease costs?

- Enhance customer relationships?
- Improve inventory and procurement management?
- Improve channel relationships?
- Improve customer service?
- Make our employees more effective in teaming and collaboration?
- Allow us to reach new markets?
- Reduce distribution costs?

This is a conversation that should be conducted with an executive (rather than an IT-focused person) who will be more able to state their business goals.

From this, you will derive a list of issues the executives have on their minds. For example, the cost per sale to customers may be above the industry average, or it could be that customers have complained about post-sales support being too difficult. These are the *business drivers*. These kinds of issues are what companies want to address with an e-business solution.

After you develop this list of business drivers, review them with the executive sponsors and gain agreement that they are complete and accurate. Then review this list with both the business and technical representatives to make sure the business drivers are understood.

Identify the true business needs and the value that the solution will add to the business. In a CRM solution, for example, some possible business drivers are:

- Reduce cycle time
- Hold down cost
- Better inventory management
- Improve Customer Service; offer new features and services like:

  - Give end customers inquiry and update access to the information related to that customer, but maintained by the business.

  - Provide customers with convenient access to services from home through the Internet. Extend the current Web-enabled publishing capability with a Web-enabled transaction capability.

  - Ensure that customer interaction is secure and confidential.

  - Provide customization of the customer's experience.

- Reduce time and effort to deploy new enterprise applications, focusing on:

  - Reducing lead time to deploy new applications

  - Supporting and enabling the branch channel by providing new capabilities and access to existing business systems and data

  - Providing broader leverage of existing centralized applications without having to rewrite or re-engineer these applications

  - Sharing and re-using business logic between different delivery systems

  - Providing a highly scalable and highly available Web-enablement of existing business transactions

- Prudent information technology (IT) investments. Key consideration are to:

  - Provide an enterprise architecture and infrastructure that scales to meet a broad range of business requirements.

- Ensure that corporate network and assets are secure from outside (Internet) attacks.
- Ensure a level of manageability for new systems equals existing systems.
- Ensure performance and response time for new systems equals existing systems for internal users and equals best-of-breed in the industry for customer Internet access.

2.5.1.2 Functional requirements

Detail the features and functions required from the e-business solution. You need to agree with the company staff and management on the priority and importance of the requirements. Possible functional requirements in different solutions scenarios are:

- **CRM solution**: Table 14 shows the key requirements and their importance to the customer reflected in the rank column:

Table 14. Example of CRM requirements

Requirement	Rank
Users can check their account status, including their recent purchases and when payments are due.	High
Update orders: Orders can be changed, created, and deleted.	High
Provide a personalized visit.	Medium
Allow user authentication.	High

- **Convenience banking (personal and business banking)**: Table 15 shows the key ranked requirements and their importance to the customer.

Table 15. Example of banking requirements

Requirement	Rank
View account balances	High
View recent transactions	High
Pay bills	Medium
Transfer funds	High
Stop payments	High

- **Supplier integration (SI)**: Table 16 shows the key requirements and their importance to the customer.

Table 16. Example of supplier integration requirements

Requirement	Rank
Automate raw materials reorder process between purchasing and suppliers.	High
Use the existing reorder rules (currently on paper) that define the individual suppliers to be used as a first and second preference for a specific product.	High

2.5.1.3 Nonfunctional requirements

These include customer requirements that are not related to a specific solution function. An example may include a requirement for platform independence and standards-based infrastructure services.

You need to agree with the customer on the non-functional requirements and specify the importance and priority of each requirement to the customer. Table 17 shows the general ranked non-functional requirements.

Table 17. Example of non-functional requirements

Requirement	Rank
Reduce the cost of project planning	High
Reuse information and knowledge between groups	High
Use the market leader's technology	Low
Adhere to industry standards	Medium
Security requirement: User authentication, access only to customer information, secure transactions	High
Operational requirement: 24 x 7	Medium
Performance requirement: Response time for business transactions is 5 seconds for page to page	High
Scalability: Number of online users is greater than 50,000; the number of concurrent online users 200 to 300	High
Availability: 95% of the time	High
Extendability: Potential for addition of new functions, services, and users for; example: financial services, stock trading	High
Flexibility: Should be able to work with all popular browsers	High
Maintainability/manageability: As in current systems	Medium

2.5.1.4 Existing customer environment

To design an effective e-business solution, you need to describe the existing customer environment. This will help to leverage the existing application and build on the existing environment based on sound and correct information. Figure 12 shows an example of an existing customer environment. You need to describe the environment details including:

- Hardware systems (S/390, iSeries, or any other server and its manufacturer)
- Server platforms and operating systems
- Applications
- Network infrastructure such as token-ring, Ethernet, Coaxial, Twinaxial, etc.
- Network protocol such as SNA and TCP/IP
- Clients platform, operating system, and interconnection
- Current problems in the existing system that need to be addressed and resolved in the subject e-business solution

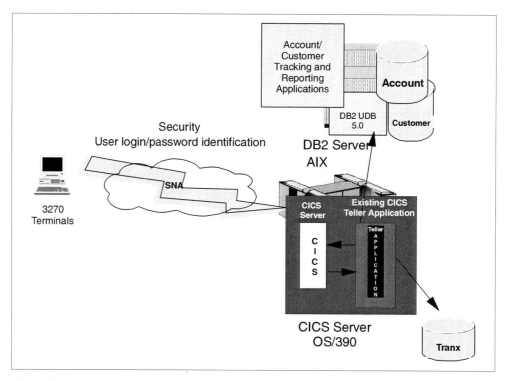

Figure 12. Sample existing customer environment

The key to designing a successful e-business solution is to understand as much as possible about your current environment.

Understanding the network infrastructure

You should assess the current network infrastructure thoroughly. Table 18 shows what information is necessary.

Table 18. Information about the current network environment

Information	Comment
Network baseline information that includes bandwidth, current network traffic, response times, and so forth	Low-speed remote links can impede intranet solutions. Intranet applications can add substantial load to the corporate network.
IP design and facilities (DNS, VPN), if an IP network exists	Existing IP network experience will expedite the implementation of an e-business solution.
Network topology diagrams including router and switch placement, sources, and sync points	Network isolation and address space separation are important elements of e-business solutions and, therefore, impact their complexity.
Application, data, and object placement principles and actual	Mature organizations tend to have placement principles, which may be mandatory for the proposed solution. Also, many e-business opportunities demand access to existing applications and data.

Information	Comment
Management and security policies	These may enable or restrict the use of certain technologies or components. For example, a firewall may restrict traffic to port 80 only, which may prohibit the use of applets that use different ports for communication.
The role of the Internet in the solution	The Internet has a whole list of security and performance issues. Those issues need to be incorporated into the solution design if the Internet is used.

Understanding the integration requirements

Providing connections to the existing servers to achieve access to existing business functions and data is relatively easy. There are a number of IBM and non-IBM middleware products that provide connectivity. The difficult issue is to understand the existing business functions and data structures so that the correct decisions can be made regarding which type of connectivity technology should be employed. If you are planning to integrate a new application with existing applications, Table 19 lists the issues that you should explore.

Table 19. The company's integration requirements

Issue	Comment
Need for real-time access	This influences the selection of middleware used for access to the existing application or server. Real time *generally* implies a synchronous logical connection to the server but could include message queueing technologies. Non-real time would permit the use of asynchronous connections used with message queueing technologies.
Ability to modify existing applications	The existing applications may be off-limits to modification. This may be the case because the source code is no longer available or is a vendor product and, therefore, never open for modification, or the application is stabilized.
Design of the existing application	The existing application's design indicates how the connection can be made. For example, an older 3270 CICS application may not be open for modification; so, some form of interface to the 3270 layer of the application is needed to access the application. However, if the application source code is open for modification, a program-to-program connection may be possible with EXCI or ECI. Also, look at how the presentation layer is abstracted from the logic and data layers. Older applications typically employed programming techniques that blended the three layers together. To the extent that the layers are logically separate in the application's design, the more flexibility you may have in making the connection.

Issue	Comment
Existing infrastructure	Evaluate the type of middleware that presently exists (if any), and determine your attitude towards maintaining that middleware or moving to a new technology. For example, in the late 1980s, *screen scraping* was a popular technique by which data from an existing application was accessed and passed to a graphical interface. Your company may have a large investment in that type of infrastructure and want to maintain all or some parts of it.
Programming skills	Connecting a new application to an existing one almost always involves some level of code customization in the new application or in the existing one, or both. Your company's programming skills are a valuable resource. And your solution design may need to use that existing resource rather than stipulating a new programming skill. That being said, many technologies, such as Java, require object-oriented programming skills. If your company has no such skills in-house, you may want to phase in a design over time or make the case to use contract skills to complete the project.
Data usage	The amount and type of data that needs to be sent and received from the client is an important factor. If your network infrastructure is robust, the amount becomes less of a factor unless some of the clients are remote and across dial lines. Similarly, the form of the data might need to be modified because it travels from data source to presentation point (the client, in other words). If the data is on an S/390 host, an EBCDIC-to-ASCII conversion needs to happen, which can be challenging for binary data types, such as packed decimal, floating point, and signed fields. Also, the issue of national language support (NLS) comes into play if the clients are located in different countries.

Understanding the target client environment

The client environment will impact the possible technology options. At issue is the degree of control your company has over the clients. If the target environment includes clients that are not under your company's control, you may not be able to specify such things as:

- The configuration of the client
- Issuing code updates to the client
- Testing new releases of the client code
- Using applets (Java, ActiveX) or other code

For example, the use of JavaScript may be restricted because of the way different browsers behave with it.

Checkpoint

At this point, you should have a prioritized list of requirements. Before you move on to developing architectural alternatives, ask yourself the following questions:

- Do you believe that all of the business needs and requirements are properly understood and agreed to by all of the customer representatives and the solution providers?

- Do you believe that you and the solution provider fully understand the company's current environment?

- Do you believe the requirements you have gathered so far with the customer are complete, accurate, understood, properly prioritized, and agreed to by all parties?

- Is everyone including the customer and solution provider in agreement that you may move to the next step?

If you can answer *yes* to each question, move on to step 2, which is explained in the following section. Otherwise, you need to go back and repeat some of the steps in this section.

2.5.2 Step 2: Developing alternatives and selecting components

Once you have gathered clear customer requirements, you need to develop architectural alternatives by:

- Making decisions on logical building blocks identified in the design space
- Using key architectural patterns, technologies, and products

After an initial check to determine whether the requirements are so clear-cut that you can base your solution on an existing design, you must create a business scenario, define some fundamental aspects of the architecture, and then develop architectural options building block by building block.

It is helpful to construct the architectural alternatives in a workshop. Conducting this phase in a workshop environment allows you and your company to arrive at agreed-upon diagrams of possible solution architectures in a very effective way.

Refer to 2.4.2, "Design space" on page 30, for a detailed discussion about consideration and suggestions for solution design blocks. After you identify the key considerations in each design block, develop the following diagrams:

- **Solution overview**: Shows the runtime environment in each tier and the communication protocol between tiers

- **Static application design view**: Shows the object, data, and function placement

- **Dynamic application view**: Traces requests from clients through the tiers to satisfy the request

- **Security walkthrough**

Is a simple e-business solution applicable?
Before you invest time in defining your architectural alternatives, you should briefly review the requirements to see whether a clear agreed-upon solution exists. For example, a requirement for a collaborative workflow system may dictate a Notes/Domino solution, or the requirements may be a close fit with the functions provided by WebSphere Commerce Suite. If all parties in the project agree, you could bypass the step of building architectural alternatives.

Note that even a simple e-business solution composed of a single component, such as Notes/Domino or WebSphere Commerce Suite, requires planning for implementation (although that topic is outside the scope of this redbook). However, even if you decide to bypass the formal construction of architectural alternatives, it is still a good idea to review the questions and comments from 2.4.2, "Design space" on page 30.

IBM intellectual capital

IBM has participated in the design of hundreds of e-business solutions. This collection of experiences is a very valuable resource. IBM's strategy is to use the results of this experience in future engagements. If you are an IBM customer, it would be beneficial for you to engage the IBM Global Services group to benefit from their vast experiences. You can find key IBM Global Services offerings at:

http://www.ibm.com/services/partners/SPfaq2a.html

At this point in the e-business solution design, you should have completed three very important tasks:

- Collected business requirements and other requirements from the customer. Moreover, you should have worked to achieve agreement from the customer that the requirements are correct, complete, and may be used to build the solution.

- Developed a business scenario that represents the business processes that your design will support.

- Started the process of developing several architectural alternatives that may apply to the business situation presented by the customer, as defined by the requirements they provided to you.

You could design the architectural alternatives without using any of this collective experience from the IBM solution designers. However, this may result in overlooking things that you had not thought of but that others had. Therefore, it would be best to use, wherever possible, this IBM intellectual capital.

2.5.3 Step 3: Choosing architectural alternative

The purpose of this step is to arrive at a decision about which alternative to implement. We do this by providing a technique for matching the requirements determined in 2.5.1, "Step 1: Gathering the requirements" on page 52, to the architectural alternatives derived in 2.5.2, "Step 2: Developing alternatives and selecting components" on page 59.

We recommend that you conduct this process in the same workshop environment that was used for selecting architectural alternatives. This keeps the customer involved in the process and ensures concurrence with the process and outcome.

Summarize the relative strengths and weaknesses of the alternative solutions by comparing and contrasting the alternative solutions according to the following defined qualities:

- **Performance**: Response time for requests
- **Capacity**: Total number of requests that can be handled
- **Security**: The ability to resist unauthorized access and allow legitimate users access
- **Availability**: The proportion of time the system is up and running

- **Usability**: Ensuring that the right information is available to the user at the right time and ensuring that the user requests go to the right service providers. This is from the end users' perspective.
- **Maintainability**: The ability to modify the system, delete unwanted capabilities, adapt to new operating environments, and restructure the system.
- **Testability**: The ease with which software can be made to demonstrate its faults through testing.
- **Scalability**: The ability to make incremental changes quickly and cost effectively, and the ability to handle ever increasing loads.
- **Portability**: The ability of the system to run under different computing environments.
- **Reusability**: The ability to reuse the systems' structure and components in other applications.
- **Business quality**: The extent to which the alternative fulfills the customer's business requirements including cost, schedule, staff, resources, and so on.

The comparison can be performed by building a matrix of requirements to alternatives.

Then grade each alternative by assessing the extent to which the alternative meets the requirement. This grading process is best kept simple by using a *plus* (+), *neutral* (o), or *minus* (-) symbol for each cell in the matrix. Table 20 defines the grading symbols.

Table 20. Definition of grading symbols

Symbol	Description
+	This indicates that the requirement is met and exceeded in some way.
o	This indicates that the requirement is met.
-	This indicates that some aspect of the requirement may not be met.

Try to narrow the architectural alternatives to one that best meets the business requirements. At this point, it may be helpful to quickly review each of the requirements with the customer. It is important that you continue to maintain consensus with the business requirements throughout this process. One of the most effective ways to accomplish this is to take every opportunity to review information that has been gathered to make sure everyone is still in agreement.

Likewise, reviewing the architectural alternatives provides an opportunity to ensure that the customer is familiar with the approach being proposed and understands the technologies being explored. If issues or concerns are raised, they need to be addressed. Assign, with the customer, the proper grade to each architecture alternative to decide on the alternative that best fits the customer's requirements.

Describing the pros and cons of each solution will help you to determine the best alternative. Make sure you use the priorities agreed upon with the customer when choosing an alternative.

Checkpoint

At this point, you should have selected an architecture for your e-business solution, documented the architecture, and gained customer commitment to the selected architecture. Ask these questions:

- Have the requirements changed by the customer since you completed this phase? If they have, you must make the appropriate updates and validations.

- Have you completely documented the selection process and agreed-to selection?

- Have you made any assumptions that have not been agreed to by the sponsors? If so, you must gain sponsor agreement on those assumptions. Based on results, you may need to go back to previous phases.

- Do all open issues have agreed-to owners, action plans, and dates for resolution assigned?

- Is the sponsor committed to the selected architecture?

If you can answer "yes" to each question, move on to the next step, which is explained in the following section. Otherwise, you may need to go back and repeat some of the steps in earlier phases.

2.5.4 Step 4: Preparing the proposal

Prepare a proposal to present the solution to the customer. The proposal should:

- Describe the requirements.
- Describe the alternative solutions and their relative strengths and weaknesses.
- Describe the recommended solution and the reasons for choosing it.
- Describe a plan for delivering a solution.

Once the proposal is accepted, an engagement is set up to deliver the solution.

2.6 Summary

This chapter conveyed the following messages:

- e-business is more than just updating technology. It is about a new way of doing business and a series of disciplines about *how* one does business.

- e-business is about transforming core processes, applications, and systems.

- An e-business transformation is crucial to a company's survival.

- e-business isn't just about technology; it is about interjecting the right technologies to remain elastic in an ever-changing world.

- A holistic approach is necessary for sustainable long-term benefits to be achieved from this new model.

- The uses and architecture of the IBM Framework for e-business in terms of:
    - System model
    - Application programming model and supported products

- The approach to develop an e-business solution is to break it into the following spaces:
  - *Problem space* defines typical e-business problem areas
  - *Technology and product space* defines key technologies and product groups in Framework for e-business that support solutions
  - *Design space* defines key decisions in n-tier logical building blocks
- To build a solution, use:
  - "Patterns" to help focus on particular solutions
  - Key decisions, impacts of the decision, and suggestions
  - Guidance in selecting options and understanding trade-offs
  - Key technologies that underlie the solution
  - Products and components that support the solution
  - IBM intellectual capital (techniques, experience, and best practices)

Chapter 3. IBM Framework for e-business products, technology

This chapter discusses the technologies and products that are used in IBM Framework for e-business. The first part of the chapter (3.1, "Technology") explains the basic technologies that the IBM Framework for e-business embraces. The technologies are separated in the logical groups, for example: protocols, Java components, and so on. The products section (3.2, "Products" on page 129) maps individual products to the corresponding technologies.

3.1 Technology

Framework for e-business addresses many important issues in the development of e-business solutions. The Framework is prescriptive; it maximizes the use of the Internet and other open standards and protocols versus proprietary technologies. However, developing in the context of the Framework still leaves a choice of technologies (including the Internet and open systems) that can dramatically affect the performance, robustness, and usability of a solution. After reading this chapter, you will better understand the many choices of client and server technologies. The first section deals with the various protocols. Then, we move on to Web technologies, Java components, e-business and objects, application patterns, CORBA, transactions, and connectors.

3.1.1 Protocols

The rapid acceptance and deployment of Internet technologies has created a fundamental shift in the nature of enterprise networks. Some of the old rules no longer apply; enterprise networks can now span companies, they can reach across unsecured networks, and they can reach users in non-office environments. These networks, often called *extranets* and *intranets*, are enabling fundamental changes in business relationships based on the development of virtual companies. This fundamental change in the nature of the enterprise network has given rise to a new type of networking infrastructure that:

- Can support open standards, building upon IP as the base networking protocol and relying on IP-based standards for higher level networking services

- Can extend across the Internet securely, so that business transactions can take place without the need for high cost private communication lines

- Can tightly integrate with existing corporate network systems, such as systems network architecture (SNA), to ensure seamless and high performance links to the massive networks in existence today

- Provides universal access to all users and devices, including those in non-office environments, such as mobile users

- Provides network-centric application deployment and management to reduce the cost of ownership

The network infrastructure focuses not only on internal networks, or intranets, but also on enabling extranets and working across the Internet. This is central to the deployment of modern enterprise networks. The term *intranet* is used to describe internal corporate networks based on an IP-backbone and other IP technologies. Extranets are relatively new. Also based on IP, an extranet allows two enterprises to merge portions of their networks and make them appear as one. This is accomplished by linking the two networks and then carving out that part of each network that is shared to create a virtual private network (VPN). The most common use of extranets today is for Supply Chain Management, but there is value to extranets in a number of business scenarios.

Reaching customers across the Internet is the third key requirement for building an enterprise network. The ability to access information stored in enterprise databases and to deliver this information securely and efficiently to a browser-based end-user is a critical requirement for the new enterprise network. The Framework's network infrastructure provides an entire set of network services to support the deployment of business applications across intranets, extranets, and the Internet. In this section, we describe the protocols for easy, secure connections to the Internet.

3.1.1.1 TCP/IP

TCP/IP refers to two network protocols (or methods of data transport) used on the Internet. They are Transmission Control Protocol (TCP) and Internet Protocol (IP), respectively. These network protocols belong to a larger collection of protocols, or a protocol suite. These are collectively referred to as the *TCP/IP suite*.

Protocols within the TCP/IP suite work together to provide data transport on the Internet. In other words, these protocols provide nearly all services available to today's "Net" surfer. Some of those services include:

- Transmission of electronic mail
- File transfers
- USENET news delivery
- Access to the World Wide Web

There are two classes of protocols within the TCP/IP suite that are addressed in the following pages. Those two classes are:

- The network-level protocol
- The application-level protocol

Network-level protocols
Network-level protocols manage the discrete mechanics of data transfer. These protocols are typically invisible to the user and operate deep beneath the surface of the system. For example, the IP protocol provides packet delivery of the information sent between the user and remote machines. It does this based on a variety of information, most notably the IP address of the two machines. Based on this and other information, the IP guarantees that the information will be routed to its intended destination. Throughout this process, the IP interacts with other network-level protocols engaged in data transport. Short of using network utilities (perhaps a sniffer or other device that reads IP datagrams), the user will never see IPs work on the system.

Application-level protocols
Conversely, application-level protocols are visible to the user in some measure. For example, file transfer protocol (FTP) is visible to the user. The user requests a connection to another machine to transfer a file, the connection is established, and the transfer begins. During the transfer, a portion of the exchange between the user's machine and the remote machine is visible (primarily error messages and status reports on the transfer itself, for example, the number of bytes in a file that have been transferred at any given moment).

For the moment, this explanation must suffice: TCP/IP refers to a collection of protocols that facilitate communication between machines over the Internet (or other networks running TCP/IP).

TCP/IP operates through the use of a protocol stack. This stack is the sum total of all protocols necessary to complete a single transfer of data between two machines. It is also the path that data takes to get out of one machine and into another. The stack is broken into layers, five of which are of concern here. To grasp this layer concept, study Figure 13.

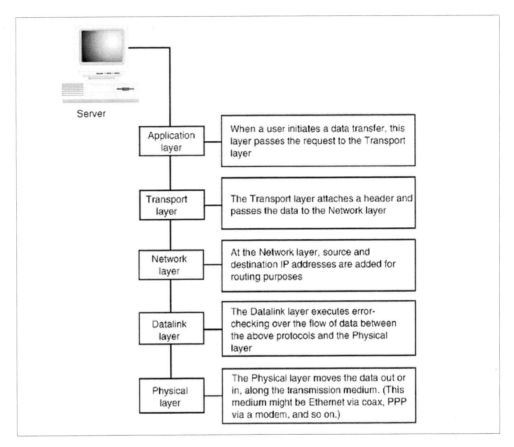

Figure 13. The TCP/IP stack

After data has passed through the process illustrated in Figure 13, it travels to its destination on another machine or network. There, the process is executed in reverse (the data meets the physical layer first and subsequently travels its way up the stack). Throughout this process, a complex system of error checking is employed both on the originating and destination machine. Each layer of the stack can send data to, and receive data from, its adjoining layer. Each layer is also associated with multiple protocols. At each tier of the stack, these protocols are hard at work, providing the user with various services.

Many TCP/IP programs can be initiated over the Internet. Most of these are client/server-oriented. As each connection request is received, the server program then communicates with the requesting client machine. To facilitate this process, each application (FTP or Telnet, for example) is assigned a unique address. This address is called a *port*. The application in question is bound to that particular port, and when any connection request is made to that port, the corresponding application is launched. Table 21 shows some of the commonly used ports and the applications that are typically bound to them.

Table 21. Common ports and their corresponding services or applications

Service or application	Port
File transfer protocol (FTP)	21
Telnet	23
Simple Mail Transfer Protocol (SMTP)	25
Gopher	70
Finger	79
Hypertext Transfer Protocol (HTTP)	80
Network News Transfer Protocol (NNTP)	119

There are thousands of ports on the average Internet server. For purposes of convenience and efficiency, a standard framework has been developed for port assignment. Although a system administrator can bind services to the ports of their choice, services are generally bound to recognized ports. These are commonly referred to as *well-known ports*.

Table 22 shows a list of protocols that are supported in the Framework. We examine some of the protocols later in this chapter.

Table 22. Protocols in the Framework

Protocol acronym	Protocol name
TCP/IP	Transmission Control Protocol/Internet Protocol
HTTP	Hypertext Transfer Protocol
LDAP	Lightweight Directory Access Protocol
IIOP	Internet InterOrb Protocol
FTP	File Transfer Protocol
NNTP	Network News Transfer Protocol
IMAP	Internet Message Access Protocol
SMTP	Simple Mail Transfer Protocol
Telnet	Terminal Emulation Protocol
SSL	Secure Socket Layer
SNMP	Simple Network Management Protocol
POP3	Post Office Protocol
JRMP	Java Remote Method Protocol

Internet topology

The Internet consists of high-speed circuits connecting routers that transmit data through TCP/IP. The network allows all of the computers to communicate with one another. A home computer is usually linked to the Internet using a normal phone line and a modem that talks to an Internet Service Provider (ISP). ISPs then connect to larger ISPs, and the largest ISPs maintain fiber-optic "backbones" for an entire nation or region. Backbones around the world are connected through fiber optic lines, undersea cables, or satellite links. This way every computer on the Internet is connected to every other computer on the Internet.

The original Internet Protocol defines IP address in four major classes of address structure, classes A through D. Each of these classes allocates one portion of the 32-bit Internet address format to a network address and the remaining portion to the specific host machines within the network specified by the address. Each machine on the Internet is assigned a unique IP Address (see Figure 14). IP addresses are normally expressed as four "octets" in a "dotted decimal number". A typical IP address looks like this:

`216.27.61.137`

The four numbers in an IP address are called *octets*, because each number is represented by 8 bits. Every machine on the Internet has a unique IP address. A server has a static IP address that does not change very often. A home machine that dials up through a modem often has an IP address that is assigned by the ISP when you dial in. That IP address is unique for your session; it may be different the next time you dial in. This way, an ISP only needs one IP address for each modem it supports, rather than one for each customer.

One portion of the address is used to identify the network, and the other portion is used to identify the host within that network. For example in Figure 14, 9.0.0.0 is the base address for IBM, and all IP addresses starting from 9.*.*.* correspond to some machine within the IBM network. Each host in a particular network has a unique address within its network. Most applications use a logical name as the designator for the target partner application. This name is resolved to an address by the name service in the network.

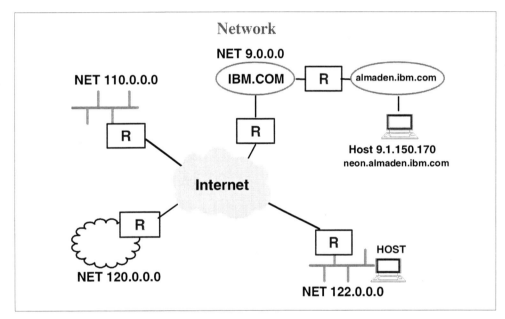

Figure 14. Internet topology

When a Uniform Resource Locator (URL) is typed into a browser, the following steps occur:

1. The browser breaks the URL into three parts:
   - The protocol (http)
   - The server name (www.ibm.com)
   - The file name (index.htm)

2. The browser communicates with a name server to translate the server name, "www.ibm.com", into an IP address, which it uses to connect to that server machine.

3. The browser then forms a connection to the Web server at that IP address on port 80.

4. Following the HTTP protocol, the browser sends a get request to the server, asking for the file "http://www.ibm.com/index.htm".

5. The server sends the HTML text for the Web page to the browser.

6. The browser reads the HTML tags and formats the page onto your screen.

3.1.1.2 Hypertext Transfer Protocol (HTTP)

HTTP is an application-level protocol for distributed, collaborative, hypermedia information systems. It is a generic, stateless, object-oriented protocol that can be used for many tasks, such as name servers and distributed object management systems, through extension of its request methods. HTTP is based on a request/response algorithm with a well-defined structure for a request/response. Web browsers use HTTP to communicate with Web servers. A feature of HTTP is the typing and negotiation of data representation, which allows systems to be built independently of the data being transferred. HTTP has been in use by the World Wide Web global information initiative since 1990.

3.1.1.3 Lightweight Directory Access Protocol (LDAP)

Any information system relies on some sort of repository to retrieve the locations of information, such as data, resources, addresses, and so forth. Those repositories are referred to as *directories*, much like a telephone directory. Information may not easily be found without these directories, and communication in distributed systems would be impossible. Directories are typically used to hold user information (for authentication purposes), resource locations (for information access), and a whole lot more.

Although directories may contain all sorts of things and every vendor may implement its own style (and many have done so in fact), the Internet more or less demands some sort of directory standard to maintain coherent information and communication among diverse systems, applications, and vendors. The directory standard of choice today is X.500, as adopted by the International Standards Organization (ISO). The more complex a directory becomes, the more overhead and cost may be involved in accessing it. LDAP specifies a simplified way to retrieve information from an X.500-compliant directory in an asynchronous, client/server type of protocol. For more information about LDAP and X.500 implementations, see RFC 1777 and RFC 2116 at: http://www.w3c.org

3.1.1.4 Internet Inter-ORB Protocol (IIOP)

IIOP is an object-oriented programming protocol that makes it possible for distributed programs written in different programming languages to communicate over the Internet. IIOP is a critical part of a strategic industry standard, the Common Object Request Broker Architecture (CORBA). Using IIOP and related protocols, a company can write programs that can communicate with their own, or other company's, existing or future programs wherever they are located and without having to understand anything about the program other than its service and a name.

3.1.1.5 File transfer protocol (FTP)

FTP is the standard method of transferring files from one system to another. Its purpose is set forth in RFC 0765 as explained here.

The objectives of FTP are to:

- Promote sharing of files (computer programs or data)
- Encourage indirect or implicit (via programs) use of remote computers
- Shield a user from variations in file storage systems among hosts
- Transfer data reliably and efficiently (FTP, although usable directly by a user at a terminal, is designed mainly for use by programs)

For over two decades, researchers have investigated a wide variety of file transfer methods. The development of FTP has undergone many changes in that time. Its first definition occurred in April 1971, and the full specification can be read in RFC 114.

3.1.1.6 Network News Transfer Protocol (NNTP)

NNTP is one of the most widely used protocols. It provides modern access to the news service commonly known as USENET news. Its purpose is defined in RFC 977, which you can find on the Web at: `http://www.ietf.org/rfc.html`

NNTP shares characteristics with both SMTP and TCP. Similarities to SMTP consist of NNTPs acceptance of plain-English commands from a prompt. It is similar to TCP in that stream-based transport and delivery are used. NNTP typically runs from port 119 on any UNIX system.

3.1.1.7 Post Office Protocol (POP3)

POP3 treats the message store as a single in-box. The user agent can retrieve and delete messages from this in-box. Once messages are retrieved and deleted from the POP3 server, it is the user agent's responsibility, if necessary, to retain messages in some local message store. While a POP3 client can leave mail on the server (by not deleting it), the POP3 protocol lacks mechanisms to categorize, file, or search the mail. Therefore, the POP3 server message store can quickly become unmanageable.

Also, most large-scale POP3 servers enforce a storage limit, so they refuse to accept new mail for a user whose limit has been exceeded. As a result, the POP3 model strongly encourages the complete transfer of mail to the client, where a well-designed client can provide many more capabilities to the user. This has the advantage that the communication with the server is simple. The disadvantage is that the user cannot conveniently use more than one computer to read mail. The mail remains on whichever computer the user reads it.

POP3 is currently widely deployed by ISPs for access to users' mail. Because of its simplicity, it may remain the major access protocol for the casual mail user for quite some time. IMAP4 is not yet widely deployed. However, due to its functionality, which is more suited to the traveling business user, it will increase its deployment throughout the business community over the next few years.

3.1.1.8 Internet Message Access Protocol (IMAP)

IMAP4 is an electronic messaging protocol with both client and server functions. Similar to POP, IMAP4 servers store messages for multiple users to be retrieved upon client request, but IMAP4 clients have more capabilities in doing so than POP clients.

IMAP4 allows clients to have multiple remote mailboxes to retrieve messages from and to choose any of those any time. IMAP4 clients can specify criteria for downloading messages, such as not to transfer large messages over slow links. IMAP4 always keeps messages on the server and replicates copies to the clients. Transactions performed by disconnected clients are effected on server mailboxes by periodic re-synchronization of client and server.

For more information on IMAP4 and its underlying electronic mail models, please see RFC 2060 and RFC 1733.

While a POP3 message can be handled only as a single block, IMAP4 allows access to individual Multipurpose Internet Mail Extensions (MIME) parts. Provisions exist to allow message stores to be replicated to a local store (and re-synchronized later) for the mobile user. The IMAP4 model, in contrast to the POP3 model, involves storing mail on the server, where it may be accessed by any client. It also involves using the client's storage only for caching messages for efficiency or for traveling.

3.1.1.9 Simple Mail Transfer Protocol (SMTP)

The objective of SMTP is to transfer mail reliably and efficiently (see RFC 821). It is an extremely lightweight and efficient protocol. The user (using any SMTP-compliant client) sends a request to an SMTP server. A two-way connection is subsequently established. The client forwards a MAIL instruction, indicating that it wants to send mail to a recipient somewhere on the Internet. If the SMTP allows this operation, an affirmative acknowledgment is sent back to the client machine. At that point, the session begins. The client may then forward the recipient's identity, their IP address, and the message (in text) to be sent.

Despite the simple character of SMTP, mail service has been the source of countless security holes. This may be due in part to the number of options that are involved. Misconfiguration is a common reason for holes.

SMTP servers are native in UNIX. Most other networked operating systems now have some form of SMTP.

3.1.1.10 Telnet

The Telnet protocol provides a standardized interface, through which a program on one host (the Telnet client) can access the resources of another host (the Telnet server) as though the client were a local terminal connected to the server. For example, a user on a workstation on a local area network (LAN) may connect to a host attached to the LAN as though the workstation were a terminal attached directly to the host. Of course, Telnet can be used across wide area networks (WANs) as well as LANs.

3.1.1.11 Secure Socket Layer (SSL)

SSL is a security protocol that was developed by Netscape Communications Corporation, along with RSA Data Security, Inc. The primary goal of the SSL protocol is to provide a private channel between communicating applications, which ensures the privacy of data, authentication of the partners, and integrity. SSL provides an alternative to the standard TCP/IP socket API, which has security implemented within it. Therefore, in theory, it is possible to run any TCP/IP application in a secure way without changing it. In practice, SSL is only implemented for HTTP connections at this time.

3.1.1.12 Simple Network Management Protocol (SNMP)

With the growth in size and complexity of TCP/IP-based networks, the need for network management became very important. The current network management framework for TCP/IP consists of:

- **Structure and Identification of Management Information (SMI)**: Describes how managed objects contained in the Management Information Base (MIB) are defined.

- **Management Information Base, second version (MIB-II)**: Describes the managed objects.

- **SNMP**: Defines the protocol used to manage these objects.

A network management station executes network management applications that monitor and control network elements such as hosts, gateways, and terminal servers. These network elements use a management agent to perform the network management functions requested by the network management stations. SNMP is used to communicate management information between the network management stations and the agents in the network elements.

3.1.2 Web technology

This section looks at the technologies that you should consider for Web applications, based on the open standards and Java-based programming model of the IBM Framework for e-business. It does not attempt to cover all technologies that can be used in developing Web applications, such as Perl or server-side JavaScript.

It looks at the technologies as they apply to both the client and the server side of the application. Some technologies, such as Java and XML, can apply to both. Also, the selection of client-side technologies used in the design will require consideration for the server-side such as to whether to store or dynamically create elements for the client-side.

3.1.2.1 Web browser

A Web browser is a fundamental component of the Web client. For PC-based clients, the browser typically incorporates support for HTML, DHTML, JavaScript, and Java. Some browsers are beginning to add support for XML as well. Under user control, there is an entire range of additional technologies that can be configured as "plug-ins", such as RealPlayer from RealNetworks or Macromedia Flash. As an application designer, you must consider the level of technology you can assume will be available in the user's browser, or you can add logic to your application to enable slight modifications based upon the browser level. Regarding plug-ins, you need to consider what portion of your intended user community will have that capability.

For an e-business application that is to be accessed by the broadest set of users with varying browser capabilities, the client is often written in HTML with no other technologies. On an exception basis, you can consider limiting the use of other technologies, such as using JavaScript for simple edit checks, based on the value to the user and the policy of the organization for whom the project is being developed. The emergence of pervasive devices introduces new considerations to your design with regard to the content streams that the device can render and the more limited capabilities of the browser. For example, Wireless Application

Protocol (WAP)-enabled devices render content sent in Wireless Markup Language (WML).

3.1.2.2 Hypertext Transfer Protocol (HTTP)

HTTP is based on request-response activity. A client, running an application called a browser, establishes a connection with a server and sends a request to the server in the form of a request method. The server responds with a status line, including the message's protocol version and a success or error code. This is followed by a message containing server information, entity information, and possible body content. An HTTP transaction is divided into four steps:

1. The browser opens a connection.
2. The browser sends a request to the server.
3. The server sends a response to the browser.
4. The connection is closed.

Figure 15 shows this in more detail. Each connection follows a sequence of packet exchanges where they exchange data. Once the request is finished, the connection is terminated. The HTTP protocol has no mechanism for keeping information about previous requests or storing information about the current request.

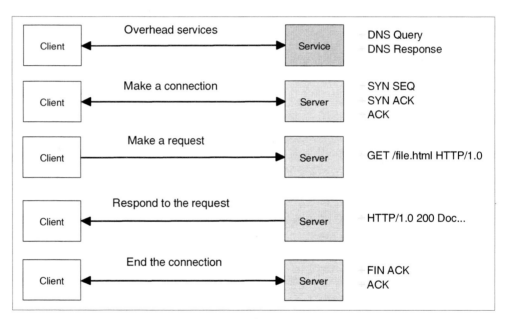

Figure 15. HTTP basic service (get or pull)

On the Internet, HTTP communication generally takes place over TCP connections. The default port is TCP 80, but other ports can be used. This does not preclude HTTP from being implemented on top of any other protocol on the Internet, or on other networks. HTTP only presumes a reliable transport, any protocol that provides such guarantees can be used. Except for experimental applications, current practice requires that the connection be established by the client prior to each request and closed by the server after sending the response.

Both clients and servers should be aware that either party may close the connection prematurely, due to user action, automated time-out, or program failure, and should handle such closing in a predictable fashion. In any case, the closing of the connection by either or both parties always terminates the current request, regardless of its status.

In simple terms, HTTP is a stateless protocol because it keeps no track of the connections. To load a page that includes two graphics, for example, a graphic-enabled browser will open three TCP connections: one for the page, and two for the graphics. Most browsers, however, can handle several of these connections simultaneously. This behavior can be rather resource-intensive if one page consists of a lot of elements as quite a number of Web pages do. HTTP 1.1, as defined in RFC 2068, alleviates this problem to the extent that one TCP connection will be established per type of element on a page, and all elements of that kind will be transferred over the same connection respectively. However, if a request depends on the information exchanged during a previous connection, then this information has to be kept outside the protocol.

As shown in Figure 16, a general HTTP frame consists of the following fields:

- Start line (with message type field)
- Message header
- Empty line indicating the end of a header
- Message body

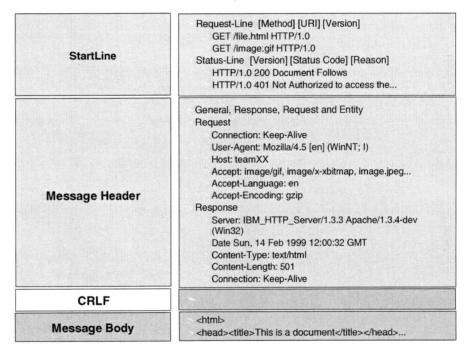

Figure 16. The HTTP frame

Message types

An HTTP message can be either a client request or a server response. The following string indicates the HTTP message type:

```
HTTP-message = Request | Response
```

Message headers

An HTTP message header field can be one of the following types:

- General header
- Request header

- Response header
- Entity header

Message body

Message body can be referred to as an "entity body" if no transfer coding has been applied. Message body simply carries the entity body of the relevant request or response.

Message length

Message length indicates the length of the message body if it is included. The message length is determined according to the criteria that is described in RFC 2068 in detail.

More information about HTTP is in RFC 2616, which is located on the Web at:
`http://www.w3.org/Protocols/HTTP/1.1/rfc2616.pdf`

3.1.2.3 HTTPS

Secure Sockets Layer provides an alternative to the standard TCP/IP socket API that has security implemented within it. In theory, it is possible to run any TCP/IP application in a secure way without changing the application. In practice, SSL is only widely implemented for HTTP connections. SSL operates at two layers:

- The lower layer is made up of a protocol for transferring data. It uses a variety of predefined cipher and authentication combinations, called the *SSL Record Protocol.*

- The upper layer contains a protocol for the initial authentication and transfer of encryption keys, called the *SSL Handshake Protocol.*

An SSL session is initiated as follows:

1. On the client (browser), the user requests a document with a special URL that begins with `https` instead of `http`, either by typing it into the URL input field, or by clicking a link.

2. The client code recognizes the SSL request and establishes a connection through TCP port 443 (default port for SSL connection) to the SSL code on the server.

3. The client then initiates the SSL handshake phase, using the SSL Record Protocol as a carrier. At this point, there is no encryption or integrity checking built in to the connection.

4. Client and server exchange the symmetric key to be used for the encryption of the data for the duration of the session.

The SSL protocol addresses the following security issues:

- **Privacy**: After the symmetric key is established in the initial handshake, the messages are encrypted using this key.

- **Integrity**: Messages contain a message authentication code (MAC) to ensure the message integrity.

- **Authentication**: During the handshake, the client authenticates the server using an asymmetric or public key. It can also be based on certificates.

SSL requires each message to be encrypted and decrypted. Therefore, it has a high performance and resource overhead.

3.1.2.4 Cookies

Cookies are a mechanism by which the server application stores persistent data on the client. The data is stored in a file called cookies.txt. The server applications can use cookies to both store and retrieve information on the client-side of the connection. Figure 17 shows the server setting the cookie after the client request. It also shows the client attaching this cookie for all further requests to the server.

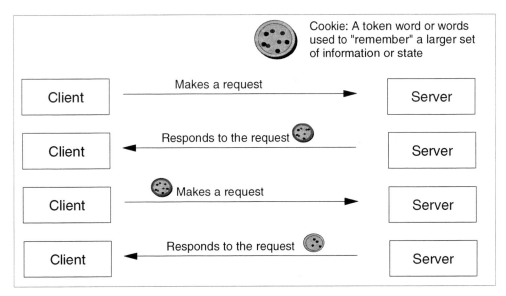

Figure 17. Session between a client and server with cookies

Because HTTP is a stateless protocol, cookies provide a way to maintain information between client requests. The addition of a simple, persistent, client-side state significantly extends the capabilities of Web-based client/server applications. A server, when returning an HTTP object to a client, may also send a piece of state information, which the client will store. Included in that state object is a description of the range of URLs for which that state is valid. Any future HTTP requests made by the client that fall in that range will include a transmittal of the current value of the state object from the client back to the server. The state object is called a *cookie*.

Cookies are extraordinarily limited in scope. Some of the limitations include:

• They contain only text, no binary code.

• Cookies can only be accessed by the page that created it, and a page can only create a single cookie.

At the same time, this simple mechanism provides a powerful new tool that enables new types of applications to be written for Web-based environments. Some are:

• Shopping applications can now store information about the currently selected items.

• Sites can store per-user preferences on the client, and have the client supply those preferences every time a user connects to the site.

3.1.2.5 Hypertext Markup Language (HTML)

HTML is a document markup language, with support for hyperlinks, that is rendered by the browser. It includes tags for simple form controls. Many e-business applications are assembled strictly using HTML. This has the advantage that the client-side Web application can be a simple HTML browser, enabling a less capable client to run an e-business application.

The HTML specification defines user interface (UI) elements for text with various fonts and colors, lists, tables, images, and forms (text fields, buttons, checkbooks, radio buttons). These elements are adequate to display the user interface for most applications. The disadvantage, however, is that these elements have a generic look and feel, and they lack customization. As a result, some e-business application developers augment HTML with other user interface technologies to enhance the visual experience. However, this is subject to maintaining access by the intended user base and compliance with company policy on Web client technologies. Because most Web browsers can display HTML Version 3.2, this is the lowest common denominator for building the client-side of an application.

3.1.2.6 Dynamic HTML (DHTML)

DHTML allows a high degree of flexibility in designing and displaying a user interface. In particular, DHTML includes cascading style sheets (CSS), which enable different fonts, margins, and line spacing for various parts of the display to be created.

These elements can be accurately positioned using absolute coordinates. Another advantage of DHTML is that it increases the level of functionality of an HTML page through a document object model and event model. The document object enables scripting languages, such as JavaScript, to control parts of the HTML page. For example, text and images can be moved on the screen, and hidden or shown, under the command of a script. Scripting can also be used to change the color or image of a link when the mouse is moved over it, or to validate a text input field of a form without having to send it to the server.

Unfortunately there are several disadvantages with using DHTML. The greatest of these is that two different implementations of Web browsers (Netscape and Microsoft) exist and are found only on the more recent browser versions. A small, basic set of functionality is common to both, but differences appear in most areas. The significant difference is that Microsoft allows the content of the HTML page to be modified by using either JScript or VBScript. Netscape, on the other hand, allows the content to only be manipulated (moved, hidden, shown) using JavaScript. Because of browser compatibility issues, DHTML is not recommended in environments where mixed levels and brands of browsers are present.

3.1.2.7 Extensible Markup Language (XML)

XML allows you to specify your own markup language with tags specified in a Document Type Definition (DTD) file. Actual content streams are then produced that use this markup. The content streams can be transformed to other content streams by using eXtensible Stylesheet Language (XSL). For PC-based browsers, HTML is well established for both document content and formatting. The leading browsers have significant investments in rendering engines based on HTML and a Document Object Model (DOM) based on HTML for manipulation by JavaScript.

The problem with data available in HTML format is that it is formatted for people to view, and not for computers to use. HTML consists of a pre-defined set of tags. This makes it a language that is easy to learn and accessible, but makes it hard to re-use the data. This is where XML enters the picture.

As its name indicates, XML is extensible, which means that you can define your own set of tags and make it possible for other parties (people or programs) to know and understand these tags. This makes XML much more flexible than HTML. In fact, because XML tags represent the logical structure of the data, they can be interpreted and used in various ways by different applications. XML seems to be evolving to a complementary role for active content within HTML documents for the PC browser environment.

For new devices, such as WAP-enabled phones and voice clients, the data content and formatting are defined by new XML schema (DTD), WML for WAP phone, and VoiceXML for voice interfaces. For most Web application designs, you should focus your attention on using XML on the server side.

XML and XSL style sheets can be used on the server side to encode content streams and parse them for different clients, and therefore, enable you to develop applications for both a range of PC browsers and for the emerging pervasive devices. The content is in XML and an XML parser is used to transform it to output streams based on XSL style sheets. This general capability is known as *transcoding* and is not limited to XML based technology. The appropriate design decision here is how much control over the content transforms you need in your application. You need to consider when it is appropriate to use this dynamic content generation and when there are advantages to having servlets or JSP files specific to certain device types.

XML is also used as a means to specify the content of messages between servers, whether the two servers are within an enterprise or represent a business-to-business connection. The critical factor here is the agreement between parties on the message schema, which is specified as an XML DTD. An XML parser is used to extract specific content from the message stream. You need to consider whether your design should use an event-based approach, for which the Simple API for XML (SAX) is appropriate, or navigate the tree structure of the document using the DOM API.

XML is a subset of Standard Generalized Markup Language (SGML), which is more powerful but also much more complex. Like SGML, XML is a meta language that allows the author of a document to provide *markup* definitions or, in other words, to associate "tags" with data. The purpose of the tags is to provide information to an application about the data through their association with the document contents. Accordingly, an XML document typically consists of *markup* and *character data*. The markup information conveys the meaning behind the document contents and is represented through tags and other XML elements, while character data represents the actual content.

In the following example, the `<author>` tag indicates that Joe Bloggs represents an author's name:

```
<author>Joe Bloggs</author>
```

Note that, in the above example, although we know that Joe Bloggs is the name of an author, it does not necessarily imply that he is the author of the document.

The meaning behind the tag depends on the context in which it will be interpreted and, therefore, on the application reading the document.

Document Type Definitions (DTD)

Like SGML from which it derives, XML supports the use of DTD. Since it is not the intent of this book to serve as an XML reference manual, we do not describe all the syntax elements of a DTD here. However, it is essential to understand the purpose and use of a DTD, and that is what we will focus on in this section.

A DTD specifies the grammatical structure of an XML document, which allows XML parsers to understand and interpret the document's contents. The DTD contains the list of tags that are allowed within the XML document and what their types and attributes are. More specifically, the DTD defines how elements relate to one another within the document's tree structure and specifies which attributes may be used with which elements. Therefore, it also constrains the element types that can be included in the document and determines its conformance: an XML document which conforms to its DTD is said to be valid.

A DTD comes in the form of a simple text file, which can be either stored in a separate file or embedded within the XML file. XML documents referencing a DTD contain the <!DOCTYPE> declaration that either contains the DTD declaration or specifies the location of an external DTD, as in the following example:

```
<!DOCTYPE LibraryCatalogue SYSTEM "library.dtd">
```

On the other hand, an XML document is not required to specify a DTD. However, with most applications, it will prove beneficial or even necessary to build a DTD that conveys efficiently the meaning behind the XML file's contents. DTDs provide parsers with clear instructions on what to check for when they are determining the validity of an XML document. Having the logical definition of an XML file stored separately allows the resulting DTD to be shared across organizations, industries, or the Web. When building XML applications, it is a good idea to look for existing DTDs that may suit your purpose.

XML applications

At the heart of every XML application is an XML processor that parses the well-formed XML document, so that the document elements can be retrieved and transformed into data that can be understood by the application and task in hand. The other responsibility of the parser is to check the syntax and structure of the document. Anyone has the freedom to implement a parser that can read and print an XML document. The XML 1.0 Recommendation defines how an XML processor should behave when reading and printing a document, but the API to be used is not defined. However, there are standards that define how to access and manipulate XML documents. Currently, the following two APIs are widely used:

- **Simple API for XML (SAX)**: SAX is an event-driven lightweight API for accessing XML documents and extracting information from them. It cannot be used to manipulate the internal structures of XML documents. As the document is parsed, the application using SAX receives information about the various parsing events.

- **Document Object Model (DOM)**: While XML is a language to describe tree-structured data, the DOM defines a set of interfaces to access tree-structured XML documents. DOM specifies how XML and HTML documents can be represented as objects. Unlike SAX, DOM also allows creating and manipulating the contents of XML documents. Basically, the DOM interfaces are platform and language neutral.

3.1.2.8 JavaScript

JavaScript is a cross-platform object-oriented scripting language. It is very useful in Web applications because of the browser and document objects that the language supports. Client-side JavaScript provides the ability to interact with HTML forms. You can use JavaScript to validate user input on the client and help improve the performance of your Web application by reducing the number of requests that flow over the network to the server.

European Computer Manufacturers Association (ECMA), a European standards body, has published a standard (ECMA-262) that is based on JavaScript (from Netscape) and JScript (from Microsoft) called *ECMAScript*. The ECMAScript standard defines a core set of objects for scripting in Web browsers. JavaScript and JScript implement a superset of ECMAScript. You can learn more about the ECMAScript Language Specification at: `http://www.ecma.ch/stand/ECMA-262.htm`

To address various client-side requirements, Netscape and Microsoft have extended their implementations of JavaScript in Version 1.2 by adding new browser objects. Because Netscape's and Microsoft's extensions are different from each other, any script that uses JavaScript 1.2 extensions must detect the browser being used, and select the correct statements to run. We recommend that you *do not use* JavaScript on the server side of a Web application, given the alternatives available with Java.

3.1.3 Java components

Java offers a wide variety of application types, which have their own strengths and weaknesses. Choosing the right Java application type for the right task and including cooperation between the application types is key to successful e-business solutions. Figure 18 compares the different Java applications.

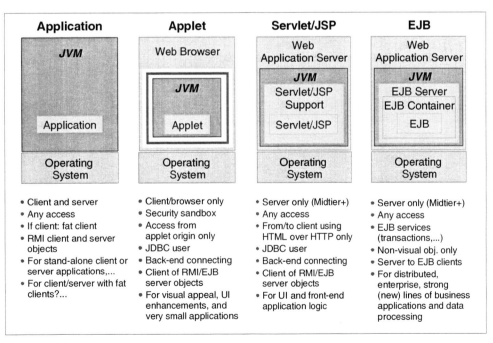

Figure 18. Java application types

The advantages of using Java are enormous:

- Java is a "write once, run anywhere" language. This means when useful applications are developed on a particular platform, they can immediately be ported to others. Regardless of what the user's hardware or operating system platform is, they can take advantage of best of breed applications. Most IT industry vendors support the Java initiative.

- "Write once, run anywhere" is very beneficial for customers. In places where distributed processing has introduced multiple platforms by using Java, you can reduce the amount of programming skill and effort required to develop the same application in several languages for various environments.

- Java allows the processing load to be distributed from the server to the client. At the same time, it provides a full function graphical user interface under the control of a browser. Any platform with a browser can use Java applets. Again, this simplifies programming efforts in a multivendor enterprise.

- Java applets enable the use of a network PC. Network PCs are workstations without any disk drive. Instead, they start up with an active browser program. They can run all user programs as Java applets downloaded from the server. They centralize software service. It greatly reduces the cost of software maintenance and distribution associated with traditional PCs.

- In the future, a consumer device that combines TV and network PC capabilities could bring the WWW into a million more homes without the cost and effort associated with today's home PCs.

Evolution of Java technology

Common gateway interface (CGI) and Server API programs had been around for some time, and can still be very useful (see Figure 19). CGI is a standard way for a Web server to pass a Web user's request to an application program and to receive data to forward to the user.

For example, when a user fills out a form on a Web page and sends it in, it usually needs to be processed by an application program. The Web server typically passes the form information to a small application program that processes the data and may send back a confirmation message. This method or convention for passing data back and forth between the server and the application is called the common gateway interface. CGI programs typically suffer the performance penalty of process activation overhead for each request. Server API programs may perform better, but errors could potentially crash the Web server. Servlets and JavaServer Pages have the advantage in these areas shown in Figure 19.

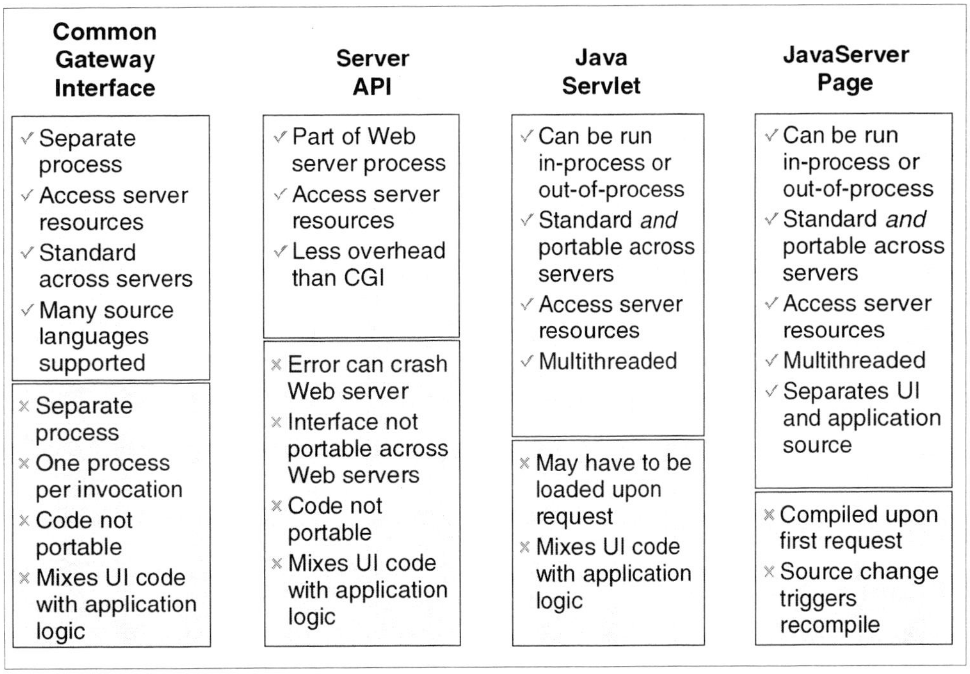

Common Gateway Interface	Server API	Java Servlet	JavaServer Page
✓ Separate process ✓ Access server resources ✓ Standard across servers ✓ Many source languages supported	✓ Part of Web server process ✓ Access server resources ✓ Less overhead than CGI	✓ Can be run in-process or out-of-process ✓ Standard *and* portable across servers ✓ Access server resources ✓ Multithreaded	✓ Can be run in-process or out-of-process ✓ Standard *and* portable across servers ✓ Access server resources ✓ Multithreaded ✓ Separates UI and application source
✕ Separate process ✕ One process per invocation ✕ Code not portable ✕ Mixes UI code with application logic	✕ Error can crash Web server ✕ Interface not portable across Web servers ✕ Code not portable ✕ Mixes UI code with application logic	✕ May have to be loaded upon request ✕ Mixes UI code with application logic	✕ Compiled upon first request ✕ Source change triggers recompile

Figure 19. Application implementation options at the server

If correctly used, JSP can provide a separation of the user interface definition and the business logic. We briefly discuss the various Java technologies in the following section.

3.1.3.1 Java applets

A Java applet is a program written in Java that is downloaded from the Web server and runs in the Web browser. The most flexible of the user interface (UI) technologies that can be run in a Web browser is offered by the Java applet. Java provides a rich set of UI elements that include an equivalent for each of the HTML UI elements. In addition, because Java is a programming language, an infinite set of UI elements can be built and used. There are many widget libraries available that offer common UI elements, such as tables, scrolling text, spreadsheets, editors, graphs, charts, etc. The applet to be run is specified in the HTML page using an APPLET tag:

```
<APPLET CODEBASE="/mydir" CODE="myapplet.class" width=400 height=100>
<PARAM NAME="myParameter" VALUE="myValue">
</APPLET>
```

For this example, a Java applet called *myapplet* will run. An effective way to send data to an applet is with the use of the PARAM tag. The applet has access to this parameter data and can easily use it as input to the display logic. Java can also request a new HTML page from the Web application server. This provides an equivalent function to the HTML FORM submit function. The advantage is that an applet can load a new HTML page based upon the obvious (a button being clicked), or the unique (the editing of a cell in a spreadsheet).

A characteristic of Java applets is that they seldom consist of one class file. On the contrary, a large applet may reference hundreds of class files. Making a request for each of these class files individually can tax any server and also tax the network capacity. However, packaging all of these class files into one file reduces the number of requests from hundreds to only one request.

This optimization is available in many Web browsers in the form of either a JAR file or a CAB file. Netscape and HotJava support JAR files simply by adding an ARCHIVE="myjarfile.jar" variable within the APPLET tag. Internet Explorer uses CAB files specified as an applet parameter within the APPLET tag. In all cases, executing an applet contained within a JAR/CAB file exhibits faster load times than individual class files. While Netscape and Internet Explorer use different APPLET tags to identify the packaged class files, a single HTML page containing both tags can be created to support both browsers. Each browser simply ignores the other's tag.

Figure 20 describes the life cycle of an applet. Although this model is well-defined and standard, different versions of the JDK and browser may implement this differently.

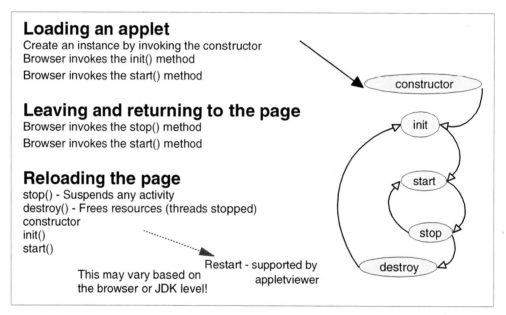

Figure 20. Applet life cycle

A disadvantage of using Java applets for UI generation is that the required version of Java must be supported by the Web browser. Therefore, when you use Java, the UI part of the application dictates which browsers can be used for the client-side application.

Another disadvantage of Java applets is that any classes, such as widgets and business logic, that are not included as part of the Java support in the browser must be loaded from the Web server as they are needed. If these additional classes are large, the initialization of the applet may take from seconds to minutes, depending on the speed of the connection to the Internet. Because of this, you *should not use* Java applets in environments where mixed levels and brands of browsers are present. Small applets may be used in rare cases where HTML UI elements are insufficient to express the semantics of the client-side Web application user interface. If it is absolutely necessary to use an applet, be careful to include, whenever possible, UI elements that are part of the core Java classes.

3.1.3.2 Java servlets

Servlets provide a replacement for CGI-based techniques in Web programming. Servlets are small Java programs that run on the Web application server. They interact with the servlet engine running on the Web application server through HTTP requests and responses, which are encapsulated as objects in the servlet.

One of the attractions of using servlets is that the APIs are easy to master. They implement a simple request and response framework for communication between the client and the server.

The Java servlet API is a set of Java classes that define a standard interface between Web clients and the Web application server. The API is composed of two packages:

- **javax.servlet**: Implements the generic protocol-independent servlets
- **javax.servlet.http**: Extends the javax.servlet generic functionality to include specific support for the HTTP protocol

This section explores the key classes and methods of the javax.servlet.http package. The subsequent sections introduce other classes and methods of this package if such services are exploited by the topic under consideration.

HttpServlet is an abstract class that provides methods for handling various HTTP requests. Typically, all servlets that respond to HTTP traffic would extend this class and override some of the methods such as doGet() to handle GET requests and doPost() to handle POST requests. WebSphere Application Server provides ways to register these servlets with the Web server. Upon receiving an HTTP request, the Web server determines if it needs to be handled by a servlet, and if so, it passes such requests to WebSphere Application Server. In turn, it calls the service() method, which then calls the HTTP-specific method based on the type of HTTP request. Some of the key methods provided by the HttpServlet class are:

- **init()**: The purpose of this method is to perform necessary servlet initialization. It is guaranteed to be the first method to be called on any servlet instance. The servlet implementer may choose to override this method to perform custom servlet initialization.

- **service (HttpServletRequest req, HttpServletResponse resp)**: The Web application server invokes this method upon receiving an HTTP request targeted toward that servlet. This method, in turn, invokes the appropriate HTTP-specific method based on the type of request. HttpServletRequest is an input parameter and contains the HTTP protocol-specific header information. HttpServletResponse is an output parameter that contains an HTTP protocol-specific header and returns data to the client.

- **doGet (HttpServletRequest req, HttpServletResponse resp)**: The service() method invokes the doGet() method if the HTTP request type is GET. The servlet implementer overrides the doGet() method if the servlet is intended to handle GET requests. HTTP GET requests are expected to be safe and read-only. They are suitable for queries.

- **doPost (HttpServletRequest req, HttpServletResponse resp)**: The service() method invokes the doPost() method if the HTTP request type is POST. The servlet implementer overrides the doPOST() method if the servlet is intended to handle POST requests. HTTP POST requests are not expected to be either safe or read-only. They are suitable for requests that result in updates to stored data.

- **destroy()**: This method is called just before unloading a servlet. It is overridden only if there is a need to perform some cleanup operations such as closing connections or files before unloading a servlet.
- **getServletContext()**: This method returns a ServletContext object that contains information about the environment in which the servlet is executing. This method is particularly useful in dispatching control from a servlet to a JSP. Developers are never expected to override this method.

HttpServletRequest represents a communication channel from the client and is passed as an input parameter into the HttpServlet.service() method, which in turn passes it to the appropriate HTTP-specific methods such as doGet() and doPost(). The servlet can invoke this object's methods to obtain information about the client environment, the server environment, and any HTTP protocol-specified header information that is received from the client.

HttpServletResponse represents a communication channel back to the client and is passed as an output parameter into the HttpServlet.service() method. It provides a number of set methods that allow servlets to manipulate HTTP protocol-specific header information and to set the response data to be returned to the client.

HttpSession represents an association between an HTTP client and an HTTP server. By design, HTTP is a stateless protocol. Over the years, a number of approaches have been developed to maintain application sessions between HTTP requests. HttpSessions are used to maintain application state and user identity across several page requests from the same user.

ServletContext object contains information about the environment in which the servlet is executing. A servlet can obtain its context by calling the getServletContext() method. The getRequestDispatcher(java.lang.String urlpath) is the key method provided by this interface. It uses the URL path of resources, such as other servlets and JSPs, as input and returns a RequestDispatcher object that implements a wrapper around a server resource. RequestDispatcher is responsible for locating such resources and forwarding any requests made by the servlet to the appropriate resource. As shown in the following example, you can use them to forward requests from the servlets to JSPs:

```
RequestDispatcher rd;
rd = getServletContext().getRequestDispatcher("Sample.JSP");
rd.forward(req, res);
```

In this example, the servlet retrieves the ServletContext. Using this context, it obtains the RequestDispatcher object for a JSP. Finally it forwards the request to the JSP by calling the forward() method in the RequestDispatcher.

The typical lifecycle of a servlet is shown in Figure 21:

1. The servlet can be loaded into memory by the application server when the first request for the servlet comes, or it can be loaded automatically when the application server starts up. There is only one instance of the servlet, with multiple threads created to handle client requests.

2. The application server initializes the servlet by calling the init() method.

3. The HTTP server receives incoming client requests. It forwards the requests to the servlet run time, which passes it on to the servlet. Depending on the type of HTTP request, either the doGet or the doPost method is invoked.

4. The servlet processes the request and returns the results through an output stream to the HTTP server.

5. The HTTP server sends the results to the client.

6. The application server unloads the servlet by invoking its destroy() method.

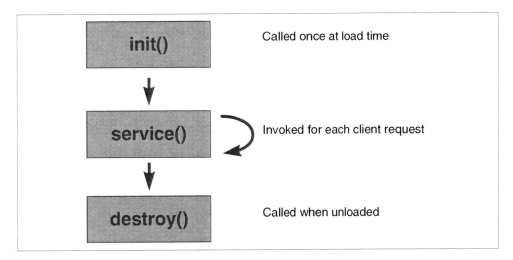

Figure 21. Servlet lifecycle

3.1.3.3 JavaServer Pages (JSPs)

JSPs were designed to simplify the process of creating pages by separating Web presentation from Web content. In the page construction logic of a Web application, the response sent to the client is often a combination of template data and dynamically-generated data. A JavaServer Page is an HTML page. JSPs can contain all the HTML tags with which Web authors are familiar.

A JSP may contain fragments of Java code that encapsulate the logic that generates the content for the page. These code fragments may call out to beans to access reusable components and back-end data. JSP files provide a simple, yet powerful mechanism for inserting dynamic content into Web pages. Dynamic content may include:

- Optional paragraphs generated based on the visitor's location, buying habits, or other attributes

- Optional tables containing one or more answers to a visitor's request for local stores or products in their price range

A JSP file looks like an HTML page with inserted Java statements. In fact, it is a script that allows a JSP processor to create a Java servlet from the embedded Java statements, which emits the HTML statements of the script. On the first reference to the JSP page, the processor constructs the servlet and then for that and all subsequent references, invokes the servlet to construct the HTML page. The steps for processing a JSP file are listed here and shown in Figure 22:

1. The JSP source is parsed.
2. Java servlet code is generated.

3. This "JSP servlet" is compiled, loaded, and run.
4. If inactive (or not current), all of the above steps are repeated.

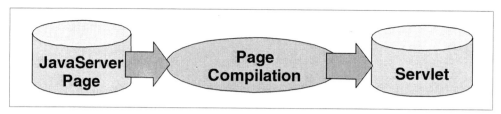

Figure 22. Compilation of JSPs into servlets

The JSP processor does its work by generating a generic HttpServlet object and creating a custom service() method for the object from the script. A statement is generated in the service() method to write each HTML statement of the script into the HttpServletResponse object. The Java statements are embedded directly into the service() method. The HttpServlet has a context that the Java statements must be able to access. The statements must be able to add text into the HttpServletResponse object. The JSP specification documents the features that are available to the author of a JSP page and that all complying JSP processors must support. For information on all the features of JSPs, refer to:

http://www.java.sun.com/products/jsp

IBM has extended this definition for the WebSphere Application Server. For a description of these extensions, refer to:

http://www.ibm.com/software/webservers/appserv/library.html

The tag and scriplets defined in a JSP specification are:

- **JSP scriptlet**:

  Syntax: `<% code %>`

  Scriptlets can be used to insert any code fragment in the specified scripting language into a JSP. By default, the scripting language is assumed to be Java.

- **JSP expression**:

  Syntax: `<%= expression%>`

  This expression stands for any valid operation that can be executed at runtime. The output from such an operation is converted into a string and is emitted into the output stream.

- **jsp:useBean**:

  Syntax: `<jsp:useBean id="beanInstanceName"`
  `scope="page|request|session|application" typespec/>`

  The server uses *id* and *scope* to look for the bean. If it exists, it is accessed. If not, it is created. *typespec* is used to specify the bean type. The `jsp:useBean` tag is used to declare the JavaBean you want to use within a JSP.

- **jsp:getProperty**:

  Syntax: `<jsp:getProperty name="beanName" property="propertyName"/>`

  <jsp:getProperty> converts the value of the specified property into a string and inserts this string into the implicit outobject. *getProperty* on a bean is usually called after declaring the bean instance using the `jsp:useBean` tag.

- **jsp:setProperty**:

  Syntax: `<jsp:setProperty name="beanName" property="propertyName" value="propertyValue"/>`

  <jsp:setProperty> is used to set the bean property value.

In addition, WebSphere supports WebSphere-specific tags that allow you to connect to databases, perform repeats, etc.

3.1.3.4 JavaBeans

JavaBeans is an architecture developed by Sun Microsystems, Inc. that describes an API and a set of conventions for reusable, Java-based components. Code written to Sun's JavaBeans architecture is called *JavaBeans* or just *beans*. One of the design criteria for the JavaBean API was support for builder tools that can compose solutions that incorporate beans. Beans may be visual or non-visual.

When discussing Java components, the Model-View-Controller (MVC) pattern is applied. According to this pattern, the process of serving a user request is split into three distinct parts:

- *Model* represents the data or business process
- *Controller* is responsible for overall flow of execution
- *View* is what a user see as a response

Beans are recommended for use in conjunction with servlets and JSPs in the following ways:

- As the client interface to the "Model Layer". An "Interaction Controller" servlet will use this bean interface.

- As the client interface to other resources. In some cases, this may be generated for you by a tool.

- As a component that incorporates a number of property-value pairs for use by other components or classes. For example, the JavaServer Pages specification includes a set of tags to access JavaBean properties.

3.1.3.5 Enterprise JavaBeans (EJB)

Enterprise JavaBeans is Sun's trademarked term for their EJB architecture (or component model). When writing to the EJB specification, you are developing enterprise beans (or, if you prefer, EJB beans). Enterprise JavaBeans are distinguished from JavaBeans in that they are designed to be installed on a server, and accessed remotely by a client. The definitions for EJBs are:

- Non-visual JavaBeans that run on a server in transactions

- Extend JavaBeans component model to support server components

- Component model for development and deployment of Object-Oriented Distributed Enterprise-Level Applications

- Programming model that ties various kinds of services together

- Components that run on any platform and are portable across EJB servers (containers)

- Component model based on a multi-tier, distributed object architecture and is a core component of the Java platform for the enterprise

Some reasons that make EJBs so powerful are:

- Standardized APIs are used for business components as well as for EJB servers:
  - EJB components have to be built, described, and profiled to the EJB standard.
  - An EJB application server has to be built to the EJB standard.
- Development tools are dedicated to the EJB components, which can reuse beans from any other EJB.
- Deployment tools are dedicated to the target EJB server, which can deploy beans created by any of the development systems.
- EJB servers can communicate with each other and are managed as a distributed object space.
- They recognize the benefit and application of the technology.
- Developers can focus on writing business logic, not plumbing.
- Development decisions are separate from deployment decisions.
- Deployment tools generate plumbing for the target server.
- Widespread reuse of software components is achieved.
- They enable the distribution of an application in an enterprise.

The EJB framework provides a standard for server-side components with transactional characteristics. The EJB framework specifies clearly the responsibilities of the EJB developer and the EJB container provider. The intent is that the "plumbing" required to implement transactions or database access can be implemented by the EJB container. The EJB developer specifies the required transactional and security characteristics of an EJB in a deployment descriptor (this is sometimes referred to as *declarative programming*). In a separate step, the EJB is then deployed to the EJB container provided by the application server vendor of your choice. There are two types of Enterprise JavaBeans:

- Session
- Entity

A typical session bean has the following characteristics:

- Executes on behalf of a single client
- Can be transactional
- Can update data in an underlying database
- Is relatively short lived
- Is destroyed when the EJB server is stopped; the client has to establish a new session bean to continue computation
- Does not represent persistent data that should be stored in a database
- Provides a scalable runtime environment to execute a large number of session beans concurrently

A typical entity bean has the following characteristics:

- Represents data in a database
- Can be transactional
- Shared access from multiple users
- Can be long lived (lives as long as the data in the database)

- Survives restarts of the EJB server; a restart is transparent to the client
- Provides a scalable runtime environment for a large number of concurrently active entity objects

Typically an entity bean is used for information that has to survive system restarts, while in session beans, the data is transient and does not survive when the client's browser is closed. For example, a shopping cart containing information that may be discarded uses a session bean, and an invoice issued after the purchase of the items is an entity bean.

An important design choice when implementing entity beans is whether to use bean-managed persistence (BMP), in which case you must code the JDBC logic, or container-managed persistence (CMP), where the database access logic is handled by the EJB container. The business logic of a Web application often accesses data in a database. EJB entity beans are a convenient way to wrap the relational database layer in an object layer, hiding the complexity of database access. Because a single business task may involve accessing several tables in a database, modeling rows in those tables with entity beans makes it easier for your application logic to manipulate the data.

EJB components

Figure 23 shows the components that participate in processing a client request to an EJB object. These components are discussed in more detail in the following sections.

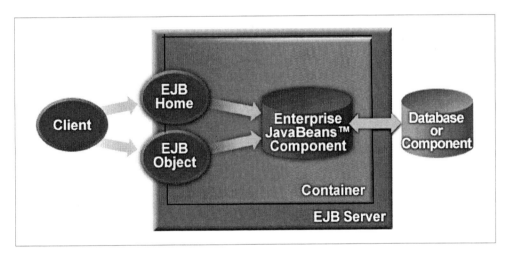

Figure 23. EJB components

EJB server

An EJB server provides the runtime environment for EJBs with the following services:

- Execution system
- Standard set of services to support enterprise bean components
- Access to a distributed transaction management service
- Activation/deactivation services
- Load balancing
- Failover support
- A home for all EJB objects

EJB container

An EJB container is the second entity required by the EJB specification to support EJBs. It adds to the list of services provided by the EJB server:

- Remote access/network inter operability
- Transaction management
- Persistence management
- Authentication and authorization
- Resource pooling
- Concurrent service for multiple clients
- Thread and process management
- Clustering and high availability
- Runtime for all EJBs

In the EJB architecture, the EJB container is the abstract entity used to explain the concept of the environment where the EJBs are deployed. EJB container services are provided through the use of two objects:

- **EJB Home interface object**: Java object that implements the Home interface for this EJB

- **EJB Remote interface object**: Java object that implements the Remote interface for this EJB

The Home interface has to extend the javax.ejb.EJBHome interface, and the Remote interface for your EJB has to extend javax.ejb.EJBObject. The inheritance chain for the Home and Remote interfaces is shown in Figure 24.

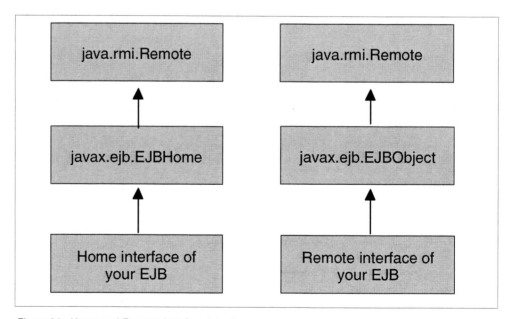

Figure 24. Home and Remote interface inheritance

The EJB Home interface and Remote interface objects are generated by the EJB container when an EJB is deployed (or "dropped") in an EJB container. All calls to an EJB object are intercepted by either of two objects to provide services guaranteed by the EJB container.

EJB Home

The EJB Home interface object is responsible for the life cycle of an EJB object. It should provide at least the following functions:

- Create an EJB object
- Remove an EJB object
- Find an EJB object by primary key (for the entity beans only)

EJB object

The EJB Remote interface object (EJB object) is responsible for routing and supporting the business methods in an EJB object. Among the methods that have to be implemented by the EJB Remote interface objects, the remove method deserves our attention. This method is similar to the remove method in the EJB Home interface object. The remove method, as one can think, removes (or destroys) the EJB object. However, for an entity bean, this method deletes the corresponding row from the database table. You must use care with this method.

EJB programming model

Figure 25 shows the flow in the EJB programming model for Web applications.

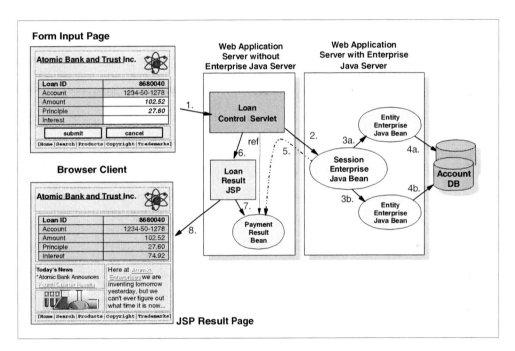

Figure 25. Programming model in EJB

The steps shown in Figure 25 are outlined here:

1. From the browser, an HTML form with name-value pairs and an action is sent to the Web application server, which triggers a so-called "control servlet".

2. The control servlet restores the state, parses the name-value pairs, connects to the transaction part of the application (which is a session EJB), and invokes the appropriate method.

3. The session EJB talks to entity EJBs or other session EJBs.

4. The entity EJBs perform basic business logic and accesses the persistent storage.

5. The result is returned in the form of a Java result bean tree and kept alive by referencing the root bean by a temporary variable, which is valid through the later JSP call.

6. The control servlet calls the proper JSP to prepare the HTML reply, which is usually an HTML form.

7. The reply JSP references the result beans to display the attributes in constant text and fields.

8. Finally, the generated HTML is returned to the browser.

3.1.3.6 Enterprise Java logical interface blocks
Full-fledged Enterprise JavaBeans containers provide all services through a set of Java interfaces (see Figure 26).

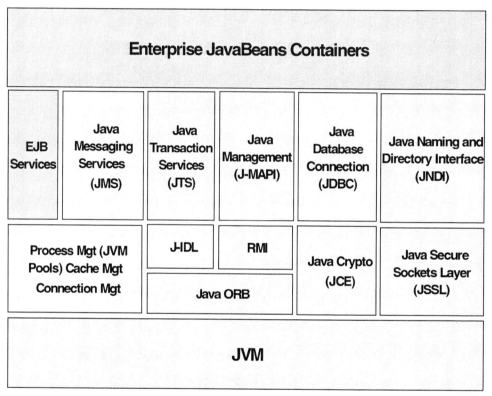

Figure 26. Enterprise Java logical interface blocks

We discuss some of these interfaces in more detail in the following sections.

JDBC and SQLJ
The business logic in a Web application accesses information in a database for a database centric scenario. JDBC is a Java API for database-independent connectivity. It provides a straightforward way to map SQL types to Java types. With JDBC, you can connect to your relational databases, and create and execute dynamic SQL statements in Java. JDBC drivers are relational database management system (RDBMS)-specific, provided by the DBMS vendor, but implement the standard set of interfaces defined in the JDBC API. Given common schemas between two databases, an application can be switched between one and the other by changing the JDBC driver name and URL. A common practice is to place the JDBC driver name and URL information in a property or configuration

file. Based on the characteristics of your application, you can choose from four types of JDBC drivers (see Figure 27).

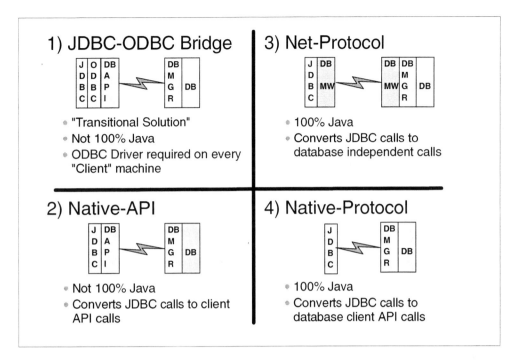

Figure 27. JDBC driver types

The JDBC driver types are:

- **Type 1: JDBC-ODBC bridge drivers**: This type of driver, packaged with JDK, requires an ODBC driver and was introduced to enable database access for Java developers in the absence of any other type of driver.

- **Type 2: Native API partly Java drivers**: This type of driver uses the client API of the DBMS and requires the binaries for the database client software. This type of driver offers performance advantages but introduces native calls from the Java Virtual Machine (JVM).

- **Type 3: Net-protocol all Java drivers**: A generic network protocol is used with this type of driver. Portability is a major advantage of this type of driver, but it has the limitation that it requires intermediate middleware to convert the Net-protocol to the DBMS protocol.

- **Type 4: Native-protocol all Java drivers**: This type of driver is portable and uses the protocol of the DBMS.

Driver Types 3 and 4 are well suited for applets that access a database server on an intranet, because they only require Java code to be downloaded. The most common drivers today are Type 2 (generally the best performer) and Type 4 (the best balance of performance and portability).

An important technique used to enhance the scalability of Web applications is connection pooling, which may be provided by the application server. When application logic in a user session needs access to a database resource, rather than establishing and later dropping a new database connection, the code requests a connection from an established pool, returning it to the pool when no longer required.

SQLJ provides a simplified syntax for JDBC that allows you to write SQL-like statements directly in your Java source code. The SQLJ preprocessor generates static SQL, which provides better performance than dynamic SQL. SQLJ also generates iterator Java classes. These iterators allow you to navigate query results using a very simple "get next" protocol.

Additional enterprise Java APIs

In developing a server-side application, you may also need to be familiar with the following enterprise Java class libraries:

- **Java Naming and Directory Interface (JNDI)**: This package provides a common API to a directory service. Service provider implementations include those for LDAP directories, RMI and CORBA object registries. Sample uses of JNDI include:

    - Accessing a user profile from an LDAP directory
    - Locating and accessing an EJB Home

- **Remote Method Invocation (RMI)**: RMI and RMI over IIOP are part of the EJB specification as the access method for clients accessing EJB services. RMI can also be used to implement limited function Java servers.

- **Java Message Service (JMS)**: The JMS API enables a Java programmer to access message-oriented middleware such as MQSeries from the Java programming model. Such messaging middleware is a popular choice for accessing existing enterprise systems.

- **Java Transaction API (JTA)**: This Java API for working with transaction services is based on the extended architecture (XA) standard. With the availability of EJB servers that support transactions, you are less likely to use this API directly.

3.1.4 e-business and objects

Developing a model for an industrial-strength software system prior to its construction or renovation is as essential as having a blueprint for a large building. Good models are essential for communication among project teams and to assure architectural soundness. We build models of complex systems because we cannot comprehend any such system in its entirety. As the complexity of systems increase, so does the importance of good modeling techniques. Implementation tools and languages are affected first and ask for changes in the abstract areas of development – the methodologies.

3.1.4.1 Methodologies

The traditional waterfall model of development is shown in Figure 28.

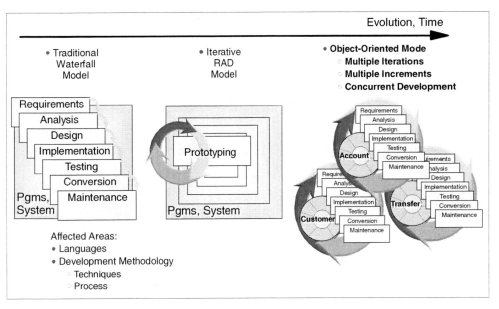

Figure 28. Software development evolution

After signing off a phase, the next phase can be started and each phase always covers the entire system. Even though we can introduce subsystems, we talk about very-course granularity. We also know the drawback: By the time we are done with the last phase, the world and its requirements have changed so dramatically, that we must throw away the new and already outdated solution and start over. Sometimes this state is already reached after the first few phases. Furthermore, we know that each phase is a big step and should include all the aspects of the system. Only after the last phase is something available to look at by the end user.

An answer to the limitations of the traditional waterfall model began about 20 years ago by the so-called *Rapid Application Development (RAD)* tools and its iterative development model. In the RAD model, a prototype is developed very fast that gives a glimpse of the final system. Through the cycles, the prototype is extended, again and again. The story is familiar: The prototype is extended and architecturally or design-wise messed up, because there is no real problem-domain related architecture or design. The cycles always deal with the entire system at any moment, which mean they are not broken down into their own individual processes. This implies that it tests the whole system. Often the developed prototype is thrown away and serves as a good insight for starting over and changing to the traditional waterfall model.

In the object-oriented model, the phases still exist, but are applied on small items with natural boundaries, the objects. And because of the nature of the object-oriented model, even extensions of objects do not affect existing functionality. With the object-oriented model, stability can be achieved, even though the system is constantly extended. Behavior changes are predictable, because the impact analyses are easy to do. The encapsulation and the fine granularity are two of the major enablers.

In the object-oriented world, once the interfaces are defined, the objects can be developed concurrently by many teams to achieve shorter time to market. You may argue that this is true as with a lot of small subsystems. To some degree, it is true. But the object orientation fulfills, by nature, the requirement for fast, easy, and only locally impacting changes. The object-oriented development process is iterative and incremental as demonstrated in Figure 29. The phases are applied to the individual objects and frameworks. That is the major difference with the waterfall model that applies the phases in a single run to the system as a whole.

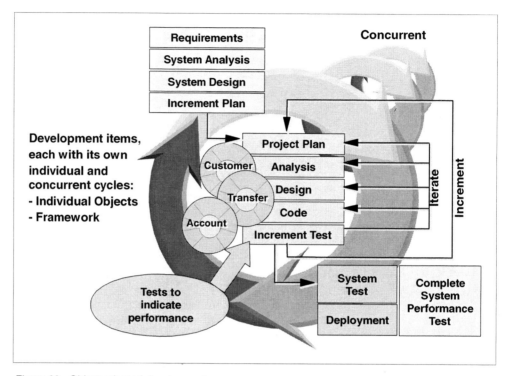

Figure 29. Object-oriented development process

The natural boundaries of the objects allow this approach to change the code without destabilizing the whole system. Beyond the functional testing, the incremental test must include performance testing to catch resource hogs in advance and to predict complete system performance.

Development items, each with its own individual an concurrent cycles, are individual objects as well as a *framework*. A framework is a cluster of objects that covers a reasonable amount of business functionality in a generic or complete way.

Project management becomes an even greater issue with so many things going on in their individual phases. The price for the reward is faster, more reliable, more flexible, and staged to the market.

3.1.4.2 Object-oriented concepts

An object class is like a blueprint, a template, or an emtpy form. It describes how the actual object instance will be built or constructed, what state or data it will carry, and what behavior or functionality it will have. All object instances share the same structure information and processing code. Changes to a class become valid to all objects of that class, no matter in what application that object is used.

Objects combine naturally the state and behavior, or the data and processing, that belong together and represent parts of the real world. That is the key difference to the procedural or structured programming, where each application program individually includes or ties together data descriptions and processing. Therefore, it is obvious that objects and object-oriented systems achieve higher maintainability and reuse than procedural-oriented modules and systems.

The individual variables or attributes of the state of an object are encapsulated and only accessible through methods. The methods are the individual functions of the behavior.

Methods are invoked by messages sent to the object, by other objects, through the object runtime environment. Invocation parameters are references to other objects. The single return value is also an object reference. Remember that objects can reference other objects in their state, which allows them to "return" basically multiple objects.

Development methodologies

Development methodologies describe the process and the artifacts that will be produced during the development stage of a project. Common artifacts are business process models, object diagrams, usecases, etc. (see Figure 30).

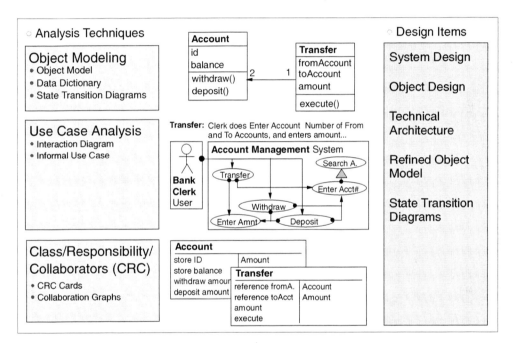

Figure 30. Object-oriented development methodologies

Object modeling is data-oriented, for example:

- What objects exist in the system?
- What are the states?
- What causes a state change?

Use Case Analysis is process-oriented:

- Describes, uniformly (text) and then formally (diagrams), how the user uses the system (no pseudo-programming; describe what you see happening)
- Finds the objects that are involved and define their methods

Class/Responsibility/Collaborator (CRC) is a relatively new, combined approach. For example, the Amount may be an object with the responsibility to store a numeric value and a reference to the Currency object, as well as perform the calculation of the amount, the numeric value exactly, for a given, different currency.

Increment and iteration have their impact on each aspects of an object. Object designs usually undergo several refinements and each of the objects become hardened and better in reuse.

3.1.5 Application patterns

A Web application is essentially a series of interactions between a client and a particular Web site. The entire Web-interaction process begins with a single page displayed in the browser. The user clicks a button or link on the page that sends a request to the Web application server. The request is processed on the server, and a new page is sent back with both the results of the request and buttons or links for the next request. The Web application consists of a set of processing steps or interactions. Each step or iteration gets a request generated from a page and must produce a response in the form of a page that serves as the input for subsequent interactions.

If you examine a single interaction at the next level of detail, you see a common set of processing requirements that map to the classical model/view/controller paradigm as follows (see Figure 31):

- **Business logic (model)**: The logic necessary to actually accomplish the goal of the interaction. This might be done by a computation, a query, an update to a database, etc. Business logic can be independent of the style or mechanism of the user interface.

- **UI logic (view)**: The logic and content necessary to construct a particular response, typically an HTML page. This logic depends on the details of the user interface. The UI logic involves the presentation form and style for the results of the interaction.

- **Interaction controller (controller)**: The logic necessary to process the HTTP request, drive the business logic, and select an appropriate response. This logic depends on the details of how HTTP requests are encoded and on the desired flow between user interactions. However, interaction control does not depend on the appearance or style of the response page.

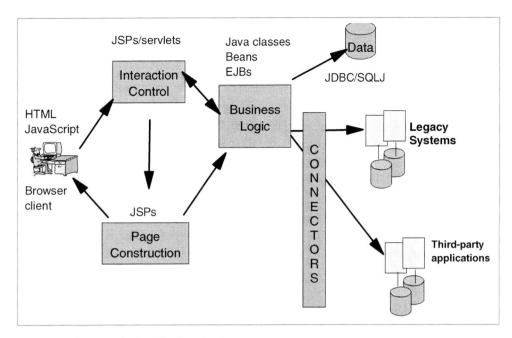

Figure 31. The standard application structure

Observing this mapping is important. The different types of logic often require different development skills and tools and evolve on different schedules. Therefore, it is critical to maintain a clean separation between the different types of program logic. As shown in Figure 31, the framework recommends that the business logic be wrapped with a JavaBean that usually represents a single function supported by the business logic of a framework application. Its usage paradigm is:

1. Create the bean.
2. Initialize by setting the bean's properties.
3. Perform by calling the bean's methods.
4. Inspect by getting the values of the bean's properties.

Using command beans of this form provides several benefits:

- *Isolation of changes*: Wrapping the business logic with command beans (as opposed to exposing the business logic model directly) allows the business logic to evolve without disrupting the rest of the Web application.

- *Distribution*: Command beans can be serialized and sent via a protocol (IIOP, HTTP, etc.) to a remote server to be executed and sent back. This allows for efficient communication.

3.1.5.1 Interaction controller
The interaction controller is the code that ties client-independent business logic to the other elements of a Web application. Some typical functions performed by the interaction controller are:

- Validating requests
- Verifying privileges
- Mapping requests to business-logic input properties
- Invoking UI logic

The framework supports the development of interaction-controller logic using either Java servlets or JavaServer Pages technology. Both of these mechanisms have significant advantages over CGI or Web-server plug-ins. You need to decide which to use in your interaction controller.

Another design issue is the cardinality of the relationship between interactions and interaction controllers. The chief advantage of JavaServer Pages over Java servlets is that they are closer to the presentation medium.

A JavaServer Page is an HTML page. It contains all the HTML tags that Web authors are familiar with. It presents them in the same way as ordinary hypertext, so an author can leverage their favorite HTML design tools. A JSP is HTML, but it may also contain fragments of Java code that select which pieces of the layout are visible and which are not. These code fragments may call out to JavaBeans or Enterprise JavaBeans to access reusable components and back-end data. The code fragments may be reinforced by expressions, which are fragments of Java code that return some value (such as a property on a bean).

If the amount of code on a page is relatively small (that is, the page is primarily for presentation), JSP offers a way to focus on the artistic creation of the page by compiling the page into a Java servlet for the author. Servlets make the Java code much easier to read (and therefore maintain) when the amount of code is proportionately larger than the amount of HTML on the page. Unlike JSPs, servlets are compiled before they become usable in runtime. They do not require a full application server runtime during the compile phase. Because servlets are deployed as .class files, they are more attractive than JSPs in instances where you do not want the source code of your Web application available on the Web server.

There are compelling reasons to use JSP whenever possible that factor business logic into JavaBeans and use JSP scripting for control flow and bean-property access. This allows rapid development of JSP and takes advantage of the maintenance benefits of the JavaBean component model. The typical functions performed by the interaction controller are described here in more detail:

- **Validating requests**: You can validate requests in JSP or servlet form in Java on the Web application server. However, if you perform this function in JavaScript on the client, you'll see a performance gain as fewer exchanges between the client and server become necessary.

- **Verifying privileges**: An e-business designer may want to obtain login information from users who have not properly logged into the application. You have a variety of choices for assigning user privileges: Web servers (such as Apache) have authentication and access-control services; most current operating systems have authentication and access-control services; and many applications "roll their own" authentication services.

- **Mapping requests to business logic input properties**: This is where command beans come into play. Command beans form a stable boundary between the business logic and user interface. The interaction controller maps input from the user request to command bean properties. The command bean hides the business logic and data behind its properties, which allows the business logic to evolve independently of the user interface and vice versa. The interaction controller may execute multiple command beans to gather output that it then routes to the UI logic.

The environment for command execution is called the *command target*. Command targets can be located on a local server, which simply calls the command bean's `perform` method. Or they can be located on a remote server that requires serializing the command bean and shipping it to a remote server for execution. However, the interaction controller needs to be aware of only the command bean interface to execute commands.

- **Invoking UI logic**: Once a command bean has executed, the interaction controller must invoke the proper user-interface logic to convey the results to the user.

3.1.5.2 UI logic

The UI logic, which is the view component of the application, is responsible for generating the HTML page that is returned to the client. The framework supports the development of UI logic using either servlets or JSP technology. Because JSP allows HTML and Java to be mixed on the same page, it is most often the better choice for implementing the UI logic. JSP offers a template-based approach, supported by visual authoring tools, for integrating dynamic data into HTML pages.

In many cases, the interaction controller passes dynamic data to the UI logic for formatting. In other cases, the UI logic invokes business logic directly to obtain dynamic data. It makes sense to have the interaction controller pass the data when it has already obtained it and when the data is an essential component of the contract between the interaction controller and the UI logic. In other cases, the data needed is not an essential part of the interaction and can be obtained independently by inserting calls to business logic directly in the UI logic.

Once the UI logic has obtained the dynamic data, either from the interaction controller, or via its own logic, it typically formats the data. This can be done several ways. The simplest mechanism is where the data is formatted using simple scripting inside the display page. An alternative is to develop reusable script or Java object formatting components that take a data set and return formatted HTML.

3.1.5.3 Business logic

The business logic part of an interaction is isolated from the details of Web technology. As a result, it is valuable to consider the interface between the Web parts of the interaction (interaction controllers and UI logic) and the business logic. The business logic part of a Web application is the piece of code that is ultimately responsible for satisfying client requests.

As a result, business logic must address a wide range of potential requirements. This includes ensuring transactional integrity of application components, maintaining and quickly accessing application data, supporting the coordination of business workflow processes, and integrating new application components with existing applications. To address these requirements and aid the development of business logic on the Web application server, the framework provides the following core services:

- Java services
- Database services
- Collaboration services
- Application integration services

3.1.5.4 Separation of UI and business logic

Command beans provide a standard way to invoke a business logic request using a single round-trip message. A command bean is a JavaBean that encapsulates a single request to a target server (the server where the command is to be executed). The target server can be the same JVM as the client or a separate JVM. The command bean infrastructure allows a command to be executed within the environment of a target server, so multiple accesses by the command to server resources avoid distributed overhead. Any server can be a target if it supports Java access to its resources and provides a protocol to copy the command bean between a Web application JVM and the command server JVM.

Command beans allow the server side of the Web application to be partitioned into efficient units of interaction. The Web application parts, such as the interaction controller and UI logic, are independent of the style of the command bean's implementation and independent of where the command bean is physically executed. Figure 32 shows the internal components that comprise the command bean execution environment.

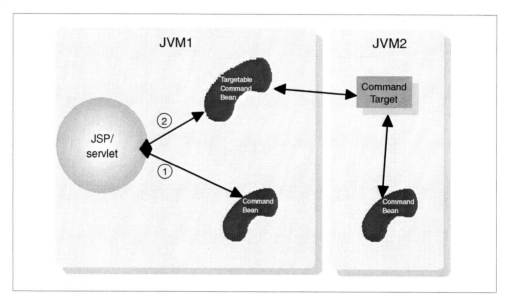

Figure 32. Command bean infrastructure

Command beans that execute locally (in the same JVM as the Web application) simply implement the `Command` interface (path 1 in Figure 32). If a command bean is to execute remotely on another server, it implements the `TargetableCommand` interface, which is an extension of the `Command` interface that allows for remote execution (path 2 in Figure 32). Regardless of whether the command bean executes locally or remotely, the JSP or servlet executes the command bean in the same way. The steps in a command bean's execution are explained here:

1. The JSP or servlet instantiates the command bean. It then sets the command bean's input properties. Finally, the JSP or servlet calls the `perform` method on the command bean. If the command bean executes locally, skip to step 2. Otherwise, these additional steps occur:

   a. The `perform` method determines the target environment for the command bean.

b. The `perform` method calls the `executeCommand` method on the `CommandTarget` object that passes itself (the command bean) as an input argument. This step may involve serializing the command bean and sending it via some protocol (such as IIOP) to the target server for execution.

c. The command target, after potentially de-serializing the command bean, then calls the command bean's `executePerform` method, which encapsulates the business logic.

2. The `perform` method, if successful, returns a copy of the command bean with its output properties set to the results of the underlying business logic task.

3. Control flows to the JSP or servlet, which is now free to query the output properties of the command bean.

3.1.5.5 Relationship of command beans and EJB

You may wonder why you wouldn't use IIOP to session beans to accomplish the same objective as commands. The answer is that commands have some advantages over session beans.

Command beans handle multiple protocols to accommodate any target server, not just IIOP to EJB servers. This includes IIOP and HTTP, as well as proprietary protocols. When the Web application and target server are not in the same JVM, command beans require fewer messages. For a session EJB whose container runs in a separate server, several remote messages are required to do a single logical request (such as add an item to a shopping cart):

1. Look up the home.
2. Narrow the home.
3. Create the SessionBean instance.
4. Call the method.
5. Destroy the SessionBean instance.

The overhead of steps 1 and 2 can often be done once for many SessionBean instances. However, there are still three round-trip messages required per instance.

On the other hand, command beans provide an `EJBCommandTarget` using a `CommandServerEntityBean`. An EntityBean is used instead of a SessionBean so many different transactions can access the same instance. This instance has the only distributed object stub required in the Web application JVM. This instance is obtained once at server startup and subsequently cached inside `EJBCommandTarget`. This allows each logical request to the EJB server to cost only a single message, because the overhead in steps 1, 2, 3, and 5 are factored out and done only once, which amortizes their cost over many command bean executions. `CommandTarget` extends `java.rmi.Remote`, so that it can potentially be an `EJBObject` (either SessionBean or EntityBean). This allows the case where the `TargetableCommand.setCommandTarget` parameter is an EJB.

3.1.6 Common Object Request Broker Architecture (CORBA)

CORBA encompasses a series of standards and protocols for interprocess communication in a heterogeneous environment. Using CORBA, developers can write applications for many different operating systems at once, in any number of languages. The CORBA specification only defines a set of conventions and protocols that must be followed by CORBA implementations. It is left to vendors and developers to translate this specification into a working implementation. CORBA does not make any restrictions on language or underlying operating system. Because of this, implementations of the CORBA specification have been created for a wide variety of operating systems, including UNIX, Windows, and OS/400, and for many languages, including C, C++, Java, Ada, LISP, Python, and even COBOL.

Any CORBA implementation that matches the defined interfaces and adheres to the defined protocols is allowed to communicate with other CORBA implementations. Such specifications as TCP/IP, HTTP, and SMTP have taken off on the Internet largely because their language- and OS-neutral specifications give them a great deal of flexibility.

Figure 33 illustrates the primary components in the Object Management Group (OMG) Reference Model architecture. These components are described in the following sections.

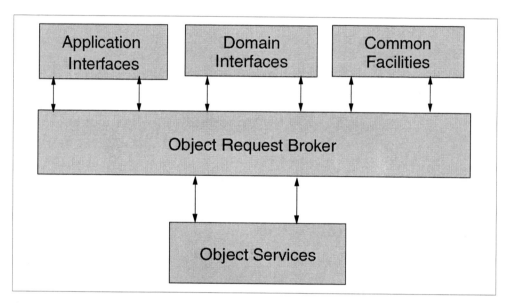

Figure 33. OMG Reference Model architecture

Object services

These are domain-independent interfaces that are used by many distributed object programs. For example, a service providing for the discovery of other available services is almost always necessary regardless of the application domain. Two examples of object services that fulfill this role are:

- **Naming Service**: Allows clients to find objects based on names
- **Trading Service**: Allows clients to find objects based on their properties

There are also object service specifications for lifecycle management, security, transactions, event notification, and many others.

Common facilities

Like object service interfaces, these interfaces are also horizontally-oriented. Unlike object services they are oriented toward end-user applications. An example of such a facility is the Distributed Document Component Facility (DDCF), which is a compound document Common Facility based on OpenDoc. DDCF allows for the presentation and interchange of objects based on a document model, for example, facilitating the linking of a spreadsheet object into a report document.

Domain interfaces

These interfaces fill roles similar to object services and Common Facilities, but are oriented toward specific application domains. For example, one of the first OMG Request for Proposals (RFPs) issued for Domain Interfaces is for Product Data Management (PDM) Enablers for the manufacturing domain. Other OMG RFPs will soon be issued in the telecommunications, medical, and financial domains.

Application interfaces

These interfaces are developed specifically for a given application. Because they are application-specific, and because the OMG does not develop applications (only specifications), these interfaces are not standardized. However, if over time it appears that certain broadly useful services emerge out of a particular application domain, they may become candidates for future OMG standardization.

3.1.6.1 CORBA Stack

Figure 34 illustrates the primary components in the CORBA Stack.

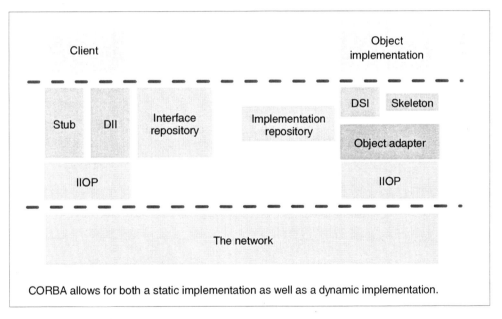

Figure 34. CORBA Stack

Each of the entities in Figure 34 are explained here:

- **Object**: This is a CORBA programming entity that consists of an *identity*, an *interface*, and an *implementation*, which is known as a *Servant*.

- **Servant**: This is an implementation programming language entity that defines the operations that support a CORBA IDL interface. Servants can be written in a variety of languages, including C, C++, Java, Smalltalk, and Ada.

- **Client**: This is the program entity that invokes an operation on an object implementation. Accessing the services of a remote object should be transparent to the caller. Ideally, it should be as simple as calling a method on an object.

- **Object Request Broker**: The ORB provides a mechanism for transparently communicating client requests to target object implementations. The ORB simplifies distributed programming by decoupling the client from the details of the method invocations. This makes client requests appear to be local procedure calls. When a client invokes an operation, the ORB is responsible for finding the object implementation, transparently activating it if necessary, delivering the request to the object, and returning any response to the caller.

- **ORB interface**: An ORB is a logical entity that may be implemented in various ways (such as one or more processes or a set of libraries). To decouple applications from implementation details, the CORBA specification defines an abstract interface for an ORB. This interface provides various helper functions. Such function include converting object references to strings and vice versa, and creating argument lists for requests made through the dynamic invocation interface.

- **CORBA IDL stubs and skeletons**: CORBA IDL stubs and skeletons serve as the "glue" between the client and server applications, respectively, and the ORB. The transformation between CORBA IDL definitions and the target programming language is automated by a CORBA IDL compiler. The use of a compiler reduces the potential for inconsistencies between client stubs and server skeletons and increases opportunities for automated compiler optimizations.

- **Dynamic Invocation Interface (DII)**: This interface allows a client to directly access the underlying request mechanisms provided by an ORB. Applications use the DII to dynamically issue requests to objects without requiring IDL interface-specific stubs to be linked in. Unlike IDL stubs (which only allow RPC-style requests), the DII also allows clients to make non-blocking *deferred synchronous* (separate send and receive operations) and *oneway* (send-only) calls.

- **Dynamic Skeleton Interface (DSI)**: This is the server side's analogue to the client side's DII. The DSI allows an ORB to deliver requests to an object implementation that does not have compile-time knowledge of the type of the object it is implementing. The client making the request has no idea whether the implementation is using the type-specific IDL skeletons or is using the dynamic skeletons.

- **Object adapter**: This assists the ORB with delivering requests to the object and with activating the object. More importantly, an object adapter associates object implementations with the ORB. Object adapters can be specialized to provide support for certain object implementation styles (such as object-oriented database (OODB) object adapters for persistence and library object adapters for non-remote objects).

3.1.7 Transactions

A transaction is a unit of work that performs an administrative function by using one or more shared system resources. It produces a definite, but reversible, change in some part of the system properties or state, such as updating several table entries in a database. A typical example is transferring money between savings accounts and checking accounts. This operation involves updating two databases. To keep the integrity of both accounts, this operation has to complete as one single unit of work.

Enterprise applications often require concurrent access to distributed data shared among multiple components. Such applications should maintain data integrity (as defined by the business rules of the application) under the following circumstances:

- Distributed access to a single resource of data
- Access to distributed resources from a single application component

In such cases, it may be required that a group of operations on (distributed) resources be treated as one unit of work. In a unit of work, all the participating operations should either succeed or fail and recover together. This problem is more complicated when:

- A unit of work is implemented across a group of distributed components operating on data from multiple resources
- The participating operations are executed sequentially or in parallel threads requiring coordination or synchronization

In either case, it is required that success or failure of a unit of work be maintained by the application. In case of a failure, all the resources should bring back the state of the data to the previous state (for example, the state prior to the commencement of the unit of work).

The concept of a transaction and a transaction manager (or a transaction processing service) simplifies the construction of such enterprise-level distributed applications while maintaining integrity of data in a unit of work.

A transaction is a unit of work that has the following properties (called ACID properties):

- **Atomicity**: A transaction is an indivisible unit of work; all of its actions either succeed or they all fail (logical units of work (LUW)). In the event of a failure of any operation, effects of all operations that make up the transaction should be undone, and data should be rolled back to its previous state.

- **Consistency**: After the transaction executes, it must leave the system in a correct state or abort (leaving the system in its initial state – COMMIT or ROLLBACK). For example, in the case of relational databases, a consistent transaction should preserve all the integrity constraints defined on the data.

- **Isolation**: A transactions' behavior is not affected by other transactions that execute concurrently. The effect of executing a set of transactions serially should be the same as that of running them concurrently. This requires two things:

  - During the course of a transaction, an intermediate (possibly inconsistent) state of the data should not be exposed to all other transactions.

  - Two concurrent transactions should not be able to operate on the same data. Database management systems usually implement this feature using locking.

- **Durability**: A transactions' effects are permanent (persistent) after it commits (information is saved in a recoverable storage resource).

Logical units of work is a sequence of processing actions (database changes, for example) that must be completed before any of the individual actions can be regarded as committed. The acronym ACID helps remember the properties of a transaction

Note: CICS defines a transaction differently than an LUW. Within CICS, a transaction can include multiple LUWs.

For a discussion of the concepts, we continue to use transaction and LUW interchangeably. However, CICS and other TP management programs make a clear distinction.

The ACID properties guarantee that a transaction is never incomplete, the data is never inconsistent, concurrent transactions are independent, and the effects of a transaction are persistent.

3.1.7.1 Distributed transactions standards

The standards for transaction processing and management in the industry are:

- **X/Open Distributed Transaction Processing Standard**: Defines a set of specifications that allows applications, resource managers, and transaction managers to synchronize distributed transactions.

- **Object Management Group (OMG) Object Transaction Services**: Defines a set of specifications to manage distributed transactions as part of CORBA.

- **Enterprise JavaBeans (EJB) Java Transaction Services**: Define a Java interface for distributed transactions based on OMG Object Transaction Services.

Each of these standards is built on the previous one.

3.1.7.2 Transaction processing

Modern transaction processing systems are increasingly complex, decentralized, and dynamic. They take advantage of evolving technologies to stay competitive and to benefit from smaller, cheaper, and more powerful computers and the proliferation of communication services. At the same time, a transaction processing system has to cope with the interaction of different types of computers, communication networks, and user devices.

A transaction may involve operations on a customer's notebook computer, a branch desktop computer, or a central mainframe, yet the system must still provide optimum service and integrity. In a transaction processing system, the application is not concerned about where operations are performed as long as the service and integrity are maintained.

An industry standard model for transaction processing is based on the X/Open XA protocol. X/Open is a consortium of users, software vendors, and hardware vendors who define programming interfaces. This model is known as the distributed transaction processing (DTP) model and is illustrated in Figure 35.

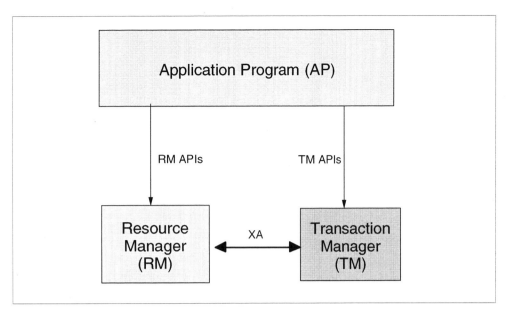

Figure 35. Distributed transaction processing model

The following section discusses distributed transaction processing and explains the components that are required for it.

Distributed transaction processing

Distributed transaction processing ensures that application processing can span multiple databases on multiple systems, coordinated by multiple transaction managers. Transaction processing in a distributed system environment requires the cooperation of three different components:

- **Transaction manager (TM)**: Serves as the transaction coordinator by providing transaction services to the applications

- **Resource manager (RM)**: Participates in the transaction by performing work on behalf of the applications

- **Application program (AP)**: Its business logic requires transaction services

Each of these roles contributes to the distributed transaction processing system by implementing different sets of transaction API and functionality.

Transaction manager

The transaction manager is typically a system component of an application server or transaction processing system. The application server provides the infrastructure required to support the application execution environment.

The transaction manager implements a set of low-level transaction interfaces that are not exposed to the applications. The low-level transaction services allow the TM to coordinate transaction processing performed by multiple resource managers, such as database connections, messaging sessions, or connections to back-end legacy systems on behalf of the application. Transaction context is propagated by the TM to all resource managers that participate in the transaction, even across network connections.

An example of low-level transaction services is the API provided by Java Transaction Service (JTS). JTS is a mapping of the OMG Object Transaction

Service (OTS) specification to the Java programming language. The JTS API is a low-level transaction management service intended for vendors who provide a transaction system infrastructure for application run-time execution.

An EJB server vendor may use JTS to provide transaction services on behalf of transactional applications, such as EJB applications. The transaction manager (TM) manages global transactions and coordinates the decision to commit them or roll them back. This ensures atomic transaction completion. The TM also coordinates recovery activities of the resource managers when necessary, such as after a component fails.

Resource manager

The resource manager supports distributed transactions by implementing a transaction resource interface and it participates in transactions that are externally controlled by a TM.

An example of a resource manager interface is the industry standard X/Open XA protocol. The X/Open XA protocol is supported by most database vendors and is also used by messaging or communications systems, such as MQSeries. In the X/Open DTP model, RMs structure any changes to the resources they manage as part of a recoverable, atomic transaction. The RM lets the TM coordinate completion of the atomic transaction with work done by other RMs.

Application program

The application program performs the business logic of a transaction. A component-based transactional application that is developed to operate in a modern application server environment typically does not need to contain any transaction logic. An example of a modern application server environment is the industry standard Enterprise JavaBeans (EJB) component architecture, which was originally defined by the EJB 1.0 Specification.

In some cases, it may be desirable for a client program or Enterprise JavaBeans to manage the transaction scope. The Enterprise JavaBeans architecture implements this capability through an interface that's defined as part of the Java Transaction API (JTA). The AP implements the desired function of the end-user enterprise. Each AP specifies a sequence of operations that may involve resources, such as a database, file, or interoperation with a legacy system. An AP defines the start and end of a global transaction, accesses resources within transaction boundaries, and usually decides whether to commit or roll back each transaction.

Atomic commit protocols

Recall that to maintain the atomicity of a transaction, either all of the operations that make up the transaction take effect or none of them take effect. In the case of a distributed transaction, the process is complicated by the fact that the operations that make up the transaction have been performed on several servers. When the client requests that a transaction should commit or abort the request, it needs to be communicated to all of the servers that have performed operations within the context of the transaction. Various strategies have been devised to perform this task. One and two-phase commit protocols are explained here:

- **One-phase commit (1PC) protocol**

  An example of a one-phase commit protocol is outlined here:

  a. The client requests a transaction to commit or abort.

  b. The transaction manager communicates this request to all of the servers that have performed operations within the context of the transaction.

  c. The transaction manager repeats the request until all of the servers have acknowledged that it has been performed.

  This simple one-phase commit protocol is inadequate because it does not guarantee the atomicity of a distributed transaction. The reason for this is that the protocol does not allow any of the servers that are taking part in the transaction to make a unilateral decision to abort the transaction.

  It is possible that any of the servers taking part in the transaction may not be able to fulfill a commit request. There are several reasons why a server may not be able to perform a commit. Examples span from the breaking of locks due to deadlock resolution to the failure and subsequent restart of the server. In any such situation, the server in question must be able to force a rollback of all of the operations performed within the context of the transaction, whether these operations were carried out on the same server or on a different server.

- **Two-phase commit (2PC) protocol**

  The two-phase commit protocol was designed to work around the limitations of the one-phase commit protocol. This protocol allows any server that is taking part in a transaction to abort its part of the transaction and, as a result, force the transaction as a whole to be aborted. To achieve this, the two-phase commit protocol breaks the commitment process into two phases. In the first phase, the transaction manager initiates a vote after it receives a commit request from the client. It sends a prepare message to each server that is participating in the transaction and waits for a response from each server that indicates whether that server can commit or whether it must rollback. Upon receipt of the prepare message, each server checks to see if it can commit its part of the transaction and then votes for either a commit or an abort accordingly. Once a server has voted to commit a transaction, it is not allowed to abort it. This has serious implications for the server because it must ensure that it can commit even in the event of a server failure and restart.

  Once a server has ensured that it can commit and has cast its vote, it is in the prepared state. When the transaction manager has collected all of votes from the participating servers, it initiates the second phase of the protocol. If all of the servers vote to commit the transaction, the transaction manager sends a message to all of the servers telling them to commit their part of the transaction. If one or more servers vote to abort the transaction, the transaction manager sends a message to the servers telling them to abort their part of the transaction.

  The process can be optimized at this point by allowing any server that votes to abort the ability to immediately perform a rollback without any further communication from the transaction manager. In this scenario, the transaction manager only needs to communicate the decision to abort the transaction to those servers that voted to commit.

The interaction diagram in Figure 36 shows an application running in the transactional environment of the Top Node.

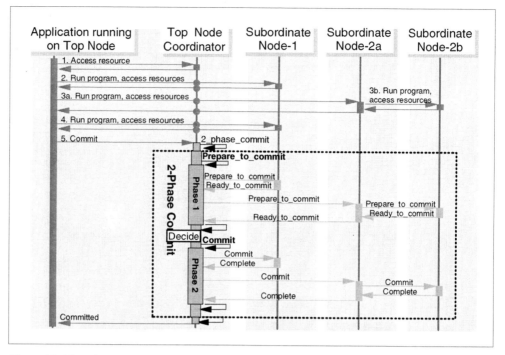

Figure 36. Two-phase commit details

It follows this process:

1. Accesses resources of the top node

2. Accesses through the Top Node program and resources of Subordinate Node-1

3. Accesses through the Top Node program and resources of Subordinate Node-2a - and this program on Subordinate Node-2a accesses program and resources on Subordinate Node-2b (3b)

4. Accesses through the Top Node program and resources of Subordinate Node-1

5. Issues a COMMIT

Note: The application always goes to the Top Node to run programs on and access resources of another nodes. This way, the Top Node's Coordinator can keep track of the involved resources and nodes (indicated by the bar and bullet on the life line of the Top Node).

Furthermore, the nesting is controlled at the each nesting level to achieve implementation and location independence between a calling and a called transaction program and a calling and a called transaction monitor. Subordinate Node-2a has to be responsible for managing transaction for Subordinate Node-2b, because Subordinate Node-2b is not visible to Top Node.

On COMMIT, the Coordinator of the Top Node remembers the involved resources and nodes. Since there is more than one node involved, two-phase commit is initiated.

Two-phase commit includes a Prepare and a Commit phase. Note that both phases involve the same nodes as the application does and with the same nesting pattern.

3.1.7.3 Types of transactional environments

The following types of transaction environments are available in the e-business framework:

- Classical transaction or transaction processing monitors (TM or TP Monitor)

    - Information Management System (IMS)
    - CICS
    - Encina

- Object transaction monitor (OTM, object-oriented, C++)

    Encina++

- CORBA ORB/IIOP model supporting transaction monitors (ORB)

    - Encina++
    - CICS (procedural/structured and object-oriented including Java/JCICS)
    - WebSphere Application Server Advanced/Enterprise Edition (Java only)
    - Component Broker

- Enterprise JavaBean container/server that include CORBA ORB/IIOP

    - CICS (Java only) - soon
    - WebSphere Application Server Advanced/Enterprise Edition (Java only)

- Database management system transactional environments (DBMS)

    DB2 (with stored procedures in SQL or Java)

- Message queuing system transactional environments

    MQSeries (can coordinate LUW between MQSeries and DB2)

3.1.7.4 Transactional models

There are many different models for performing transactions and each has its own features and complexities. The two most popular models are *flat transactions* and *nested transactions.*

Flat transactions

These are the simplest to understand. A flat transaction is a series of operations that are performed as a single unit of work. After a flat transaction begins, your application can perform any number of operations. When a transaction ends, there is always a binary result, either a success or a failure.

It is considered flat because all work is performed at the same level inside a single Begin/End Work bracket. The work may be performed by many different servers and may be distributed across many different platforms. Based on the result, the series of operations is committed or rolled back.

Nested transactions

A nested transaction allows you to embed atomic units of work within other atomic units of work. The unit of work that is nested within another unit of work can be rolled back without affecting the full transaction to roll back. Therefore, the large unit of work can retry the embedded unit of work. If the entire operation succeeds, then a commit is made or else the entire transaction is rolled back. The following points summarize nested transactions:

- A nested transaction is a tree of transactions, of which the sub-trees are either nested or flat transactions.

- Transactions at the leaf level are flat transactions. The distance from the root to the leaves can be different for different parts of the tree.

- The transaction at the root of the tree is called the *top-level transaction*, the others are called *sub-transactions*. A transaction's predecessor in the tree is called a *parent* and a sub-transaction at the next lower level is called a *child*.

- A sub-transaction can either commit or roll back. Its commit does not take effect unless the parent transaction commits. By induction, any sub-transaction can finally commit only if the root transaction commits.

- The rollback of a transaction anywhere in the tree causes all of its sub-transactions to roll back.

Chained transactions

Chained transactions are similar to hard save points. The work is broken into pieces, with each piece being under control of a flat transaction. Once a piece of work is complete it is committed or rolled back without regard to the state of the other pieces. If the chained transaction succeeds and is committed, and if the transaction under which the original requester is working is rolled back, the committed work remains durable. That is, the transactions are isolated, and one has no affect on the other.

3.1.7.5 Transaction Processing Monitor (TP Monitor)

TP Monitor is a program that monitors a transaction as it passes from one stage in a process to another. The TP Monitor's purpose is to ensure that the transaction processes completed successfully or, if an error occurs, it takes the appropriate actions.

You can think of a TP Monitor as a kind of message queuing service. The client connects to the TP Monitor instead of the database server (see Figure 37). The transaction is accepted by the monitor, which queues it and then takes responsibility for managing it to correct completion. An example of a TP Monitor is the Encina Monitor.

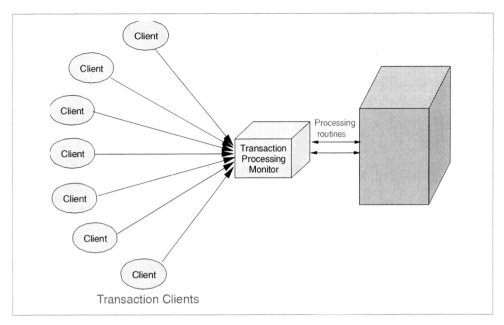

Figure 37. Transaction processing monitor technology

A TP Monitor provides the following services:

- Process management

  - Starting server processes
  - Dispatching work to processes
  - Monitoring process execution
  - Balancing process workloads

- Persistent data management:

  - Files and queues in CICS/Encina; hierarchical DB and queues in IMS
  - Coordination with key resource managers (RDBMS, multisystem, transactional environments)

- Transaction management

  Guarantees ACID properties for all applications

- Secure client/server communications management

  Allows clients with a user ID and password to invoke registered and protected services of a server in variety of ways including:

  - Request-Response
  - Conversations
  - Queuing
  - Publish and subscribe
  - Broadcast

Persistence management systems or database management systems are usually resource-owning subsystems, but that are tightly integrated with the TP Monitor. It is difficult to determine whether the TP Monitor itself or the integrated or connected DBMS provides persistency. Because of the close relationship between both transaction and persistence functions and the coordination duty of the TP Monitor, persistence can be viewed as provided jointly by the TP Monitor and DBMS. This is evident for IMS, CICS, and Encina in their original implementations.

TP Monitors provide the following performance advantages (see Figure 38):

- Optimize the resource usage
- Queue the requests for a continuous, overall high throughput (funneling)
- Provide tools for managing (monitoring and tuning) production
- Include workload management and balancing function
- Allow scaling with multiple transaction servers

TP Monitors prevent the flooding of a system with requests. The requests are queued for continuous, high throughput. The queuing function of TMs is not limited to usage by users of the TM. Applications can also define their own queues and get and put messages. Transaction monitors optimize the resource usage (sharing connections, keeping connections open, keeping program modules loaded, and preloading on startup).

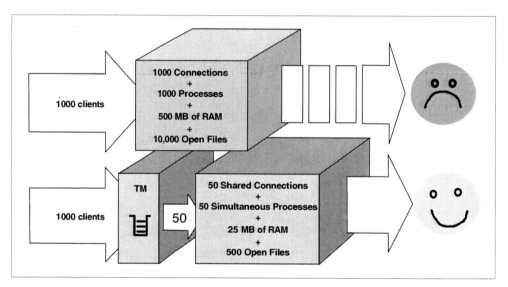

Figure 38. TP Monitor manages high volumes easily

Transaction monitors can cope with very high transaction rates. Transaction monitors even support the direct access from Web browsers that use HTTP over TCP/IP.

General purpose or standard TP Monitors fulfill most business requirements. There are a few dedicated TP Monitors for special businesses, for example, for flight reservation systems.

Consider a scenario of application implementation without a TP Monitor (Figure 39). The issues that arise include:

- Each application has to implement everything on its own
- High complexity and maintenance/low flexibility
- Business logic falls short beside all other code
- Programmer needs to know everything
- Heavy operating system dependency

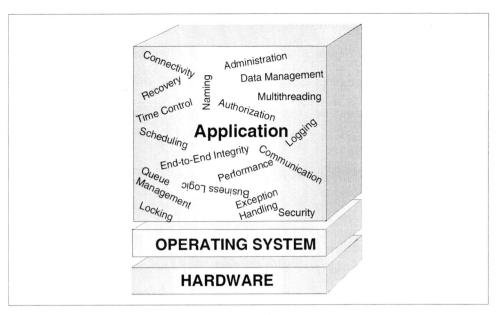

Figure 39. Application implementation without a TP Monitor

As discussed earlier, a transaction monitor provides a high-level application implementation platform with many of ready-to-use services. It also shields the applications from underlying operating system specifications. The application logic is lean, clean, and easy to follow. Lets consider a scenario where the application implementation is done using a TP Monitor (see Figure 40).

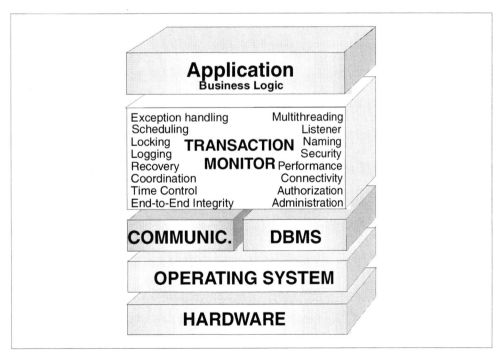

Figure 40. Application implementation with a TP Monitor

As you can see, this approach has many advantages over the one shown in Figure 39:

- Applications can focus on business logic
- Lower complexity/maintenance/enhanced flexibility
- Business logic concise and clean
- Programmer can use powerful TM services
- Operating system independence

3.1.7.6 EJB transaction service

As an application server framework, the EJB servers address transaction processing, resource pooling, security, threading, persistence, remote access, life cycle etc. However, this section focuses only on the distributed transactional model of the EJB framework.

The EJB framework specifies construction, deployment, and invocation of components called *enterprise beans*. The EJB specification classifies enterprise beans into two categories: entity beans and session beans. While *entity beans* abstract persistent domain data, *session beans* provide for session specific application logic. Both types of beans are maintained by EJB-compliant servers in the environment called *EJB container*. A container provides the run time environment for an enterprise bean. Figure 41 shows a simplified architecture of transaction management in EJB compliant application servers. This figure shows only the essential interactions between the constituent parts of the architecture.

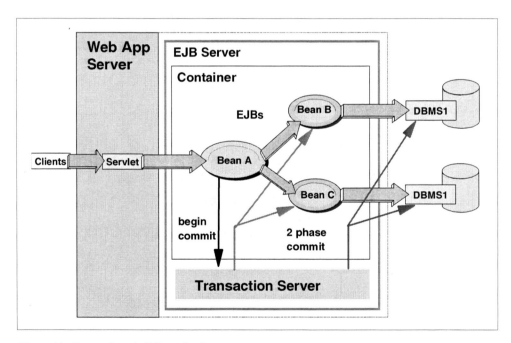

Figure 41. Transactions in EJB application server

The EJB framework does not specify any transaction service (such as the JTS) or protocol for transaction management. However, the specification requires that the `javax.transaction.UserTransaction` interface of the JTS be exposed to enterprise beans. This interface is required for programmatic transaction demarcation as discussed in the next section.

The EJB framework declares the demarcation of transactions. The container performs automatic demarcation depending on the transaction attributes specified at the time of deploying an enterprise bean in a container.

The following attributes determine how transactions are created:

- **NotSupported**: The container invokes the bean without a global transaction context.

- **Required**: The container invokes the bean within a global transaction context. If the invoking thread already has a transaction context associated, the container invokes the bean in the same context. Otherwise, the container creates a new transaction and invokes the bean within the transaction context.

- **Supports**: The bean is transaction-ready. If the client invokes the bean within a transaction, the bean is also invoked within the same transaction. Otherwise, the bean is invoked without a transaction context.

- **RequiresNew**: The container invokes the bean within a new transaction irrespective of whether the client is associated with a transaction.

- **Mandatory**: The container must invoke the bean within a transaction. The caller should always start a transaction before invoking any method on the bean.

The EJB framework supports three types of transaction demarcation:

- **Declarative demarcation**: This is also called as container managed demarcation. The container demarcates transactions on behalf of the bean. The required attribute is specified in a deployment descriptor at the time of deploying the bean on an EJB server. The bean can use the `javax.ejb.EJBContext.setRollbackOnly()` method to mark the transaction for rollback.

- **Client-managed demarcation**: Java clients can use the `javax.transaction.UserTransaction` interface to demarcate transactions programmatically.

- **Bean-managed demarcation**: This is similar to the client-managed demarcation.

3.1.8 Connectors

e-business connectors are gateway products that enable you to access enterprise and legacy applications and data from your Web application. Connector products provide Java interfaces for accessing database, data communications, messaging, and distributed file system services. IBM provides a significant set of e-business connectors with tool support for CICS, Encina, IMS, MQSeries, DB2, SAP, and Domino. IBM bases its tool support on a Common Connector Framework (CCF). For resources on System 390, IBM delivers native connectors based on CCF. The command bean model allows you to code to the specific connector interface or interfaces of your choice while hiding the connector logic from the rest of the Web application.

A fundamental principle of Framework for e-business is to protect investments in existing applications and systems so that businesses can realize the competitive advantages of the Web more quickly. Connectors play a key role in linking and extending the framework's Web application programming environment to other programming environments. That means existing, reliable business applications can be extended to the Web without change. Specifically, connectors enable Web access to:

- Relational and hierarchical data as stored in IBM and other vendor's databases

- Application programs that run in transactional environments such as CICS, IMS, and Encina

- Applications written for object-oriented programming environments such as OMG's CORBA

- Industry applications from vendors such as SAP, Baan, and PeopleSoft

- Services outside the enterprise such as payment system clearinghouses and security key registry services

By protecting investments in proven, reliable applications and systems, connectors allow businesses to realize the competitive advantages of the Web more quickly and less expensively.

3.1.8.1 Connector role in Web application programming environment

A fundamental characteristic of the Framework's Web application programming model is the acknowledgment that most Web applications integrate with existing computing assets. This greatly reduces the complexity and cost of developing mission-critical Web applications because, in many cases, the hard transactional business logic is complete and already running in a robust, managed environment.

Framework for e-business connectors provide Java programmers with high quality access to existing assets without requiring the programmer to write C or other non-Java code. The Framework greatly improves programmer productivity by supporting a CCF that provides a uniform Java access API to all connectors. For example, a common communication interface is supported for connecting or disconnecting to or from a connector and executing a specific connector interaction. In addition, the Framework is "pleadable" to allow additional connectors to be supported in the future.

In many cases, it is necessary to establish a connection to an external resource before it can be used. Since connection setup is a very time consuming operation, many performance-sensitive applications require that open connections be maintained and reused across Web interactions. To satisfy this requirement, the CCF includes support for connection pools and appropriate pool management.

Development tool environments also benefit from the single, consistent interface provided by the CCF. Development tools can more easily provide or support the creation of Java components built on top of the CCF.

3.1.8.2 Common Connector Framework

The task of connecting an application to a back-end data store is relatively standard and follows the same basic pattern whether you are considering the interactions between applications, servlets, EJBs, message queueing systems, relational databases, transactional systems, or some other piece of enterprise infrastructure. The typical approach to integration has been to hand-craft the code required to drive each component of a system. This approach has a number of clear drawbacks, including:

- Each interaction seems very different, but each is actually very similar semantically.

- Each connector may require a different style of use, so each developer needs to spend time and effort learning how to work with each new connector.

- Each developer has to deal with the low-level aspects associated with driving an interaction along, as well as with higher-level infrastructure issues, such as security, transactions, and so on.

- It becomes very hard to develop adequate tool support.

- The approach often results in a severe restriction of extensibility and adaptability.

The IBM Common Connector Framework recognizes that most interactions follow a standard pattern. It provides a standard Java-based infrastructure for integrating various system components together. As shown in Figure 42, the CCF solves the problems by providing:

- A common client programming model for connectors that greatly reduces the learning curve for an application developer

- A common infrastructure programming model for connectors

- A plug-in interface for higher-level tools, which makes them independent of a particular connector

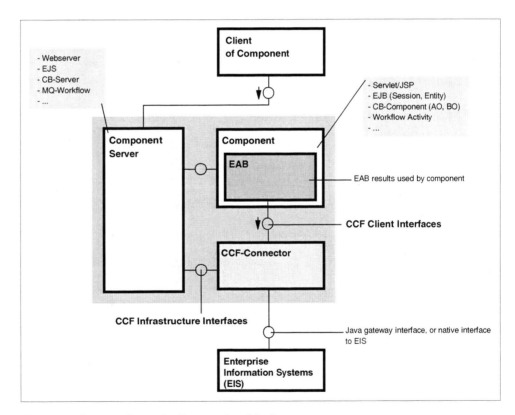

Figure 42. Common Connector Framework architecture

With the common client programming model, the learning curve for switching from one connector to another becomes drastically reduced. Another major benefit is that the CCF also functions as the plug-in interface for higher-level tools (such as VisualAge for Java), making those independent of a particular connector. VisualAge for Java provides the Enterprise Access Builder (EAB) tool. Using the EAB tool, you can create an EAB command that wraps all the complexities behind the command. With this functionality, programmers can easily use this command as JavaBeans that provides enterprise access functionality in the same manner for all the connectors. Connectors currently exist for:

- CICS (both External Call Interface (ECI) and External Presentation Interface (EPI) modes)
- IMS
- MQSeries
- Host On-Demand
- DCE Encina Lightweight Client (DE-Light)
- SAP R/3

3.1.9 Java 2 Platform, Enterprise Edition

With the industry's acceptance of Java technologies (like servlets, JSP, EJB, and so on), the time has come to set the stage for the standard way of defining an enterprise-level application that would use these technologies. The name of the new standard (specification) is Java 2 Platform, Enterprise Edition (J2EE). The latest approved version of the J2EE specification, at the time this redbook was written, is version 1.2.

The idea behind this specification is to simplify the process of building enterprise-level applications. J2EE provides a clear demarcation line between application's specific business logic and system-level services that are used by most of the enterprise applications (for example, database connectivity, transaction support, networking, and so on). With this approach, an application developer has to concentrate on a business logic implementation. System-level services are provided by the J2EE product provider (such as IBM with its WebSphere Application Server).

J2EE includes several parts:

- **J2EE specification**: Defines J2EE architecture, how tiers communicate between themselves, what components of the J2EE platform reside on what tier, and so on.

- **Reference implementation**: Provides Sun's implementation of the J2EE platform. The reference implementation is useful for two reasons:

  - Let the I/T community experiment with the new platform
  - Compare Sun's implementation with other implementations of the J2EE platform

- **Compatibility test suite**: A comprehensive set of tests to ensure the compliance of a platform implementation with the J2EE specification.

- **J2EE blueprints design guidelines**: They provides "best practice" recommendations for the developers and designers of the enterprise applications for the J2EE platform.

3.1.9.1 J2EE application model

Figure 43 provides a graphical view of the J2EE application model. It is based on the notion of *containers*. Containers are the standard runtime environments that provide a certain range of services for the components deployed in the containers.

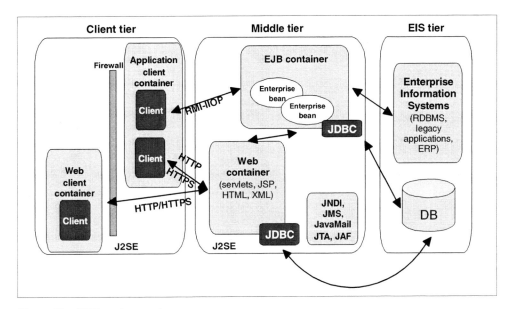

Figure 43. J2EE environment

Examples of these container services may be transaction support, database connectivity, and persistence.

J2EE is built on top of Java 2 Platform, Standard Edition (J2SE). It adds a number of Java standard extensions (APIs) to J2SE. These extensions are defined in the corresponding specifications. Each specification outlines the interfaces, rules, and recommendations for a certain part of J2EE platform. Table 23 shows these specifications (at the level required by J2EE v1.2) and which have to be implemented in which containers. "Y" means the APIs have to be implemented. "N" means the opposite.

Table 23. J2EE required specifications

Specification	Applet container	Application client container	Web container	EJB container
JDBC 2.0 Extension	N	Y	Y	Y
JTA 1.0	N	N	Y	Y
JNDI 1.2	N	Y	Y	Y
Servlet 2.2	N	N	Y	N
JSP 1.1	N	N	Y	N
EJB 1.1	N	Y (EJB client APIs only)	Y (EJB client APIs only)	Y
RMI/IIOP 1.0	N	Y	Y	Y
JMS 1.0	N	Y	Y	Y
JavaMail 1.1	N	N	Y	Y
JAF 1.0	N	N	Y	Y

If you want to implement a Web container that complies to J2EE platform, for example, you know what APIs your container have to support.

In general, J2EE specification divides all elements of the J2EE application model into three main categories:

- **Application components**: Includes EJBs, servlets, JSPs, applets, and so on.
- **Containers**: All application components reside in a container (Web container, EJB container, and so on).
- **Connectors**: Even though a connector framework is not defined in the J2EE v1.2 specification, it will be included in the next version of the specification. Besides, you can think about JDBC as a connector to a database.

The *application components* encapsulate a business logic and provide an application specific processing. The J2EE specification defines the *application component provider* role to implement these components (in real life, this role maps to the developers, I/T specialists, architects, and so on).

A *container* intercedes between the application components and the client or underlying server platform. It provides system-level services to the application components. As such, it removes a lot of complexity from the application components. A container is available from the J2EE product provider (as defined in the J2EE specification).

To achieve a higher level of abstraction, J2EE allows the application component provider to design a component without targeting a particular container or J2EE product. This abstraction is achieved through the file called *deployment descriptor*. This file provides a way for the application component provider to declare any external dependencies in textual format using XML. A J2EE product provider is required to supply a tool that helps the deployer (another role in J2EE specification) to map these dependencies to the J2EE environment where an application component is deployed. You can think of a deployment descriptor as a *contract* between the application component provider and the deployer.

Using the J2EE specification and the J2EE blueprint design guidelines, the application component provider can create a component that will be portable across any J2EE compliant product. As a result, the new market of the portable business components will develop in the near future.

For more information about the J2EE platform, see: `http://java.sun.com/j2ee/`

3.1.9.2 J2EE Connector architecture

Today's constantly changing world requires most companies to reconsider the way they do their business. Many new business opportunities, as well as the customers' expectations, push companies to create their presence on the Internet, and therefore, change their existing I/T architecture.

But what should the companies do with their existing Enterprise Information Systems (EIS)? Is it wise for them to abandon the proven applications, processes, and investments for the sake of the new paradigm?

The answer to these questions is the integration of the company's existing I/T resources with Internet technologies. This is a challenging task. With existing integration technique, a separate adapter (driver) has to be created for each EIS.

As a result, if a company has several legacy applications, it has to create or buy the same number of adapters. To meet this challenge, the J2EE Connector architecture was proposed. It describes a unified way for accessing EISs.

The J2EE Connector architecture is part of the upcoming J2EE v1.3 specification. This architecture defines a standard way of accessing the EIS tier (see Figure 43 on page 125) and is based on the IBM Common Connector Framework.

The Connector architecture is implemented in two places:

- A J2EE application server
- EIS resource adapter (you can think of an EIS resource adapter as a plug-in or a driver)

An EIS resource adapter is a system library for a specific EIS that is provided by an EIS vendor. An EIS vendor can create one adapter, which should work with any J2EE compliant application server.

Figure 44 shows the Connector architecture with these three main components:

- System-level contracts between an application server and an EIS resource adapter (think about the system contracts as Java interfaces)
- Common Client Interface (CCI) for accessing an EIS resource adapter by the development tools (an application component can access adapter too, but this access is discouraged)
- Packaging and deployment tools for an EIS resource adapter

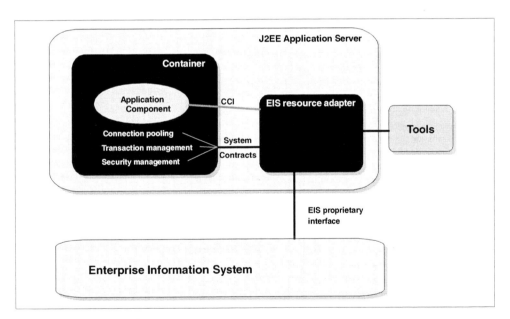

Figure 44. J2EE Connector architecture

The system contracts include:

- Connection pool management
- Transaction management, both local and XA transactions
- Security management

The J2EE application server provider implements the system contracts. The J2EE Connector architecture doesn't impose any rule on the way the contracts are implemented.

The EIS resource adapter provider implements its part of the system contracts and the interface to the EIS.

CCI is designed to help the development tool provider to simplify access to the heterogeneous EISs. The CCI APIs provide a unified way of accessing any EIS, shielding the tool provider or the application component provider from EIS-specific details (see Figure 45). The CCI APIs allow remote functions in the EISs to run and retrieve results. The implementation of CCI APIs is not required by J2EE Connector architecture v1.0. However, this requirement will be added in future versions of the Connector architecture.

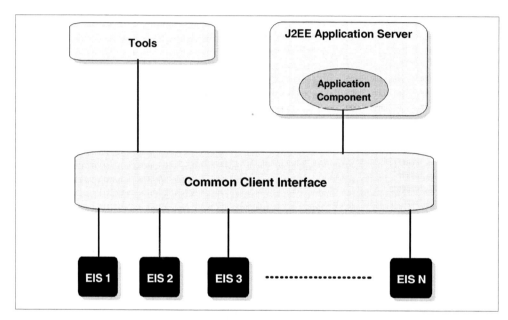

Figure 45. CCI architecture

The last piece of the Connector architecture is the packaging and deployment tools. They help the resource adapter provider to package all classes, native libraries, documentation, and the deployment descriptor in a Resource Adapter Module. The deployment descriptor is a contract between the resource adapter provider and the deployer. Following the same modular architecture as the rest of the specifications in the J2EE platform, a resource adapter can be plugged into a J2EE application server.

You can find more information about the J2EE Connector architecture at: http://java.sun.com/j2ee/connector/

3.2 Products

As we've mentioned already, the advantages of using Framework for e-business include:

- A standards-based model that enables multi-platform/multi-vendor solutions
- Portfolio of leadership products
- Quick to deploy, easy to use
- Server-centric with single model across servers
- System can be managed for 24 x 7
- Leverage core system by extending existing applications into the world of e-business
- Rich capabilities to support simple to sophisticated applications
- Rapid application development environment based on cross-platform standards including Java
- The availability of components for development can bring a high-speed, high-quality project to completion in a time span that has seldom previously seen

To support these features of Framework for e-business, IBM has developed a number of products. We discuss the products in Framework for e-business based on the Build, Run, and Manage cycle shown in Figure 46.

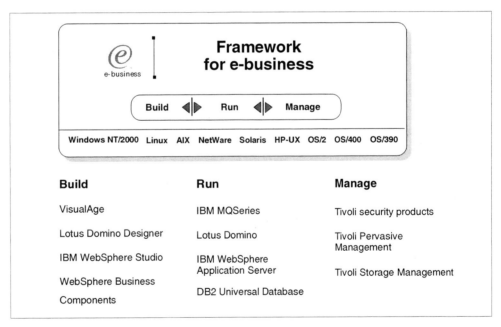

Figure 46. Framework for e-business

3.2.1 Build cycle

IBM delivers a growing set of development tools and reusable application components, including the VisualAge family for professional programmers, WebSphere Studio, Lotus Domino, and WebSphere Business Components (see Figure 47).

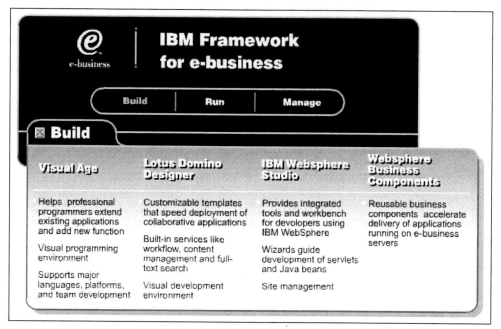

Figure 47. Tools used for application development in the framework

Before we go into the specifics of each tool, it is very important to understand that e-business applications require several different kinds of skills for building an end-to-end solution. Each of kind of skills needs a different type of tool to complete its work. The role to skill/tool mapping is shown in Figure 48.

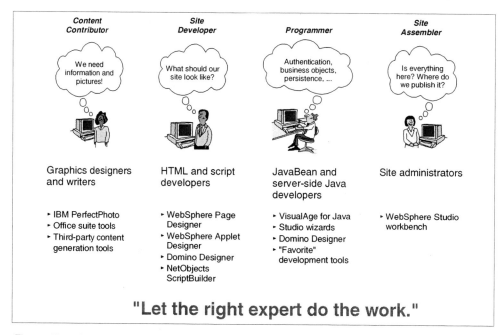

Figure 48. e-business application development tool users

3.2.1.1 VisualAge for Java

IBM WebSphere Studio Workbench

While this book was written, IBM announced the new tool called WebSphere Studio Workbench. The IBM WebSphere Studio Workbench is the foundation for IBM 's next generation of application development tools and for IBM Business Partners who want to build tools that integrate with the WebSphere software platform. The Workbench offers state-of-the art tool technology and is designed to enable an unprecedented level of inter-tool integration.

In short, Studio Workbench include functionality of two existing tools, WebSphere Studio and VisualAge for Java, that are plugged into the Eclipse. The Eclipse Platform is designed for building integrated development environments (IDEs) that can be used to create applications as diverse as web sites, embedded Java programs, C++ programs, and Enterprise JavaBeans. Eclipse Platform is an open source project. You can find more information about Eclipse at: http://eclipse.org/

You can find more information about WebSphere Workbench at: http://www.ibm.com/software/ad/workbench/

IBM VisualAge for Java (VAJ) is an award-winning, highly graphically-oriented, integrated development environment (IDE) for creating Web-enabled enterprise applications. It delivers advanced support for building, testing, and deploying 100% pure Java applications, EJB, JavaBeans components, servlets, and applets. VAJ is a key element of the IBM Framework for e-business. VisualAge for Java is available in four editions:

- VisualAge for Java Entry Professional Edition
- VisualAge for Java Professional Edition
- VisualAge for Java Entry Enterprise Edition
- VisualAge for Java Enterprise Edition

The basic differences between the Professional and Enterprise editions are shown in Figure 49.

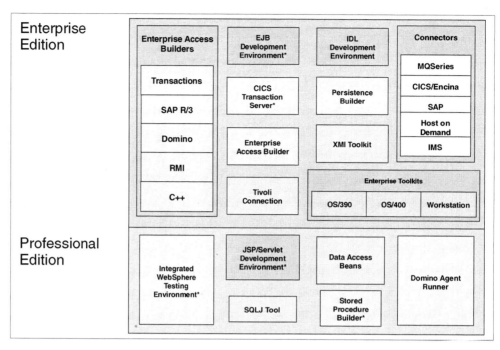

Figure 49. Features of VisualAge for Java (Advanced and Enterprise Edition)

Features of VisualAge for Java Enterprise Edition

VAJ Enterprise Edition provides an extremely rich IDE for developing a wide variety of software for different platforms, from stand-alone applications, though applets and servlets to Enterprise JavaBeans. VAJ is closely linked with the WebSphere Application Server, which enables developers to locally test and debug applications and cuts development time. Tight integration with WebSphere Studio makes it easy for teams to communicate and work together to develop Web-based, e-business applications. The following components are included with VisualAge for Java Enterprise Edition:

- **Integrated development environment**: A set of windows that provide the user with access to development tools. The primary windows are the Workbench, Log, Console, Debugger, and Repository Explorer.

- **Visual Composition Editor (VCE)**: A tool you can use to create graphical user interfaces from prefabricated beans and to define relationships (called *connections*) between beans. This process of creating object-oriented programs by manipulating graphical representations of components is called *visual programming*.

- **Team programming support**: The product provides an integrated team development environment that is based on a shared source code repository.

- **WebSphere Test Environment (WTE)**: VAJ includes almost a complete runtime environment of WebSphere Application Server Advanced Edition. As a result, you can test your applications on the fly!

- **Builders**:

  - *Enterprise Access Builder for Transactions (EAB)*: Helps developers to quickly and easily extend existing applications to the Web. It consists of frameworks and tools that allow you to access the function and data assets of your EIS. It provides a standard access builder interface for connectors that adhere to the IBM CCF. EAB uses e-business connectors that are based on CCF. Connectors are provided for CICS (both ECI and EPI), Encina DE-Light, IMS Connect, MQSeries, Host On-Demand (HOD), and SAP R/3.

CCF will form IBM's implementation for the emerging Java 2 Platform, Enterprise Edition (J2EE) standard for enterprise connectivity (JCX API).

- **Access Builder for SAP R/3**: A complete toolkit for creating Java applications, applets, and beans that allow access to an SAP R/3 system. The Access Builder for SAP R/3 helps you to retrieve complete meta information within the R/3 system, keep it locally for multiple R/3 systems, access without an R/3 connection, and search for business objects. It includes a connector for SAP R/3 that generates EJB proxies for business objects.

- **RMI Access Builder**: Enables you to provide remote access to JavaBeans in a distributed, client/server environment. You can use it to generate proxy beans and associated classes and interfaces, so you can distribute code for remote access, enabling Java-to-Java solutions. It also creates the distribution-specific code that supports the distribution of bean events and integrates with the application-specific code contained in your bean.

- **C++ Access Builder**: Provides access from Java applets or stand-alone Java applications to services written in C++. You can use it to generate beans and C++ wrappers that let your Java programs access C++.

- **Domino Access Builder**: Allows you to create Java applications that access databases and services located on a Domino server or on a Notes client. Domino Access Builder provides generic beans, based on the Domino Java classes from Lotus, plus a SmartGuide to create user-defined beans. The generic beans include wrapper classes for databases, forms, views, and other Domino design elements. You can use the SmartGuide to select a database and to configure the code generator, which creates customized beans that match the selected Domino design elements. Domino Access Builder also enables developers to specify which view, field, or columns are represented in the JavaBeans.

- **CICS Transaction Server support**: Allows you to create Java applications that use CICS services and that execute under CICS Transaction Server for OS/390 Release 1.3. You can develop these applications on a workstation, or in the OS/390 UNIX System Services shell. JCICS, a Java class library, allows you to access CICS resources and integrate your Java programs with programs written in other languages.

- **Data Access**:

  - **Data Access Beans**: Are provided with VisualAge for Java to develop programs that access relational databases.

  - **DB2 Stored Procedure Builder (SPB)**: A tool that enables you to write Java-stored procedures to run on a DB2 server.

  - **SQLJ support**: Provides you with a standard way to embed SQL statements in Java programs. The SQLJ standard has three components:

    - *Embedded SQLJ*

    - *A translator*: The translator translates SQLJ files that contain embedded SQLJ to produce .java files and profiles that use the runtime environment to perform SQL operations.

- *A runtime environment*: The runtime environment usually performs the SQL operations in JDBC and uses the profile to obtain details about database connections.

  - *Enterprise Access Builder for Persistence (Persistence Builder)*: Enables you to map objects and relationships between objects to information stored in relational databases. It also provides linkages to the mapping between Enterprise JavaBeans and relational data.

- **Distributed Debugger**: A client/server application that enables you to detect and diagnose errors in your programs. You can use it to debug Java applications that are developed outside the IDE.

- **Domino AgentRunner**: Helps you build, run, and debug Domino agents in VisualAge for Java. It uses a set of debug classes that access Lotus Notes context information so that you can run and debug an agent in the VisualAge for Java IDE.

- **EJB Development Environment**: Enables you to develop and test EJB and access (adapter) beans for use in your enterprise applications. In addition, the EJB Development Environment provides all of the necessary run-time support for the IBM WebSphere Application Server Advanced Edition. It includes a new incremental consistency checker that ensures that an enterprise bean conforms to the EJB programming specification and indicates whether changes are needed to fix inconsistencies.

- **Enterprise Toolkits**:

  - *Enterprise Toolkit for Workstations (ET/Workstation)*: Enables you to develop Java code that is targeted to specific platforms. The high-performance compiler compiles Java source code or bytecode into optimized, platform-specific code for execution on OS/2, Windows NT, or AIX.

  - *Enterprise Toolkit for AS/400 (ET/400)*: Allows you to develop enterprise applications in Java for the iSeries and AS/400 platform. You can use ET/400 to export Java class and source files to the iSeries, compile Java code optimized for the iSeries, and run and debug iSeries Java applications from the VisualAge for Java IDE.

  - *Enterprise Toolkit for OS/390 (ET/390)*: Lets you code Java programs at your workstation, and then export your class and source files to the OS/390. You can also use the ET/390 to bind Java bytecode into optimized code that runs in the OS/390 shell or CICS/ESA environment. In addition, you can run and debug OS/390 Java applications from the IDE and use the Performance Analyzer to fine-tune your compiled Java application.

- **External Software Configuration Management (SCM) system tool**: A bridge that allows you to use an external SCM system from within VisualAge for Java. You can add classes to the source control, check classes in and out, and import the most recently checked-in version of a class into VisualAge for Java.

- **Interface Definition Language (IDL) Development Environment**: Provides an integrated IDL and Java development environment that works with a user-specified IDL-to-Java compiler. You can work with both your IDL source and the generated Java code in one convenient browser page to perform such tasks as importing IDL files and creating new IDL groups and IDL objects.

- **JSP/Servlet Development Environment**: Enables you to develop and test JavaServer Pages. You can use all of the Java APIs that are available to any Java applet or application. For example, you can use JavaBeans, enterprise beans (EJB beans), and servlets.

- **Migration Assistant**: Use this to create a code framework for a JavaBean to replace an ActiveX control. It creates a set of methods, properties, and enums (enumerations) that an equivalent JavaBean needs to achieve the same function as an ActiveX control.

- **Tivoli Connection**: Helps you create business-critical distributed Java applications that can be managed by Tivoli Enterprise management software. Tivoli Connection allows you to generate Tivoli events and to interface to the Tivoli Enterprise Console. Tivoli provides an application management solution that covers the life cycle of an application, from deployment to monitoring and administration.

- **Tool Integrator**: A VisualAge for Java mechanism that lets you integrate Java applications that reside on the file system to launch them from within the IDE.

- **XML Metadata Interchange (XMI)**: A toolkit for integration with the Rational Rose modeling tool. VisualAge for Java converts the Rose model (.mdl files) into an XMI format. Since VisualAge understands the parsing of XMI (the XML data type definition for UML), the generation of the Java code is done inside the development environment. A comparison tool reconciles what is contained in Rose with the implementation in VisualAge for Java. This facilitates the rapid transformation of business models.

- **XML Parser for Java**: Provides a way for your applications to work with XML data on the Web. The XML Parser provides classes for parsing, generating, manipulating, and validating XML documents. You can include the XML Parser in B2B and other applications that manage XML documents, work with meta content, interface with databases, and exchange messages and data. The XML Parser is written entirely in Java and conforms to the XML 1.0 Recommendation and associated standards, such as Document Object Model (DOM) 1.0, Simple API for XML (SAX) 1.0, and the XML Namespaces Recommendation.

- **XML Generator**: This is an application for editing a Document Type Description (DTD) and generating sample XML documents based on that DTD. XML Generator helps users see the kind of XML documents generated by their DTD. It also helps them test applications that are designed to use those documents.

3.2.1.2 Domino Designer

Domino Designer is the next step toward a Web-friendly development environment. While Notes has always been a powerful tool for developing applications, Domino Designer builds on this power by making it easier and faster for Web developers to create rich, robust, and secure applications with a new IDE. For a Web developer, it is now easier to use HTML and JavaScript in their designs because Designer supports them natively, meaning that a conversion process is no longer required. They can also use frames and Java applets, both supported by the Domino server and available in Designer. For a Notes developer that is familiar with application development in previous releases, they can now design more visually appealing applications that use the new features and still leverage the strengths of the Domino infrastructure.

The goal of Domino Designer is to support rapid development of applications for the Domino server. The themes driving the development team are:

- **Usability**: Reducing the "time to Web", creating an intuitive set of design tools, providing more templates and examples (and documenting them), and incorporating additional Web design constructs.

- **Openness to alternate tools**: Adding new tools to enable partners to extend the design environment themselves and providing integration with third-party tools (for example, NetObjects Fusion, IBM VisualAge for Java, or any HTML created with any HTML authoring tool).

- **Mixed client design**: Narrowing distinctions between the Notes client and Web browsers with a number of features, including native image support, the Web color palette, framesets, and pages, and establishing a common model for user interface (UI) events.

- **Industry-standard programmability**: Leveraging existing and emerging languages, including Java, JavaScript, and HTML 4.0, and maintaining the existing investment in LotusScript.

- **Global applications**: Integrating more closely with Domino Global WorkBench, which allows you to create multilingual databases that let users choose their preferred language from a list of available languages. In addition, you can tag Domino application design elements with a specific language attribute and automatically serve the application, in that language, to the client.

- **Tools for Enterprise Access from within the Domino environment**: Domino Designer provides these tools, which are designed to leverage the Domino features. They are also built around Web standards to provide compatibility with standard Web browser environments.

Features overview
Domino Designer comes with everything you need to rapidly build e-business applications:

- **Page Designer**: WYSIWYG HTML authoring with complete control over page design and layout. Add styled text, image maps, tables, Java, and ActiveX components to applications.

- **Frameset Designer**: Easily create multi-paned interfaces for your Web applications, without HTML coding. Automatically maintains target links.

- **Outline Designer**: Design an entire site, link the content to the site design, manage the links, and automatically generate a personalized site map.

- **Domino Objects**: Rapidly build applications that access system services such as security, messaging, and workflow in your applications, using your choice of Java, JavaScript, CORBA/C++, or LotusScript.

- **Domino UI Java Applets**: Enhance the functionality of browser-based applications with popular Notes design elements such as a view with resizable columns, multiple document selection, and rich text — with no programming.

- **Forms Designer**: Create professional-looking forms (surveys, visitor registration, etc.) in minutes.

- **Programmer's Pane**: Provides universal, consistent access to all programming languages and scripts.

- **Instant Feedback**: Preview as you go in your choice of client, including Lotus Notes, Microsoft Internet Explorer, and Netscape Navigator.

Domino Designer gives you live access to enterprise data and applications, via support for Domino Enterprise Connection Services (DECS):

- **Comprehensive connectivity**: DECS supports a wide range of enterprise systems, including DB2, Oracle, Sybase, ODBC, EDA/SQL, SAP, PeopleSoft, JD Edwards, Oracle Applications, MQSeries, CICS, and more.

- **High performance, real-time connectivity**: DECS manages persistent, parallel, pooled connections from Domino to external data sources, enabling efficient, simultaneous data access.

- **Your choice of development options**: Connect to enterprise data non-programmatically via the easy-to-use DECS interface, or programmatically from LotusScript. Domino Designer lets you work with your choice of popular Web development tools.

- **Extensive Java support**: Develop Domino Web applications in your favorite Java IDE, like IBM VisualAge for Java, Symantec Cafe, or Borland JBuilder. Embed and manipulate Java applets, integrate Java servlets, and even create Domino server agents in Java.

- **Integration with NetObjects Fusion and Microsoft FrontPage**: Create HTML pages and links in your favorite site authoring tool and save them directly to the Domino object store.

- **Use with Lotus eSuite DevPack**: Domino Designer templates enable easy integration with a powerful set of pre-built, pre-tested, Java applets including spreadsheet, word processor, calendar, address book, and CGI gateway.

Domino Designer lets you create and maintain multilingual Web applications, with Domino Global WorkBench:

- **Make your applications multilingual**: Display Web pages in the language of the country where the user is located. Maintain multilingual Web sites with minimal additional overhead, while slashing translation costs.

- **Synchronize translated content**: Manage the release of documents across different language versions of your site.

3.2.1.3 WebSphere Studio

WebSphere Studio (see note on page 131) is a project-based workbench environment that provides a central point of source control for a development group. It allows for each type of file to be associated with the developer's choice of tools, and provides wizards to speed the development of WebSphere applications. It also provides the necessary tools to publish content to a Web server.

WebSphere Studio is a suite of tools that brings all aspects of Web site development into a common interface. Content authors, graphic artists, programmers, and Webmasters can all work on the same projects, each having access to the files they need. With WebSphere Studio, it is easier than ever to cooperatively create, assemble, publish, and maintain dynamic interactive Web applications. The Studio is composed of the Workbench, the Page Designer, the Remote Debugger, and wizards. It also comes with companion Web development products.

WebSphere Studio enables you to do everything you need to create interactive Web sites that support advanced business functions, including:

- *Create Java beans, database queries, and Java servlets using the Studio wizards*: The wizards make it easy to produce input forms, output pages, and the Java code that makes it all work.

- *Group Web site files into projects and folders*: You decide what organization makes sense and group your files accordingly. Filters and global search capabilities let you find the files you need.

- *Maintain the files individually or in a shared version control system*: Store files locally on your own workstation, on other systems in your network, or in a full-function version control system (VCS).

- *Edit and update the files with your preferred tools*: You get to choose which editing and viewing programs to use for each file type. When opening a Studio file, you can quickly launch your default selection, or you can choose one of your alternative tools.

- *Quickly assess file relationships and find broken links*: The Relationship view provides a visual representation of how your files link to each other. You can quickly see how many other files link to a particular file, which files have broken links, and which files are not linked at all.

- *Publish your Web site during any stage of development on any of your WebSphere Application Servers*: Go directly from site development to site publishing, right within the Studio Workbench. You can publish all or part of a Web site during any stage of development and quickly view and test the results of your work. When the Web site is ready for release, you can easily transfer the files to your final stage and publish them to your production servers.

The Studio Workbench helps you manage and maintain your Web site applications and files. It also provides the following capabilities:

- A graphical display of the link relationships between the files in a project

- The automatic updating of links whenever files change or move

- The ability to register multiple authoring tools, giving you a choice each time you edit your Web site files

- The ability to stage your Web site production cycle and publish various stages to different (and to multiple) servers

- An import wizard that simplifies the transfer of existing site content directly into a Studio project

- A quick way to archive Web sites or sub-sites in a single file

- The ability to easily integrate third-party tools right into the Workbench environment

- An enhanced team environment with a common view of work-in-progress through the integration of popular source control-management software, such as IBM VisualAge Team Connection, Microsoft SourceSafe, PVCS, Rational ClearCase, and Lotus Domino

The Studio Page Designer (see Figure 50) provides a visual design environment that enables you to create JavaServer Pages, Java servlets, and other Java-based Web components.

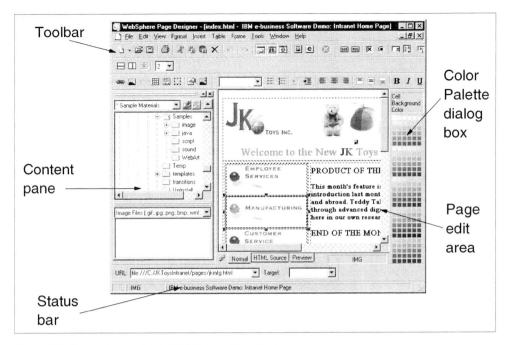

Figure 50. Content assembly in WebSphere Page Designer

For example, you can use the visual environment to drag and drop JavaBean components into JSP files. The Studio Page Designer can also be used to create DHTML and HTML pages and includes the capability to easily edit and toggle between the HTML or DHTML source and the browser view. This capability is based on the new IBM NetObjects TopPage product. The Studio Remote Debugger provides source-level debugging of JSP files and Java servlets within the Studio environment. Remote debugging is possible on any machine that contains WebSphere Application Server 3.0 or higher.

3.2.1.4 WebSphere Business Components

IBM WebSphere Business Components are easy-to-use software implementation packages. This initiative came out of IBM SanFrancisco, which has been discontinued. These components provide a coherent set of functions that:

- Can be independently developed and delivered
- Can be composed from other components
- Have explicit and well-specified interfaces for the component services they provide and require

IBM has developed WebSphere Business Components to help you reduce development time, create applications that operate across diverse infrastructures, and deliver value to your company faster with a whole project solution.

The value of component technology is increasingly apparent in today's application development environment. Component technology enables a faster and lower cost method for assembly of e-business applications. It facilitates rapid development and supports Enterprise Application Integration. IBM WebSphere Business Components allow you to reap the rewards of component technology, by presenting the tools and the context within which you can develop packages of software implementation that are easy to use, that can be combined with other components, and that have explicit interfaces for the services they provide and expect from others.

The power of WebSphere Business Components allows you to:

- Reduce development time
- Improve time to market
- Build flexible applications
- Simplify portability
- Improve performance, availability, and scalability
- Focus on unique needs
- Mix and match solutions
- Operate across diverse infrastructures
- Modify quickly
- Lower the cost of code maintenance
- Support new business models
- Deliver value to your company faster

Products in WebSphere Business Components Family

The IBM WebSphere Business Components family of products has a strong foundation based on IBM's experience with component and object technology. Several Java and EJB-based WebSphere Business Components products are available now. Additional EJB-based components and associated development environments will be made available on an ongoing basis as IBM enriches the WebSphere Software Platform with leading edge component technology. The following products are currently included in the IBM WebSphere Business Components family:

- **Studio**: Provides the supporting services that application developers use to develop applications in various industries. It also includes a set of tools that support the creation, configuration, and deployment of components. The Studio also includes a starter set of components. The highlights of this component are:

    - Provides tools for creating and deploying components to improve developer productivity

    - Contains advanced components that let you solve specific business problems with platform neutral elements of IBM Framework for e-business

    - Provides pre-built and reusable components to help reduce development cycle time and cost

    - Lets you seamlessly mix and match the best of breed IBM and ISV WebSphere Business Components, along with your own applications to result in tightly integrated working software

- **Order Capture**: This is an advanced component for capturing information on sales orders, pricing, handling credit checks, and determining product availability. The Order Capture component can be easily customized. It has industry standard interfaces that allow for much easier implementation in capturing orders from multiple channels such as phone, e-mail, B2B, and shopping carts. The Order Capture component provides the server mechanisms necessary to:

    - Create a customer profile
    - Create, modify, and delete sales orders and sales order line items
    - Query sales orders and line items

- Provide pricing and discount functions
- Integrate inventory availability and credit availability checking functions
- Integrate with an existing fulfilment system

- **Text Analyzer**: This is an advanced component that solves text document categorization problems such as information routing, office automation, and customer resource management. Text Analyzer can rapidly categorize any object that can be represented by text. This makes it well suited to large volume applications such as e-mail, snail mail, Web site comment fields, text chat, and any other application where text documents must be categorized. The highlights of this component are:

  - It is the most accurate categorization engine in the market.

  - It is simple to use. It has a simple set of APIs for you to build your top performing application. It is also simple to put into production because you can set up the document categories easily, and once started, you can add categories without requiring expert assistance.

  - It is unique in the number of languages it can process. It can categorize double-byte character languages, such as Chinese, Japanese, and Arabic.

  - It is fast. It quickly generates analysis rules, sorts documents very fast, up to 20 to 40 messages per second, and adds up to a million messages per day.

  - It is unique in that it can return multiple categories with different confidence levels to enable a richer set of routing choices.

- **Components Composer**: Provides transaction components and the infrastructure Java components that allow you to deploy applications, using a reliable, compact, and fast transaction processes. The highlights for this component are:

  - Shorter development cycles for branch teller applications and transactional projects (IBM Bank Teller Business Components require the Components Composer product)

  - A member of the IBM WebSphere Business Components family, which enables multichannel solutions and provides a consistent service through multiple delivery channels

  - Proven solution aligned with well-established technologies ready to be deployed

  - Preserves investment in back-end and enterprise-wide systems, networks, financial devices, etc.

  - High degree of components reuse

  - High performance solution to implement effective e-business (for example, banking service) solutions that result in maximum satisfaction from your customers

  - Can be customized to meet specific requirements

  - Integration with other IBM WebSphere Business Components as the foundation to build effective enterprise-wide customer relationship management solutions

With these specialized components for transaction processing, you are ready to deploy applications, using a reliable, compact, and fast transaction processor.

- **Bank Teller Business Components**: Help you maximize the efficiency of your administrative and customer transactions by enhancing WebSphere Business Components Composer with additional components that enable you to provide superior customer service. You can seamlessly integrate sales and service functions at every branch workstation for better customer service with greater productivity.

    The business benefits of using Bank Teller Business Components are:

    - Maximize the efficiency of administrative and customer transactions at the branch

    - Ability to seamlessly integrate sales and service functions at any branch workstation

    - Service transactions are executed in an integrated manner for greater customer throughput, streamlined efficiencies, and reduced costs

    - Can be integrated with other components to achieve enterprise-wide Customer Relationship Management

    - Highly customizable to meet the service-specific requirements of your financial institution

    - Friendly user interface allows users to train quicker and smarter in order to be more effective front-line agents

    The technical benefits of Bank Teller Business Components include:

    - Support multiple standard branch devices (Passbook printers, Card Swipes, MICR readers, etc.)

    - Integrate with existing host systems to complete financial transactions and provide legacy data to agents

    - Open and scalable architecture makes the solution easy to implement and flexible to grow as your financial institution expands

    - Designed to preserve investments in existing host systems, computing infrastructure, and IBM WebSphere Business Components Banking Components itself

3.2.2 Run cycle

At the heart of the Framework is a family of secure, feature-rich application servers and integration services that are fortified by years of experience delivering mission-critical applications in a wide variety of environments (see Figure 51). The IBM products in this segment include:

- Lotus Domino Application Server
- WebSphere Application Server
- IBM DB2 Universal Database
- WebSphere MQSeries

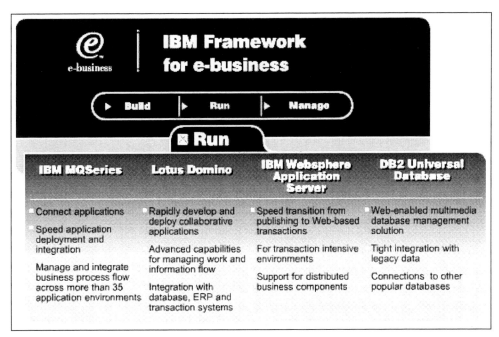

Figure 51. Servers for mission-critical applications

3.2.2.1 Lotus Domino

Domino Family of Servers provide a multi-platform foundation for collaboration and e-business. Lotus Domino brings messaging, Internet integration, and scalability to a whole new level. The new Domino server includes:

- The latest innovations in Internet messaging, with native support for all the major Internet standards

- Industry-leading support for Web applications, including CORBA support and integration with Microsoft Internet Information Server (IIS)

- Increased server reliability and scalability, including improvements in performance, capacity, availability, and maximum database size

- A new administration interface, with a task-oriented approach that makes Domino easier to deploy, use, and manage

Domino continues to support a wide variety of clients, in addition to the traditional Notes client. Messaging features are available to Web browsers and Internet mail clients (such as POP3 and IMAPv4 clients). Directory features are available to browsers and LDAP clients. Discussion features are available to browsers and NNTP newsreader clients. Administration features are available to browsers and the Notes client. Plus, Domino continues to be the best platform for designing dynamic Web applications. With Domino Designer, you can easily build a single application that looks and runs the same for both the Web and Notes clients. There are three types of Domino servers:

- **Domino Mail Server**:

    This is the newest member of the Lotus Domino server family. Domino Mail combines support for the latest Internet mail standards with the advanced messaging capabilities and enterprise-scale reliability and performance of Lotus Domino. Its integrated, cross-platform services include Web access, group scheduling, collaborative workspaces, and newsgroups, which are all accessible from a Web browser or other standards-based client. Domino Mail Server is used for messaging only. Customers that want to deploy their own applications on the Domino server should consider Domino Application Server or Domino Enterprise Server.

- **Domino Application Server**:

  This is the leading integrated messaging and applications server. It delivers best-of-breed messaging as well as an open, secure Web application platform. The server easily integrates back-end systems with front-end system business processes. This is the natural evolution of the Lotus Notes server from which Lotus Domino originates.

- **Domino Enterprise Server and Domino Advanced Enterprise Server**:

  This server is for customers who require mission-critical, highly scalable deployments with uninterrupted access, and maximum performance under all conditions. It extends the functionality of Domino Mail and Domino Application Servers with high availability services such as partitioning, clustering, and billing. This product was previously called Domino Advanced Services.

Services offered by Domino Servers
Lotus Domino Servers offer a wide range of services. We briefly describe the most important ones here.

Object store
Documents in a Domino database can contain any number of objects and data types, including text, rich text, numerical data, structured data, images, graphics, sound, video, file attachments, embedded objects, and Java and ActiveX applets. A built-in full text search engine makes it easy to index and search documents. The object store also lets your Domino applications dynamically present information based on variables such as user identity, user preferences, user input, and time.

Directory
A single directory manages all resource directory information for server and network configuration, application management, and security. Domino includes user account synchronization between Windows NT and Domino and is LDAP-compliant. The directory is the foundation for easily managing and securing your Internet and intranet applications.

Security
The Domino security model provides user authentication, digital signatures, flexible access control, and encryption. Domino security enables you to extend your intranet applications to customers and business partners.

Replication
Bidirectional replication automatically distributes and synchronizes information and applications across geographically dispersed sites. Replication makes your business applications available to users around your company or around the world, regardless of time or location.

Messaging
An advanced client/server messaging system, with built-in calendaring and scheduling, enables individuals and groups to send and share information easily. Message transfer agents (MTAs) seamlessly extend the system to SMTP/MIME, X.400, and cc:Mail™ messaging environments. The Domino messaging service

provides a single server that supports a variety of mail clients; Post Office Protocol V3 (POP3), Internet Message Access Protocol V4 (IMAP4), Message Application Programming Interface (MAPI), and Lotus Notes clients.

Workflow

A workflow engine distributes, routes, and tracks documents according to a process defined in your applications. Workflow enables you to coordinate and streamline critical business activities across an organization, and with customers, partners, and suppliers.

Agents

Agents enable you to automate frequently performed processes, which eliminates tedious administration tasks and speeds your business applications. Agents can be triggered by time or events in a business application. Agents can be run on Domino servers or Lotus Notes clients.

Development environment

Domino Designer is general-purpose client software that features an IDE that provides easy access to all features of the Domino server.

Domino object model

Domino offers a unified model for accessing its objects through back-end classes, whether you use LotusScript or Java. This allows you to switch programming languages without having to learn new ways to program for Domino.

Live integration with enterprise data

Domino Enterprise Connection Services (DECS) is part of the Domino server. It is a Lotus developed technology, first shipped with NotesPump 2.5, that supplies an easy-to-use forms-based interface to achieve deep, integrated connectivity to external data from Domino applications. This allows developers to map fields in forms directly to fields in relational database tables, without storing any data within the Domino database.

Scalability and reliability

Domino Enterprise Server allows you to cluster up to six Domino servers to provide both scalability and failover protection. This maximizes the availability of your groupware and messaging applications. Real-time replication technology keeps the clustered servers synchronized.

> **Note**
>
> A Domino server is not the same as a file server. A file server provides access to shared resources, such as printers and applications, and also manages network activity. Domino is an application-level server process that provides services necessary for the effective management of communications and applications.

Connectors

Lotus Domino Connectors provide the foundation for native connectivity to enterprise systems. The connectors are driven by all Lotus EI tools and technologies, including programmatic interfaces for LotusScript and Java. Figure 52 shows the different connectors for Domino.

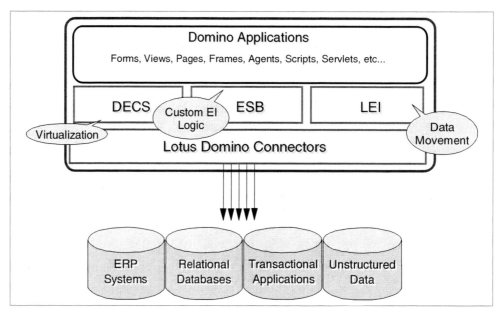

Figure 52. Connectors with Domino

Incorporating back-end data into everyday business processes maximizes the value of Domino applications. Domino applications provide core technologies for the security and control of business processes, forms routing, and approvals management. With new enterprise integration technologies, Domino applications can now incorporate traditionally difficult-to-reach data into those applications, becoming a key component of managed business processes.

Domino includes the ability to create Web applications that contain connectors to relational databases (for example, Oracle DB2), Enterprise Resource Planning systems (for example, SAP), and transaction systems (for example, CICS, IBM MQSeries, and IMS). You can accomplish this either programatically (as available in previous versions) or with visual tools to native database drivers. Figure 53 shows you how you can access other systems from the agent. Do not confuse MQSeries Enterprise Integrator (MQEI) with the MQSeries Integrator (MQSI). MQEI is just a way to talk to base MQSeries from a Domino agent. Similarly you can use other connectors. The added advantage with MQEI is that you can configure it to wake up an agent when a message is received on an incoming queue.

Integration Tools	Connectors	
Domino Enterprise Connection Service (DECS) *Real-time access* *Non-programmatic (forms-based)*	DB2 Oracle Sybase EDA/SQL ODBC File SAP PeopleSoft Oracle	Applications JD Edwards Lawson Infinium Tuxedo** MQSeries** CICS** IMS** TXSeries**
Lotus Enterprise Integrator (LEI): Formerly NotesPump *Schedule- & Event-driven access* *Non-programmatic (forms-based)*		
Domino Connector LotusScript Extension Domino Connector Java Class Library Formula Language *Programmatic access*		
MQSeries and CICS Connections for Domino*** • MQSeries Enterprise Integrator (MQEI)		

* Any integration tool can be used with any connector.
**Tuxedo, MQSeries, CICS, IMS, and TXSeries connectors are currently in development for 2H99 delivery.
***Use *MQSeries and CICS Connections for Domino* as an interim solution for MQSeries, CICS, and IMS integration with Domino.

Figure 53. Extending Domino to the enterprise

Domino Enterprise Connection Services (DECS) offers developers a visual tool and high performance server environment used to create Web applications that provide live, native access to enterprise data and applications. The visual tool presents an application wizard and online documentation to assist you to define external data source connections — DB2, Oracle, Sybase, text-based files, EDA/SQL, and ODBC — and fields within the Domino application that will be automatically updated with external connector data. DECS provides the following advantages:

- Real-Time Web client or Notes Client Access
- Declarative interface
- High performance
- Persistent, parallel, pooled connections
- Filter formulas, metalinks, stored procedures

New Domino classes for enterprise data access will be available in LotusScript and Java. These classes enable you to customize applications to incorporate information from relational databases, transaction systems, and ERP applications from Domino according to your business needs. The Domino driver for JDBC, which provides standard JDBC access to data in Domino databases, is also available. Using this driver, you can write Java applets and applications that use JDBC to access information in Domino databases.

Lotus Enterprise Integrator is the Lotus tool for server to server data management. It's considered "middleware" to connect to and transfer or synchronize information between Lotus Connector enterprise sources on a scheduled or event driven basis. Lotus Enterprise Integrator supports high-volume data exchange or synchronization, and should be positioned as complementing the live access capabilities provided by DECS. The LEI product will continue to support RealTime "live" access to external Connector source data from Domino applications, via the RealTime Notes Activity, which is functionally equivalent to DECS. LEI consists of three components:

- **Lotus Enterprise Integrator Administrator database**: This is a Domino application. System managers create Domino documents, called *activities*, that serve as the instruction set for the second product component.

- **Lotus Enterprise Integrator Server**: The LEI Server processes instructions, connecting to external data sources and moving data according to activity-defined conditions.

- **LEI server log**: Records data transfers and error messages.

LEI supports the exchange of data between all Lotus Connector sources. Available Lotus Connectors include DB2 UDB, Oracle, Sybase, OLE-DB to Microsoft SQLServer 7.0, Text, File, Notes/Domino, ODBC, EDA/SQL (over 70 data sources via Information Builders, Inc. EDA Server product). LEI 3.0 introduced support for new Lotus Connector sources, including SAP R/3, J.D. Edwards OneWorld, Oracle Applications/Financials, and PeopleSoft. A new Lotus Connector for IBM MQSeries is under development. Lawson and SSA/BPCS have built Lotus Connector for their enterprise systems using the Lotus Connector Toolkit. These Lotus Connectors may be purchased from their respective vendors.

LEI also supports programmatic data transfers via LotusScript and Java classes.

3.2.2.2 WebSphere family

Part of the WebSphere family of products that provides the runtime environment for the applications is shown in Figure 54. This section discusses the WebSphere Application Server, WebSphere Commerce Suite, and WebSphere Edge Server.

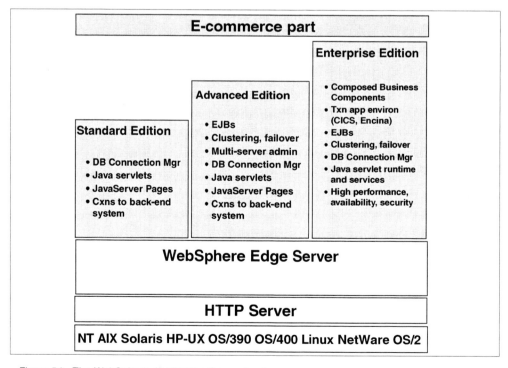

Figure 54. The WebSphere Application Server family

WebSphere Application Server

An *application server* is a middle-tier application that combines three components:

- Pieces for communicating with back-end systems (for example, business applications or databases)

- Pieces for communicating with front-end clients (often, but not necessarily Web clients)

- A framework providing a runtime environment for business logic

Because many databases cannot interpret commands written in HTML, the application server works as a translator, allowing, for example, a customer with a browser to search an online retailer's database for pricing information.

IBM WebSphere Application Server provides a scalable, industrial-strength deployment platform for your e-business applications. There are three editions of WAS:

- **Standard Edition**: Intended for use by Web application developers who focus on the issues of presentation logic, data access, and the business logic that resides in the middle tier.

- **Advanced Edition**: Adds support for EJBs, which includes bean-managed persistence and container-managed persistence, full support for sessions beans, relational database connectivity using JDBC, and support for EJB to MQSeries and CICS. It also provides the ability to scale your application by distributing it across multiple physical machines, and the administrative tools you need to manage your distributed site. By using WebSphere and its supported technologies, you can rapidly build sophisticated applications that are well structured, and maintainable and extensible at e-business space.

- **Enterprise Edition**: Adds services to WebSphere Application Server and includes IBM TXSeries to meet the most sophisticated needs of rapidly evolving, highly-distributed e-business infrastructures. This edition extends the Java programming model and provides additional qualities of service.

Standard Edition

WebSphere Standard Edition is a single system, extremely easy-to-use Web Application Server. You can use Standard Edition for applications producing both static and dynamic Web pages that contain:

- Static HTML (HTML, .gif, .wav, etc.)
- HTML with imbedded client-side scripts, for example JavaScript
- Servlets
- JSPs

WebSphere Standard Edition's objective is to be a simple, easy-to-use, but complete solution for building an active Web site and basic Web applications that integrate with databases. WebSphere Standard Edition does not provide the workload management (WLM) functionality that is available in WebSphere Advanced Edition. However, it allows for multiple JVMs on a single physical server. The JVMs can be mapped to multiple virtual hosts on a single HTTP server to support hosting multiple Web sites on a single application server.

Advanced Edition

WebSphere Advanced Edition extends the WebSphere Standard Edition's functions across multiple machines to provide complete support for developing new high-performance, scalable and available, transactional Web-driven applications. WebSphere Advanced Edition focuses on new applications (JSPs and EJBs) that access relational databases for persistent data. WebSphere Advanced Edition also supports distributed system management across multiple nodes. The set of nodes that are administered collectively comprise a WebSphere administrative domain. You can administer an entire WebSphere domain from a single administrative console. The distributed WebSphere Advanced Edition architecture also requires other fundamental services which include:

- **Naming**: In an object-oriented distributed computing environment, clients must have a mechanism to locate and identify the objects as if the clients and objects were all on the same machine. A naming service provides this mechanism. WebSphere uses the Java Naming and Directory Interface (JNDI) to provide a common front end to the naming service.

- **Security**: WebSphere Advanced Edition allows you to control access to Web resources, such as HTML pages and JSPs, and to control access to EJBs and the business methods they provide. Authorization to access a resource is permission-based. You can grant access permissions to users or groups and control which users or groups can access the resource.

- **Transactions**: A transaction is a set of operations that transforms data from one consistent state to another. Any realistic business application has operations that require several updates be made to a database. Either all these operations should complete or none should complete. For example, a money transfer should debit one bank account and credit another; it would be a serious error if only one of the two updates were to occur. Traditional implementations of such business process would require the programmer to place explicit transaction BEGIN and COMMIT statements in the application code. One benefit of the EJB programming model is that you specify your transactional requirements when you configure the EJB, not in the code. The code is much simpler to write. WebSphere Advanced Edition in supporting EJBs provides full transactional capabilities. These are implemented using the mechanism defined in the Java Transaction API (JTA).

- **Workload management**: The WLM functionality in WebSphere Advanced Edition introduces the notion of modeling application server processes. Clones, which are instances of a model, can be created either on a single machine or across multiple machines in a cluster. In either case, the WebSphere Advanced Edition WLM provides workload distribution and failover.

Enterprise Edition

IBM WebSphere Application Server Enterprise Edition enables full e-business transactions over the Web. Using open standards-based technologies, such as interoperable CORBA and EJB components, Enterprise Edition provides comprehensive, high quality middleware runtime services for distributed component applications. It also contains the industry's most complete support for integrating existing IT applications and resources for reuse on the Web. The features for enterprise edition are same as Advanced Edition plus:

- The ability to compose new business applications
- EJB-based interfaces to existing resource managers
- Extensive horizontal and vertical scalability
- Performance enhancing technology
- Distributed component technology (formerly called IBM Component Broker)
- Transaction application environment (CICS, Encina)

Table 24 compares the J2EE standards with what WebSphere supports today.

Table 24. J2EE standards with WebSphere

Java 2 technologies and profile requirements	Current version	WebSphere today and Version 3.5	WebSphere Version 4
EJB	1.1	1.0 plus extensions (RMI/IIOP, transactions, CMP, etc.)	1.1 including XML descriptor support
HTTP	1.1	Yes, plus across multiple Web servers	Yes, plus across multiple Web servers
JavaIDL/CORBA	_	Enterprise Edition supports 10 different CORBA services. WebSphere also supports Java IDL	Same as 3.5
JavaMail	1.1	No, but supports third-party	Yes, plus Domino support
JDBC	2.0	Yes, across all databases plus partnership with Merant	Yes, 2PC across heterogeneous databases
JDK	1.2	In 3.5, JDK 1.2.2 across Win NT, Win 2000, AIX, Solaris, HP-UX	Upgrade to 1.3 and include Linux, OS/400, OS/390
JMS	1.0.1	Yes, MQSeries native support	Yes, plus JMS-based EJBs, Message Beans
JNDI	1.2	JNDI 1.1 for EJB lookup and COSNaming	Yes, plus JNDI over LDAP
JRMP (Java Remote Message Platform)	1.0	Fully supported via RMI/IIOP	Fully supported via RMI/IIOP
JSP	1.1	JSP 1.0 and 0.91 API levels with some 1.1 features, investigating earlier 1.1	JSP 1.1
JTS/JTA	1.0	Yes, with distributed transactions	Yes, with distributed transactions
LDAP (Lightweight Directory Access Protocol)	_	Client/server support for LDAP; Domino, Netscape, Novell, IBM	Same as 3.5
RMI/IIOP	1.0	Yes, fully supported	Yes, fully supported
Servlet	2.2	Servlet 2.1 API with many 2.2 features, investigating earlier 2.2	Servlet 2.2 API
SQLJ	_	Support via DB2 UDB	Support via DB2 UDB
SSL Security (Secure Sockets Layer) **JCE** (Java Cryptography Extension)	2.0 1.2	Complete end-to-end EJB security, partial Java security APIs	Complete, except for JCE

Java 2 technologies and profile requirements	Current version	WebSphere today and Version 3.5	WebSphere Version 4
XML DOM/SAX (Document Object Model/Simple API for XML) **XSL** (Extensible Stylesheet Language)	–	IBM is industry leader	Perf. in XML Parser, XML in EJBs

WebSphere Application Server Version 4.0

At the time this book was written, IBM has announced the availability of WebSphere Application Server Version 4.0 on most of the platforms (WAS Version 4.0 on OS/400 will be available later). This is a tremendous step for IBM to bring more standards, more features, and more functionality to the customers. Current enhancements solidify WAS's role as the foundation of the WebSphere software platform.

The new features in version 4.0 include:

- Integrated support for key Web services open standards, such as simple object access protocol (SOAP), Universal Description, Discovery and Integration (UDDI), and Web Services Description Language (WSDL). It makes WebSphere Application Server the industry's premier production-ready Web application server for the deployment of enterprise Web service solutions for dynamic e-business.

- Full Java 2 Enterprise Edition (J2EE) v1.2 platform certification. It enables powerful interoperability between Web services and J2EE applications and offers key solutions for collaboration, B2B, portal serving, content management, commerce, and pervasive computing.

- Unparalleled connectivity provided by a preview implementation of Java 2 Connectivity (J2C) and an enhanced set of application adapters for enterprise systems, including SAP, PeopleSoft, IBM CICS, and IBM IMS.

- Performance and scaling attributes that support bean-managed and container-managed persistence for entity beans and session beans with transaction management and monitoring.

- Enhancements for security and control.

- An easy-to-use XML technology-based administrator client and friendly server environment for easy set up.

- Integration with IBM WebSphere Studio Workbench, the new open development environment.

- Bidirectional CORBA connectivity, including CORBA interoperability and coexistence.

- ActiveX client and server integration through an ActiveX bridge.

- Integration between messaging and component-based paradigms through Java Message Service (JMS) listener and message beans.

- Support for global applications through the accommodation of different cultural conventions, geographical boundaries, and time zones.

- Enhancements to the J2EE programming model to allow for transparent access to shared information across a distributed computing environment with shared work areas.

- Support for business rule beans that allow for dynamic updates to application logic to quickly meet evolving business requirements.

- Specialized configuration options that offer businesses the flexibility to decide how they want to respond to the changing marketplace.

IBM has changed the packaging strategy for WAS v4.0. It will be sold in three editions:

- **WebSphere Application Server Advanced Single Server Edition (AEs)**: As the name suggests, this edition can run on a single system, but it doesn't include the workload management support for multiple nodes. Note that even this edition can host EJBs. This edition is available free of charge for testing and evaluation purposes.

- **WebSphere Application Server Advanced Edition (AE)**: This is a full-blown version of the application server.

- **WebSphere Application Server Enterprise Edition (EE)**: This edition is based on WAS AE and adds the Enterprise Services and TXSeries. The Enterprise Services add value to the application server. They plug into the AE server and augment it. The Enterprise Services do not add a separate runtime environment but instead build directly on top of the AE runtime environment.

WebSphere Commerce Suite

WebSphere Commerce Suite (WCS) is available in several editions:

- The Start edition
- The Pro edition
- The Service Provider edition
- The Marketplace edition

The WebSphere Commerce server runs within the environment of the WebSphere Application Server, which, in turn, interacts with the HTTP server. WCS has a very modular solution architecture (see Figure 55) that makes the platform easier to customize or extend. For example, the subsystems shown in the chart can usually either be extended to meet a customers specific needs, or replaced, without hindering the rest of the solution component subsystems. One example would be if a customer had their own auction application or systems management solution. They could replace their own components for the WCS subsystems (assuming they are Java and follow the EJB programming model).

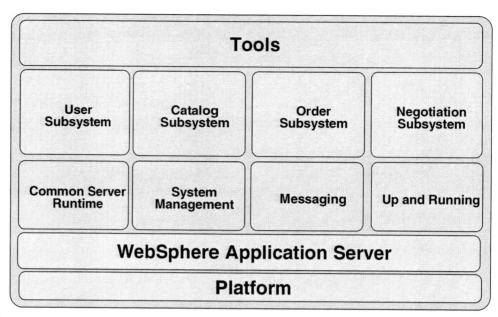

Figure 55. WCS modular architecture

The WebSphere Commerce Suite is packaged with the following award-winning software to provide a complete end-to-end solution:

- IBM DB2 Universal Database provides a scalable, reliable database to store your data.

- IBM HTTP Server provides a powerful Web server and is based on the popular Apache Web server.

- IBM WebSphere Payment Manager provides a secure system for managing payments.

- IBM WebSphere Application Server Advanced Edition for servlets, JSP, and EJB technologies.

- IBM SecureWay Directory is a robust directory server.

- Blaze Rules Server provides rules processing for personalized product recommendations.

It can also be integrated with other software products.

WebSphere Commerce Suite exploits the WebSphere Studio platform. WebSphere Studio provides content-creation tools for site creation. The enablement of JSP technology for catalog display provides further evolution into a more open standards. The key to increasing e-commerce sales is to leverage the same proven merchandising techniques used in traditional commerce ventures. The WebSphere Commerce Suite uses an advanced rules-based framework to provide unique customer shopping experiences and to implement marketing campaigns that improve site traffic and sales. With WebSphere Commerce Suite, you can create your own marketing campaigns. Or you can use packaged campaigns such as:

- **Merchandising**: Highlight related items based on cross-sell, up-sell, accessory, or substitution strategies.

- **Inventory reduction**: Recommendations and discounts for overstocked items.

- **Legal policy**: Sales based on country-specific legal policies.

- **Time based**: Promotions based on seasons, special events, or holidays.

The WebSphere Commerce Suite also supports the increasingly popular auctions sales model. You can add the excitement of an auction to attract site traffic, increase sales, and to move excess inventory. The WebSphere Commerce Suite has rich and extensible functionality. You can tailor the interface to meet your individual needs. You can integrate your e-commerce system with existing in-house systems and middleware. You can even add on more than 100 applications for WebSphere Commerce Suite that were developed by independent software vendors.

WebSphere Commerce Suite features

The industry has moved beyond a simple Web-based sales-from-a-catalog approach to e-business. Now WebSphere Commerce Suite offers:

- A feature-rich, scalable, and customizable e-commerce platform

- Full integration with business processes and applications

- A powerful, flexible application development and management workbench

- An open industry standards-based architecture

- A flexible, scalable family of offerings, from the WebSphere START edition for small and medium businesses, to the PRO edition for large enterprises, to the Service Provider edition for application service providers (ASPs)

- Content management capabilities that enable catalog information management and site asset management

- Marketing functionality such as pricing and promotions, advertising, catalog browsing, personalization, up-sell and cross-sell programs, loyalty programs, and Business Intelligence

- Order management features, including negotiations, shopping cart and order form, inventory management, order calculation, and tax calculation

- Customer relationship management capabilities, such as customer service, order and shipment tracking, and user registration and profiling

- Payment processing for proofs, settlements, and billing

- Fulfillment, including shipping and delivery calculation and logistics

WebSphere Commerce Suite architecture

You can view the WebSphere Commerce Suite architecture as layers of data and functionality (see Figure 56), with each layer building on the layer beneath it. When you customize your store, you may modify one of the higher levels without modifying the lower levels. This abstraction hides implementation details and makes it easier to customize the store.

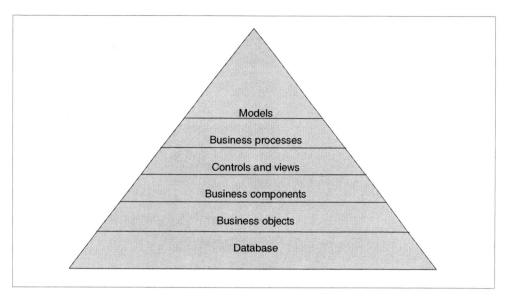

Figure 56. Layered view of WebSphere Commerce Suite architecture

Each layer of the application architecture is described here:

- **Database**: WebSphere Commerce Suite uses a database schema designed specifically for e-commerce applications and their data requirements. User, order, and product are examples of tables in the schema.

- **Business objects**: Business objects represent entities within the commerce domain and encapsulate the data-centric logic required to extract or interpret information contained within the database. These entities comply with the EJB specification. The beans act as an interface between the commerce application and the database. The beans model entities in a more natural way that provides easier comprehension than a complex relationship between columns in database tables.

- **Business components**: Business components are units of business logic. They perform coarse-grained procedural business logic. The logic is implemented using the WebSphere Commerce Suite model of controller commands and task commands. An example of this type of component is the OrderProcess controller command. This particular command encapsulates all the business logic required to process a typical order. The e-commerce application calls the OrderProcess command, which, in turn, calls several task commands to perform individual units of work. For example, individual task commands ensure that enough inventory is available to meet the requirements of the order, process the payment, update the status of the order, and when the process is complete, decrease the inventory by the appropriate amount.

- **Controls and views**: Results of the commands and actions taken by the user are displayed using views implemented by the JSP templates. Examples of views include ProductDisplay (returns a product page that reflects the relevant product information the shopper has selected) and OrderPrepare (presents the shopper with a form to submit appropriate order information).

- **Business process**: Together, sets of business components and views create workflow and site-flow processes that are known as *business processes*. Examples of business processes include user registration and catalog navigation.

- **Models**: Collectively, the lower layers support the B2B and B2C markets. The actual implementation of a particular e-commerce environment determines the specific processes used. For example, you could choose a purchase order system for a B2B environment as opposed to a credit-card-based system for a B2C environment.

Implementation of the architecture

While the previous section introduced the architecture that WebSphere Commerce Suite uses, this section discusses how the architecture is implemented in a WebSphere programming environment.

The commerce server, operating within the WebSphere Application Server environment, provides the functionality to run your store. Figure 57 illustrates the main components of the commerce server.

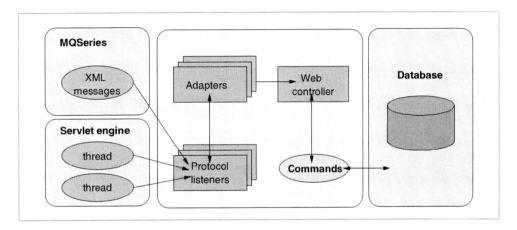

Figure 57. Commerce server components

The following list describes the commerce server components:

- **Servlet engine**: The servlet engine is part of the WebSphere Application Server runtime that acts as a request dispatcher for incoming URL requests. The servlet engine manages a thread pool and removes the need for the commerce application to implement its own task dispatcher. The WebSphere Application Server plug-in code works with the Web server for effective receipt and processing of HTTP requests for the WebSphere Application Server.

- **Protocol listeners**: WebSphere Commerce Suite commands can be invoked from various devices, each of which may use a different communication protocol. Examples of devices that can invoke commands include Internet browsers, mobile phones using an Internet browser, and B2B applications that send XML messages using MQSeries.

    A commerce server run-time component, a protocol listener, receives inbound requests from transports and then dispatches the requests to the appropriate adapters. WebSphere Commerce Suite protocol listeners include the request servlet and the MQSeries listener.

    When the request servlet receives a URL request from the servlet engine, it passes the request to the HTTP adapter manager. The HTTP adapter manager then queries the adapter types to determine which adapter can process the request. Once the specific adapter is determined, the request is passed to the adapter.

- **Adapters**: WebSphere Commerce Suite adapters are device-specific components that receive and process incoming requests and call the Web controller. WebSphere Commerce Suite includes adapters for browsers, XML messages, pervasive computing devices, and the scheduler.

- **Web controller**: The Web controller processes the request, calls the appropriate controller and view commands, and returns the appropriate result. The Web controller provides services such as session management, transaction control, access control, and authentication.

Commands

WebSphere Commerce Suite commands are beans that contain the programming logic associated with handling a particular request. The WebSphere Commerce Suite command framework is shown in Figure 58.

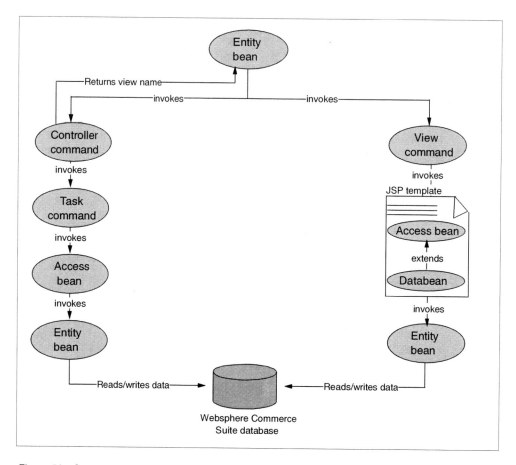

Figure 58. Command framework for handling incoming requests

The types of commands are described here:

- **Controller command**: A controller command encapsulates the logic related to a particular business process. It contains the control statements (for example, if, then, else) and invokes task commands to perform individual units of work in the business process. Upon completion, a controller command returns a view name. The Web controller then determines the appropriate implementation class for the view and executes the view task.

- **Task command**: A task command implements a specific unit of application logic. Together, a controller command and a set of task commands implement the application logic for a URL request.

- **Databean command**: A JSP template invokes a databean command when a databean is to be instantiated. The primary function of a databean command is to populate the databean with data.

- **View command**: A view command is used to compose a view as a response to a client request.

- **Access beans**: Access beans provide a simplified interface for entity beans. VisualAge for Java generates the access beans.

- **Entity beans**: An entity bean is a persistent, transactional commerce object. WebSphere Commerce Suite uses entity beans to access commerce data from the database. Entity beans are implemented according to the EJB component model.

- **Databean manager**: Using WebSphere Commerce Studio, when a WebSphere Commerce Suite databean is inserted into a JSP template, by invoking the databean manager, a line of code is generated populating the databean at runtime.

Transitioning to version 5

Previous versions have a programming model built on C++ and use commands, tasks, and overridable functions. Commands are C++ components that service major functions such as placing an order. Tasks represent subunits of work within a command. Overridable functions are the C++ components that actually perform the work of the tasks.

The version 5.1 programming model is based on WebSphere Application Server, Java technology, and EJB. The Net.Data display functions are completely replaced by JSP. The C++ command, task, and overridable function structure is replaced by a single command structure that uses Java technology and EJB. The new version 5.1 programming model provides more flexibility for customers to extend business logic. Figure 59 shows the changes in the technology between the current version of WCS and the older versions. Because of the complexity in running C++ and EJB in the same environment, C++ and Net.Data are no longer supported in version 5.1.

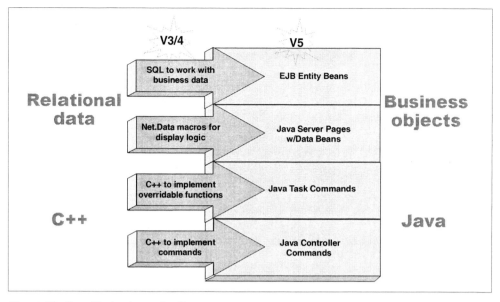

Figure 59. Transitioning to version 5

Standards in WCS

WCS is standards-based to provide an open platform since customization is both a key requirement and a strength for WCS. It has a Java programming model, with a complete set of robust tooling to support users in customizing and managing their environment:

- **WCS Java environment**: Provides support for EJBs, JSPs, servlets, JDBC, JTA/JTS, JNDI, JMS, and JavaBeans

- **Directory services**: Support for LDAP directory (Secureway and Domino); WCS supports single sign-on with WAS and Domino

- **XML**: Is used pervasively throughout the application (server configuration, store creation, messaging, and mass load)

- **Connector tools**: WCS provides a direct connection to back-end systems using the emerging J2EE standard (Common Connection Framework)

Mobile commerce support

WCS is architected to be device agnostic. This means that the same commerce application can serve the customer across multiple delivery channels and do it intelligently. WCS provides the infrastructure that enables shoppers and buyers to access the right display and the right shopping flow that is best suited for the device they are using at that time. Think of it as customized JSPs for each specific device. This ensures that the display is always perfect and the end customer does not receive information that cannot be read or doesn't fit the device they are using.

This is possible because the device type is in the header information for the request to the server. Logic is invoked to render the proper JSP and can direct the request through a specific shopping flow. You may not want to cross-sell someone on a cell phone, but rather send that customer through a quick and efficient shopping flow or interaction that is more conducive to the device they are using. The wireless protocols supported in WCS are listed in Figure 60.

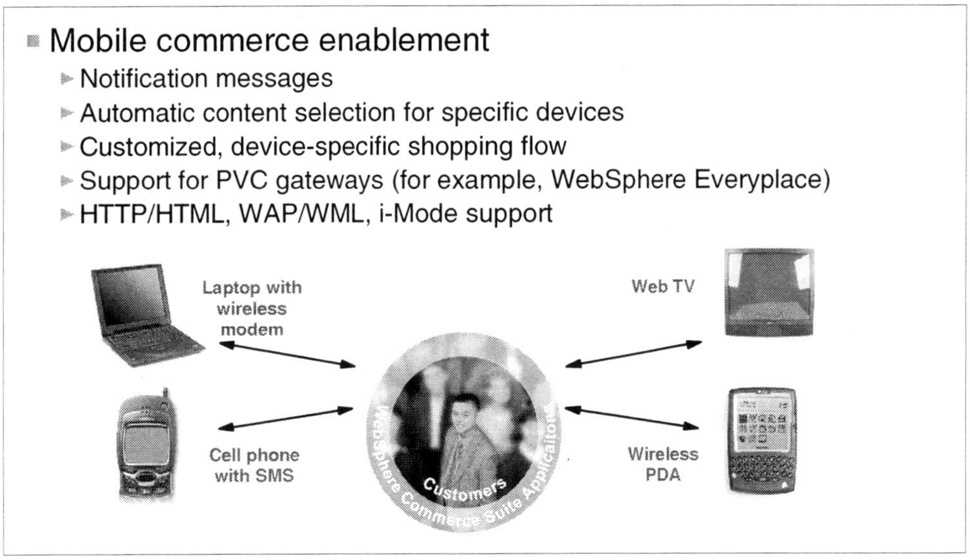
Mobile commerce enablement
Notification messages
Automatic content selection for specific devices
Customized, device-specific shopping flow
Support for PVC gateways (for example, WebSphere Everyplace)
HTTP/HTML, WAP/WML, i-Mode support
Laptop with wireless modem
Web TV
Cell phone with SMS
Wireless PDA
Customers

Figure 60. Mobile commerce support in WCS

WebSphere Edge Server

The WebSphere Edge Server (WES) provides software building blocks to reduce Web server congestion, increase content availability, and improve Web server performance. It serves as the workload management node for multiple WAS servers. WES is available for all of the WebSphere Application Server editions. It provides sophisticated detection of system utilization and error events across multiple networks and servers. It is extremely robust and scalable, providing caching of content across multiple servers and automating the replication and mirroring of data and applications. WES is geared for ISPs, whether they are in the ISP business or in the business of providing access to internal users of corporate information technology (IT). WES is designed to help you provide Internet access and content hosting. It includes the following components:

- **IBM Network Dispatche**r: Load-balancing software with high availability features. Network Dispatcher can dynamically monitor and balance requests to available TCP/IP servers and applications in real time. Load balancing allows heavily-accessed Web sites to increase capacity by linking many individual servers to a single logical server.
- **IBM Caching Proxy**: A server with Platform for Internet Content Selection (PICS) filtering. Web Traffic Express provides highly-scalable caching and filtering functions associated with receiving requests and serving URLs. With tunable caching capable of supporting high cache hit rates, the server can reduce bandwidth costs and provide more consistent rapid customer response times.

For more information, refer to 9.3.1, “WebSphere Edge Server” on page 409.

3.2.2.3 MQSeries

The MQSeries family is integrated middleware that provides the intelligence and infrastructure to drive rapid and flexible business change. It transforms and integrates business applications and processes both within the enterprise and through the firewall, across the extended enterprise.

The MQSeries Family provides assured operational integrity across the widest range of IT and e-business environments with the most powerful, complete, and proven solution portfolio, complemented by highly skilled Business Partners.

The MQSeries family comprises five key elements:

- **MQSeries**: The core of the MQSeries family, integrates over 35 platforms. Providing the base messaging functions for servers and clients, and assuring once-only message delivery, it can be used alone or with other members of the family.

- **MQSeries Adapter Offering**: Provides the framework and tools to build and customize MQSeries adapters for existing and new, pre-packaged, or custom-developed applications.

- **MQSeries Everyplace**: Brings the benefits of assured message delivery and rock-solid security to the failure-prone environment of mobile working.

- **MQSeries Integrator**: A powerful information broker, includes a one-to-many connectivity model plus transformation, intelligent routing, and information flow modelling across multiple, disparate business systems.

- **MQSeries Workflow**: A business process management system. It enables the definition, execution, and swift change of complete business processes that span systems, applications, and people.

MQSeries

The IBM MQSeries range of products provides application programming services that enable application programs to communicate with each other using messages and queues. This form of communication is referred to as *commercial messaging*. It provides assured, once-only delivery of messages.

Using MQSeries means that you can separate application programs, so that the program sending a message can continue processing without having to wait for a reply from the receiver. If the receiver, or the communication channel to it, is temporarily unavailable, the message can be forwarded at a later time. MQSeries also provides mechanisms for providing acknowledgements of messages received. The programs that comprise an MQSeries application can run on different computers, different operating systems, and at different locations. The applications are written using a common programming interface known as the Message Queue Interface (MQI), so that applications developed on one platform can be transferred to another. Figure 61 shows two applications communicating using messages and queues, one application puts a message on a queue, and the other application gets that message from the queue.

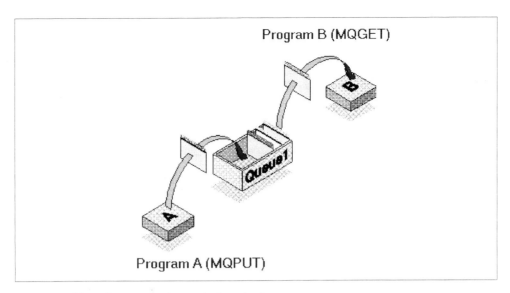

Figure 61. Shows how messaging works in a simple case

Queue managers

In MQSeries, queues are managed by a component called a *queue manager*. The queue manager provides messaging services for the applications and processes. The queue manager ensures that messages are put on the correct queue or that they are routed to another queue manager. Before applications can send any messages, you must create a queue manager and some queues.

How applications identify themselves to queue managers

Any MQSeries application must make a successful connection to a queue manager before it can make any other MQI calls. When the application successfully makes the connection, the queue manager returns a connection handle. This is an identifier that the application must specify each time it issues an MQI call. An application can connect to only one queue manager at a time (known as its *local queue manager*), so only one connection handle is valid (for that particular application) at a time. When the application has connected to a queue manager, all the MQI calls it issues are processed by that queue manager until it issues another MQI call to disconnect from that queue manager.

Opening a queue

Before your application can use a queue for messaging, it must open the queue. If you are putting a message on a queue, your application must open the queue for "putting". Similarly, if you are getting a message from a queue, your application must open the queue for "getting". You can specify that a queue is opened for both getting and putting, if required. The queue manager returns an object handle if the open request is successful. The application specifies this handle, together with the connection handle, when it issues a put or a get call. This ensures that the request is carried out on the correct queue.

Putting and getting messages

When the open request is confirmed, your application can put a message on the queue. To do this, it uses another MQI call on which you have to specify a number of parameters and data structures. These parameters define all the information about the message you are putting, including the message type, its destination, which options are set, and so on.

The message data (that is, the application-specific contents of the message your application is sending) is defined in a buffer, which you specify in the MQI call. When the queue manager processes the call, it adds a message descriptor, which contains information that is needed to ensure the message can be delivered properly. The message descriptor is in a format defined by MQSeries; the message data is defined by your application (this is what you put into the message data buffer in your application code).

The program that gets the messages from the queue must first open the queue for getting messages. It must then issue another MQI call to get the message from the queue. On this call, you have to specify which message you want to get.

Messaging using more than one queue manager

This arrangement is not typical for a real messaging application because both programs run on the same computer and are connected to the same queue manager. In a commercial application, the putting and getting programs would probably be on different computers, and therefore, would also be connected to different queue managers. Figure 62 shows how messaging works where the program putting the message and the program getting the message are on different computers and connected to different queue managers.

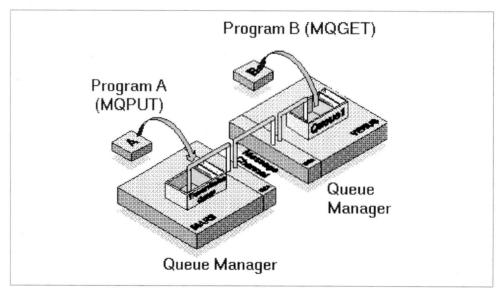

Figure 62. Messaging: When programs are on different computers

In this situation, you also need to create message channels to carry MQSeries messages between the queue managers.

MQSeries Adapter Offering

Adapters simplify the connection of applications by allowing them to exchange information with each other despite using different message formats. The MQSeries Adapter Offering is part of the MQSeries family of products. It provides the framework and tools to build and customize MQSeries adapters for existing and new, pre-packaged, or custom-developed applications.

It consists of the MQSeries Adapter Kernel for Multiplatforms and the MQSeries Adapter Builder for Windows NT and Windows 2000. The MQSeries Adapter Kernel is the runtime component, which enables the deployment of adapters built using the MQSeries Adapter Builder. The latest versions enhance the offering for the Java environment.

The MQSeries Adapter Builder tool is used to build adapters that connect applications, including pre-packaged applications such as those from Baan, J.D. Edwards, SAP, Siebel, PeopleSoft, and many others to MQSeries messaging environment.

Until now adapters had to be custom developed or bought and modified. They were usually expensive, often non-standard, and required an external transformation engine. But MQSeries Adapter Offering is based on XML, and optionally the Open Applications Group (OAG) standards. Therefore, its adapters are intelligent and perform transformation without the need for a transformation engine. However, if the number of connections required increases to a level where a message broker is justified, one (ideally the MQSeries Integrator) can be easily added.

Highlights of MQSeries Adapter Offering include:

- Reduces the risk and cost of managing point-to-point application integration
- Provides generic support for adapters, such as message creation, parsing and error logging, and the interface to MQSeries messaging
- Builds interfaces for applications with the provision of the MQSeries Adapter Builder
- Provides a safe, predictable migration path
- Can be used by enterprises, Business Partners, or service providers to create open XML standards-based adapters
- Reduces the costs of application development and application maintenance, and brings applications on stream faster
- Ensures easier integration with existing applications
- MQSeries Adapter Builder is now available on Windows NT and Windows 2000
- MQSeries Adapter Kernel supports IBM AIX, IBM OS/400, HP-UX, Sun Solaris, Windows NT, and Windows 2000

MQSeries Everyplace
MQSeries and MQSeries Everyplace are complementary offerings within the MQSeries base messaging family. IBM MQSeries Everyplace for Multiplatforms is an innovative messaging product that extends the reach of the MQSeries family to a wider range of distributed and mobile environments. It provides functionality that is particularly suited to lightweight platforms, devices, and unmanaged networks. It is the ideal way to provide MQSeries messaging in a world of fragile communications.

MQSeries Everyplace provides an assured messaging infrastructure where small footprints and optimized communication protocols are required. It is frugal in its use of system resources and minimizes the costs of set-up and administration, making it suitable for unmanaged networks. It offers tailored functions and interfaces appropriately to its customer set, for example, both synchronous and asynchronous messaging support, local and remote queue access, direct and indirect routing, rock-solid security, and extensive customization capabilities.

MQSeries Everyplace provides cross-platform compatibility and function extensibility. It extends support to a wider range of distributed and mobile environments. It is suitable for use over public networks and for access through firewalls.

MQSeries Everyplace offers:

- The introduction of an input node to MQSeries Integrator (extending MQSeries Integrator to new applications and information sources)
- A Retail Edition designed specifically for IBM 4690 system users
- Direct support of HP-UX and Linux platforms
- A simplified pricing model

The highlights of MQSeries Everyplace include:

- Allows mobile workers to access corporate data and applications on any of the 35-plus platforms in an MQSeries network
- Runs on laptops, PDAs, and telephones allowing mobile workers to choose personal workstations to suit their current needs
- Operates on 4,690 retail systems, allowing transactions captured from cash drawers (tills) to be "fed" more efficiently to host systems or MQSeries Integrator
- Can be easily customized and adapted, and requires minimal administration and management
- Ensures messages are delivered once and only once, so high value transactions are safe
- Includes rock-solid, end-to-end security (128-bit encryption) as standard, ensuring access to data is fully controlled
- Has simple setup options for security and can easily work through firewalls using HTTP
- Provides full support for both synchronous and asynchronous messaging
- Tightly integrated with other MQSeries family members and WebSphere Everyplace Suite
- Now talks directly to MQSeries Integrator V2.0.2 via an MQSeries Everyplace input node

MQSeries Integrator
Often enterprises need to address the issue of incompatible message formats between many applications within the enterprise (see Figure 63). To solve this incompatibility problem, IBM offers MQSeries Integrator.

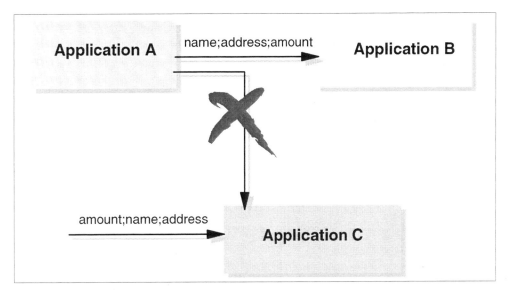

Figure 63. Incompatible message format

MQSeries Integrator is a powerful information broker that selects and distributes information to the applications, databases and people that need it. Users can implement realtime, application-to-application message transformation and intelligent message routing quickly and easily. Business effectiveness across the enterprise is improved by tighter integration with existing applications, leading Enterprise Resource Planning (ERP) systems, and other software packages.

It uses rules to enable the business intelligence of an enterprise to be implemented and applied to business events. Operations include dynamically manipulating and routing messages, such as augmenting in-flight data with that from corporate databases (for example, data enrichment) or storing information in corporate databases (for example, data warehousing).

Figure 64 shows the integration architecture before using MQSeries Integrator.

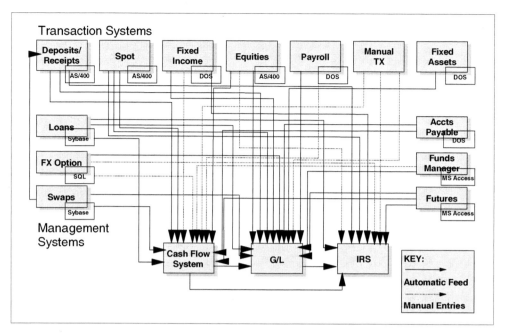

Figure 64. Example of a financial service company: Before

Let us introduce MQSeries Integrator in the system and see what difference it brings to the application integration architecture. As shown in Figure 65, the communication becomes seamless with the communication logic now pulled out of individual components and onto the MQSeries Integrator.

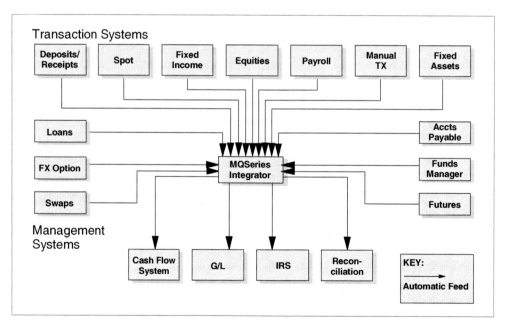

Figure 65. Example of a financial service company: After

Sophisticated, yet easy-to-use, GUI tools are used to exploit a wide range of capabilities to ensure a flexible and scalable application integration solution. Business analysts can design, use, and manipulate business rules as needed, without detailed product knowledge. Applications can be added, extended or replaced easily, which allows them to interact and respond rapidly to changing requirements.

Using MQSeries to deliver messages, MQSeries Integrator establishes a hub through which they pass. It simplifies connections between applications, integrates information from databases and other sources, applies enterprise-defined business rules intelligently, dynamically directs the flow of information, and transforms and reformats the data to suit the recipients.

MQSeries Integrator has an open framework, so built-in components can be combined with those from third parties. Message formats are defined either in supplied message dictionaries or as self-defining XML messages.

The latest release is available in 10 national languages and extends support for existing AIX, Sun Solaris, and Windows NT/2000 platforms to include HP-UX and a solution for iSeries, which significantly increases integration opportunities. It also supports MQSeries Everyplace and Supervisory Control and Data Acquisition (SCADA) protocols to enable closer integration with remote users.

Other features include improved integration with New Era of Networks (NEON) Version 5.2 rules and formatter to provide backward compatibility with rules, formats, and templates. In addition, a new integrated, interactive visual message flow debugger and a node development wizard enhance usability in the development environment.

The highlights of MQSeries Integrator include:

- Transforms, augments, and applies rules to message-based data, and routes and distributes it between high performance systems

- Integrates both existing and new applications

- Integrates application and business data using dynamic content and topic-based publish and subscribe functions

- Visualizes the application flow through a graphical development environment

- Allows message formats to be defined through a variety of dictionaries, either those supplied with the product or from a third party

- Simplifies support for multiple environments with a variety of application adapters, templates, and tools

- Provides a fully scalable architecture to meet growing business needs

- Has an open, architectural framework that allows the use of built-in components with third-party offerings

- Exploits and complies with industry standards such as SQL and XML

- Provides compatibility with relevant standards such as OMG, EJB, XML/EDI, ERP, CRM, and SCM formats

- Allows database updates under transactional control

- Integrates with MQSeries transaction control and allows end-to-end transaction coordination of application integration

- Optimizes the functions of MQSeries Integrator Version 2, and supports and exploits the functions of MQSeries Version 5.2, which is shipped with the product

- Improves usability in the development environment via a new integrated, interactive visual

- Offers a message flow debugger and a node development wizard

- Enhances support for remote users with direct support for MQSeries Everyplace and SCADA clients

- Improves support for NEON Version 5.2 and the Message Repository Manager (MRM) to provide backward compatibility with rules, formats, and templates

- Supports 10 national languages

- Significantly increases integration opportunities; in addition to enhancements to the AIX, Sun Solaris, and Windows versions, the latest release also supports HP-UX and the iSeries (using the Integrated xSeries Server for iSeries (IXS) to implement MQSeries Integrator for Windows)

MQSeries Workflow

IBM MQSeries Workflow is the powerful process engine at the heart of IBM's Business Process Management software. It enables business agility, service-level management, and rapid process deployment based on WebSphere and MQSeries. It executes process definitions captured during modeling and ensures that business functions are performed reliably and correctly using the transactional integrity of MQSeries. It is scalable and takes full advantage of multiple processors and clustering. It is particularly well suited to Web server farms. It executes processes running from sub-seconds to many months.

Its full restart and recovery capability makes it truly fault tolerant. When you require high availability, essential in today's e-business environment, MQSeries Workflow is the engine you can bet your mission-critical business processes on. The powerful process engine facilitates the integration of services provided by IT and organizational infrastructures. Managing business process logic separately from participating services enables your organization to be and remain agile in a constantly changing and dynamic market place – so vital in the competitive world of e-business.

Integrating business applications into a workflow management system means that you remove the flow dependency from the application. The routing features of a workflow management system allow you to extract all information that is related to the process flow from an application program. Equally, process-relevant data is under control of the workflow system. MQSeries Workflow is "middleware" and, therefore, is similar to a database management system that allows you to extract standard data-management functions from an application program.

Whenever changes to the process flow need to be done, you do not need to change the applications that are part of the process model. This means that you can reuse your software components in other processes and consequently, achieve significant cost savings.

IBM MQSeries Workflow enables businesses to:

- Increase their agility so they can act, and react, in a timely way

- Deliver new services and products that leverage new and existing investments in infrastructure

- Make their processes visible so they reveal what is actually happening

- Ensure processes are visible and usable by employees, customers, business partners, and suppliers
- Ensure their processes are auditable and measurable
- Separate what needs to be done from how it is implemented
- Execute business without being limited by IT
- Manage fluctuations in demand and support rapid business growth
- Perform business functions reliably and correctly

The features of MQSeries Workflow include:

- Allows you to quickly integrate applications and the flow of work and data
- Provides scalability, reliability, and security through the IBM Relational Database DB2
- Provides coverage across multiple platforms from Windows to the mainframe
- Provides transaction and messaging support
- Integrates people and automated applications
- Makes it possible to achieve a high degree of reuse for processes and applications
- Supplies a middleware infrastructure for process-based solutions
- Provides a build-time graphical editor to enable the design of complex business processes

MQSeries Workflow allows you to have your business processes comply with ISO 9000. As far as standards for workflow products are concerned, MQSeries Workflow adheres to the specified standards of the Workflow Management Coalition (WfMC). The WfMC was founded in 1993. It is an organization that focuses on the advancement of workflow management technology and its use in industry. It is equally important for vendors and buyers of workflow products. The WfMC has more than 170 members, located in 24 countries around the world. IBM is a member of the WfMC organization.

3.2.2.4 DB2 Universal Database (UDB)

The DB2 Universal Database builds upon the stability and performance of DB2 on the mainframe and provides the features required in a distributed database product. DB2 UDB is IBM's relational database server solution for the UNIX, OS/2, and Windows NT/2000 operating environments. DB2 UDB supports the following key capabilities and benefits:

- *Superior scalability*: DB2 Universal Database can run on everything from laptops supporting mobile users to massively parallel systems with terabytes of data or thousands of users. It is the only database in the industry capable of scaling this breadth of systems with the same function. This allows you to minimize costs and maximize personnel skills by using a single database for all your application needs, regardless of the scale. You can also rest assured that your applications will not fail because your database will not scale.

- *Multimedia extensibility*: DB2 Universal Database allows you to extend the capabilities of the database to meet your specific organizational requirements. This includes the ability to support more advanced applications involving multimedia data such as documents, images, audio, and video. You can now develop applications that use technology to gain competitive advantage in ways that were not previously possible or practical. You can also save costs by extending DB2 UDB to support these new applications.

- *Complete Web-enablement*: One of the key new application areas is e-business. DB2 Universal Database is fully integrated with Web technology so that data can be easily accessed from the Internet or from your intranet with complete security. This allows you to quickly build e-business or Internet applications that will provide a competitive advantage, greater customer service, or reduced costs.

- *Universe of partner solutions*: DB2 Universal Database is capable of supporting a broad range of data management applications with excellent performance and reliability. As a result, a large number of industry solution providers, including SAP, Baan, Peoplesoft Seibel, and thousands more, have adopted DB2 UDB to support their applications. Some have even adapted their tools to support DB2 UDB. This allows you to more quickly satisfy your requirements by buying, rather than developing, solutions.

- *Business Intelligence powerhouse*: DB2 Universal Database has particular strengths in supporting Business Intelligence applications such as data warehousing and Online Analytical Processing (OLAP). DB2 UDB leads the industry in parallel database technology and query optimization resulting in the proven ability to help customers find competitive advantage, better customer service, or reduced costs by mining their data for the knowledge required to make better decisions. This does not require the additional expense of a specialized database. DB2 UDB provides a single database that can be used across an enterprise for all data management requirements from OLAP to OLTP.

- *Ease of use and management*: DB2 Universal Database is one of the easiest databases in the industry to set up, use, and manage. It includes a complete suite of GUI administration tools that allow for easy installation, administration, and remote operations. It includes programmer-friendly tools to get an application up-and-running quickly and user-friendly tools to make end-users immediately productive. Everything you need comes in the box, ready to go.

- *Universal access*: DB2 Universal Database can be accessed from almost any client workstation over almost any network. Through built-in data replication and distributed transactions, it provides you with the flexibility of placing data anywhere in your network required for optimum service and productivity. Further, DB2 UDB provides the most efficient and seamless integration of data on mainframe and midrange data servers in the industry allowing you to reduce costs and improve cycle-times by leveraging your current investments in data, hardware, software, and skills.

- *Multi-platform support*: DB2 Universal Database is one of the most open database platforms available. It runs on the most popular UNIX and Intel server platforms including AIX, HP-UX, Solaris, Linux, NUMA-Q, OS/2, and Windows NT/2000. It supports all major industry standards relevant to distributed data so that it can be accessed using thousands of existing tools and applications. It can also be easily managed within an open, network computing environment.

- *Bullet-proof reliability*: DB2 Universal Database is setting the standard for quality and reliability in the client/server database industry. As more mission-critical applications are implemented on UNIX and Intel platforms,

IBM's ability to bring mainframe-level reliability to this environment has become a major factor in choosing DB2 UDB. Better reliability and availability can reduce your costs, while scalability both within and across platforms can reduce the risk of dead-end projects.

- *Market leadership*: IBM entered the client/server database market late. However, with its core competency in database technology and its renewed emphasis on software marketing, IBM has delivered more high-quality database technology to market faster than anyone else in the industry. DB2 Universal Database is the culmination of this effort. With DB2 Universal Database, you can rest assured that you are getting the best database technology available today from a vendor with a bright future and the best record of service and support in the industry.

With DB2 Universal Database, you can:

- Support applications from Business Intelligence to transaction processing with a single high-value database that allows you to minimize costs, leverage the skills of your support personnel, and maximize your return on investment

- Easily Web-enable enterprise data for your intranet or the Internet, which allows you to go to market faster, gain a competitive advantage, and increase customer satisfaction

- Extend applications with new function, or scale them for more users or data, so you can increase productivity and provide more useful information to your user community

For more information, visit: `http://www.ibm.com/software/data/db2/udb/`

3.2.2.5 Transaction systems

Transaction processing and TP Monitors represent an important part of general Web application computing. As Web applications mature and become the basis for mission-critical solutions, it becomes apparent that for such solutions to be effective requires that there be some component in the system that manages the interactions between all the participants (sometimes likened to the software equivalent of the symphony orchestra's conductor). This is the traditional role of the TP Monitor, in which transactions, rather than being mere business events, really represent a philosophy of application design that guarantees robustness in a distributed system.

IBM has created several transaction systems that have proven to be the top notch products:

- Information Management System
- Customer Information Control System
- Encina/Encina++
- TXSeries

Information Management System

When immediate access to mission-critical information is imperative, major corporations rely on IMS to provide a continuous link to data that is accurate, up-to-date, and quickly accessed by many end users. Customers rely on IMS systems to process billions of vital transactions a day. Any time you make an airline reservation, rent a car, get cash from an ATM, or pick up a prescription from the pharmacy, chances are you've used IMS.

IBM Information Management System was once, 30 years ago, created as a single, almost closed system with three components (see Figure 66):

- IMS DataCommunication to communicate with terminals, printers, and other systems

- IMS Transaction Monitor to monitor transaction processing

- IMS Database, a hierarchical database system using the Data Language/1 Data Manipulation Language (DL/1 DBMS was made available for other system environments)

Today IMS is as open as other systems to participate in distributed logical units of work with processing, message queuing, and database accessing.

The main difference between IMS and other Transaction Processing Monitors is the fact that IMS works directly with messages in queues. IMS uses similar technologies in its format and formatting management such as XML and XSL. The tagged message sent to the terminal by the formatter includes the format information. The tagged message in the queue is like an XML data/document that contains the semantic tags and a reference to the format such as a reference to an XSL formatting information.

Because of the persistent input/output message concept, a crash at any time leaves the input message in the request message in the input queue and everything else is backed out. Therefore, IMS never loses a request (as most other systems do). Once an input or request message is successfully put, it is not destroyed until the corresponding output message is successfully written. A successful write of the output message commits everything. Messages can be multi-segmented to achieve large messages, and not all message have to go to terminals or printers and use the formatting services.

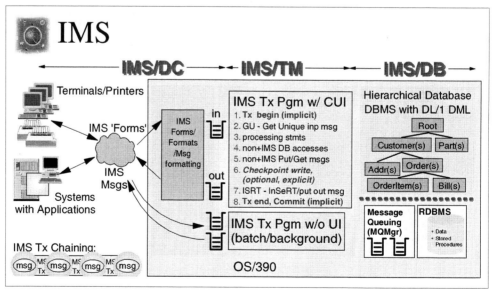

Figure 66. IMS transaction monitor

IMS chains programs over messages in queues, where with other TP Monitors, a call starts a program and passes the arguments in record format and queuing is not visible to the outside.

IMS Tx has to be chained with messages, but each of it is a single LUW. This leads a multi-screen online transaction to a construct, in which only the last one in the chain updates resources to rollback. The data is accumulated and handed over in the message (for background Tx) or in the scratch pad area (for terminal Tx).

IMS provides the Open Transaction Monitor Access (OTMA) interface and protocol to access IMS transaction program modules to participate in distributed LUWs. Any master resource manager coordinator or master sync point manager can control the LUW in an IMS TP Monitor, for example, a CORBA ORB through its OTS. It can also let other objects participate in an IMS transaction under the same LUW. EJBs can encapsulate or hide IMS transactions when WebSphere's Application Server Advanced and Enterprise Editions, with the built-in EJB server and CORBA-Java-compliant ORB, implement the mapping from IIOP to the OTMA protocol.

IBM Customer Information Control System

CICS is IBM's general-purpose online transaction processing (OLTP) software. It is a powerful application server that runs on a range of operating systems from the smallest desktop to the largest mainframe. It is flexible enough to meet your transaction-processing needs. For example, you may have thousands of terminals or a client/server environment with workstations and LANs exploiting modern technology such as graphical interfaces or multimedia. It takes care of the security and integrity of your data while looking after resource scheduling. It makes the most effective use of your resources. CICS seamlessly integrates all the basic software services required by OLTP applications. It also provides a business application server to meet information-processing needs of today and the future.

Each product in the CICS family is designed to run on a particular operating system and hardware platform. They have powerful functions to allow inter-product communication with other members of the CICS family. CICS provides a cost-effective and manageable transaction processing system. It allows you to write your own applications or choose from many existing vendor-written business products. CICS clients and gateways provide a lightweight, small footprint platform to easily access and control transactions running on CICS servers.

CICS/TXSeries features

Some of the features that are offered by CICS include:

- **Integrity**: Many transactions may access the same data at the same time. It is important that all transactions can complete successfully, without interfering with any other transaction. Changed data must be available immediately to all other transactions.

  An online transaction processing system can become quite complex, with a large number of concurrent users and a high volume of transactions. Despite this complexity, a transaction processing system must still allow users to share data and resources with full integrity.

- **Security**: Users must have security of access to the CICS system, with no one being able to sign on and run programs unless they are authorized to do so. Supervisors can assign authority for a user to run specific transactions and can restrict access to specific resources.

- **Recoverability**: In the event of an application or system failure (for example, if there is a power loss and the computer system shuts down), when the system restarts, any uncompleted work that was in progress at the time of shutdown, including changes to data, must be backed out to a point where the system was last in a consistent state.

- **Connectivity**: Transactions are generally invoked by online input and generate online output. To be online, the end user needs a terminal or workstation connected to a computer system. That system configuration could be:

  - A *standalone workstation*

  - A *local area network (LAN)*: A communication network offering a physical, hardwired connection to a group of users across a limited area. Separate LANs can be interconnected.

  - A *wide area network (WAN)*: Must consist of several LANs connected by telecommunication links.

- **Scalability and affordability**: Client/server technologies enable applications to be split and distributed to meet diverse business needs. The CICS family is growing all the time.

  Using members of the CICS family, you can execute transactions anywhere in the network. CICS programs can communicate with other programs on the same CICS system or on a remote system. They can also access data held remotely, elsewhere in the network. CICS gives you the opportunity to have the resources you need where you need them; you have the choice.

- **Portability**: With the CICS family, programming skills and programs are portable across the different platforms. The CICS application programming interface means that applications using a range of EXEC CICS commands can run on hardware ranging from workstations up to mainframes without needing a major change. It also means that existing programming skills can be used across multiple CICS platforms. CICS client APIs also allow applications to be ported across different client platforms.

CICS transaction

A typical OLTP transaction consists of many computing and data-access tasks to be executed in one or more machines. The tasks may include handling the user interface, data retrieval and modification, and communications. In CICS terms, these operations are grouped together as a unit of work or a *transaction*.

A transaction management system (sometimes called a *transaction monitor*) such as CICS:

- Handles the start, running, and completion of units of work for many concurrent users

- Enables the application (when started by an end-user) to run efficiently, to access a number of protected resources in a database or file system, and then to terminate, normally returning an output screen to the user

- Isolates many concurrent users from each other so that two users cannot update the same resource at the same time

In particular, CICS provides an easy-to-use application programming interface (API), EXECUTE CICS or EXEC CICS, which allows a rich set of services (including file access, scratchpad, and presentation services). This API is to be used in the application and ported to and from a wide variety of hardware and software platforms where CICS is available.

Communication mechanism in CICS

This section discusses the different interfaces and links in CICS. Table 25 shows the interfaces and links in CICS and a brief definition.

Table 25. Interface in CICS

Interface	Definition
LINK (Program Link)	CICS server link to a program on the same CICS
DPL (Distributed Program Link)	DPL enables an application program executing in one CICS system to link (pass control) to a program in a different CICS system. The linked-to program executes and returns a result to the linking program. This process is equivalent to remote procedure calls (RPCs). You can write applications that issue RPCs that can be received by members of the CICS family.
ECI (External Call Interface)	ECI enables a non-CICS application running on a workstation to call a CICS program located on the CICS server. To the called program, an ECI call is indistinguishable from a distributed program link call issued by a remote CICS application program. ECI is a flexible model for designing new client/server applications. The client logic that manages the presentation, graphical user interface (GUI), for example, is cleanly separated from the CICS server business logic.
EPI (External Presentation Interface)	EPI allows a non-CICS application running on a workstation to appear to the CICS server as one or more standard 3270 terminals. The application can, therefore, start CICS transactions and send and receive standard 3270 data streams to and from the transactions. EPI allows a workstation interface to be added to an existing CICS application, and appears as transaction routing at the server. The application can present the 3270 data to the user by emulating a 3270 terminal, or by using a GUI such as Presentation Manager.
EXCI (External CICS Interface)	Non-CICS application on OS/390 to call a CICS program

In a CICS client presentation program, even though you can implement updates of data that resides on the CICS client platform, it is not useful, because the data can never be part of a logical unit of work. Table 26 compares the CICS call types.

Table 26. Comparing CICS call types

Call type	Communication from:	Communication to:	Bi-directional/ recursive	Synchronous/ asynchronous
DPL	Full Function CICS System	Full function CICS system	Yes	Synchronous
ECI	CICS Client	Full function CICS system	No	Either
EPI	CICS Client	Full function CICS system	No	Synchronous

Call type	Communication from:	Communication to:	Bi-directional/ recursive	Synchronous/ asynchronous
EXCI	non-CICS, OS/390 subsystem (TSO, batch, IMS)	Full function CICS system	No	Synchronous

In a CICS client presentation environment, you may implement business logic. However, you would then use a server transaction program via ECI or EXCI to update the data.

Options for Web enabling CICS

As shown in Figure 67, there are four basic methods of Web enabling a CICS application. The following sections show the flow of each method, which is followed by a discussion of the advantages and disadvantages.

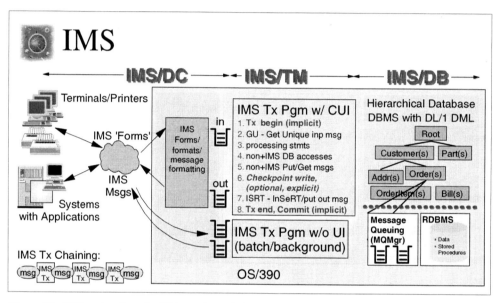

Figure 67. Different options for Web enabling CICS

CICS Web Support

CICS Web Support (formerly CICS Web Interface) offers three options to write DPL, called Web-aware CICS Transaction Programs:

- Native input form processing and native output HTML creation by the application.

- Use the Template Manager with HTML templates for input parsing and output formatting. Templates and input and output data include named tags for matching items. In modern terms, we would say: Data from the program is XML, the template includes the XSL, and the parsed or produced HTML form is the source or result. Note that the Template Manager is not strategic and kept for compatibility reasons.

- Use the Web APIs, which offer a rich set of functions built into CICS Web Support to parse the input form and to build the output HTML.

A Web server with the CICS Web server plug-in in a separate or the same system unloads CICS (and CICS OS/390) from processing HTTP requests and replies.

The plug-in connects to back-end CICS program modules by EXCI (see Figure 68).

We now show the flow of triggers/data through the Web enabled CICS application which uses the CICS Web Server plugin (see Figure 68).

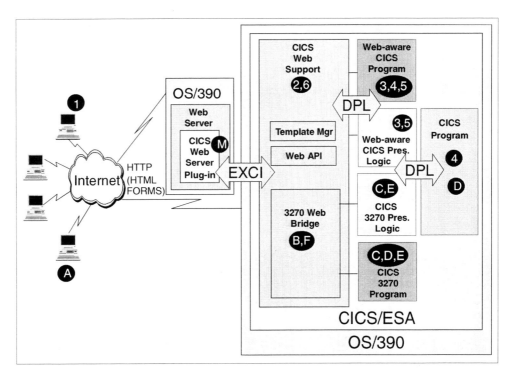

Figure 68. CICS Web support

The numbers and letters in Figure 68 are used to differentiate the flow through 3270 and DPL applications:

1/A A browser requests a URL from CICS Web Support using HTTP.

2/B The URL references a CICS program that is to be executed and a Web-aware program that "decodes" the request. The CICS Web Support starts the Web-aware program.

3/C The Web-aware program decodes the request (for example, it takes the input from the browser and formats it for the CICS program to be executed) and links to the CICS program.

4/D The CICS program processes the request and returns the reply to the Web-aware program.

5/E The Web-aware program encodes the request (for example, it takes the reply from the CICS program and puts it in HTML).

6/F CICS Web Support returns the HTML to the browser.

Note: Points 3, 4, 5 and C, D, E in a single oval indicate programs without separation into presentation, business, and data logic modules.

The advantages of this model are that:

• You can use existing enterprise server skills.
• It can support both 3270 and DPL applications.

- It can be used with no, little, or a lot of programming.
- It provides HTML Forms Document manipulation support.
- It offers SSL support.
- It is strategic.

The disadvantages of this method are that:

- It does not do much for the user interface without programming.
- Some programming is required for implementation.
- The application has to manage the state.
- There are no plain HTML pages from files (an extra server is required).

EXCI User Interface
As shown in Figure 69, EXCI is used for communicating with CICS applications.

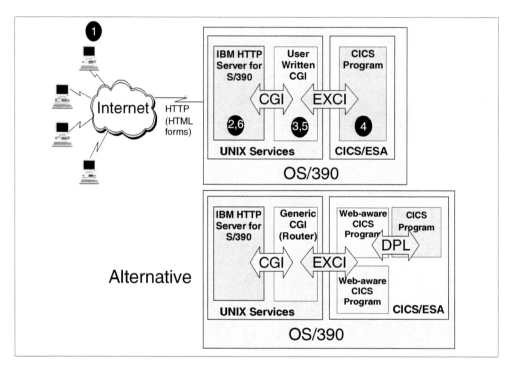

Figure 69. EXCI user interface

The flow of triggers and data through the model follow this sequence:

1. A browser requests a URL from the Web server – the IBM HTTP Server for S/390.

2. The URL references a CGI program that is started by the Web server.

3. The CGI program formats the input from the browser for the CICS program to be executed and links to the CICS program using the EXCI.

4. The CICS program processes the request and returns the reply to the CGI program.

5. The CGI program takes the reply from the CICS program and puts it into HTML.

6. The Web server returns the HTML to the browser.

The alternative part in Figure 69 shows a user-written, but generic CGI program, which works like a router. The logic in the CICS server is the same as described under CICS Web Support (Figure 68).

The advantages of using the EXCI interface are:

- No HTTP server is required for transactions.
- You can use existing Web skills.

The disadvantages are:

- The HTTP server works for plain HTML pages.
- Some programming is required for implementation.
- State management is required.

CICS Java Gateway

Servlets in the Web application server and Java applications on any system can use the CICS Java Gateway and the related Java Gateway, ECIRequest, and EPIRequest to communicate with CICS applications (see Figure 70).

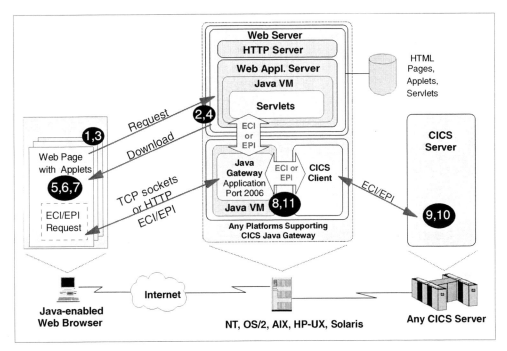

Figure 70. CICS Java gateway

The flow of the triggers and data through the model follow this sequence:

1. A browser requests an HTML page from the Web server using HTTP.

2. The server returns the HTML page that contains a tag identifying a Java applet.

3. The browser starts loading the applet and requesting related Java classes from the Web server.

4. The Web server returns Java gateway classes as requested.

5. As classes are returned, the Java applet starts.

6. In processing, the Java applet creates a Java gateway object to connect to the Java gateway using sockets.

7. The Java applet creates an ECIRequest or EPIRequest object and sends it to the gateway using the Java gateway flow method.

8. The gateway receives the request and makes a corresponding ECI or EPI call to the CICS client, which forwards the call to the CICS server.

9. The CICS server processes the call, including verifying the user ID and password if required, and passes control and user data to the application program.

10. After processing, the application returns control and data to CICS, which returns the requested data to the gateway through the CICS client.

11. The gateway returns the data to the Java applet.

The advantages of using the Java gateway are that it supports:

- *Security - security classes*: ECI can pass a user ID and password
- *State maintenance*: An applet maintains connection during LUW
- Protocols and connectivity
- Better performance
- Lightweight, multi-threaded, and never-ending gateway
- Application development
- Processing of an applet, servlet, or Java application

CICS access using MQSeries

CICS access via MQSeries is not limited to applets. Both applications and servlets can use the MQSeries Client for Java Classes to access an MQServer. The MQSeries Client for Java Classes uses the communication-over-listener approach to talk to any MQServer MQQueueManager in the TCP/IP network. Java applications and servlets can use the much faster MQSeries Language Bindings to access MQServer MQQueueManagers, if they run on the same system. Figure 71 shows the architecture model when using MQSeries with CICS.

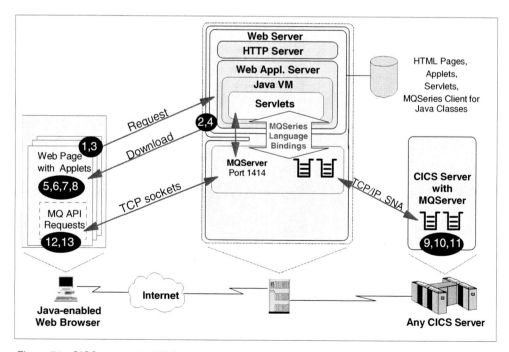

Figure 71. CICS access via MQSeries messages

The flow of the triggers and data through the model is outlined here:

1. A browser requests an HTML page from the Web server using HTTP.
2. The server returns the HTML page that contains a tag identifying a Java applet.
3. The browser starts loading the applet and requesting related Java classes from the Web server.
4. The Web server returns Java classes, including the MQSeries Client for Java Classes, as requested.
5. As classes are returned, the Java applet starts.
6. In processing, the Java applet connects to an MQSeries queue manager on the Web server using sockets.
7. The Java applet opens a queue and puts a request message.
8. The Java applet does a get on the queue and waits for a reply message.
9. The MQSeries queue manager on the Web server passes the request message to another MQSeries queue manager on the CICS server.
10. The arrival of that message triggers a CICS program that opens the queue, gets the message, processes the request, and puts a reply message on a queue.
11. The MQSeries queue manager on the CICS server passes the reply message to the MQSeries queue manager on the Web server.
12. The applet gets the reply message.
13. The applet closes the queue and disconnects from the MQSeries server.

The advantages of using MQSeries with CICS are:

- Loose Web to transaction coupling
- Platform flexibility as with Java

The disadvantages are:

- Additional subsystem and infrastructure to build, run, and maintain
- Applications are more difficult to debug
- Access to other back-end systems

Encina

Encina extends the power of Distributed Computing Environment (DCE) to simplify the construction of reliable distributed systems and provide the integrity guarantees required for business-critical computing. In addition, Encina is its own transaction monitor. It is also the "engine under the hood" for CICS on the non-OS/390 platforms. Encina's core technology is also "under the hood" of the IBM WebSphere Application Server container and Enterprise JavaBean Server.

Encina enables companies seeking industry-leading, enterprise-class distributed computing capabilities to develop and deploy three-tiered applications on a variety of platforms. The simplified security, transactional mainframe connectivity, scalable and resilient three-tiered infrastructure of Encina, as well as its distributed objects support (through Encina++) provide value-added services. Encina gives organizations a network computing environment that not only delivers reliable performance and data integrity, but that also can be tightly controlled.

To expand its object-oriented programming capabilities, Encina supports the Object Management Group's (OMG) Object Transaction Service (OTS) and the Object Concurrency Control Service (OCCS) on top of a commercial object request broker. This enhanced object support lets users develop C++ clients and servers, as well as Java clients, that work with the Orbix ORB.

The Encina architecture

The Encina product family is based on a modular, layered architecture (see Figure 72). It builds upon the basic services supplied by the OSF DCE, and extends DCE to provide a rich set of facilities for distributed transaction processing.

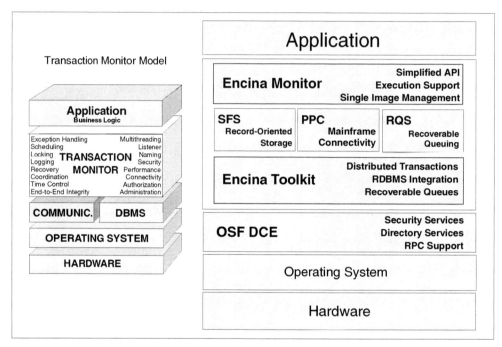

Figure 72. Encina components

At a high level, these facilities are divided into the Encina "toolkit". The toolkit implements the fundamental services for executing distributed transactions and managing recoverable data. They also offer various Encina extended services, which expand the functionality of the toolkit to provide a comprehensive environment for developing and deploying distributed transaction processing applications.

The lower layers of the Encina product family extend the DCE to form a "toolkit" of core technologies that enable client-server transaction processing and the management of recoverable data. The components that make up the Encina toolkit are:

- **Encina Base Services**: The Encina Base Services module provides services that permit a node to initiate, participate in, and commit distributed transactions. These services include:

  - *Transactional-C*: A high-level API that provides for transaction demarcation and concurrency management.

  - *Transactional RPC (TRPC)*: An extension of the DCE RPC that transparently ensures transactional integrity over distributed computations

Encina Base Services also supports nested transactions, which is a feature that provides failure containment and simplifies the application development task.

- **Encina Server Core**: Built upon Encina Base Services, the Encina Server Core provides facilities for managing recoverable data, for example, data that is accessed and updated transactionally. These facilities include a locking library to serialize data access, a recoverable storage system to allow transactions to roll back or roll forward after failures, and an X/Open XA interface to permit the use of XA-compliant resource managers (such as Oracle, Informix, Ingres, or Sybase).

The upper layers of the Encina product family provide extended services. The various Encina extended services build on the Encina toolkit to provide the higher-level facilities typically needed to develop and deploy distributed transaction processing applications. Current Encina extended services include (refer to Figure 72):

- **Encina Monitor**: The Encina Monitor is a full-featured transaction processing monitor that provides a powerful, reliable environment for the development, execution, and administration of distributed transaction processing applications. It allows application servers to be replicated to increase availability and performance, supports automatic load balancing and restart of failed application servers, and provides facilities to monitor and control Encina-based applications. The Encina Monitor can also do automatic authorization checking for security.

- **Encina Structured File Server (SFS)**: The Encina Structured File Server is a record-oriented file system that provides full transactional integrity, high performance, and log-based recovery for fast restarts. It is highly scalable to support very large databases. It is also fully capable of participating in two-phase commit protocols, to allow multiple SFS servers to be used in a single transaction. For increased availability, SFS supports online backup and restore.

- **Encina Recoverable Queuing Service (RQS)**: The Encina Recoverable Queuing Service enables the transactional enqueuing and dequeuing of data. This allows transactional tasks to be queued for later processing while ensuring that system failures do not result in lost information. RQS provides multiple levels of priority and readily scales to support large numbers of users and high volumes of data.

- **Encina PPC Executive**: The Encina PPC Executive supports transactional peer-to-peer communications using the CPI-C and CPI-RR application programming interfaces to provide LU6.2 connectivity over TCP/IP.

- **Encina PPC Gateway/SNA**: In conjunction with the Encina PPC Executive, the Encina PPC Gateway/SNA module provides transactional interoperability over an SNA protocol implementation of LU6.2. This allows Encina applications to ship or accept transactions from mainframe transaction processing systems that use LU6.2, such as IBM CICS, without requiring Encina software on the mainframe. The Encina PPC Gateway/SNA module is unique in its ability to deliver full two-phase commit from an open, distributed environment to the mainframe.

For distributed transactions, Encina selects a two-phase commit coordinator for the transaction. The coordinator is responsible for logging the commit/rollback status of the transaction. Whenever a participant in a transaction performs recovery, it must contact the coordinator to obtain the status of transactions that are undecided. Only the coordinator can determine the outcome of such transactions. For example, if a back-end database fails and is restarted, it contacts the TM-XA service for the outcome of in-doubt transactions. The TM-XA service contacts the transaction coordinator for such transactions and then informs the database of the transaction outcome. The database must then roll back the effects of aborted transactions.

Encina++

Encina++ is a set of C++ classes and language extensions that combine the benefits of objects with the production-quality distributed computing infrastructure of the Encina Monitor. Encina++ enables developers to leverage the power and flexibility of C++ when building Encina Monitor-based applications. Encina++ also enables organizations that are committed to an object-based strategy to begin developing business-critical distributed applications. It does this without many of the current compromises presented by popular alternatives such CORBA-compliant ORB products.

Organizations that use Encina++ can build sophisticated distributed applications more quickly, reduce total system complexity, take advantage of the Monitor's substantial systems management capabilities, and leverage the benefits of object-oriented design and programming. In fact, using Encina++ today enables companies to use distributed objects and lay the groundwork for future standards-based ORBs.

The Encina++ distributed object model

Encina++ client applications are written in C++ and can invoke methods on both local objects and remote server objects written in C++. Remote server objects are created by Encina Monitor application servers, using one of two mechanisms. *Static server objects* are created once and persist across requests from multiple clients. Server objects usually can also be created *dynamically* by application server-based *factories*. Factory-based server objects are created, used and destroyed by a single client. Static server objects and factories remain available to clients until the application server that started the server object or factory is shut down by the system administrator (see Figure 73).

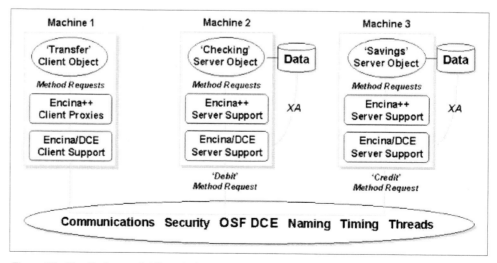

Figure 73. The Encina++ distributed object model

The interfaces to remote server objects and factories are specified by developers using the OSF DCE Interface Definition Language (IDL). In the case where the interface specifies transactional objects, developers use Transarc's Transactional IDL (now an X/Open standard), an extension of the DCE IDL that includes transactional keywords. The information contained in an interface's TIDL file includes the names of methods that can be invoked on remote objects, the parameters required and returned by each method, and an indication of whether a method is expected to be invoked as part of a transaction. Because the server object interfaces are defined in the DCE IDL or Encina TIDL, Encina++ servers can also be called by non-Encina++ clients using normal Transactional RPC calls. Encina++ also includes a utility program, called TIDL++, that automatically generates client-side proxy classes and server-side skeleton classes from IDL files.

Encina++ transaction models

Encina++ supports a transaction model that enables developers to group multiple method requests, on one or more server objects, into a logical unit of work. If a target server object invokes methods on any other server objects, the new servers join the transaction. Then, if any server object experiences any sort of exception, such as a database or network error, all updates performed by all methods in the transaction are automatically rolled back.

Transactions are created in Encina++ applications using one of two transaction demarcation interfaces: Transactional-C++ or a version of OMG's Object Transaction Service (OTS). Transactional-C++ is based on Encina's Transactional-C and provides a simple and intuitive way to structure transactions in C++. Encina++'s OTS support enables developers to construct transactions using the OMG standard. Both the implicit and explicit forms of the OTS transaction demarcation interface are supported.

As with standard Encina Monitor application servers, transactions in Encina++ server objects can include updates to all popular RDBMS systems, including any XA-compatible resource such as IBM's MQSeries and Encina's RQS or SFS. Transactions can also include calls that invoke mainframe applications. If any update in any resource fails, or an object signals an application error, all updates to all resources, including those done on the mainframe, are automatically rolled back by Encina's transaction manager.

Web enabling Encina

The explosive growth of the Internet has created a need for a product that allows access to Encina applications from the World Wide Web. The increasing use of PCs has created the need for an easy way to build PC clients using GUIs to access Encina applications without using DCE on the client PC. The DCE Encina Lightweight Client (DE-Light) product addresses these two needs.

As shown in Figure 74, DE-Light is a set of APIs and a gateway server that enable you to extend the power of the DCE and Encina to PCs and other systems not running as DCE clients. You can use DE-Light to build clients that require less overall effort to create compared to the standard DCE and Encina clients and still take advantage of the benefits of distributed transactions, security, load balancing, scalability, and server replication formerly restricted to full DCE and Encina clients. DE-Light clients use simplified RPCs to communicate with a DE-Light gateway. The clients do not use DCE for communication with the gateway. The gateway translates the simplified RPC into full DCE RPC or Encina

TRPC and communicates with DCE or Encina servers on behalf of the clients. The gateway also translates communications from these servers into responses for the clients, which completes the communications loop between the clients and servers.

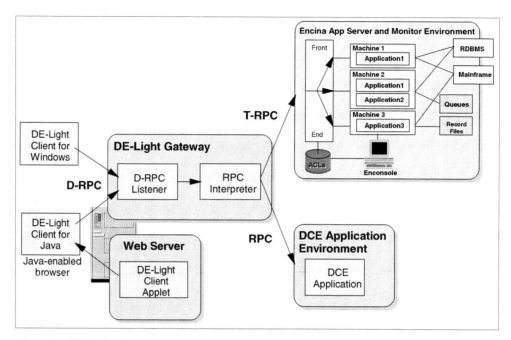

Figure 74. DE-Light client

The DE-Light package consists of three components:

- Gateway server
- C API
- Java API

The gateway server provides the RPC translation to the DE-Light clients. The two APIs provide a set of calls to be used by C and Java programs for accessing DCE and Encina servers through the simplified RPC.

TXSeries

IBM TXSeries is middleware designed to support and simplify transactional connections across increasingly diverse and complex networks. In addition to offering secure, cross-enterprise integration, TXSeries delivers the following features that are necessary for large scale transaction processing:

- **Scalability**: Whether customers are using the Internet as a platform for e-business or are looking to the latest technologies to expand internal networks into an extranet, most IT departments face the challenge of developing systems and applications that can handle unlimited, or at least, unknown numbers of clients. TXSeries is based on industry-proven technology that leverages replication and workload management to meet customers' needs – from managing thousands of clients to processing one billion transactions in 24 hours.

- **Availability**: Business-critical applications must be available 24 x 7. TXSeries incorporates replication, operational and runtime support, and online management capability to centrally administer multiple servers, eliminating single points of failure and ensuring that applications always are available.

- **Integrity**: System integrity is the cornerstone of a solid transaction processing foundation. In addition to delivering the well-known ACID properties (Atomicity, Consistency, Isolation, and Durability), TXSeries offers functionality to eliminate bottlenecks and failure points. It enables fast commit processing for transactional integrity across heterogeneous servers.

- **Longevity**: IBM is committed to being a Business Partner with its customers. As a result, maximizing customers' return on their investment is a core aspect of any IBM solution. To ensure the longevity of transactional applications, TXSeries focuses on two aspects of leveraging applications:

  - Enabling existing applications to be extended to meet new business goals, such as bringing mainframe applications to the Web

  - Allowing new applications to use information and services from existing applications

- **Security**: Security is a fundamental requirement for any transactional system, regardless of its deployment. Through IBM DSSeries, TXSeries provides the most comprehensive security that leverages both Kerberos and public key technology with authentication control, authorization control, session security and Web security. Since TXSeries incorporates these vital security features, it eliminates the need for programmers to develop large amounts of code.

TXSeries is IBM's transactional middleware solution for UNIX and Windows NT platforms. It is the evolution of IBM Transaction Server. It brings together and extends the functionality and offering all of the capabilities of the Transaction Server, CICS, and Encina. Like Transaction Server, TXSeries offers multiple programming models and related TP Monitors with a common infrastructure. In addition to enhancements to the transaction monitors and inclusion of the appropriate infrastructure servers (DSSeries Servers), TXSeries includes a connectivity suite for e-business and messaging to further extend TXSeries application connectivity. It also provides all the tools necessary to deliver highly secure and scalable e-business solutions.

In addition to the core transactional services and infrastructure, TXSeries' connectivity suite for e-business and messaging includes:

- CICS and Encina clients
- CICS and Encina servers
- DE-Light Client and Gateway
- CICS Transaction Gateway

3.2.3 Manage

When you transform your business into an e-business, you need the same level of security and management you have enjoyed within the walls of the enterprise. IBM Tivoli security products (formerly known as *Tivoli SecureWay*) provide integrated directory, connectivity, and security between users and applications for e-business in a networked world. To manage the availability and performance of your e-business solution, IBM has extended the Tivoli family to manage your entire environment (refer to Figure 75), from systems and network management all the way through application management.

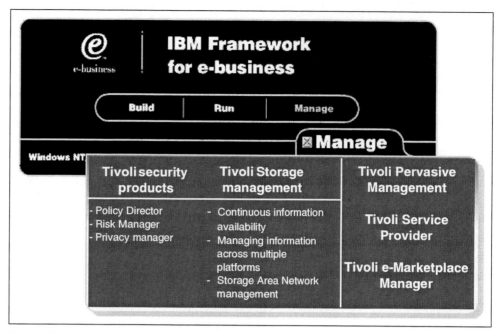

Figure 75. Secure network and management software

3.2.3.1 Tivoli security products

Tivoli security products provide a comprehensive and scalable solution for centralized security management and access control. Figure 76 shows the products in the Tivoli security product family that are part of the Tivoli security products solution.

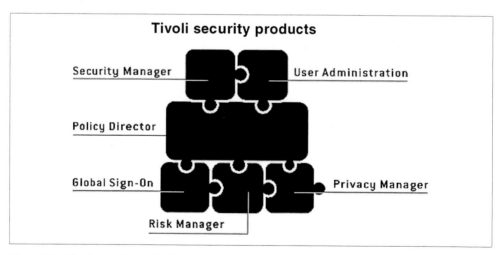

Figure 76. Tivoli security product family

Tivoli security products remove many of the security barriers to fully exploiting e-business by:

- Enabling companies to quickly deploy secure e-business applications
- Allowing consistent enforcement of security and privacy policies
- Providing centralized enterprise risk management
- Simplifying security administration

Tivoli security products provide a single interface for maintaining security profiles and policies across heterogeneous systems in mainframe, distributed, and desktop environments. This allows e-businesses to decrease their costs while increasing productivity and customer satisfaction.

Tivoli Policy Director

Tivoli Policy Director provides authentication and access-control services for Web resources. It manages access to all your Web servers, regardless of their platforms. This allows you to centrally control your Web resources as a single, logical Web space. By performing intelligent load balancing over replicated servers, Tivoli Policy Director lets your organization scale its deployment of servers without increasing management overhead. It also provides a failover capability, which allows Tivoli Policy Director to automatically switch to a backup Web server.

Tivoli Policy Director supports authentication and access control for Web browser users through user IDs and passwords, client-side certificates, or RSA SecurID tokens. It can also provide authentication and access control for users of pervasive devices, such as Web-enabled wireless phones.

Tivoli Policy Director enables you to implement flexible, step-up authentication for environments that need to address multiple levels of trust.

Tivoli Policy Director provides single sign-on access to the Web servers it secures. Users simply log on once to Tivoli Policy Director, and subsequent logons are handled transparently.

Tivoli Policy Director for MQSeries

This is a comprehensive security solution for IBM MQSeries. It enables MQSeries-based applications to communicate securely across a variety of platforms. This scalable, high-performance solution provides access control to govern which applications or users of those applications can put or get messages to specific queues. It also allows MQSeries applications to exchange data with a guarantee of message integrity and confidentiality by using public encryption keys associated with those applications. These services are provided transparently to MQSeries applications.

Tivoli User Administration

Ensuring consistent user access, while safeguarding corporate information assets, is the system manager's biggest juggling act in an enterprise. Tivoli User Administration, one of Tivoli's core applications for security management, provides an automated, secure way to manage user attributes and user services across heterogeneous, distributed networks. Designed to give your IT staff centralized control, Tivoli User Administration features several breakthrough management concepts:

- Policy-based management
- Management by subscription
- Secure delegation
- A platform-independent interface

These capabilities give you an unparalleled level of control and security and greatly improve the productivity of your administrators. Table 27 shows the features of, and advantages of using, Tivoli User Administration.

Table 27. Tivoli User Administration features

Feature	What it does	What it means to you
Single-action management	Allows you to create, modify, and delete users across platforms with a single tool in a single action	Requires fewer administrators, creates fewer mistakes, and provides a faster process
Secure delegation of authority	Enables a senior administrator to centrally define user-account policies, then delegate activities to junior administrators	Leverages best practices and knowledge
Scalability	Enables you to manage every user account in the enterprise from a single point	Requires fewer administrators, and enables you to consolidate help-desk activities
Integration with Tivoli Software Distribution and other applications	Enables you to manage everything a user needs (software, system, etc.) from a single point=	Automates and streamlines a user setup process (define accounts, deploy software, set up monitoring—all with a task-driven approach)
Integration with Tivoli Security Manager	Provides an integrated product suite (although neither product is a prerequisite)	Simplifies enterprise-security management

Tivoli Risk Manager

Tivoli Risk Management enables you to manage external and internal threats throughout the enterprise. For the first time, customers can proactively address vulnerabilities and exposures in an enterprise context by harnessing the intelligence across the different security checkpoints to gain knowledge and insight into the root cause of these problems and use decision support to quickly upgrade their security policies.

Tivoli Risk Manager provides the following benefits to your enterprise:

- Provides a simple, easy-to-use enterprise security console to monitor, view, and manage alert events across the enterprise.

- Provides a common data format and naming convention for alerts using Intrusion Detection Exchange Format (IDEF), a draft IETF specification, and a Common Vulnerability and Exposure (CVE) standard.

- Provides an out-of-the-box solution for integrated management of the perimeter security (demilitarized zone) in the customer's e-business environment.

- Leverages advanced correlation techniques to reduce, aggregate, correlate, and classify the thousands of individual security alerts into severity categories that can be administered and answered. Eliminates clutter, such as false-positive alerts, and quickly identifies real security threats to help speed response time.

- Provides decision support using an analytical and Web-based historical reporting decision support guide. Security administrators can apply decisions to gain insight into patterns of intrusions, systems and network usage, and compliance with security policies using graphs, charts, and trend analysis techniques to pinpoint vulnerable hotspots.

- Provides a variety of predefined reaction tasks to quickly resolve urgent security issues, such as denial of service attacks, viruses, or unauthorized access. Predefined tasks include reconfiguring a firewall, revoking user accounts on servers, or deleting viruses from a desktop.

- Leverages integration with the full range of Tivoli network, system, and security management products to take long-term corrective actions and constantly improve enterprise security policies.

- Integrates with multivendor security technology products to provide comprehensive security management. The Tivoli Risk Manager Integration Toolkit enables you and your business partners to add new technology endpoints to Tivoli Risk Manager.

- Includes optional intrusion detection, developed by Tivoli in collaboration with IBM research. Components include a powerful, low-overhead network intrusion detection system that detects more than 200 known attacks and a Web intrusion detection system that detects attacks launched using HTTP or SSL (HTTPS) against Web servers.

Tivoli Privacy Manager

Managing e-business is often considered a risky proposition because of the constant threat that information collected will be illegally accessed in ways unknown and unapproved by consumers. New regulations and lack of consumer confidence are pressuring companies to address the e-business privacy issue. Any company involved in e-business faces the challenge of preserving consumer privacy and maintaining the integrity of consumer information in a diverse enterprise. The need to protect privacy, alleviate consumer concerns about e-business, and avoid legal action based on privacy invasion requires a cost-effective, efficient way to centralize the administration of privacy policies and control access to personally identifiable data.

Tivoli Privacy Manager supports these capabilities:

- Centralizes administration of privacy policies to help enforce access to personal data so that consumer trust and brand integrity are protected

- Pre-defines privacy roles and categories of data or e-commerce to save implementation time and simplify access administration

- Allows you to modify pre-defined roles and categories through its flexible, scalable architecture

- Supports dynamic roles to enable access decisions based on the relationship between the requestor and the subject of the data

- Leverages Tivoli Policy Director standards-based authorization services to keep access control consistent across the entire enterprise

Tivoli Security Manager

Managing today's multi-platform, multi-vendor enterprise represents a serious challenge. To confront this challenge, IT departments must thoroughly understand each platform¦s security requirements, monitor systems constantly, apply vendor patches to newly discovered security holes, and continually edit configuration files. Traditional security tools rarely integrate with each other and are insufficient for today's geographically dispersed, diverse environments.

Tivoli Security Manager supports these features:

- Provides an open solution for role-based distributed and OS/390 access-control management

- Enables you to enforce a security policy consistently across multiple platforms with a single security model

- Reduces administrative overhead by integrating with other security-management solutions as part of a larger IT management strategy

Tivoli Security Manager is the most comprehensive solution for actively preventing unauthorized access to your systems. This solution includes a security engine for UNIX servers in addition to the Tivoli Security Manager functions and productivity tools. The UNIX component, Tivoli Access Control Facility (TACF), finally solves the UNIX root-user problem and provides an innovative architecture that is consistent with the IBM RACF solution for OS/390.

Tivoli Security Manager also provides flexible auditing capabilities and allows you to focus auditing on particular groups or resources. By taking care of the details, Tivoli Security Manager lets you focus on security priorities, including enterprise-security policy and the protection of business resources. Table 28 shows the features of Tivoli Security Manager and the advantages of using it.

Table 28. Features and advantages of Tivoli Security Manager

Feature	What it does	What it means to you
Comprehensive security policy	Enables implementation of consistent security policy across an enterprise using a role-based security model.	Helps you proactively prevent security breaches across your enterprise.
Centralized security management	Provides role-based security administration from central location.	Increases the availability and integrity of systems, and produces a complete security audit trail.
Enhanced network security	Protects files to ensure Internet security; provides login restrictions; and prevents abuse of UNIX root ID by partitioning root privilege.	Significantly reduces or eliminates many user-access problems.
Enhanced network management	Integrates with Tivoli applications using consistent user interface: Tivoli User Administration, Tivoli Enterprise Console, and Tivoli Distributed Monitoring.	Integrates seamlessly with other critical enterprise-management tools and automates many tasks.
Simplified installation and maintenance	Requires no OS kernel modifications. Allows simple installation for all supported platforms.	Ensures quicker realization of benefits and more efficient use of time and personnel.
Extended native security	Manipulates native security on most platforms. UNIX security enhanced with permission database on each UNIX server.	Protects investments in native security products, such as RACF and Windows NT.

Tivoli Global Sign-On
This provides a highly secure solution that gives users seamless access to resources, reduces corporate security risks and reduces help-desk costs associated with password management. By using Tivoli User Administration to manage Tivoli Global Sign-On information, companies have a powerful solution for administering and managing access to resources from a single administrative interface.

Tivoli Public Key Infrastructure
Tivoli Public Key Infrastructure is a highly customizable public key infrastructure (PKI) solution that manages digital certificates for e-business. At the heart of this solution is a Web-based enrollment and approver framework that lets you tailor the certificate registration process according to existing business processes. Its powerful workflow features allow you to integrate online enrollment with legacy and Web applications in less time and by using established Web development methods. This way, you can quickly deploy digital certificates according to your secure Internet application requirements without having to train developers on specific vendor APIs.

Tivoli FirstSecure
Tivoli FirstSecure is an integrated security solution comprised of interoperable components that can help companies secure all aspects of networking via the Web and other networks. The unique advantage of this solution is the integration of core security technologies with Tivoli Policy Director, which defines and implements policy across security components.

The components of Tivoli FirstSecure include:

- **Tivoli Policy Director**: Allows for the update or modification of security policy without having to use various product-specific configuration consoles.

- **IBM Boundary Server**: Provides protection for Internet-based business transactions through the use of firewall, virtual private networking, and content-filtering technologies. This solution includes:
    - IBM Firewall
    - IBM Network Security Auditor
    - Content Technologies MIMEsweeper
    - Finjan SurfinGate
    - RSA ACE/Server
    - SecurID tokens

- **Tivoli Public Key Infrastructure**: Enables e-business by providing registration and certification that shields data and transactions against unauthorized access.

- **Intrusion Immunity**: Provides proactive protection and detection against a broad range of security exposures through the use of Symantec Norton AntiVirus to address viral attacks.

- **IBM SecureWay Toolbox**: Protects your data and its integrity, as well as access to your files and data.

3.2.3.2 Tivoli Storage Management Solutions
Tivoli offers a centralized storage solution that enables IT organizations to deploy, access, share and protect mission-critical business information in the SAN, WAN, and LAN environments.

Tivoli Storage Management Solutions

There are several Tivoli products in this arena:

- **Tivoli Storage Manager**

  Tivoli Storage Manager is a full-function storage software product that addresses the challenges of complex storage management across distributed environments. It protects and manages a broad range of data, from the workstation to the corporate server environment. More than 39 different operating platforms are supported–all include a consistent GUI. Tivoli Storage Manager provides:

  - Centralized administration for data and storage management

  - Efficient management of information growth

  - High-speed automated server recovery

  - Full compatibility with hundreds of storage devices, as well as local area network (LAN), wide area network (WAN), and emerging storage area network (SAN) infrastructures

  - Customized backup solutions for major groupware, enterprise resource planning (ERP) applications, and database products

- **Tivoli Space Manager**

  Tivoli Space Manager facilitates enterprise-wide storage management deployment, helping improve administrator productivity and providing virtually unlimited disk storage. Tivoli Space Manager uses hierarchical storage management (HSM) to automatically and transparently migrate infrequently accessed files to Tivoli Storage Manager server while more frequently used files remain in local file systems for fast access. By migrating rarely accessed files to server storage, Tivoli Space Manager frees administrators and users from manual file-system pruning tasks.

  It also helps ensure sufficient storage space is available at your workstation or file server-deferring the purchase of additional disk storage. Tivoli Space Manager:

  - Provides enterprise-wide, scalable storage management
  - Migrates rarely accessed files without administrator help
  - Integrates and coordinates with Tivoli Storage Manager automatically
  - Provides quick retrieval of current and archived data

- **Tivoli Disaster Recovery Manager**

  Most organizations agree that backing up data is a critical part of business continuance. Without the proper safeguards, an equipment malfunction or physical catastrophe can cause mission-critical data to be lost. To complicate matters, data protection has become a more difficult task as information is more widely distributed-geographically and organizationally. In the flurry of activity following a disaster, when operational chaos can make key storage management decisions more complex, you cannot afford to worry about these issues. An airtight, organized roadmap to fast recovery must be in place.

  Tivoli Disaster Recovery Manager can ensure recovery and help an enterprise function and operate quickly. Tivoli Disaster Recovery Manager helps you maintain business continuance by:

  - Managing server databases and storage pool backup volumes
  - Establishing a thorough disaster recovery plan

– Tracking and reporting systems destroyed, in the event of a disaster
– Automating vital recovery steps to bring your business back to normal
– Performing restores in order of priority

Tivoli Storage Area Network Solutions

Tivoli Storage Area Network (SAN) Solutions provide a comprehensive open systems SAN solution built upon a scalable architecture to allow customers to cost effectively manage new and emerging SAN technologies. As shown in Figure 77, Tivoli's SAN Solutions enable customers to fully exploit even the most complex SAN configurations, by offering the SAN management and exploitation capabilities to deploy, allocate, maintain, protect, and share SAN resources.

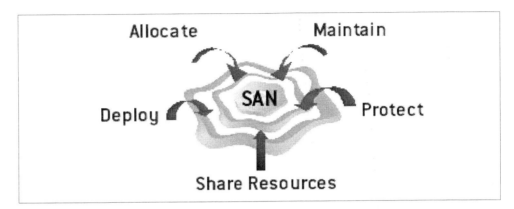

Figure 77. Tivoli Storage Area Network Solutions

Tivoli has established itself as a leader in the SAN environment by offering the following state-of-the-art SAN software products:

- **Tivoli Storage Network Manager**

  Tivoli Storage Network Manager is a comprehensive ANSI standards-based solution that manages storage area network infrastructures and their associated storage resources. This unique solution discovers, monitors, and manages SAN components while automating and allocating attached disk resources. It is built upon an architecture that can scale to handle very large and complex configurations. Tivoli Storage Network Manager provides features to manage SAN topology, assign available disk resources to managed hosts, and automatically extend file systems using administrator-defined policies.

  Tivoli Storage Network Manager moves beyond the traditional industry definition of SAN management, in which management functions are typically made available through fibre channel (FC) switch vendor interfaces. Although these functions are necessary, Tivoli Storage Network Manager provides additional functionality by enabling you to more effectively use existing and new SAN resources.

  With Tivoli Storage Network Manager, you can:

  – Monitor the SAN for problem identification and resolution techniques to assist in maintaining the SAN infrastructure for continuous application availability

  – Identify and allocate heterogeneous disk storage resources using logical unit numbers (LUNs) for a simple, secure, and efficient method of assigning resources to host systems

- Monitor file systems to automatically assign and extend additional disk resources to maintain continuous application processing while reducing administrative workload and costs

- **Tivoli SANergy**

  With Tivoli SANergy, customers can efficiently centralize their storage resources for reduced administration overhead, improved performance, and greater ROI. Tivoli SANergy enables users implementing storage area networks (SANs) to transparently share access to common storage, volumes, and files. Storage resources can be shared across UNIX, Microsoft Windows NT, and Apple Macintosh systems at the volume, file, and byte level with increased throughput and lower overhead than server-based sharing. The resulting high-performance shared storage environment can significantly reduce IT costs by consolidating storage space and eliminating the replicated data common to multihost environments.

  Tivoli SANergy helps you reach your full SAN potential because it can:

  - Simplify SAN storage centralization and administration through the power of heterogeneous sharing at the volume, file, and byte level

  - Extend industry-standard networking to utilize the high bandwidth of any SAN media, including Fibre Channel, SCSI, SSA, iSCSI, and InfiniBand

  - Enable storage centralization without the performance-limiting overhead of server-based file sharing

  - Increase data availability by eliminating the single-point-of-failure potential of server-based sharing

  - Reduce the total amount of storage required in a SAN by eliminating redundant or replicated data

  - Reduce the number of disk volumes required in a SAN and improve the efficient deployment of unused space

  - Increase the server-to-storage scalability ratio, eliminating the expense and bottleneck of dedicated file servers

  - Use industry-standard file systems and SAN and local area network protocols

  - Work with almost any SAN and LAN product, regardless of hardware and software

3.2.4 Pervasive computing

Pervasive computing is a series of technologies that enable people to accomplish personal and professional tasks typically using a new class of portable, intelligent device. Technologies in pervasive computing are still under development, and this field is growing at a very swift rate. It gives people convenient access to information that is relevant to them at the time, whenever and wherever they are, with appropriate levels of security. The key feature of these devices is that they provide usability that is comparable to everyday devices such as telephones or domestic appliances. Meanwhile, they still allow users access to the information that they need, typically provided by today's e-business solutions over increasingly intelligent networks.

The new pervasive computing paradigm enables a single user to use multiple clients connected to multiple servers in the network (see Figure 78) and to do so in a consistent and natural manner. The pervasive computing model is enabled by the introduction of a connectivity services (that is, gateway and proxy server) between the clients and the servers. It is also enabled by the introduction of content formats that can be rendered on the diverse range of client devices.

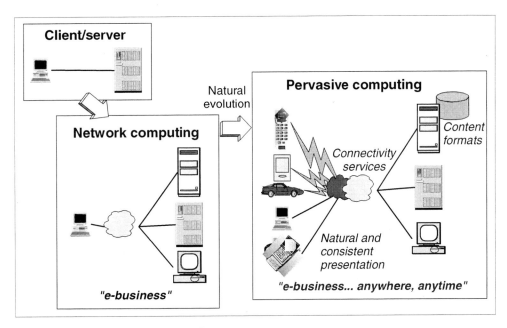

Figure 78. Pervasive computing paradigm

This new model is a logical evolution of the movement from client/server (which supported a client connected to a single server) to network computing (which supported a client connected to multiple servers in the network). Pervasive computing enables e-business anywhere, anytime.

Figure 79 shows the end-to-end view of the technical elements of pervasive computing. This includes connectivity services, content format definitions, and an application model.

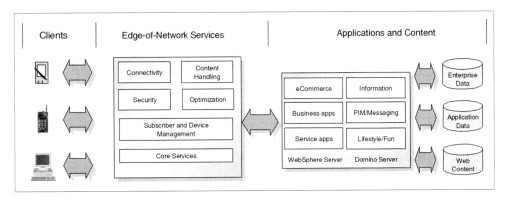

Figure 79. Architectural elements

The elements of the architecture are:

* The components that reside on the client devices

* The components that reside on the network as connectivity services, that is the gateways and proxy servers

- Server-based components that execute application logic and provide application data, and components that support the management and infrastructure for the devices, network, and applications

- Tools that support the development and deployment of pervasive computing solutions

The pervasive computing model exploits the ideas of e-business design, including a lightweight browser-based client, moving computation to the server, and the use of existing and emerging Internet standards (for example, HTML, TCP/IP, and Java). It also borrows heavily from the common architecture evident in current industry technologies, for example, Wireless Application Protocol, and existing products. It leverages Internet standards to remain consistent with the tools and technologies used for mainstream Internet development and to achieve portability of both applications and data across the diverse and evolving device types. IBM has a number of independent activities underway that are targeted to particular customer segments in the pervasive computing space. This architecture incorporates those efforts, as well as other IBM technologies, especially those addressing Internet enablement and wireless access.

3.2.4.1 WebSphere Everyplace Suite (WES)

As the name suggests, this is not a single product, but rather an integrated suite of existing products. IBM WebSphere Everyplace Suite provides the functionality necessary to enable both network access, applications, and content serving to multiple device types. It also provides the functionality to extend e-business applications to the new classes of pervasive computing devices discussed previously, including WAP phones, Personal Device Assistant (PDA), Internet appliances and screenphones in addition to the large installed base of Internet browsers.

The pervasive computing model extends the availability of e-content, e-commerce, and e-collaboration services from traditional desktop users to the users of a broad class of devices ranging from mobile phones to digital assistants to automobiles.

Everyplace Suite is not part of the infrastructure that comprises those business applications and data, but rather it provides the infrastructure to enable many different devices to access those applications and data via networks. WES has become the primary platform for IBM to provide the following services:

- Connectivity
- Content handling
- Security
- Optimization
- Subscriber and device management
- Base services

If we examine these abstract functional areas in more detail, we can see more detailed functionality contained within each of them. Refer to Figure 80 for a description of the technologies that are contained within each major functional area.

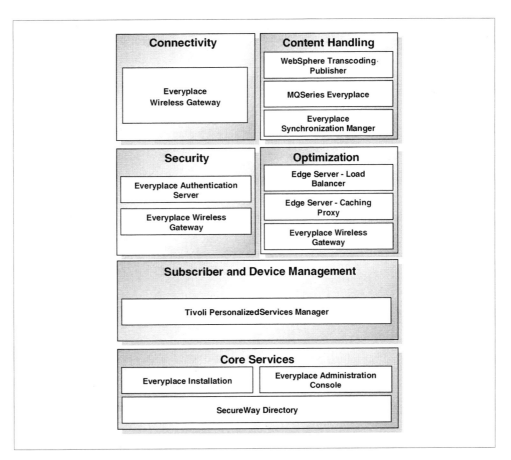

Figure 80. WebSphere Everyplace Suite infrastructure

3.2.4.2 Mobile e-business products

In addition to WES, IBM has an array of other products for extending the reach of e-business applications, enterprise data, and Internet content into the realm of pervasive computing:

- Domino Everyplace Quick Start
- Secureway Wireless Software
- eNetwork Web Express/Emulator Express
- IBM Mobile Connect

Domino Everyplace Quick Start

In today's increasingly mobile business environment, providing travelling users with access to strategic corporate information while on the move gives companies the edge they need to stay ahead of their competitors. The most critical resource required by the mobile worker is normally their collaborative environment: their e-mail, corporate directory, shared calendar and to do list, and the informal workflow processes built on their messaging infrastructure. The Domino Everyplace Quick Start solution responds to this need by providing employees with access the corporate directory, and their mail, calendars and to do items, allowing them to use Lotus Domino anytime, anywhere on any WAP device. Beyond that, Domino Everyplace Quick Start can be used to provide access to existing or new Domino applications from a mobile phone, allowing the enterprise to extend its value far beyond basic collaborative applications. It can provide mobile users with access to a Domino-based line of business applications, enterprise data (through the Enterprise Integration capabilities of Domino), and even other enterprise WAP applications (through its integrated WAP Gateway).

Domino Everyplace Quick Start includes:

- A WAP connector for Domino databases
- Integration to users' mail databases and the Domino Directory
- Installation Services for the complete package
- Mobile Notes Client Access Licenses for 100 users
- One year of maintenance on all software components
- A WAP Gateway (may be omitted if a Wireless Operator WAP Gateway used)
- Mobile Services for Domino for SMS support (as an optional component)

It may optionally also include the following add-on components:

- A 56-bit or 128-bit Security Pack for over the air encryption
- An IMAP4/SMTP client for WAP
- Mobile Services for Domino to provide SMS support
- WAP Sametime support

The solution is designed to deliver the application software you need to get an initial pilot group of up to one hundred users accessing their e-mail, calendar and corporate directory (excluding all hardware).

Secureway Wireless Software

IBM SecureWay Wireless Gateway and Client extend IP connectivity across a diverse set of wireless and wireline networks to enable TCP/IP applications to seamlessly access enterprise networks. SecureWay Wireless Gateway and Client, sometimes referred to as middleware, are components of SecureWay Wireless Software. These components work together to provide security for communications and improve the performance for mobile computing applications. The SecureWay Wireless Client supports the mobile worker who needs real-time access to the same information that is available in the office.

SecureWay Wireless Client resides on a user's mobile PC or handheld device and communicates with the Wireless Gateway over any IP-based connection, including wireless or dial-up networks. SecureWay Wireless Gateway integrates the mobile networks and provides the connection to the enterprise network.

Mobile users can use the same Wireless Gateway and access the same enterprise applications. SecureWay Wireless Gateway also enables mobile users to connect to multiple applications, as they can do using desktop computers within the enterprise network.

eNetwork Web Express/Emulator Express

eNetwork Web Express is designed for organizations that use the Web to distribute information or applications to mobile users through Internet services or corporate intranets. It provides affordable and seamless integration of standard network applications for wireless use, without complex reprogramming.

The features of eNetwork Web Express are:

- Operating with leading Web browsers, it can significantly reduce network traffic and improve response time of data transfers, making wireless Internet connectivity cost-effective.

- It features a disconnect mode, in which mobile users work offline before sending, therefore, minimizing network connection charges.

- In addition to wireless access, it works over standard telephone lines.

eNetwork Emulator Express extends your existing 3270 and 5250 applications to mobile employees over wireless networks. The eNetwork Emulator Express Client resides on the mobile device with a TN3270 or TN5250 emulator (such as IBM eNetwork Personal Communications) where it communicates over a local TCP/IP connection. It also communicates using TCP/IP with a remote eNetwork Emulator Express Server, which in turn, communicates with a Telnet server, such as IBM eNetwork Communications Server.

The eNetwork Emulator Express Client and Server work together to lower connection costs by significantly reducing the amount of data sent over the network. Therefore, performance over wireless or low bandwidth wireline connections may improve.

Mobile users can run existing IP-based wireline network applications over leading international data packet radio, analog and digital cellular and wireline networks with a single interface. eNetwork Emulator Express communicates over any IP connection, including the IBM SecureWay Wireless Gateway and Client.

The features of eNetwork Emulator Express are:

- **Differencing and caching**: This improves performance by not sending static data that is not updated between screen changes.

- **Data compression**: After applying differencing and caching, the data is compressed

- **Protocol reduction**: Because of the unique relationship between the eNetwork Emulator Express Server and Client, the standard Telnet connection protocols can be reduced by more than 50 percent.

IBM Mobile Connect

IBM Mobile Connect 2.5 is a pervasive computing technology solution that helps enable handheld devices, such as IBM WorkPads, Palm, EPOC, and Windows CE devices, to be integrated into Enterprise Solutions.

Mobile Connect allows organizations to directly transfer information from multiple handheld devices directly to corporate systems, without needing to synchronize via the PC. It enables two-way relational database synchronization, two-way file transfer, and the remote installation of applications. IBM Mobile Connect also supports direct synchronization with Lotus Notes and Microsoft Exchange for server-based synchronization of e-mail, calendars, contacts, and tasks.

Mobile Connect also supports IBM DB2 Everyplace and Palm personal information manager (PIM) applications. DB2 Everyplace includes the DB2 relational database engine and a set of APIs that allow developers to take advantage of DB2 on these platforms. IBM Mobile Connect provides the support for synchronizing relation database information between DB2 Everyplace and a server or mainframe relational database.

All of these transfers are supported over any networking infrastructure that supports IP, such as Wireless GSM, Internet, as well as standard LAN and WAN. Additionally, the product uses a Visual Basic (VB) scripting engine that enables a company to "plug" its core business logic components directly into their server. Events handled by these components can then be triggered automatically by the captured data that is being transmitted from the remote hand-held devices.

For example, consider a nurse practitioner. Visiting nursing professionals need to keep a great deal of information (appointment schedules, driving directions, client medical histories, etc.) with them at all times. During home visits, nurses input patients' vitals into their PDAs and synchronize them with the hospital's server. Medical files are accurately updated instantly without returning to the hospital or re-entering data.

Chapter 4. Security

In the traditional environment, transactions are carried out face to face. There is an implied security there because the parties involved can perform a verification of each other via business credentials, driver's license, and so forth.

In e-business, you still need to perform the traditional tasks, but you need to do things differently (for example, you can't identify and authenticate a person by looking at a driver's license). The electronic environment requires the same level of security but requires some different techniques. The e-business security challenge is to recognize the parties in the transaction and protect the databases, applications, and objects of the organization.

This chapter discusses security in e-business applications. It discusses the principles of cryptography and explains three main cryptographic methods:

- **Symmetric (secret) key cryptography**: A single key is used to encrypt and decrypt information.

- **Asymmetric (public) key cryptography**: Two keys are used, one for encryption, the other for decryption.

- **One-way functions**: Information is encrypted to produce a "signature" of the original information that can be used later to prove its integrity.

The discussion also covers the products used in IBM Framework for e-business to provide security and management of your e-business:

- **Tivoli security products**: Provides an integrated security solution that will assure continuity of service for Web and legacy applications with a single centralized management point.

- **WebSphere Application Server**: Provides authentication and authorization of your applications down to the method level of your servlets. It can use Lightweight Directory Access Protocol (LDAP) and Lightweight Third Party Access (LTPA).

4.1 Security for e-business

Implementing and managing a secure e-business environment is one of the most challenging tasks today. The basic approach of implementing firewalls is extended widely to allow access to your enterprise on a more fine-grained basis. Sophisticated use of digital signature (certificates) and other authentication and authorization mechanisms have to be included in the enterprise security architecture.

Enabling security means enabling e-business, because users, customers, and companies want to be sure that their data (for example, credit card number, and other personal data) cannot be corrupted or misused by unauthorized people. Therefore, it is essential in running an e-business that you focus on centralized authentication and authorization. To enable e-business, you have to build a "chain of trust" and let everybody know about it.

As time matters, you have to provide a quick, but highly secure, solution. That means, you need to integrate your existing applications into a secure environment without changing your applications in order to participate in the security gain.

One of the fundamental components of e-business is the ability for employees and customers to work with a company's resources over the Internet. As these new business practices emerge, most enterprises are finding that their existing security infrastructure is not capable of meeting the rapidly changing and more rigorous demands of doing business over the Internet. The demands of network security have gone far beyond simply managing user accounts and restricting access between internal and external networks to electronic mail and Web traffic. These demands now require a sophisticated system that allows fine-grained access control to resources, yet that is manageable enough to be tailored to protect systems from many types of security threats.

It is important to adopt a systematic approach to security. One of the major concerns that emerges with security solutions is the overall complexity and cost. In fact, the following inhibitors to deploying security solutions are frequently mentioned:

- Security is too complex.
- Security policies are becoming impossible to implement.
- The total cost of security is escalating.
- Security topics are stopping e-business initiatives.

What is needed is a solutions framework that includes the major disciplines of IT security as part of an overall architecture, rather than a set of unrelated products that solve point problems. These areas include:

- Comprehensive security policies, their proper definition, handling, and implementation, and their centrally controlled enforcement

- Secure boundary services to securely connect computer networks using firewalls as well as virtual private networks (VPN) functions and mobile code security solutions

- A real time intrusion detection systems (IDS) and centralized IDS correlation, as well as virus immunity to detect potential threats

- A public key infrastructure (PKI) to securely identify and handle identities

- Toolkits that provide a set of application programming interfaces (API) for incorporating specific security needs into the software

How much security you implement is based on your assessment of the risks involved in not providing it as compared with the benefit you achieve when you do. Your decision to apply security to your e-business application will involve a series of decisions and policies, not a binary declaration of whether to "do" security. Which, and how many, of the security mechanisms described in this chapter you use depend in part on the nature of the application you're working with and the business value of the transactions you're supporting. Usually the amount of money you spend on technology to protect your assets, coupled with the cost of managing and maintaining that technology, must be less than the values of your assets for you to stay in business.

The following sections discuss the various security techniques that will feed your final security decision.

4.2 Cryptography principles

On unsecured networks, such as TCP/IP, there is a concern for both the sender and the receiver about the security of the data that is sent over the network. The network protocol itself doesn't provide any protection against tampering with the data. Figure 81 illustrates an end-to-end model that is not secure. The enterprise data and applications are not guarded from external access via the connection provided by the Web server to the Internet. This exposure has threats of information theft, malicious destruction of business applications, or general access violations.

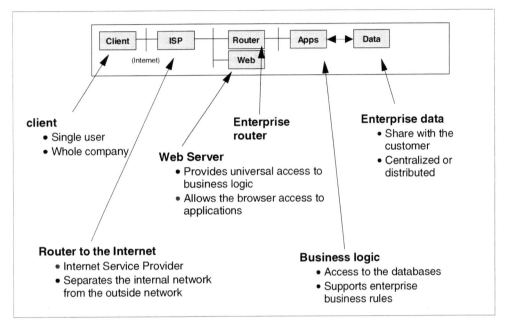

Figure 81. The basic "no-security" end-to-end model

When pushing the enterprise onto the Internet, four security issues need to be addressed:

- **Confidentiality**: e-business transactions are protected against access by attackers who seek to make copies of them or to insert fraudulent data into the process. Simply said, no one can access or copy the data.

- **Integrity**: e-business data and applications are protected in such a way that any effort to change them is detected and prevented. This way, data is not altered as it goes from the sender to the receiver.

- **Authenticity** (access control): Access to e-business applications and data is restricted to those who can provide the appropriate proofs of identity. This ensures that the parties should be able to identify each other beyond doubt.

- **Accountability** (non-repudiation): The flow of data through an e-business application and the flow of transactions that drive the data are logged and reported in such a way that should a dispute arise about any transaction, proof of what actually happened can be produced. The sender of the data cannot deny that they didn't send it, and they cannot deny the content of the data.

You address these issues by using cryptography in your e-business security solution.

4.2.1 Symmetric (secret) key cryptography

Symmetric key cryptography, also known as *secret key cryptography*, is a technique used to encrypt and decrypt data using a single secret key. Both parties have the same key for encryption and decryption. Some well-known secret key algorithms include DES, 3DES, and IDEA.

In Figure 82, the *Sender* is sending a text message to *Recipient* using a single key (the symmetric or secret key). Both the sender and the recipient of the text must have the secret key. Both the sender and the recipient encrypt and decrypt the message using the same secret key.

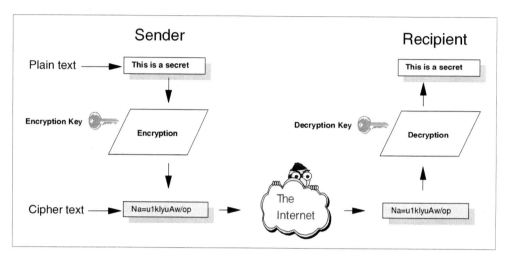

Figure 82. Symmetric or secret key cryptography

Using symmetric key cryptography aids in *authenticity*, since only the known parties involved should have the secret key. Even though the message could be altered, the hacker who does not have the key cannot read the message. This aids in *confidentiality* since the data is encrypted and the parties with the keys are the only ones who can read the message. The main advantage of symmetric key cryptography is that it is fast.

The issues with symmetric key cryptography are:

- *Distribution of the secret keys*: When one party creates a secret key, how is the other party going to get the secret key? Sending the key in e-mail is not secure. Sending the key in normal mail takes too long and is difficult to automate.

- *Secret key administration*: For each party, you want to communicate with, you must create a different secret key. If you do not use different keys with different parties, all parties with the same key will be able to read each others communications. The end result is administering a lot of keys, which can become hard to manage.

4.2.2 Asymmetric (public) key cryptography

Asymmetric key technology uses two keys: a public key and a private key pair. The two keys always work together to encrypt and decrypt the message. The most well-known asymmetric key or public key algorithm is RSA.

Figure 83 illustrates a message encrypted with a public key of the recipient. The message is then sent over the Internet and can only be decrypted with its matching private key. The private key is a secret key that the recipient keeps. Both keys are different, and the key used for encrypting data cannot be used for decrypting the same data. The public key is made available to the world while the the private key should never be revealed.

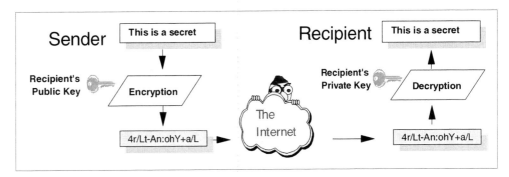

Figure 83. Asymmetric key cryptography

Asymmetric key cryptography is a technique that overcomes the problems of secret key distribution of symmetric key cryptography. This form of cryptography ensures that the data is provided confidentially to the recipient. This level of cryptography does not achieve accountability or non-repudiation. Since the public key is available to the world, the sender can be anyone.

To overcome the issue of accountability, data signing can be used in conjunction with the public key encryption to provide both confidentiality, integrity, and non-repudiation. Figure 84 show how the signing and encryption work together.

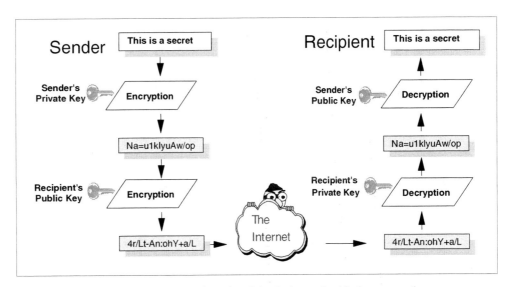

Figure 84. Asymmetric key cryptography using data signing and public key encryption

The following steps describe the process shown in Figure 84:

1. The sender creates a message "This is a secret".
2. The sender encrypts (signs) the message with their (sender's) private key.
3. The sender further encrypts the message using the recipients public key.
4. The message is transported to the recipient over the Internet.

5. The recipient decrypts the message using their (recipient's) private key.
6. The recipient further decrypts (unsigns) the message using the senders public key.
7. The recipient has the message "This is a secret" from the sender.

The issues with asymmetric key cryptography are:

- *The asymmetric key cryptography process is computation intensive.* Signing and encrypting the whole data stream implies a long encryption time. The difference in speed between symmetric key and asymmetric key can be excess of 1,000 times.

- *The public key of the recipient may be fraudulent.* It is possible that somebody publishes a public key that claims to be the recipient and access communications intended for the true recipient.

4.2.3 Digital signature algorithm (DSA)

Symmetric cryptography presented a technique that was fast, but had management problems. The asymmetric key overcame the management problems of the symmetric key, but presented performance issues and concerns that authenticated the recipient of the message. A technique to address these problems is to use a digital signature algorithm.

In DSA, a hash function uses a Hashed Message Authentication Code (HMAC) to generate a small fixed-size block of data (a message digest) from the message. Instead of signing the whole message and encrypting it afterwards, the encryption/decryption process follows the sequence of events shown in Figure 85.

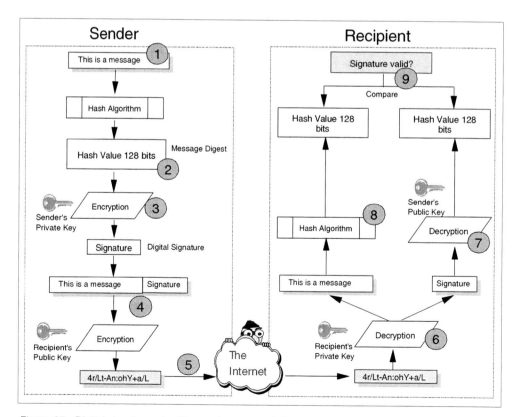

Figure 85. Digital signature algorithm and asymmetric key cryptography

The process flow shown in Figure 85 is explained here:

1. The sender creates a message.

2. The sender creates a message digest using a hash algorithm.

3. The message digest is encrypted using their (sender's) private key to create a digital signature.

4. The digital signature is appended to the original message and encrypted using the recipient's public key.

5. The encrypted message is sent to the recipient via the Internet.

6. The recipient decrypts the whole message with their (recipient's) private key. This produces the message and a digital signature that are now separated.

7. The digital signature is decrypted using the sender's public key to obtain the message digest.

8. The recipient uses the hash function to create a message digest from the message.

9. The sender compares the two message digests. If both are the same, then the recipient is sure who the message came from and that the message is unchanged.

Digital signatures are often used in conjunction with public key systems where some performance gains are achieved from encrypting less information. The use of digital signatures guarantee integrity and authenticity. If the data is altered, the hash algorithm on the receiving side would know the message was altered when the two message digests are compared. Some well-known DSA algorithms are SHA-1, MD5, and RIPEMD.

4.2.4 Digital certificates

Using digital certificates can solve the problem of authenticating the public key. A digital certificate binds the owner of the public key to the public key itself. It is a data structure that contains a public key, necessary details about its owner, and some other information. All this information is signed by a trusted third party called a Certificate Authority (CA).

The role of a CA and digital certificates is explained here:

- When a public/private key pair is generated, the public key, together with the identity of the owner, must be submitted to a CA.

- The CA signs the data with their own private key. The data becomes a Digital Certificate, and returns it to the owner.

- A certificate does not contain any confidential data and should be made available to the world, so that other people can use this certificate for sending data to the owner of the certificate and decrypt data from the owner.

The CA may be operated locally by an organization that takes the form of a server (or servers) running a service. However, CAs are often commercial organizations, such as VeriSign, Thawte, or Entrust.net, that operate on the Internet and whose identities are already programmed into most browsers.

To obtain the digital certificate you want, so that you can have the public key of the recipient (B shown in Figure 86), there is a challenge mechanism that allows safe capture of B's public key.

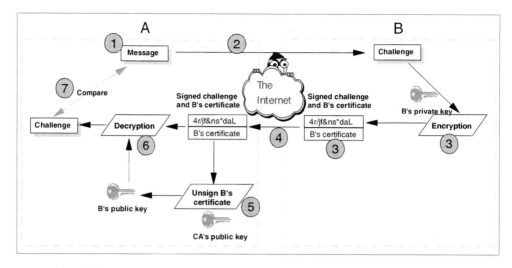

Figure 86. Challenge for digital certificate

The process flow in Figure 86 provides a challenge for the public key:

1. A must obtain B's digital certificate so that it can gain access to B's public key.

2. A sends a challenge message (a piece of arbitrary data) to B (or to the perceived address of B).

3. B signs the challenge from A with its private key and also attaches B's digital certificate.

4. B sends the signed challenge and the digital certificate back to A.

5. A receives the message and uses the CA public key to unsign B's digital certificate. This will create and obtain B's public key.

6. A uses the obtained B's public key to unsign the challenge response.

7. A compares the decrypted challenge response to the original challenge message sent.

8. If the two messages match, then B is who and where A perceives them to be.

Now that you have the digital certificate of B, you can send messages to B with the confidence that the intended recipient is receiving your message (Figure 87).

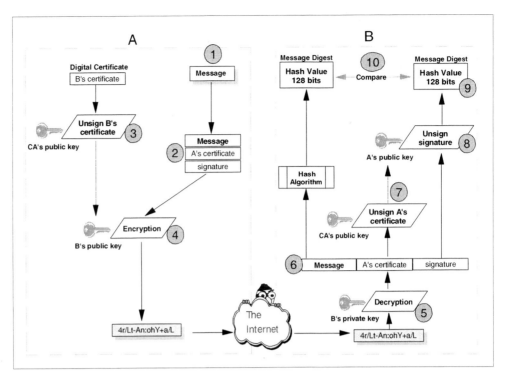

Figure 87. Digital certificates

The flow shown in Figure 87 is explained here:

1. A composes a message for B.

2. A packages its message with its own (A's) digital certificate, signature, and message.

3. A uses the CA's public key to obtain B's public key from the digital certificate.

4. A uses B's public key to encrypt the whole message and sends it to B.

5. After receiving the message, B decrypts it with B's private key.

6. B has access to A's digital certificate, the message, and the signature of the message.

7. B unsigns A's digital certificate to obtain A's public key.

8. B unsigns A's signature using A's public key and obtains the message digest.

9. B generates a message digest from the original message using the hash algorithm.

10. B compares the two message digests.

11. If the two message digests are the same, the integrity of the message is intact.

Using digital certificates establishes a secure way to transfer messages through asymmetric key cryptography without having the authentication problems associated with it. The problem that remains is performance. It would be nice to marry the performance of symmetric key cryptography with the management and scalability of asymmetric key cryptography. This can be achieved by using a secret key for the duration a communication session. The simple steps are:

1. When two entities want to communicate, they set up communication channels using asymmetric (public) key cryptography.

2. During this set up, a secret key is created and transferred to the parties involved. This secret key will only be used for this session and will be destroyed afterwards.

3. Once all parties have the secret key, they can send information to each other with symmetric (secret) key cryptography.

4. When the communication channel is closed, the secret key is destroyed.

4.3 Secure Sockets Layer (SSL) protocol

Secure Sockets Layer was created by Netscape to ensure a secure session on TCP/IP networks. SSL uses a combination of certificates, digital signatures, and cryptography (based on RSA). The client initiates an SSL Web connection by using a URL starting with `https:` instead of `http:`. With SSL, the data flowing back and forth between the client and server using a secret key algorithm. This technology is evolving into Transport Layer Security (TLS).

SSL performs the following functions:

- It authenticates the server to the client.
- Optionally, it authenticates the client to the server.
- It creates an encrypted connection between both machines.

The authentication of the server to the client, and vice versa, happens through the exchange of certificates. The Certificate Authority that signed the certificate can be a different CA for the server than for the client. They must be trusted by the client and the server respectively.

The encryption of the connection keeps the data sent over the connection confidential. On top of that, it also checks whether the data has been changed during the transfer.

SSL sits between the TCP/IP protocols and application protocols. TCP/IP is responsible for the transport and routing of data over the Internet. Application protocols are HTTP, LDAP, or IMAP. This is shown in Figure 88.

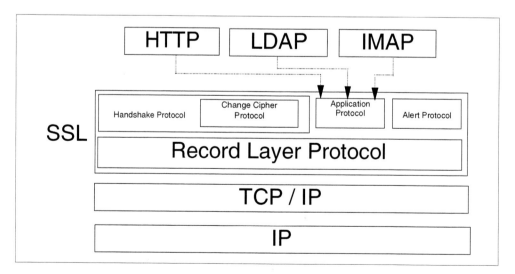

Figure 88. SSL structure and place in the protocol stack

SSL consists of two protocol levels:

- Record layer protocol
- Communication protocols

    - Handshake protocol
    - Change Cipher Specification protocol
    - Alert protocol
    - Application protocol

4.3.1 Record layer protocol

All messages coming from the higher level protocols go through the record layer before going to the transport layer. The record layer sends blocks of data called *records*, which are of fixed length. A record contains the content type, the protocol version number, the length, and the data, which is compressed and encrypted. Each message passes the following three functions:

- Fragmentation of data, where the message is divided or combined to fit into a record. Records have a fixed length.

- Compression before sending the data.

- Encryption of the data part of the record.

4.3.2 Communication protocols

There are four communication protocols:

- **Handshake protocol**: Defines the sequence of events to establish an SSL session between two entities.

- **Change Cipher Specification protocol**: A subset of the handshake protocol. It's primary function is to indicate to the other party that there has been a change in the cryptographic options.

- **Alert protocol**: Deals with errors. An alert message contains two parts the actual error description and the severity level of the error. There are two levels of errors:

    - *Warning*: This indicates a potential problem. An example is the `close_notify` error, which specifies that the sender will not send any more messages in the current session.

    - *Fatal*: This interrupts the current session and means that the current session cannot be resumed in the future. An example of this is the `bad_record_mac` error, which indicates that the message or its hash code has been tampered with.

- **Application protocol**: Is responsible for passing messages from the application layer protocol to the record layer protocol.

SSL communication is set up using the Handshake protocol. Both entities negotiate the version of the protocol to be used (2.0 or 3.0), the cryptographic algorithms, and the setup of the keys. It is also possible to include entity authentication in this step (one-way or mutual). If this happens, the server will authenticate itself to the client using asymmetric (public) key cryptography. Then, the server will use symmetric (secret) key cryptography to achieve better operating performance.

The sequence of the messages exchanged during the handshaking is illustrated in Figure 89.

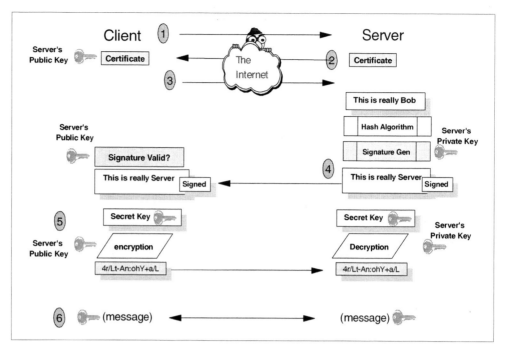

Figure 89. Secure Sockets Layer handshake

The series of events in Figure 89 is explained here:

1. The client (browser) contacts the server.

2. The server sends a certificate to the client; this contains the server's public key.

3. The client contacts the server asking for proof (this can be eliminated if a trusted CA is used).

4. The server creates a message with a digital signature that has been encrypted with the server's private key. The server sends the message to the client. The client validates the message.

5. The client creates a secret key, encrypts the secret key with the server's public key, and sends the encrypted secret key to the server.

The secure session is established. Further communication is encrypted with the secret (symmetric) key.

4.4 SET Secure Electronic Transaction protocol

SET is an industry-standard protocol sponsored by MasterCard and VISA for a secure (encrypted), "end-to-end" payment process. SET is a group of protocols designed for safe credit card payments over the World Wide Web. The main parties of the SET transaction include:

- **Merchant**: A person or organization that has goods or services to sell to the shopper. SET advantages to the merchant include:

– Difficulty to commit fraud with a stolen or fictitious credit card
– Consumers are authenticated as legitimate cardholders
– Bank processing fees are reduced
– Dispute resolution is easier
– Currency independent

- **Cardholder**: A person, or organization, with a credit card who, or that, wants to buy goods or services from a merchant. SET advantages to the customer include:

    – Difficulty to commit fraud with a stolen or fictitious credit card
    – Merchants are authenticated as legitimate businesses
    – A merchant cannot submit altered orders or additional orders
    – Dispute resolution is much easier
    – Alternatives to credit cards for payment
    – Currency independent

Figure 90 shows the main parties that contribute to a SET for e-commerce transaction.

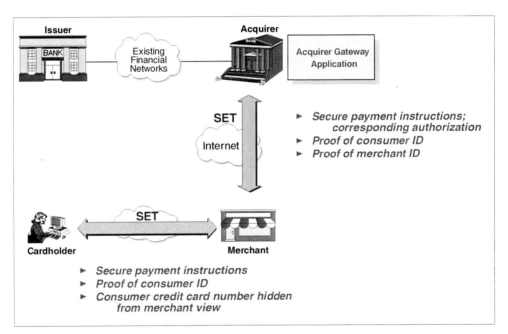

Figure 90. Using SET in e-commerce transactions

There are several more parties in the SET transaction besides shopper and merchant:

- **Issuer**: This is the company that provides the cardholder with the credit card. Ultimately the issuer is responsible for the payment of the debt of the cardholder. In other words, the issuer balances the risk of a cardholder defaulting against the income from interest payments. Issuers are financial institutions, such as banks. There is no reason why the cardholder should have any relationship with the issuer except for the credit card account. However, in practice most cardholders have at least one card from the bank that holds their checking account.

- **Brand**: Brand recognition and loyalty are key to the marketing of credit cards. Some brands are owned by a single financial organization, which is also the card issuer. Other brands are owned by bankcard associations, consortium of financial institutions that promote and advertise the brand, establish operating rules, and provide a network for payment authorizations and fund transfer. SET provides controlled access to these networks from the Internet.

- **Acquirer**: This is an organization that provides card authorization and payment capture services for merchants. A merchant will normally want to accept more than one credit card brand, but does not want to have to deal with multiple bankcard associations. They achieve this by using the services of an acquirer. These services include such things as verbal or electronic telephone authorization support and electronic transfer of payments to the merchant's account. Now the services can include SET protocol support as well. Acquirer services are paid for by the merchant in the form of a small percentage charge on each transaction.

- **Payment gateway**: This is a function provided by, or on behalf of, an acquirer. It is more accurately called the *acquirer payment gateway*. The payment gateway interfaces between SET and the existing bankcard association networks for authorization and capture functions. To put it another way, the payment gateway acts as a proxy for the bankcard network functions.

- **Certification Authority**: This is a function that provides public key certification. There are separate certifiers for each of the different key-using roles in SET (cardholders, merchants, and payment gateways). However, they are all bound together in a hierarchy so that any SET party can use public key certificates to establish trust in any other.

Many of the inter-role relationships are implicit in the definitions of the roles themselves (above). We can divide the relationships into three types:

- **Contractual relationships**: These represent agreements in law between the different parties to provide services and accept responsibilities. They have nothing to do with SET directly, except that SET assumes the relationships already exist.

- **Administrative relationships**: These are relationships required to set up the SET environment before any payments can flow. They also maintain the environment and keep it secure. Some of these are actual SET protocol flows.

- **Operational relationships**: These are the short-term relationships that take place when a payment happens. These are all defined by SET protocol flows.

The contractual relationships are defined as:

- The *cardholder* has a contract with the issuer in which they promise to pay the minimum monthly payment and stay within a credit limit.

- The *issuer* has a contract (or other legal instrument) with the bankcard association in which it agrees to accept the risk of card debt and to support the association.

- The *acquirer* has an agreement with the bankcard associations in which it agrees to operate securely and within their rules. In practice, the acquirer is often part of a financial institution itself, so different parts of a company may play different roles.

- The *merchant* has a contract with the acquirer in which it receives payment processing services in return for a percentage fee.

The administrative relationships (Figure 91) are defined as:

- The cardholder has a relationship of trust with a software provider. This will probably be the bank that provided his or her credit card. Based on this trust, the cardholder will install the SET code and upgrades on his or her personal computer. Trust is necessary, because the cardholder needs to be sure that the code is genuine.

- The merchant has a contract with a software and services provider. This may be an Internet Services Provider (ISP) or other organization, probably related to the acquirer. Whatever the organization is, it will supply and (possibly) install the merchant SET code, so the merchant needs to trust it not to install a Trojan horse or otherwise damage the integrity of the system.

- The different certification authorities have hierarchical relationships between them based on public key certificates.

- The cardholder, merchant and payment gateway have relationships with the appropriate certification authorities. They must each prove their legitimacy, for which they receive a signed public key certificate. The details of these relationships are part of the SET specification.

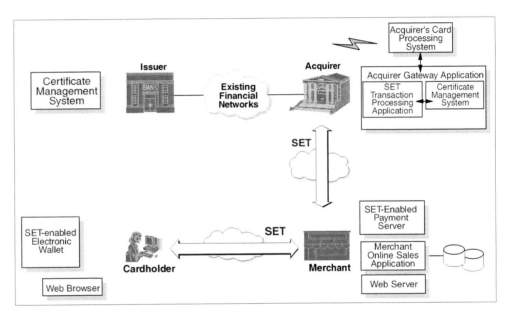

Figure 91. Enabling SET for e-commerce transactions

Finally, we get to do some shopping. The operational relationships are the heart of SET (Figure 92):

1. The cardholder connects to the merchant system to perform payment, inquiry, and refund transactions.

2. The merchant system connects to the payment gateway to perform authorization and capture transactions.

3. The payment gateway connects to the bank card association networks to relay the requests from the merchant.

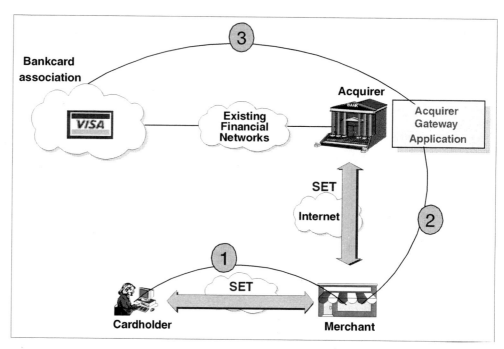

Figure 92. SET operational relationships

SET protocol is used with cryptography for e-commerce applications. It provides confidentiality of information and ensures payment integrity. SET authenticates both merchants and cardholders for credit card. It also makes payment processing on the Internet faster, safer and more secure.

SSL provides a secure "electronic pipe" between the consumer and the merchant for exchanging payment information. Data sent through this pipe is encrypted, so that no one, other than these two parties, will be able to read it. In other words, SSL can give us confidential communications. Once this secure pipe is open, SET can be used to conduct the financial transaction.

SET is an open standard for conducting secure bank card payments over the Internet. First, the consumer must prove their identity to the bank that issued the credit card. That bank, in turn, vouches for the customer by putting its digital signature on the customers certificate. The merchant get their bank to digitally sign their certificate as well. But, since the customer and the merchant are unlikely to use the same bank, they both need a trusted third party that can vouch for both banks. Since the credit card company (for example, Visa, MasterCard, etc.) is best positioned to do this, it becomes the common entity that both trust.

This explanation only scratches the surface of SET and its cryptographic basis. Many of the actual mechanisms that the protocol employs have been simplified here to demonstrate the underlying concepts.

4.5 Techniques for securing the end-to-end model

An e-business must provide assurance that the infrastructure and application resources, including systems, networks, and data, are protected with regard to confidentiality and integrity. This includes protecting the enterprise network and systems from various forms of attack. It also requires that the communications between the consumer and the application are secure and confidential.

4.5.1 Firewalls

A firewall is a combination of hardware and software that sits in the entry point to the company network (or the point where a company network is connected to the Internet). It monitors the type of traffic that comes into the company network. And, it decides whether a packet is allowed to enter. All traffic (data packets) must be screened by the firewall and only allows authorized packets to gain entry into the network.

Firewalls are used in boundary protection (as illustrated in Figure 93), where there is a logical and physical separation of the Internet and internal IT systems. It is often accomplished by using two firewalls, one on each side of the Web server or other bastion hosts inside the demilitarized zone. Firewalls police "who" enters and leaves an enterprise network and "what" goes in and out.

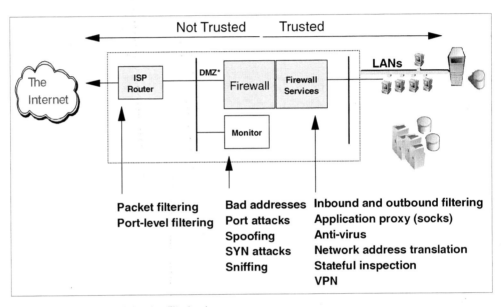

Figure 93. Firewall and the demilitarized zone

The components of a firewall are:

- Packet filtering (also called *screening routers*)
- Application proxies
- Circuit level gateways
- Virtual private networking

4.5.1.1 Packet filtering (screening routers)

Screening routers can look at the packet IP address (network layer) and the types of connections (transport layer). Then they provide filtering based on that information. A screening router may be a stand-alone routing device or a computer that contains two network interface cards (dual-homed system). The router connects two networks and performs packet filtering to control traffic between the networks. Administrators program the device with a set of rules that define how packet filtering is done. Ports can also be blocked as part of packet filtering. If your company security policy only allows Web browsing (HTTP), but not the rather dangerous FTP, packet filtering by the screening routers can achieve this by implementing appropriate rules.

4.5.1.2 Application proxies

An *application-level proxy* server provides all the basic proxy features and extensive packet analysis. When packets from the outside arrive at the gateway, they are examined and evaluated to determine if the security policy allows the packet to enter into the internal network. Not only does the server evaluate IP addresses, it also looks at the data in the packets to stop hackers from hiding information in the packets.

In case any company employee wants to access a server on the Internet, a request from the computer is sent to the proxy server. Then the proxy server contacts the server on the Internet with its address as the source address (not the actual computer which requested it). The proxy server then sends the information back from the Internet server to the actual computer that requested the data. By doing this, the IP address of the internal (company) computer is never known outside its own network. Proxy servers also log the information on who has requested and what the transfer details are to make an analysis of the Internet access. The IBM SecureWay Firewall provides application-level proxies (FTP, Telnet, and HTTP).

Application-specific proxies require a different one for each application (for example, FTP and HTTP as illustrated in Figure 94). Depending on the service required, they act on the client's behalf. A socket secure proxy or a SOCKS server performs the same functions as a proxy except they are not application-specific. They work just below the application layer at the sockets layer. SOCKS servers are often used to cater for larger client loads. Performance gains are achieved because they do not perform the extensive packet analysis (which is computation intensive) of application proxies.

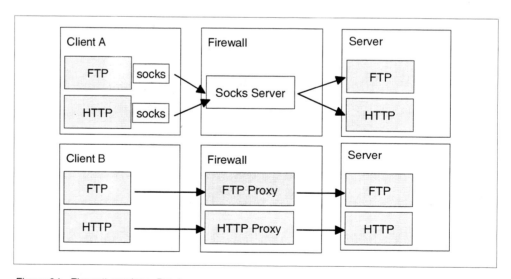

Figure 94. Firewall services: Proxies

4.5.1.3 Circuit-level gateways

Circuit-level gateways are a type of proxy server that provides a controlled network connection between internal and external systems. A virtual "circuit" exists between the internal client and the proxy server. Internet requests go through this circuit to the proxy server. The proxy server delivers those requests to the Internet after changing the IP address. External users only see the IP address of the proxy server. Responses are then received by the proxy server and sent back through the circuit to the client. While traffic is allowed through, external systems never see the internal systems.

4.5.1.4 Virtual private networks

Virtual private networking is a process by which organizations take advantage of the public network (Internet) to achieve connectivity for their branches as well as their remote users (illustrated in Figure 95). The security of this connection is achieved by authentication and encryption. This section looks at the various options to build a VPN.

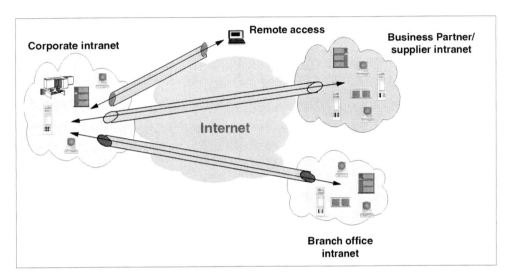

Figure 95. Virtual Private Network overview

VPNs are deployed at two layers:

- Data Link layer VPN (Layer 2)
- Network Layer VPN (Layer 3/IPSec)

The protocols used for establishing VPN layers are:

- Point to Point Tunneling Protocol (PPTP)
- Layer 2 Tunneling Protocol (L2TP)
- Layer 2 Forwarding (L2F)

The protocol that is used to establish the network layer VPN is IPSec. IPSec, in turn, has three component protocols:

- Authentication Header (AH)
- Encapsulated security payload(ESP)
- Internet key exchange (IKE)

This section discusses only IPSec-based VPN. There are two modes of IPSec operation:

- **Tunnel mode**: This is a type of operation deployed between two gateways (for example, intranets) or a server to a gateway scenario. In this method, the traffic is tunneled between the client and the gateway of the destination network, not the exact host in the network. Technically speaking, the IP header is modified and a new header is added before the original IP header to reflect the gateway address, not the host address.

- **Transport mode**: This is a type of operation deployed where there is a requirement of end-to-end encryption (for example, between two users). The resource demands on the communicating partners in this type of operation are tremendous. Technically, in this mode, a new IP header is inserted after the original IP header. This facilitates an end-to-end transport mode.

4.5.1.5 Firewall objectives and rules

There are a number of ways to configure a firewall, depending on the size of your organization and what you are trying to achieve. Some objectives that are common to all firewall cases are:

- You want to only allow traffic to flow that you have determined is safe and in your interest.

- You want to give away a minimum of information about your private network.

- You want to track of firewall activity and be notified of suspicious behavior.

These common objectives translate into a number of rules that you should always keep in mind:

- Anything that is not explicitly permitted should, by default, be denied. This means that when you set up your firewall, you should be able to state exactly what traffic you want to pass through it. It should not be possible for any other traffic to pass.

- You should keep outside users out of your internal network wherever possible. Even if you are providing a legitimate service for outsiders to use, you should not trust them. If possible, you should place such services outside the firewall (possibly within a DMZ), isolated from your internal systems.

- You should do thorough auditing and logging. You should assume the worst, that at some time, your systems will be compromised by a hacker. At this point, you need good logging functions to allow you to detect the hacker, retrace their movements, and prevent further damage.

Firewall technology must wage a continuous battle against the ingenuity of the hacker. This means continuing to be vigilant in preventing the misuse of legitimate IP network services and new security holes. One area that has become part of this battlefield in recent times is the potential for exploitation of "smart" client function. As the Web browser becomes the complete do-everything client, Web-based applications start to rely on client-side execution of programs, using such techniques as Java, ActiveX controls, and other plug-in functions.

4.5.2 Directory services

Directories are used in security for authentication and permissions. A directory service is simply a repository of information. Directory security combines an access method and related services, location information, and other detailed information about resources such as users and servers. A good example of a directory is the telephone book, which contains the names, addresses, telephone numbers, and (in some cases) services of people and businesses. Such information can be retrieved by name (white pages) or service categories (yellow pages).

A directory should support the basic capabilities needed to implement a security policy. The directory, in this case, is one of the components by which a security mechanism is put in place for the whole network. It is also one of the network resources that, itself, needs protecting.

First, a method is needed to authenticate users, that is to verify that they are who they say they are. A user name and password are a basic authentication scheme. Once a user is authenticated, it must be determined if they have the authorization or permission to perform the requested operation on the specific object.

Authorization is often based on access control lists (ACLs). An ACL is a list of authorizations that may be attached to objects and attributes in the directory. An ACL lists what type of access each user or a group of users is allowed or denied. To make ACLs shorter and more manageable, users with the same access rights are often put into security groups.

4.5.2.1 Directory service standards

Directory services provide the ability to store, modify, delete, and retrieve information in a logically centralized repository using open, standard APIs. Information stored in the directory is typically accessed for read only, changes infrequently, and is centrally managed and updated by an administration facility. As part of Framework for e-business, IBM has defined a standards-based directory architecture to address the requirements of directory-based enterprise computing.

Standards-based LDAP client and server

Lightweight Directory Access Protocol (LDAP) was developed to provide standards for accessing the data in network directories. The LDAP distributed architecture (in Figure 96) supports scalable directory services with server replication capabilities ensuring that directory data is available when needed. For security, LDAP supports both basic client authentication using a distinguished name and password, and SSL, which provides mutual authentication between the client and server. It also supports data security via encryption. LDAP version 3 supports the Simple Authentication and Security Layer (SASL), a framework for adding additional authentication mechanisms.

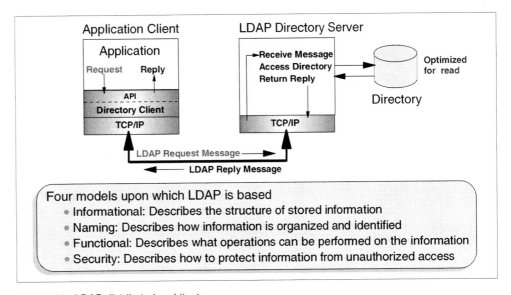

Figure 96. LDAP distributed architecture

Common directory schema

A directory schema defines the rules by which objects are stored and retrieved in the directory. A common schema allows different applications to share the same set of objects (user, address, etc.) so that the information for a person or resource is not created and stored in multiple places within the network. In addition, a common schema definition allows directory-enabled applications to be developed independent of a specific directory implementation.

Meta directory

To ensure interopretability with non-LDAP based directory and synchronization of their contents, a set of meta directory functions is defined (see Figure 97). The meta directory serves two purposes:

- It is used as the "master" for directory information by all other directories.

- It synchronizes the information between the different directories in an organization, allowing users accessing any of the directories to see the same information.

The meta directory provides the basis for common administration of the information stored in the directory by different applications, such as configuration and security data.

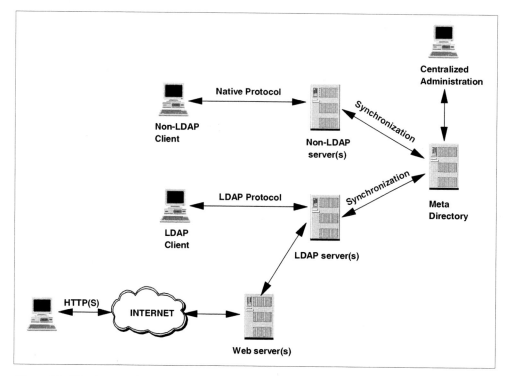

Figure 97. Directory services components

4.5.3 Security architecture

Security architecture is described by using *screen routing*, the *bastion model*, and a *dual-homed gateway*. As the architectures are described throughout this section, refer to Figure 98.

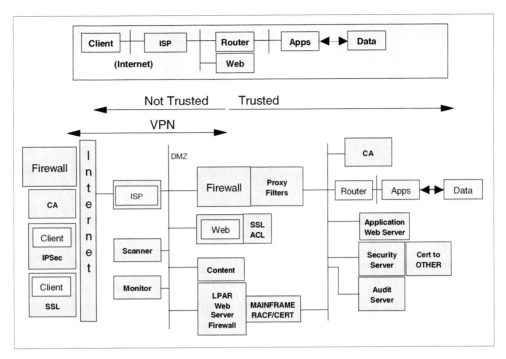

Figure 98. Security architecture overview

4.5.3.1 Screening router
The first and most commonly used strategy is to separate the private IP network from the Internet by inserting a router between them. This router filters all IP packets passing through and is called a *screening filter*. This way you can prevent access to machines or to ports in the private network. You can also do the reverse, which is to prevent an inside machine from accessing the Internet.

The connections are made through a proxy filter as shown in Figure 98. If you do this, there is no way to control what's happening at the application layer. That is, you may want to allow one type of traffic across the gateway, but not another. You could manage this at the application host itself, but the more machines on which you have to impose controls, the less control you have. Nonetheless a screening filter is a useful tool to use in conjunction with other tools as a security building block.

4.5.3.2 Bastion
A bastion is a machine placed between the secure and non-secure network where the IP forwarding is broken, which means no IP packet can go through this machine. As the routing is broken, the only place from which you can access both networks is the bastion itself. Therefore, only users who have an account on the bastion, with double identification (one for the bastion and one for the remote host), can use services on both the networks. This has some disadvantages, because the bastion may have to support many users.

It is important to enforce good password control here. If a hacker manages to break into a user ID, they can then impersonate the user and get into the private network. Besides this security point, supporting a great number of users requires a big machine. To avoid having users logged into this machine and to reduce the load on the machine, application proxies and SOCKS are now being used.

4.5.3.3 Dual-homed gateway

In this case, you can protect the dual-homed gateway from external attacks with filtering. For example, if you forbid external access to the Telnet daemon, you reduce the threat of an external attack. If you have some nomadic machines that are hosted outside, but need to connect to hosts inside the private network, you can limit the exposure by using a proxy server and perhaps using smartcard authentication techniques. The IBM SecureWay Firewall for Windows NT comes as a configuration similar to a dual-homed gateway.

A further development of a dual-homed gateway is to use the sub-network between the screening router and the bastion as a site for application services. This is increasingly common, as organizations want to provide machines that are widely available (such as Web servers) but still have strong protection for their private network. The screening router provides some protection for the service machines, without unduly limiting access. This network is composed of two screening routers and one or several bastions. When you start considering this sort of solution, the cost becomes a major factor since, for reasons of integrity, each component in the design should ideally be a dedicated machine.

4.6 WebSphere Application Server security

The WebSphere Application Server security model strives to:

- Provide a unified security model for both Web resources and enterprise beans (such a security model allows a single policy to govern the security of Web pages, servlets, and enterprise beans)

- Manage the security policies and services provided by WebSphere Application Server Standard or Advanced Editions in a distributed manner consistent with the WebSphere systems management facility

- Leverage the Enterprise Java Server environment by integrating an EJB-based WebSphere Security Application with the WebSphere systems management infrastructure

- Integrating an HTML, JSP file, servlet, and enterprise bean security

- Integrating an HTTP Single Sign-On solution

- Supporting modes of delegation between WebSphere servers

- Supporting secure Java clients

- Lightweight Directory Access Protocol directory support

- Provide client certificate-based authentication and authorization for Web clients

Security policies for Web resources and enterprise beans are configured using the security application that resides within every WebSphere Administrative Server attached to a node. A security application represents the collection of security server and security-related components that reside in the WebSphere Administration Server. In essence, security in WebSphere Application Server Standard or Advanced Editions is a collaborative effort between the WebSphere security application and the security runtime support found in the WebSphere middleware servers. The WebSphere-supported Web servers and the WebSphere Application Server (WAS) interact with the security application in providing the security support in WebSphere Application Server Standard or Advanced Editions.

A WebSphere Administrative Server hosts the enterprise beans that make up the WebSphere Application Server system management facility including the security application. The security runtime consists of two core components:

- **Security plug-in attached to a Web server**: The plug-in helps make security decisions when users request Web resources (such as, HTML files, servlets) from Web clients (over HTTP).

- **Security collaborator attached to every application server**: The collaborator makes security decisions on method calls on resources hosted by the application server.

These two runtime components collaborate with the security server present within the security application, to make authentication, authorization, and delegation decisions.

WebSphere security runtime components consult the security server, which controls security policies and performs authentication and authorization services. The security runtime components attached to the Web server (security plug-in) and the application server (security collaborator) enforce security policies based on the configured policies specified in security server.

4.6.1 Security server

The security server, which is part of the security application, has essentially two purposes:

- To centralize control over the security policies (for example, permissions, delegation)

- To provide central security services (for example, authentication, authorization)

In both respects, the security server is a trusted third party for security policy and control. The security server supplements the security runtime components namely the WebSphere security plug-in and the WebSphere security collaborator executing in each application server. To be more specific, the Web server and the application servers call on the security server to provide:

- Authentication, authorization, and delegation policies

- Authentication and authorization services (including Token services when the LTPA authentication model is used)

The security runtime components (the plug-in, collaborator) acquire security policy information from the security application. Because the security application is coupled with the system management facility, all the configuration information resides in the persistent datastore (for example, a DB2 UDB database) associated with the system management facility. The security plug-in uses the security policies to determine which authentication and authorization services to invoke. The security collaborator uses these policies to make the authorization and delegation decisions.

4.6.2 Security plug-in

When a user attempts to access Web resources, including static HTML pages, servlets, and JSP files, the Web server plug-in performs initial security checks. Note that the plug-in protects the URL name space, not the physical file name space. Therefore, even if two URLs point to the same physical resource, access may be allowed for one URL, but denied for another. If a Web resource is protected using the WAS security configuration, the security plug-in consults the security application to make authentication and authorization decisions.

4.6.3 Security collaborator

The security collaborator is a component of every application server that interacts with the security server. For every remote method invocation of a servlet or an enterprise bean, the security collaborator:

- Drives authentication, if required
- Performs the authorization check
- Performs pre- and post-security trace logging
- Enforces the delegation policy

4.6.4 WebSphere Application Server security architecture

The key to the WAS security architecture is the central security application that runs in the administration server. It provides the services for authentication and authorization for the Web server (for HTML files and JSP files), the servlet engines, and the EJB server.

The authorization information is maintained in the shared administration server database. Therefore, this is a logical centralized security server. You can protect resources not served by WebSphere. The plug-in forwards authentication requirements or requests on to WebSphere as a separate step from the processing request.

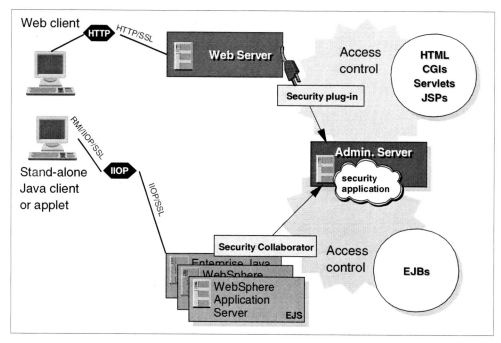

Figure 99. WebSphere Application Server security architecture

The security model of WebSphere, Standard and Advanced Editions, secures the operations of a Web server and servlets. This security model is optimized for protecting Web objects, such as HTML content pages, files, Java Server Pages, Java classes, Java Archives (JARs), Enterprise JavaBeans, servlets, and so on. The security model consists of:

- **Policy services**: Enforced and administered by a security plug-in module and security collaborator through the security server

- **Authentication services**: Enforced through a platform-dependent mechanism

- **Authorization services**: Implemented through a security plug-in or security collaborator

- **Secure delegation services**: Implemented through the security server

Figure 100 illustrates the building blocks that comprise the operating environment of WebSphere security.

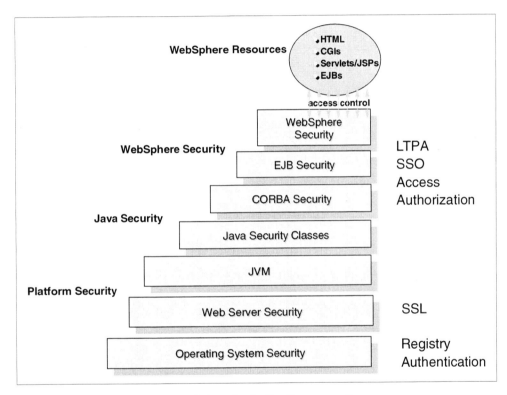

Figure 100. Building blocks for WebSphere Application Server security

The building blocks are:

- **Operating system security**: The security infrastructure of the underlying operating system provides certain security services to the WebSphere Security Application. The WebSphere system administrator can configure the product to obtain authentication information directly from the operating system user registry, for example the Windows NT Security Access Manager (SAM).

- **JVM**: The Java Virtual Machine security model provides a layer of security above the operating system layer.

- **CORBA security**: Any calls made among secure Object Request Brokers are invoked over a Secure Association Service (SAS) layer that sets up the security context and the necessary quality of protection. After the session is established, the call is passed up to the enterprise bean layer.

- **EJB security**: The security collaborator enforces EJB security by communicating with the security server for authentication and authorization services.

- **WebSphere security**: WebSphere security enforces security policies and services in a unified manner on access to Web resources and enterprise beans.

You can find more information on WebSphere security at:
http://www.ibm.com/software/webservers/appserv/security_v35.pdf

4.7 Approaches for securing e-business solutions

This section summarizes the security solutions using the architectures described in 4.5, "Techniques for securing the end-to-end model" on page 220.

4.7.1 Securing e-business using packet filtering and application firewalls

In the scenario illustrated in Figure 101, there is a business requirement to provide external access to enterprise data and applications.

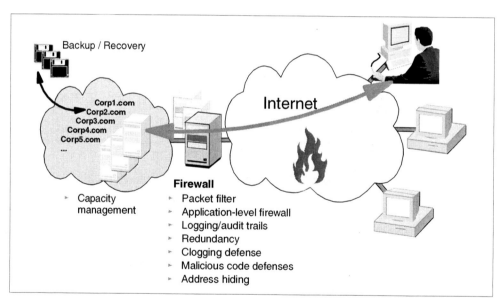

Figure 101. Hosting solution using packet filtering and application proxies

In this scenario, the security and management requirements include:

- Address hiding to provide a level of confidentiality

- Protecting the integrity of the enterprise against attacks from malicious code

- Availability of components via redundancy, backup/recovery, fault tolerance, and capacity management

- Audit trails and logging to provide non-repudiation

- Single sign-on for authentication using access control lists

There are two firewall security components that are used to protect the enterprise applications and databases from potential external intruders over the Internet:

- **Screening routers**: Perform effective packet filtering.
- **Application proxies**: Extend the protection by analyzing the packets to protect the enterprise data and applications from unauthorized or malicious attacks.

4.7.2 Securing e-business using circuit-level gateways

In the scenario illustrated in Figure 102, there is a business requirement to provide external access to enterprise data and applications.

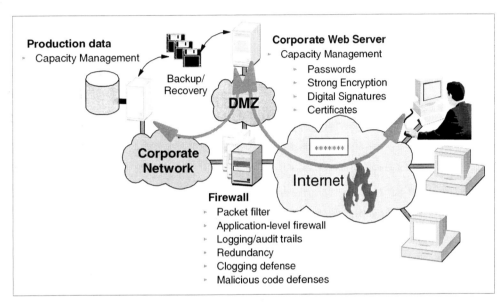

Figure 102. Production access solution using firewall and digital signature access via DMZ

In this scenario, the security and management requirements include:

- Strong encryption to ensure confidentiality

- Protect integrity of the enterprise against attacks from malicious code

- Availability of components via redundancy, backup/recovery, fault tolerance, and capacity management

- Audit trails and logging to provide non-repudiation

- Digital signatures used for authentication

The firewall security components used to protect the enterprise applications and databases from potential external intruders over the Internet are screening routers, application proxies, and circuit-level gateway. The corporate Web server in the DMZ performs the role of authenticating the clients via digital signatures and certificates. The client access to the enterprise databases and applications is through the corporate Web server in the DMZ.

4.7.3 Securing e-business using SET

In the scenario illustrated in Figure 103, there is a business requirement to provide e-commerce services to external customers via the Internet.

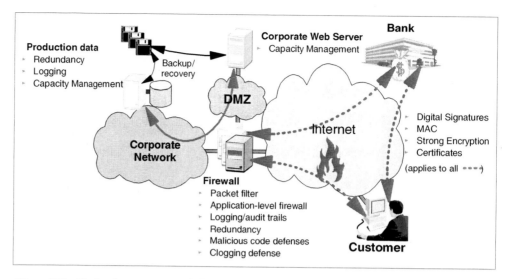

Figure 103. Electronic commerce solution using SET

In this scenario, the security and management requirements include:

- Strong encryption to ensure confidentiality

- Protect integrity of the enterprise against attacks from malicious code

- Availability of components via redundancy, backup/recovery, fault tolerance, and capacity management

- Audit trails and logging to provide non-repudiation

- Challenge response (for digital certificates) used for authentication and non-repudiation

The corporate firewall security components are based on the SET protocol. The firewall components used to provide this secure and managed environment include screening routers, application proxies, and circuit level gateway. The corporate Web server in the DMZ performs the role of authenticating the clients via digital signatures and certificates. The banks participates in the transaction to provide secure payment services. There is a certificate authority (not in the illustration) that make sure that the participants in the transaction are who they say they are, to avoid misrepresentation.

4.7.4 Securing e-business using VPN

In the scenario illustrated in Figure 104, there is a business requirement to provide connectivity between branches as well as remote users via the Internet. This is achieved using VPN. In this scenario, the security and management requirements include:

- Strong encryption and IP tunnelling to ensure confidentiality

- Protect integrity of the enterprise against attacks from malicious code

- Availability of components via redundancy, back/recovery, fault tolerance, and capacity management

- Audit trails and logging to provide non-repudiation

- Access control to include packet filtering, application gateway, and access control lists

In this scenario, IP tunneling is deployed between two intranets or gateways. The network traffic is simply tunneled between the client and the destination gateway. This way, the host address is always protected from external parties as only the gateway address is visible. When remote users require access to the enterprise applications and databases, they use the IPSec transport mode as the type of operation deployed.

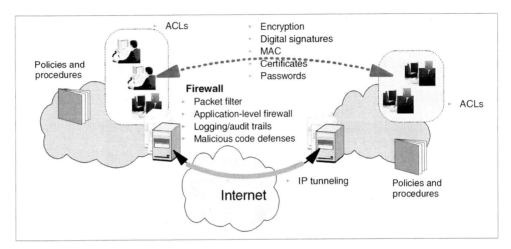

Figure 104. Collaboration solution using VPN components

Chapter 5. Customer Relationship Management (CRM)

This chapter discusses the key technologies, products, decisions, and experiences in building solutions for Customer Relationship Management e-business problems. Figure 105 illustrates the problem space for CRM.

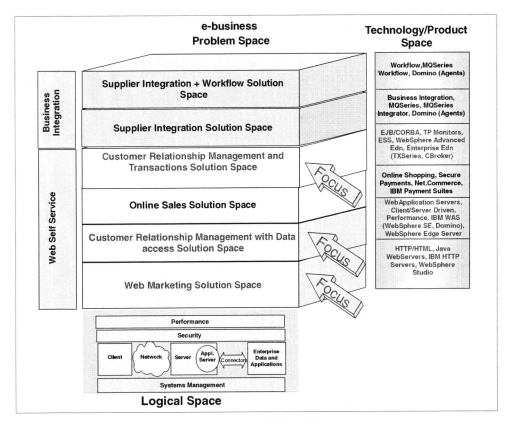

Figure 105. Customer Relationship Management (CRM) solution space

In this chapter, CRM is divided into the following areas:

- **Web marketing**: Allows customers to view information regarding a business (products, services, contact information, etc.). The technologies include HTML/HTTP, Java, and Web servers. The IBM products focus on WebSphere Studio, IBM HTTP Server, Lotus Domino Server, and Lotus Domino Designer.

- **CRM with data access**: Applies to CRM situations where users are allowed to access data and information related to their interactions with the business. The technologies focus on Web application servers, client- versus server-driven interactions, and performance issues. The products include IBM Web application servers (WebSphere Application Server Standard Edition and Lotus Domino), and IBM Edge Server (formally known as Performance Pack). This section emphasizes the key decisions regarding the client, network, server, application server, security, and performance-related to designing an e-business solution for a CRM application.

- **CRM with transactions**: Applications that involve pushing the "enterprise down" to the Internet. This section focusses on the characteristics of user-to-business CRM and the transactions used for integration to back-end applications and data. It discusses secure transactions and authorized access. The technologies that are presented include Enterprise JavaBeans

(EJB), CORBA, transaction processors and monitors, and Enterprise Solution Structure. The products that are discussed are WebSphere Application Server Advanced Edition (using Enterprise JavaBeans), and WebSphere Application Server Enterprise Edition (TX Series, Component Broker). This section emphasizes the key decisions in the application server, connectors, enterprise applications and data, security, and performance decision blocks.

5.1 Web marketing

This section explains:

- An overview of the Web Marketing problem space
- The business and technology requirements for the solution space (Web server technology)
- The decision blocks for Web marketing
- The products and solutions for Web marketing

5.1.1 Overview of the problem space

Web marketing e-business problems involve situations where a user accesses the information about a company on the Web. The information may be displayed via static Web pages or dynamically using Web server technology.

5.1.2 Requirements of the e-business solution space

Web marketing allows customers to view information regarding business (products, services, contact information, etc.). The technologies include HTML/HTTP, Java, and Web servers. The IBM products include WebSphere Studio, IBM HTTP Server, Lotus Domino Server, and Lotus Domino Designer.

5.1.2.1 Using Web servers in Web marketing

Web server technology is a tightly integrated, single platform client/server model (refer to Figure 106).

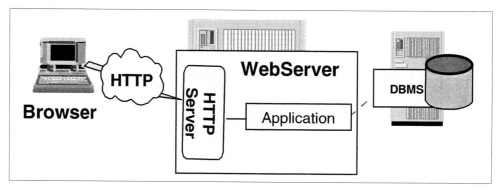

Figure 106. Web server topology

Typically Web servers are used for single platform applications developed and deployed quickly. Web servers use gateways to connect back-end databases and do not integrate.

The client is the "browser" (Netscape, Microsoft IE) that makes requests and controls the "session". It is also known as the "universal client". The network is everything between the server and the client (HTTP, TCP/IP, and so on).

The Web server (Apache, IBM HTTP Server, Lotus Domino server, Netscape, Microsoft IIS) responds to a request from the client.

The limitations for Web servers in e-business are that they:

- Do not scale to enterprise level (performance/capacity)
- Have limited reuse of components across applications
- Have limited integration with existing applications and data
- Are difficult to integrate with other enterprises (for example, for supply chain business integration)

5.1.3 Decision blocks for Web marketing

The section emphasizes the key decisions regarding the client, network, server, application server, security, and performance related to designing an e-business solution for a CRM application.

5.1.3.1 Client decisions and options

Table 29 describes the client decisions and options.

Table 29. Client decisions and options

Decisions	Impacts	Suggestions
Is normal HTML presentation adequate, or should the user interface be enhanced through the use of Java applets?	Applets take time to download and may be a concern over dial-up connections.	Java applets can be used to make the presentation more flexible and user friendly.
How will the choice of client affect end-to-end response?	- If an HTML page has many complex objects, the number of connections required by HTTP may be large, download time may be impacted, and rendering time on the browser workstation may suffer. - The use of Java applets will slow down the initial response while the applet loads, but may allow subsequent interactions to be faster.	You should consider key Internet technologies and how they might affect response time. Compare response times of HTML versus Java applets.

5.1.3.2 Network decisions and options

Table 30 describes the network decisions and options.

Table 30. Network decisions and options

Decisions	Impacts	Suggestions
What protocols will you use?	HTTP is the standard protocol used by browsers. Other protocols that you might find are FTP (for file transfer) and HTTPS (HTTP over Secure Sockets Layer). Application protocols may include IIOP, RMI, Messaging, or RPCs.	Try to stay with standard protocols as much as possible and ensure that the firewalls will support the selected protocols. Determine which parts of the interaction necessitate HTTPS, since HTTPS will affect performance.

5.1.3.3 Server decisions and options

Table 31 describes the server decisions and options.

Table 31. Server decisions and options

Decisions	Impacts	Suggestions
Should the server provide indexing and searching or other site navigation aids?	Some servers, or server packages, provide these capabilities as standard, but depending on your requirements you may need a special purpose indexing/search engine.	Do not try writing your own search engine. It is a good idea to use the standard capabilities provided by the server. List the searching capabilities that you need: Do you need to be able to search a single server or many? What should be indexed: HTML files, word processor files, PDF files, other formats, databases?

5.1.3.4 Performance decisions and options

The performance considerations are divided into three parts:

- Client design and development considerations:

    - Implement Network Computing Web UI usability guidelines
    - Implement Network Computing Web site design guidelines
    - Reduce development task fragmentation
    - Understand performance trade-offs in choice of technology (for example, Java or HTML)

- Network design and development considerations:

    - Quantify the latency impact on performance. This includes quantifying the number of systems in the solution, number of round trips among systems, and the variance across multiple round trips.

    - Analyze the application flow to determine whether it is simple or very complex.

- Web server design and development considerations:

    - Analyze workload segments into informational and transactional. It is important to deploy on a system or systems of appropriate strengths.

    - Plan for peak access and design a "load shedding" option.

Refer to the document "Designing e-business solitons for performance" at:

`http://www.ibm.com/developerworks/patterns/`
`ebusiness-performance-customer-v2.pdf`

5.1.4 Products and solutions used for Web marketing

This section presents the products that are recommended as part of IBM Framework for e-business.

5.1.4.1 IBM HTTP Server, WebSphere Studio, and NetObjects Fusion

IBM HTTP Server powered by Apache is based on the Apache HTTP server, which is the most popular server on the Web. This HTTP server runs on AIX, OS400, Solaris, Windows NT, HP-UX, and Linux. IBM has enhanced the

Apache-powered HTTP server by adding SSL for secure transactions. It offers full support, as it would with any other IBM product.

IBM WebSphere Studio is a tool set that helps reduce time and effort when creating, managing, and debugging multiple platform Web applications. The tool provides a visual layout of dynamic Web pages. Studio supports JSPs, full HTML, JavaScript, and DHTML; uses wizards (for generating database-driven pages); and updates and corrects links automatically when content changes. WebSphere Studio allows developers to integrate their favorite content creation tools and provides local and remote debugging with a JSP debugger.

NetObjects Fusion builds Web pages and has Web authoring options. The tool's single package addresses each step in a Web site life-cycle (create, publish, update). It requires no programming knowledge (point-and-click, drag-and-drop ease-of-use) and can be easily used for data-driven Web sites (database publishing). It also provides support for the latest Web browser standards' (DHTML) open, flexible approach to third-party tool integration.

Figure 107 shows the topology and interactions for a Web marketing solution using IBM HTTP Server to dynamically present HTML pages to the client browser.

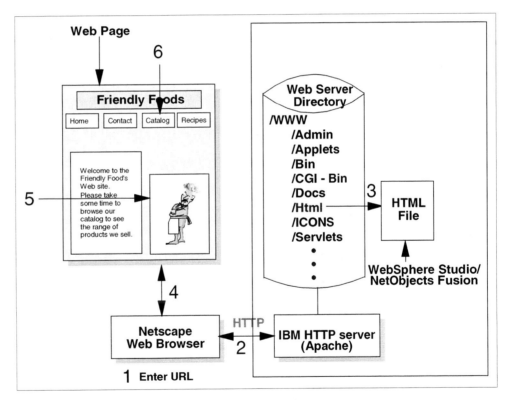

Figure 107. IBM HTTP server: Dynamic application view for a request

The following steps walk you through the flow of a request from the Web browser client as shown in Figure 107:

1. The user enters a URL.

2. The URL request is routed to the Web server.

3. The Web server looks for the appropriate file in the Web server directory. In this case, it looks for the index.html file if only the directory name is specified.

4. The HTML page and the animation gifs are sent to the user's browser.

5. When the user moves the mouse over the Chef's image, it waves.

6. When the user clicks a link, the corresponding HTML page is served by the Web server.

The associated security diagram in Figure 107 shows:

- No user authentication is required.
- The firewall is used to prevent any other protocol, except HTTP from entering.

You can find more product information about the IBM HTTP Server, WebSphere Studio, and NetObject Fusion at the following Web sites:

- IBM HTTP (Apache) server:
  http://www.ibm.com/software/webservers/httpservers/
- WebSphere Studio: http://www.ibm.com/software/webservers/studio/index.html
- NetObjects Fusion: http://www.netobjects.com/products/html/nfmx.html

The relative strengths and weaknesses of using IBM HTTP Server
The advantages of using this product solution are:

- Web sites are up and running very quickly and with minimal application development.
- Only HTML and HTTP standards are used. Therefore, performance should be very good.
- Web sites are easy to modify and maintain.

The disadvantage of using this product solution is that user interaction is limited.

5.1.4.2 Domino Web server and Domino Designer
Lotus Domino Application Server includes all functions of the Lotus Domino mail server plus support for custom intranet and Internet applications in a single Domino partition. These custom applications can be generated from standard database templates or written using Domino Designer. Domino Designer is the interactive, graphical development environment for creation of powerful intranet and Internet applications.

Figure 108 shows the topology and interactions for a Web marketing solution using a Domino server to dynamically present HTML pages to the client browser.

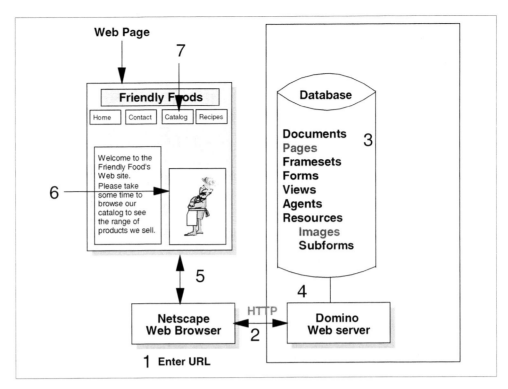

Figure 108. Domino: Dynamic application view for a request

The following steps walk you through the flow of a request from the Web browser client as shown in Figure 108:

1. The user enters a URL.

2. The URL request is routed to the Domino server.

3. Domino interprets the URL, and retrieves the page and its associated image resources.

4. The page is converted into HTML by Domino.

5. The HTML page and the animation gifs are sent to the user's browser.

6. When the user moves the mouse over the Chef's image, it waves.

7. When the user clicks a link, the corresponding Domino object (for example, page, document, view, and so on) is converted into HTML and served by Domino.

The associated security flow in Figure 108 shows:

- No user authentication is required.
- The firewall is used to prevent any other protocol, except HTTP, from entering.

You can find more product information on the Lotus Domino Web server and Lotus Domino Designer at these Web sites:

- Lotus Domino Webserver:

  http://www.ibm.com/software/webservers/dgw/index.htm

- Lotus Domino Designer:

  http://www.lotus.com/home.nsf/welcome/dominodesigner

The relative strengths and weaknesses of using Domino

The advantages of using this product solution are:

- The Web site can be up and running quickly and with minimal application development or HTML skills.

- Domino provides for dynamic Web serving, even with a simple site.

- The Web site is easy to modify and maintain.

The disadvantages of using this product solution are:

- There is limited user interaction.
- The site creator must understand the basics of Domino database design.
- Domino dynamically converts objects into HTML, so performance is not as good as HTML file serving.

5.2 CRM with data access

This section presents:

- An overview of the problem space
- The business and technology requirements for CRM with data access:

  - Web application server
  - Client-driven versus server-driven processing
  - Session/state management
  - Connectors to enterprise applications and data
  - Performance and scalability

- The decision blocks for CRM with data access
- The products used in CRM with data access
- A solution using WebSphere Application Server
- A solution using Domino Application Server

5.2.1 Overview of the problem space

CRM with data access looks at a typical self-service solution scenario that is referred to simply as "content access". Characteristics include providing multiple connections to heterogeneous systems that contain data and information and many different forms and formats. Using this data, we need to dynamically generate content to serve back to the Web clients. Also, we may need to eventually provide highly-transactional execution environments that are initiated by many simultaneous Web clients. Some examples include:

- Providing flight and gate information to travellers
- Allowing insurance claim filling online
- Financial services and loan applications via the Web
- Creating a manufacturing call center for service and support online
- Building an infrastructure for travel agency communications

All of these examples require the use of open standards across a broad range of operating platforms and systems. They require quick access in real-time to up-to-date latest information and data. They may require persistent connections for performance and scale as well as object-oriented components for ease-of-use. They may require support for national languages for worldwide business. Typical components within this scenario include:

- A Web server (as the first point of contact for our universal client)

- A development environment for building these portable and reusable application parts

- A deployment environment with a Web application server

- Possibly additional infrastructure enhancements for scaling and performance

5.2.2 Requirements for the e-business solution

The business requirements gathering process:

- Defines business drivers
- Defines functional requirements
- Defines nonfunctional requirements
- Describes existing customer environment

Defining business drivers

Business drivers include such things as:

- Improving customer service
- Holding down costs
- Protecting customer information

> **Note**
>
> For more complex businesses, these lists of requirements may be longer. Ranking the items high, medium, and low will give the solution design process more focus, where the solution architecture delivers the "high" ranked items as a priority. Ranking is a useful tool to start the business thinking about the critical features they want to deliver in an e-business.

Defining functional requirements

The functional requirements for the online account self-service example include:

- Users can check their account status, including their recent purchases and when payments are due

- Update orders: Change, create, and delete orders

- Provide personalized visit

- Allow user authentication

See Figure 109 for an illustration of the business environment.

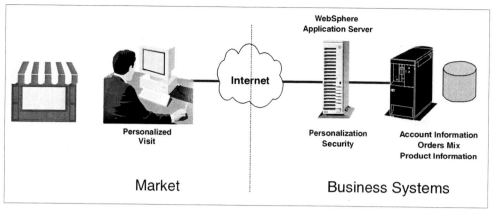

Figure 109. Functional requirements for CRM account self-service example

Defining non-functional requirements

Non-functional requirements for this CRM account self-service example include (the following requirements have been ranked high, medium, low):

- **Security requirement**: User authentication (high)

- **Operational requirement**: 24x7 (medium)

- **Performance requirement**: Response time is 5 seconds for page to page (high)

- **Scalability**: Number of online users > (greater than) 5000, number of concurrent online users is 100, with a potential of going to 200,000 customers in two years (high)

- **Availability**: 95% of the time (high)

- **Extendibility**: Potential for adding new functions, including account report generation and personalized promotional (medium)

- **Flexibility**: Should be able to work with all popular browsers (high)

Often the non-functional requirements determine the technology used in the final solution architecture. These requirements establish how robust the solution needs to be. This knowledge focuses the technology selection to deliver an architecture that fits the purpose. Depending on the outcome of the solution, it may also present the customer with solution architecture options, with advantages and disadvantages for each case.

Finally we need to describe and understand the current business environment. We must make the effort to thoroughly understand the business environment to ensure that legacy information is leveraged appropriately. Figure 110 illustrates the business system environment for this CRM account self-service example. As you can see, the legacy systems are not integrated to the current Internet services that the business current provides. The Web services would be simple static Web pages.

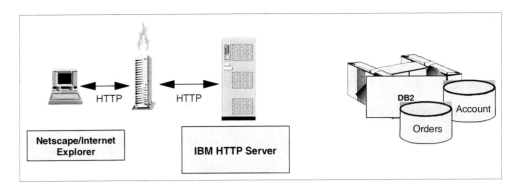

Figure 110. Current business system environment

5.2.2.1 Web application servers

Web application servers are a standards-based development and deployment approach. A conceptual model of where a Web application server fits in the Framework is shown in Figure 111. In this diagram, the client can access data and services anywhere in the system. A call is made from the client using HTTP through the firewall. The Internet dispatcher sends the request to the Web server for processing into the application server. Directory and security services are used to make sure that the content entering the internal system domain does not compromise internal security. The business logic that is developed in the Web application server uses connectors to access enterprise data or applications. The Web application server gathers the content that is requested and serves it through the Web server as HTML for the client to render in its native environment (for example, a browser).

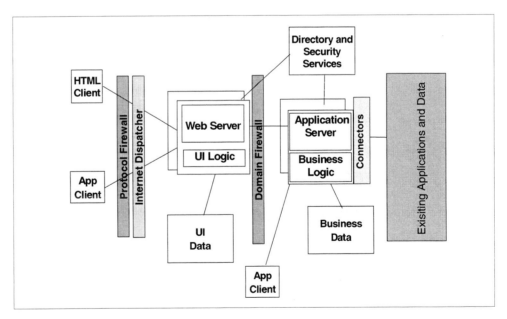

Figure 111. Web application server topology

The services that a Web application server provides include:

- Work load management
- Reliability, availability, security
- Management and monitoring

- Location and service transparency (naming service)
- Resource management and pooling (for example, database connections)
- State/session management
- Caching of results
- Integration (Connectors) to back-end applications and data

The IBM e-business Web application server strategy is to:

- Deliver software that enables a robust infrastructure for consistent Web application deployment on IBM and other leading platforms, based on Java servlets and JavaBeans

- Foster and implement industry standards for all Web application development

- Provide the ability to scale Web environment to meet and exceed user demands

- Deliver solutions for end-to-end design, development, and deployment of Web applications

5.2.2.2 Client-driven versus server-driven processing model

Figure 112 describes the conceptual differences between a client-driven processing application model and a server-driven processing application model. It is important to know the components that are used in each of the processing models and their location, either on the client or on the server.

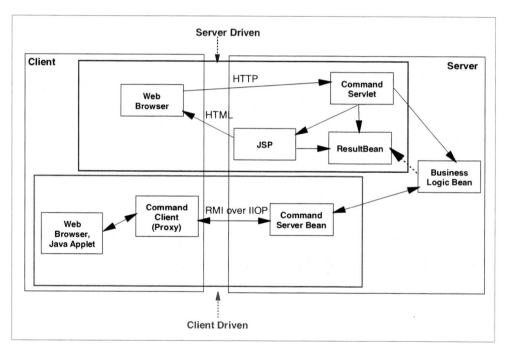

Figure 112. Client-driven versus server-driven processing model

Interaction control is of interest because the client-driven interaction can be much "richer" and easier for programming sophisticated actions. The time to download or install this client-resident code, plus the issues of maintaining and changing this code, often encourage the use of server-resident programs. However, if the interaction is "chatty", with lots of packets moving back and forth between the client and server to complete the application function, this becomes a performance issue. Trade-offs must be made to achieve optimal functionality.

There is also a data aspect to consider. If the client controls the interaction, data must be sent over the network for all of the "intermediate" interactions, as well as for the final one, where the data requested is transferred. This intermediate step data may be a significant security exposure.

The uses of the client model and the server model are summarized in the following points:

- The client-driven model (applets) is used when:
    - Applications require a high level of user interaction.
    - There is a need to provide real-time multimedia effects.
    - Coding can be accomplished in a small footprint.
    - There is a requirement to pull unsolicited information.

- The server-driven model (servlets/JSP) is used when:
    - There needs to be a separation of concerns (decouple client from the application).
    - Browser dependencies are required to be minimized.
    - Applets are too big to download.
    - There is a need for greater scalability.
    - There is a need for better control of the user experience.

The server driven processing model promotes the use of Java servlets. Figure 113 describes the role that Java servlets play in the server (in particular the Java Virtual Machine (JVM)). The steps in the process are:

1. The controller HTTP servlet receives an HTTP request.
2. The servelet invokes business logic.
3. The command bean retrieves the information for processing.
4. The controller servlet invokes a process to determine the result.
5. The controller servlet invokes the JSP servlet to create results view.
6. The JSP access the result information from the result bean.
7. The JSP creates an HTTP reply.

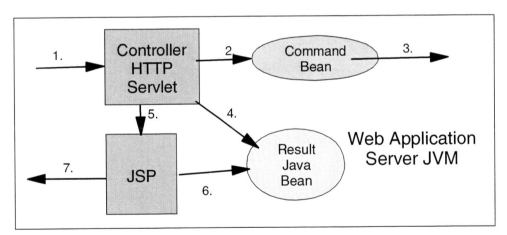

Figure 113. Dynamic view of servlet-based interaction

Java servlets are an open Java standard for executing code on a server that:

- Includes all the advantages of Java
    - Easy to code object model
    - Platform independent

- Are called within the server process

  Have access to security and transaction context

- Remain resident once they are loaded for performance reasons

  Service method handles one or more requests

- Are stateless themselves

    - Servlets scale across clustered, multiprocessor, multi-threaded environments

    - Have access to various Java standard services to maintain state

The ways to use servlets include:

- Creating and returning a portion or an entire HTML page in real time
- Personalization
- Managing dialog with a user
- Synchronizing the handling of multiple requests to back-end systems

The server-driven CRM application model is illustrated in Figure 114. The server application:

- Controls application flow
- Accesses enterprise resources
- Generates the UI shown by the client (for example, generates HTML from JSP)

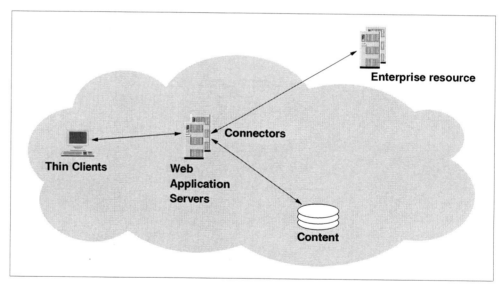

Figure 114. Server-driven CRM applications

Data access applications, by their very nature, imply integration with enterprise resource and services. They also may make use of existing Java components, enabling the reuse of business logic and data access policies.

General programs requiring access to multiple backends can use XML as a common format for sharing information. XML is a tag language to specify the actual data (content) and a structure for the data. XML can allow easy interaction between data stores and applications, which allows general programs to retrieve data and pass it back to the requester.

Figure 115 shows where XML is used in CRM applications. Some types of uses that are highlighted are:

- XML messaging provides interaction with applications hosted on other systems.

- Published XML interfaces provide interaction between components and subsystems that execute on local or remote systems.

- JSP 1.1 requires the ability to represent JSP as XML documents, which allows the use of HTML or XML to define template data.

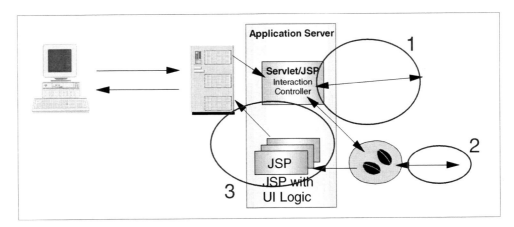

Figure 115. Where XML is used in CRM applications

The application programming model in Figure 116 shows the interaction of the Java servlets in the overall framework of the e-business application:

1. The client sends a request to the Web server when the user clicks the Submit button on the Web page.

2. Web application server gets the request, and the loan servlet involves "loan business logic" to access some data from the account database.

3. A DB2 UDB connector bean is used to make the call to the account database.

4. The call is made to the account database, and the data is retrieved into the *loan business logic*.

5. The payment results bean processes the result.

6. The final result is published using a *loan JSP*.

7. The loan JSP gets the information from the *payment result bean*.

8. The Web server publishes the Web page for the client to render in the browser.

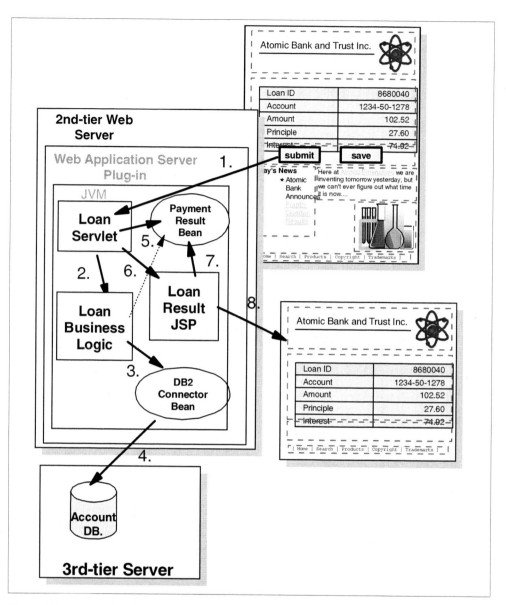

Figure 116. Java application programming model

The advantages with the Java application programming model shown in Figure 116 include:

- Modifying the layout easily without changing the servlet controlling application flow

- Using What You See Is What You Get (WYSIWYG) editing tools for Web page editing

- Easily choosing a different JSP based on class of service, user preferences, client type, and connection information

The disadvantages with the Java application programming model are:

- Many objects are involved.
- Developers must understand the programming model.

5.2.2.3 Session state management

A session state is used to maintain data across multiple (stateless) HTTP requests from a given user. The session ID is passed back to the client to get around IP address correlation problems (for example, firewalls and sockservers often hinder unique addressing). There is an option to use cookies (default) or URL encoding (implicit or explicit) to pass around this session information.

You should consider the following cases when dealing with session management:

- Creating, joining, and rejoining a session are not standardized.

- Session size can be an important performance consideration.

  Use in conjunction with directory and database information.

- Persistence is not guaranteed across a Web server's lifetime.

  - Can configure time-out, paging characteristics
  - Use notification capability to store or reload at session lifecycle events

You can use a session state for:

- Multi-stage functionality:

  - To keep variables between related HTTP requests in a session state

  - Final submit retrieves values and initiates back-end business application logic

  - Typical scenarios include:

    - New loan application
    - Shopping
    - Travel reservations

- Coordinating multiple users:

  - Each user has an individual session state
  - Others are accessed from session context
  - May use notifications
  - Typical scenarios:

    - Games (for example, checkers, bridge)
    - Online auction

5.2.2.4 Connectors to enterprise applications and data

Data accessed through a servlet must be requested through some client that can send the formatted data request to the data manager program. Connectors are generic clients that allow ease in connectivity to the enterprise data using JavaBeans. One such client on the WAS is the JDBC driver for DB2 UDB, which connects to the server "partner" at the database (Figure 117).

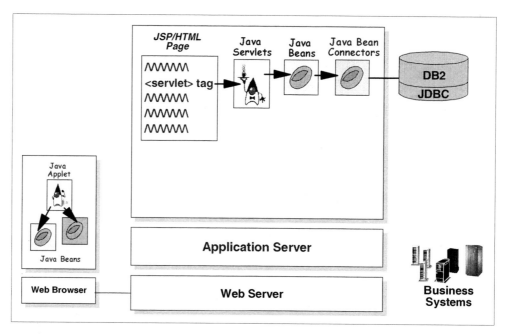

Figure 117. Connector beans to access back-end resources

Connection capabilities of an application server (such as WebSphere Application Server) include:

- Support for Java for Enterprise APIs (JDBC, JMS, JIDL, JTS, EJB, JSQL, JNDI)
- Relational databases (DB2 UDB, Oracle, etc.) using JDBC
- CICS using EPI and ECI
- Encina using Encina TIDL or DCE IDL over TCP/IP
- IMS using JITOC (IMS TCP/IP OTMA Connection) over TCP/IP
- MQSeries using MQI over TCP/IP
- SAP using BAPI
- Host On-Demand using 3270 or 5250 VT streams

Access to business components include:

- CORBA and Component Broker (CB) through CB Java Client transparently using IIOP

- WebSphere Business Components that are objects distributed transparently using extended Remote Method Invocation

- Enterprise JavaBeans

Java programming depends on whether the backend is:

- Data, code, or object-centric (synchronous)
- Message-centric (asynchronous)

5.2.2.5 Performance and scalability issues

The issues that affect performance require analysis of where the bottlenecks are in the system. Figure 118 illustrates, in a simple network topology, where potential bottlenecks could occur. Performance can clearly be addressed by improving latency throughout the network or improving processing time in the application.

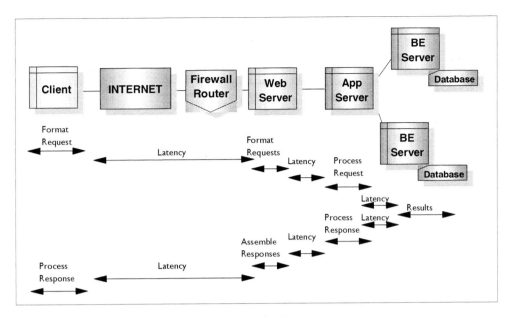

Figure 118. Areas in a system where performance bottlenecks may occur

Performance considerations include:

- Intranet versus Internet
- *Client time*: Application, connections, tables, images)
- *Network*: Bigger isn't always better, but it usually helps
- *Load balancing*: For performance and availability
- *Web server*: Caching
- *Application*: Programming models – *CGI* versus *fast CGI* versus *ICAPI* versus *servlet*
- *Security*: Symmetric, asymmetric key cryptography
- *Database*: Pools of pre-established connections
- *File server*: DFS, AFS
- Server scalability clustering versus symmetric multiprocessing

The issue of performance and the trade-off options is discussed in 5.2.3.6, "Performance decisions and options" on page 262.

5.2.3 Decision blocks for CRM with data access

The decision blocks for CRM with data access describe the key decisions that need to be made. The tables also discuss the impact of the decision on the solution and suggestions on how to make the decision. Figure 10 on page 30 shows the logical decision areas that require you to identify known options or products for each block. The decisions, impact, and suggestions discussed as part of the logical decision blocks create a checklist for you to ensure that all aspects of the CRM problem domain have been explored and addressed in your solution.

5.2.3.1 Client decisions and options

Table 32 describes the client decisions and options.

Table 32. Client decisions and options

Decisions	Impacts	Suggestions
Is this an Internet or an intranet-based application?	This will impact the type of client technology selected. For the Internet, use a "universal" client. For an intranet, you have some control over the hardware and software specifications.	For Internet applications, use standard browsers. For an intranet application targeted towards specific users, it would be feasible to consider Java applets and applications.
Is client-side scripting needed? At what level?	JavaScript, JScript, or ECMAScript are languages, interpreted by the browser and can be used to enhance the user interface and perform some basic input validation.	Because of implementation incompatibilities between the different levels of browsers from Netscape and Microsoft, you should plan to test against all likely clients.
Will the client control the interaction?	A client-driven interaction may increase traffic between the client and the server. Be careful about authentication and authorization issues; know who is in charge and how to ensure integrity throughout the session. Security is also impacted.	An applet is a reasonable choice to interface directly (usually through a gateway in the Web server) to back-end applications and data. This can be a straightforward way to Web-enable back-end systems with a minimum of modification.
Will the state or session be managed by the client?	If the client manages a state or session, then consider the appropriate technologies, along with the security concerns of maintaining information on the client.	Refer to Table 33 for state-management options on the client.
Will the site use proprietary scripts, tags, or plug-ins?	The use of proprietary features limits the application's portability.	Only use proprietary scripts, tags and plug-ins when you can control the type of clients (for example, in intranet solutions) and when their use is mandated.

Table 33 describes the client session state management decisions and options.

Table 33. Options for client session state management

Type	Uses	Comment
Cookies	Maintain session state	Users may set their browser to refuse cookies because of (unfounded) fears that they introduce privacy exposures. For that reason, your application should be designed to work when cookies are unavailable.
Hidden fields or URL component (Hidden fields or strings appended as options to a URL can be used to contain an encoded field which defines the session state.)	Maintain session state	These fields or strings are visible to users either directly or via the browser View Source command. They should not contain passwords in clear text. The server should also destroy the session variable at the completion of a transaction because the information could persist in the browser's cache. This would allow a subsequent user of the workstation to attempt to continue the previous user's transaction.
Applet (An entire transaction consisting of several interactions with a server can be performed by a single Java applet, which therefore maintains the state.)	Manage session	This is more complex to implement because it involves selecting and implementing a protocol for communicating between the applet and its partner on the host.
Options for the client: • Browser • Notes client • Applet • Java application		

5.2.3.2 Network decisions and options

Table 34 describes the network decisions and options.

Table 34. Network decisions and options

Decisions	Impacts	Suggestions
Will the network traffic be a major bottleneck for performance?	To understand the impact of the e-business application on your network, you need to know the data and application placement. Analysis of projected transaction volumes, amount of data typically being requested, and amount of interaction are required to help with decisions on network options.	Lack of attention to this area could cause severe performance problems. Think of using HTTP sprayers to help ease the network traffic by distributing it across a set of Web servers.
Options for the network: • HTTP/HTTPS • IIOP • Remote Procedure Call • Remote Method Invocation • MQSeries		

5.2.3.3 Server decisions and options

Table 35 describes the server decisions and options.

Table 35. Server decisions and options

Decisions	Impacts	Suggestions
Is the server primarily used as a gateway to connect to back-end applications?	A gateway runs on the server and interfaces between a client and the back-end system. This can be a straightforward way to Web-enable back-end systems with a minimum of modification.	Usually this is a good approach if there are hard time constraints since usually no modifications are required to the back-end application code. Try to use existing gateways to access back-end databases, CICS Transaction Gateway to access CICS applications, and MQSeries Internet Gateway to access MQSeries-based applications.
Will the site use Java applets? What are the connectivity requirements?	As part of the standard security built in to Java, an applet can only communicate with the server from which it was downloaded.	If the applet needs to communicate with another server, this has to be done indirectly via its own server or through the use of digitally signed applets.

Decisions	Impacts	Suggestions
How will the application be split between client-side logic and server-side logic?	Assuming a logical three-tier architecture, determine how to distribute presentation, business and data access logic. For example, you can use HTML on the client. This implies that all user field validations will be carried out on the server. However, if interaction is needed from the user, can the application support the amount of client-to-server interaction?	Use an interaction model that separates the model (that provides the business logic) from the controller (that supports the interaction with the user) from the view (that is concerned with displaying information to the user.) Use a servlet as the controller, JSP as the basis for the view, and a command bean that interfaces with the business logic.
Options for the server: • Generic HTTP server • Combined Web and application server • Mail server • News and special purpose multi-media server		

5.2.3.4 Application server decisions and options

Table 36 describes the application server decisions and options.

Table 36. Application server decisions and options

Decisions	Impacts	Suggestions
Is this a logical two-, three- or n-tier solution?	The main impact is the placement of logic (presentation, business, and data access) on the tiers.	To directly access back-end applications, use the middle tier as a gateway. The client should be thin (HTML-based), the server should manage interaction, and the application server have the business logic and data access logic. Even in a physical 2-tier, client/server approach, ensure that the client is thin, and the server separates the management of interaction (Web server) from the application/ business logic and data access (Web application server).
How will the application be split between the Web server and the Web application server?	A clear separation of responsibilities between the Web server and Web application server will facilitate ease of change, impact performance, allow the application to scale, and facilitate portability.	The Web server should be responsible for handling the interaction with the user. The Web application server should be in charge of business logic and access to back-end applications and data.

Decisions	Impacts	Suggestions
How will the presentation logic be separated from the business logic?	Most applications need to support multiple client types. The user interface logic and the business logic will evolve independently.	Wrap the business logic with a simple task-based interface, for example, by using a command bean. Don't expose the details of the business logic object model.
Options for the application server: • WebSphere Application Server • Lotus Domino Application Server		

Table 37 describes the application development tools decisions and options.

Table 37. Application development tools decisions and options

Decisions	Impacts	Suggestions
Will the application development tools facilitate different parts of the application to be built by personnel with appropriate skills?	Developing the presentation, business, and data access logic requires different skill sets. It is difficult to have one person or one team build the entire e-business application.	The development environment should facilitate building an application from many parts developed by different teams. Also, debugging in such an integrated environment should allow all the parts in the application to be executed together.
How much integration is provided by the application development tool set?	The degree to which the type of e-business application development is integrated into a single development environment can help provide productivity for the development team.	Ensure that all tools can inter operate, for example the parts produced in one tool are usable in another tool using round trip engineering. Ensure that the parts that make up the entire project can be managed and controlled in a consistent manner.
How will a team development environment be supported?	The team development environment has a direct impact on productivity and the quality of code.	Make sure that the different tools (for example, for Web page creation, Web site management, UI building, application development, and connecting to the back-end systems) all work well together. The development tools should support a team environment providing integrity of code.

Decisions	Impacts	Suggestions
Will the code be developed on one platform and deployed on another? How is the application deployed across n-tiers?	The development tools should allow the development of code on the platform that is most productive for developers, and then assist in deployment to other platforms. Deployment and its tools have a direct impact on the quality and testability of the code.	The development tools should include the ability to package modules for deployment on different servers. This functionality can be provided by the development environment or by allowing development tools to interoperate with system management tools.
How does the tool assist the developer in ensuring all parts of complex components have been completed?	Components have very complex interfaces that need to be implemented correctly and completely to allow them to function correctly. For example, a server component may need to define a client side proxy, a copy helper, a key to find the component, an interface to store/restore the component, etc., to allow it to function properly in a n-tier solution.	Tools should provide smart guides that assist the developer in a step-by-step process to ensure that all the necessary parts of the components are properly defined.
Options for application development tools: • VisualAge for Java • WebSphere Studio • Domino Designer		

5.2.3.5 Security decisions and options

Table 38 describes the security decisions and options.

Table 38. Security decisions and options

Decisions	Impacts	Suggestions
Is this an Internet or an intranet-based requirement?	This will impact how much security is required based on trusted versus non-trusted parties.	Internet access requires proper security to authenticate and authorize valid users, and protect from attacks. If you are accessing back-end applications and data, then establish a DMZ to protect back-end applications from attacks. The application server (with the business logic) should be placed in the trusted internal network behind the DMZ.

Decisions	Impacts	Suggestions
Does communication across the network need to be encrypted?	Encryption is an expensive operation and impacts your end-to-end budget. Deciding such things as which parts of a message need encryption, and the levels of encryption needed inside the firewall versus outside the firewall, may impact the design and certainly the technologies.	Where applicable, use proven standard technologies such as SSL.
If servers or clients are located outside the USA, is a 40-bit or 56-bit encryption acceptable?	The U.S. is relaxing some controls over the export of cryptographic products. Financial institutions in many countries can now obtain export licenses.	If the cryptographic products cannot be exported to the country, ask the customer to seek strong cryptography from non-U.S. sources.
How will users be identified and authenticated?	Decide what information will be open to all visitors and at what point users need to be authenticated.	Cookies can be used to recognize repeat visitors to the site without needing to know any of their personal details. User IDs and password are the minimum required for authentication. Use digital signatures if possible.
What privacy rules should be applied to information provided by users?	Policies should be in place for the use of collected user data.	Ensure that the policies are consistent with the legislation of the countries in which the servers will reside governing the holding of personal data on computer files.
Options for security: • Basic authentication • Client certificates • Application specific • Cookies		

5.2.3.6 Performance decisions and options

Performance considerations span the range from a client to the back-end system, so we discuss this topic in relation to each tier or block of the e-business solution.

Considerations for client performance are to:

- Define client response time budget based on detailed flows. Include such considerations as:

  - Formatting the request:

    - Client startup delays, loading, initialization, memory management
    - Number and size of graphics

- Submitting the request

  - Number of requests, serialization of requests
  - Number of TCP/IP connections verses persistent connections
  - Number and protocol of Java connections

  - Formatting the response

  - Data aggregation/coalescing should be done on server-side
  - To and from format conversions (for example, encrypt or decrypt) latency
  - Table construction
  - Use client-side browser caches (memory, disk, image)

- Define the client system configuration

  - Where possible (that is, intranet solutions), establish a "minimum" client configuration

  - Where not possible (Internet, etc.), establish a design point for the solution, for example, "thin" client - lowest common denominator

  - In any case, avoid a mismatch between development and deployment systems

  - Java versus HTML

- Test the application on the full range of deployed clients

  - Processor size and configuration, operating system release, browser, JVM
  - Avoid mismatch "but it ran OK on my PC"

Considerations for network performance are to:

- Use application profiling and technology to understand how your application uses the network, number of round trips, etc.:

  - Serialized versus parallel flows
  - Number of objects
  - Multiple record versus summary data flow

- Understand the deployment network

  - Packet size
  - Packet loss
  - Typical and peak round trip latency (network load from existing traffic)
  - Paths between each node
  - Number of protocol/format conversions (TCP/IP to SNA and so on)

- Allocate appropriate budget

- Gather data about application performance

  - Instrument limited logging
  - Track end user response time as metric

Considerations for the Web server are to:

- Monitor server statistics

  - Matrix differ by workload type
  - Set alerts to inform you about performance problems

- Use fast devices for Web server logs

- Cache all objects that are frequently used
- Java servlets are much faster than CGI-BIN programs

Considerations for load balancing include:

- Growth path must be defined *up front*
- Type of load balancing design can affect response time and consistency
    - *Round Robin*: Limited user balancing, not true load balancing
    - *"Intelligent" load balancing*: Work is distributed based on each server workload
- Load balancing (cluster) design and e-business application design must be done in concert

5.2.4 Products in Framework for e-business supporting CRM

This section describe the products in the IBM Framework for e-business that will deliver the functionality for your CRM application with data access.

5.2.4.1 WebSphere Application Server Standard Edition

WebSphere Application Server Standard Edition (Figure 119) is an IBM Web application server product that may deliver the functionality for your CRM application with data access.

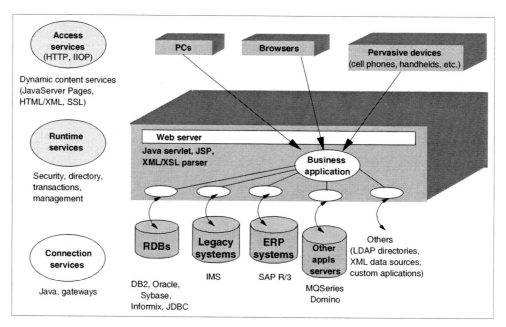

Figure 119. WebSphere Application Server Standard Edition

WebSphere Application Server Standard Edition offers:

- Session tracking
    - Records the referral page that led a visitor to your site
    - Tracks the visitor's position in your site
    - Associates user identification with the session

- Dynamic page content
  - Supports variable substitution in your Web pages
  - Specialized servlets to allow administrators to dynamically post site-wide bulletins or news flashes
  - Specialized servlets to enable visitors to exchange messages with other visitors connected to the site
- Connection management (using WebSphere Connection Manager)
- Security

Additional IBM WebSphere products may be added to WebSphere Application Server Standard Edition that perform the following functionality:

- Personalization (using WebSphere Personalization) and user profile management:
  - Uses rules-based personalization and collaborative filtering to personalize Web page content for each site visitor
  - Provides the ability to maintain detailed, persistent information about your Web visitors
  - Makes the information available for use in your Web applications
- Site activity (using WebSphere Site Analyzer) monitor
  - Has site traffic measurement and reporting, dynamic language translation
  - Java application that provides a dynamic, real-time view of the activity on your Web-site

WAS improves performance by using the technique called *connection pooling*. The technology is illustrated in Figure 120. The following steps describe the process:

1. WAS passes a user request to a servlet.
2. The servlet requests a connection from the pool.
3. The pool gives the servlet a connection.
4. The servlet uses the connection to the data server.
5. The data server returns data back.
6. When the servlet ends, the connection is returned to the pool.
7. The servlet sends the response back.

If the connection is not available, the following actions occur:

1. The CM requests a new connection.
2. The new connection is added to the connection pool.

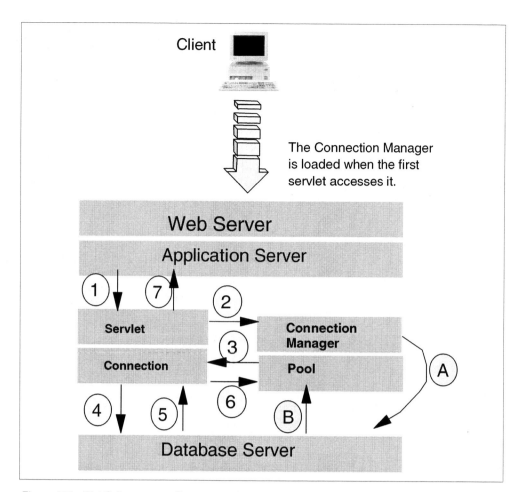

Figure 120. WebSphere connection manager

5.2.4.2 WebSphere Edge Server

When there is a requirement to enhance the performance of the site, WebSphere Edge Server is used. It is a robust caching and load-balancing product for mission-critical, high-volume sites (previously version known as WebSphere Performance Pack).

5.2.4.3 Lotus Domino Application Server

Lotus Domino Application Server is a product that may deliver the functionality of your CRM application with data access. Figure 121 illustrates the components of Domino Server and some of the technologies used in the e-business application.

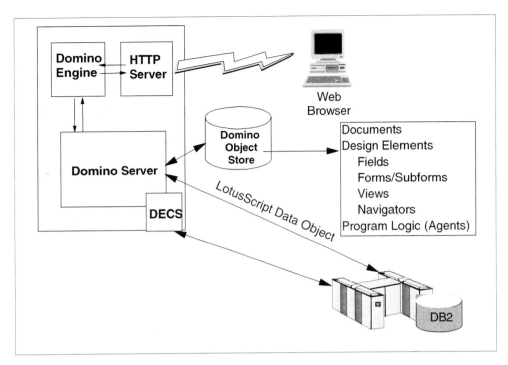

Figure 121. Domino Application Server

Domino forms are used to create the presentation layer of the application. They include all the fields and graphics to be presented to the user.

The program logic in Domino Web applications is created in Agents. Agents can be created in the Notes formula language, LotusScript, or Java. Agents are programs that are triggered to execute by event. Typical events that trigger agents are:

- On a schedule (that is, 8 AM on weekdays)
- If documents have been created or modified
- When a document is opened
- When a document is closed
- If called by another agent program
- When a button is clicked
- When hypertext is clicked

To access enterprise data with Domino, LotusScript Data Object (LS:DO), and Domino Enterprise Connection Services (DECS) are used. LS:DO gives access to relational data (for example, DB2 UDB) through LotusScript. It is good for occasional access, but must be programmed. DECS is real-time access to any external data source (for example, DB2 UDB) and does not require any programming. The database connection is continuous and connections are shared.

5.2.5 CRM with data access solution: WebSphere Application Server

IBM WebSphere Application Server is an e-business application deployment environment that is built on open standards-based technology. It is the cornerstone of WebSphere application offerings and services. The Standard Edition lets you use Java servlets, JavaServer Pages (JSP), and XML to quickly transform static Web sites into vital sources of dynamic Web content. WebSphere

Application Server Standard Edition is a reliable, scalable, and secure deployment environment that is available on Intel and UNIX technology-based platforms versions, including IBM AIX, Sun Solaris, Novell NetWare, Mircosoft Windows NT, IBM OS/390, IBM OS/400, Red Hat Linux, and Caldera Linux.

5.2.5.1 Static view of the solution

In Figure 122, the solution overview introduces a candidate technology, WebSphere Application Server Standard Edition in the middle tier of the architecture. This component is responsible for the application business logic. It also manages the interface to the back-end database or application. Using JSP, it creates the Web pages dynamically and serves them up to Internet via the Web server.

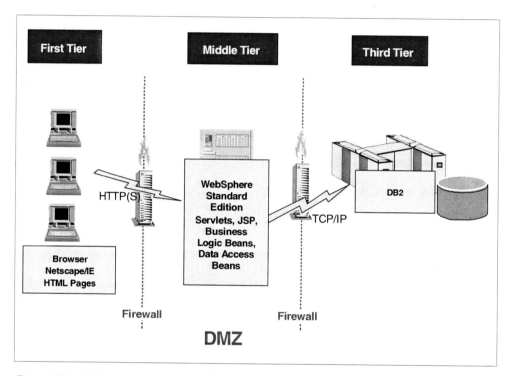

Figure 122. WebSphere account self service: Static application view

5.2.5.2 Dynamic view of the solution

Figure 123 shows the programming components used in a simple scenario of retrieving user account information and changing order mix. The interactions and roles of the illustrated business components are described in the application walkthrough.

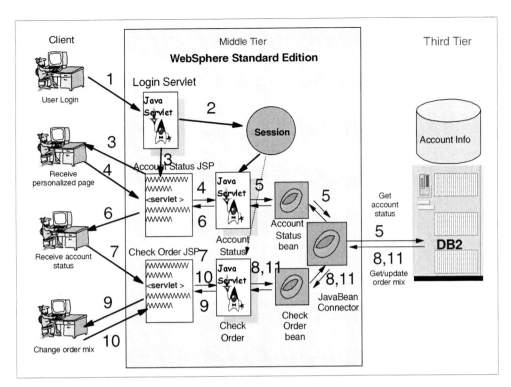

Figure 123. WebSphere account self service: Dynamic application view

Each step in the application flow shown in Figure 123 is explained here:

1. The user submits a login form, via their client (for example, a browser) through the firewall, which requests the Web server to execute a login servlet using the data that was entered.

2. The servlet creates a session object, which is used to maintain the state during all subsequent user requests.

3. The servlet invokes the Account Status JSP, which causes a personalized page to be sent as HTML to the user.

4. The user clicks a button to request the account status, and the request is sent through the firewall. The JSP executes a servlet (servlet tag statement).

5. The servlet uses a JavaBean and JavaBean connector to connect to DB2 UDB and run an account status query.

6. The JSP is returned to user with account status information.

7. The user selects the Order from account status page and a request is sent through the firewall. JSP executes a servlet (servlet tag statement).

8. The servlet uses JavaBeans and JavaBean connectors (with the same connection that was established in step 5) to run the order query.

9. The JSP is returned to the user with order information.

10. The user changes the order mix and submits a change request through the firewall.

11. The servlet uses a JavaBean and JavaBean connector (with the same connection that was established in step 5 and used in step 8) to update the order.

5.2.5.3 Security walkthrough

In Figure 124, the solution covers security architecture. The walkthrough steps describe the interactions of the components in the architecture. It highlights the technologies and components used to provide security in the solution environment.

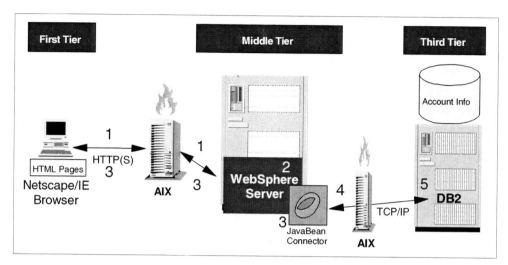

Figure 124. Security solution architecture using WebSphere and dynamic application design view

The following list explains the security walkthrough shown in Figure 124:

1. The user logs in through the login form by providing a user ID and password. The user ID and password are transmitted via HTTPS through the firewall, which routes it to the Web server.

2. The Web server authenticates the user ID and password, and a session object is created to manage user requests and maintain state.

3. The user requests their account status or order information. This information is transmitted via HTTPS through the firewall. The request invokes the appropriate servlet. The servlet invokes a JavaBean, which in turn, uses the JavaBean connector to attempt to run the account status query on DB2 UDB.

4. The JavaBean connector sends the query along with the user ID and password, which have been saved in the session object, via TCP/IP through the firewall to DB2 UDB.

5. DB2 UDB security compares the user ID and password with the directory and either allows the query to execute or rejects the query.

The architecture components selected using WebSphere include:

* Netscape/Internet Explorer Web browser
* VisualAge for Java Enterprise Edition as a development tool
* WebSphere Standard Edition
* DB2 UDB server

5.2.6 CRM with data access solution: Domino Application Server

Domino is an environment that makes it easier for you to productively perform unstructured work using a wealth of rapidly changing information and knowledge. It's middleware that lets you customize the Web interactions.

Domino is appropriate for Web applications that focus on information sharing, collaboration, and business process automation. A Domino database is a collection of documents (just like a Web site). It has built-in capabilities for sorting and viewing in different ways, for managing the documents (complete with built-in workflow for approval), and for e-mail integration.

5.2.6.1 Static view of the solution

The solution overview, shown in Figure 125, introduces another candidate technology, Lotus Domino Application Server, in the middle tier of the architecture. This component is responsible for the application business logic. It also manages the interface to the back-end database or application. Using forms, it creates the Web pages dynamically and serve them up to the Internet via the Web server.

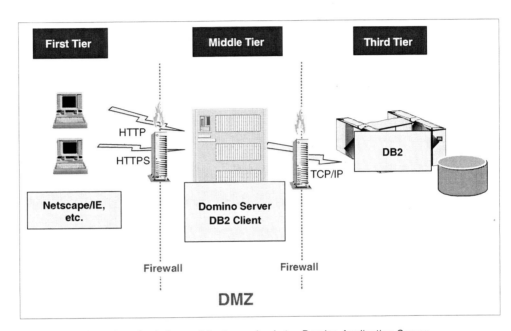

Figure 125. Overview of solution architecture using Lotus Domino Application Server

5.2.6.2 Dynamic view of the solution

Figure 126 examines the programming components used in a simple scenario of retrieving user account information and changing the order mix. The interactions and roles of the illustrated business components are described in the application walkthrough.

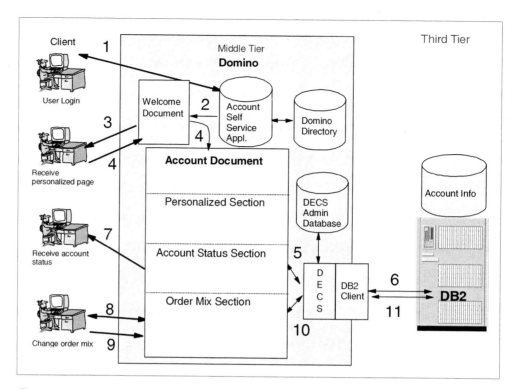

Figure 126. Domino account self service: Dynamic application view

The application walkthrough for Figure 126 is outlined here:

1. The user points their browser to the account self-service URL. The Domino account self-service application rejects the anonymous request and prompts for a user ID and password.

2. The user successfully logs in to the application. Domino opens the welcome document and populates the document with personalized account information based on the user ID. The account information is stored in the account self-service application database.

3. Domino converts the welcome document into HTML and serves it to the user.

4. The user clicks a button on the welcome page to request the account status. The account document is opened on the application server.

5. The DECS server task, which is monitoring the account self-service application, intercepts the account document, opens the document, and sends a predefined query to obtain the account status and order information.

6. DB2 UDB runs the query and returns the results to DECS. DECS maps the results to the fields in the account document.

7. The account document is converted into HTML, with the personalized and account status sections visible and the order mix section hidden (no generated HTML).

8. The user clicks a button to view the orders. Domino converts the account document into HTML again, but includes the order mix section.

9. The user changes their order mix and submits the change.

10. DECS intercepts the document, saves it, and sends an update command to DB2 UDB.

11. DB2 UDB updates the database that contains customer orders. The original account document, which is stored in the Domino database, remains unchanged. Only DB2 UDB data is altered in this application.

5.2.6.3 Security walkthrough

The solution in Figure 127 covers security architecture. The walkthrough steps describe the interactions of the components in the architecture. It highlights the technologies and components used to provide security in the solution environment.

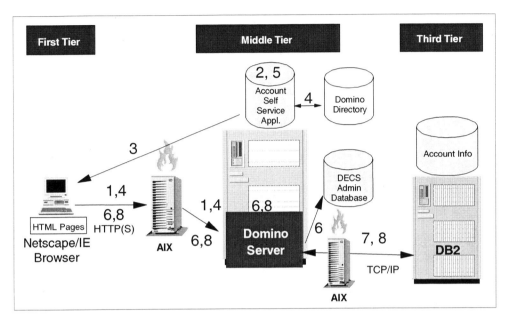

Figure 127. Security solution architecture using Domino and the dynamic application design view

The security walkthrough for Figure 127 is outlined here:

1. The user points their browser to the account self-service application URL. The request is transmitted through the firewall, which routes it to the Domino server.

2. The access control list (ACL) associated with the Domino database file is queried to determine if anonymous has access control rights to the database.

3. The database ACL does not have an entry for anonymous, so Domino responds with a user ID and password prompt.

4. The user submits a valid user ID and password through the firewall to the server. Domino finds the user ID in the Domino directory and compares the entered password with the registered user's password.

5. The ACL associated with the Domino database file is queried again to determine access control rights to the database. The welcome document is served.

6. The user clicks a button to request the account status, which is sent via the firewall to the server. DECS intercepts the account status document, opens it and checks the DECS administrator database for the appropriate user ID and password to send to DB2 UDB.

7. DECS creates a connection to DB2 UDB, sends the SQL command to DB2 UDB via TCP/IP through the firewall, and receives the results.

8. The user submits the order change, which is sent via the firewall to the server. DECS intercepts the document, save it, and sends the update command to DB2 UDB via TCP/IP using the firewall with the same connection established in step 7.

The architecture components selected using Domino include:

- Netscape/Internet Explorer Web browser
- Domino Designer for developers
- Domino server (includes DECS)
- DB2 UDB client
- DB2 UDB server

5.2.7 Strengths and weaknesses of the solutions

This section summarizes the relative strengths and weaknesses of the alternative solutions by comparing and contrasting them according to the following defined qualities:

- **Performance and capacity**: The response time for requests and total number of requests that can be handled.

- **Security**: The ability to resist unauthorized access and allow legitimate users access.

- **Availability**: The proportion of time the system is up and running.

- **Usability**: Ensuring that the right information is available to the user at the right time and ensuring that the user requests goes to the right service providers. This is from the end users' perspective.

- **Maintainability and manageability**: The ability to modify the system, delete unwanted capabilities, adapt to new operating environments, and restructure the system.

- **Testability**: The ease with which software can be made to demonstrate its faults through testing.

- **Extendibility and scalability**: The ability to make incremental changes quickly and cost effectively, and the ability to handle ever increasing loads.

- **Portability**: The ability of the system to run under different computing environments.

- **Reusability**: The ability to reuse the systems' structure and components in other applications.

- **Business quality**: Cost, schedule, staff, resources,...

Performance and capacity
Performance and capacity are the measure of response time for requests and the total number of requests that can be handled. To measure performance, response time targets are required. For the WebSphere solution, multiple objects are involved in handling a request (servlet, JavaBean, JavaBean connector) that would affect performance. Both solutions need additional software and hardware to handle load balancing across replicated servers. The number of concurrent users supported in the Domino solution will be lower.

Security
Security is the ability to resist unauthorized access and allow legitimate users access. Both solutions provide security through the use of:

- DMZ to isolate the core business data and protect it from outside attacks
- Authentication of user via a user ID and password
- Authorization to access back-end data

Both solutions have security problems because:

- The server on the second tier inside the DMZ maintains the user IDs and passwords

- The server on the second tier inside the DMZ has the application and business logic

Availability
Availability is the proportion of time the system is up and running. Availability for both solutions greatly depends on the platform and its architecture on which the application is deployed. Both solutions are based on products that can be deployed on platforms that have high availability, such as the iSeries server.

Usability
Usability ensures that the right information is available to the user at the right time. It also ensures that the user requests go to the right service providers. This is from the end users' perspective. Both solutions are developed using development tools that can create the most effective user interface for the user.

Maintainability and manageability
Maintainability and manageability are the ability to modify the system, delete unwanted capabilities, adapt to new operating environments, and restructure the system. WebSphere Studio and Domino Designer both support this functionality.

Testability
Testability is the ease with which software can be made to demonstrate its faults through testing. WAS solution has multiple objects that might be deployed on multiple systems. This makes the testing of WAS solution more complex.

Extendibility and scalability
Extendibility and scalability is the ability to make incremental changes quickly and cost effectively, and the ability to handle ever increasing loads. The WebSphere solution can take advantage of Java's inheritance, interfaces, and encapsulation to facilitate extensions. The Domino-based solution can be easily extended to include discussion groups, bulletin boards, e-mail, etc.

Both solutions do not have any inherent capabilities to scale. A Domino solution has defined limitations on the number of concurrent users it can manage, which makes scalability an issue. WebSphere Application Server Standard Edition has some load balancing features, but they are not as sophisticated as those found in WebSphere Application Server Advanced Edition. A WebSphere solution could manage the growing requirements of a business using Standard Edition. And when the requirements exceed their limits, Advanced Edition could be the platform of choice to be the deployment environment for the same application.

Portability
Portability is the ability of the system to run under different computing environments. The WebSphere solution can be ported to any system that has a JVM (which is available for most operating systems and across all platforms). The Domino solution will only run on Domino, which may be deployed on most popular platforms.

Reusability

Reusability is the ability to reuse the systems' structure and components in other applications. The WebSphere solution is based on Java and, therefore, the servlets or JavaBeans can be used as components in other applications. The Domino solution is form based. Forms require the entire form to be used "as is" in another Domino-based application.

Business quality

Business quality refers to costs, schedules, staff, resources, etc, to the company to develop the solution. The WebSphere solution requires Java skills. However, the VisualAge for Java visual development environment is an advantage. The Domino-based solution is form-based, easy to develop, and can leverage any existing Domino skills.

The selection of the technology to deliver the solution is often determined by the non-functional requirements. Based on the requirements stated in "Non-functional requirements" on page 281, both WebSphere and Domino solutions described could fulfill these retirements. The only requirement that could sway the decision toward a WebSphere solution would be in a scalability requirement where the increased number of users in the future could lead to a transaction-intensive environment.

5.2.7.1 The advantages and disadvantages of the WebSphere solution

The advantages of the WebSphere Application Server solution include:

- Java-based servlets and beans are easy to extend and reuse.
- VisualAge for Java provides an IDE to build the solution and visual tools to connect to DB2 UDB.
- Can be ported to systems supporting JVM (which is available on most platforms).

The disadvantages of the WebSphere Application Server solution are:

- Needs Java skills to develop.
- Many objects involved in handling a request may affect performance.

5.2.7.2 The advantages and disadvantages of the Domino solution

The advantages of the Lotus Domino solution include:

- DECS is forms-based for easy development and maintenance.
- DECS gives you real-time access to external data using pooled connections.
- Applications can be easily extended to include discussion groups, bulletin boards, e-mail, etc.
- It leverages existing Domino development skills.
- Applications are easy and fast to develop.

The disadvantages of the Lotus Domino solution are:

- The number of concurrent users supported is lower.
- Applications only run on Domino and cannot be easily ported.
- Requires Domino development skills.

5.3 CRM with transactions

CRM with transactions looks at e-business problems where a user is interfacing with existing business applications. Typically, these applications are considered as pushing the enterprise "down" to the Internet. Transactions are used for integration to back-end applications and data. They are secure transactions and have authorized access.

The technologies cover component architectures (EJB/CORBA), transaction monitors (transaction processors and monitors), and Enterprise Solution Structure (patterns for e-business CRM applications with transactions). The products discussed include WebSphere Advanced Edition and WebSphere Enterprise Edition (TX Series, Component Broker).

The logical decisions, in the subject area, emphasize making recommendations in the application server, connectors, enterprise applications, and data, security, and performance decision blocks.

5.3.1 The problem space for CRM with transactions

Many of the e-business basic building blocks can be involved in transactions. It is important to distinguish where the transaction demarcation takes place and where the actual transactional environment is implemented (Figure 128).

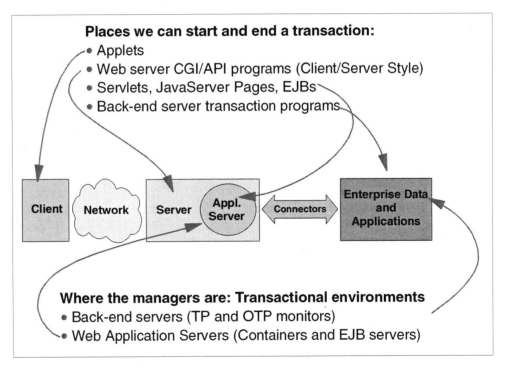

Figure 128. Building blocks and transactions

A single transaction is implemented by a set of API calls in a single program that executes in one place in the end-to-end logical space. The Web server, the Web application server, and the back-end server, with the enterprise data and applications, can be on a single, or many, distributed physical boxes.

The calls (for begin and end of transaction) are processed by the transaction manager. Placing this manager is one of the critical design decisions in an e-business transaction application. If there is an existing transaction manager in the system, then it is a "placement" decision.

A sample scenario of a CRM application with transactions problem space is shown in Figure 129. Here, a business flow is described where a transaction of transferring an amount from a savings account to a checking account is performed.

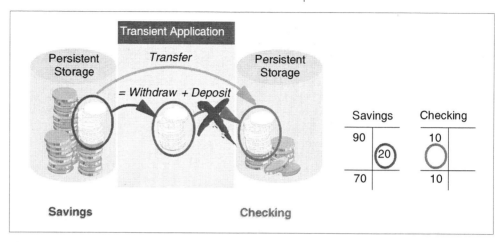

Figure 129. Bank account transaction problem

The following steps describe a successful transaction when an amount of money is transferred from a savings account to a checking account, as illustrated in Figure 129:

1. There is a savings account and checking account.
2. The savings and checking accounts are in persistent storage (file, database).
3. The transaction is to transfer funds from the savings to checking account.
4. A transient application is run to perform the transaction.
5. The application performs a withdrawal from the savings account.
6. The savings balance is reduced and a new savings balance is recorded.
7. The application performs a deposit into the checking account.
8. The checking balance is increased and a new checking balance recorded.

The following steps replace step 8 in the above scenario and show an incomplete transaction. The deposit fails to update the checking account. The end result describes the consequence of performing the transfer with no transaction manager in place.

a. The application fails to complete the deposit into the checking account.

b. The money does not show up in the checking account, and the balance is not updated.

c. There are inconsistent balances. The funds have been removed from the persistent storage of the savings account and not deposited anywhere.

d. The money and transient application are gone. The transaction has finished incomplete.

Working in a transactional environment

Transactions need to satisfy the following requirements:

- *Atomic*: Where a transaction is and indivisible unit of work where all its actions succeed or they all fail. This is also known as a logical unit of work.

- *Consistent*: Where after the transaction executes, it must leave the system in a correct state or abort.

- *Isolated*: Where a transaction's behavior is not affected by other transactions that may execute concurrently.

- *Durable*: Where a transaction's effect is permanent after it commits (for example, the information is saved in a recoverable storage resource).

The acronym ACID helps you remember the properties of a transaction. It is worthwhile to note that some transaction management programs may define transactions differently than a LUW (for example, CICS can include multiple LUWs).

A typical online transaction processing (OLTP) transaction consists of many computing and data-access tasks to be run in one or more machines. An LUW is a sequence of processing actions (database changes, for example) that must be completed before any of the individual actions can be regarded as committed.

A transaction program (TP) is the implementing program that manages LUWs. The application program's role is to mark the beginning and end of the transaction. The begin can be implicit. The end must be marked through a COMMIT or ROLLBACK call to the transactional environment.

The transaction monitor (TM) oversees the transaction by monitoring and logging each access and change of the persistent storage (also known as *recoverable resource*). It monitors transaction activity to enable restoration of a previous consistent state in case of failure. The recoverable resource monitoring unit of the transactional environment is called *resource manager* (RM).

In case of an application crash, the transactional environment does an automatic ROLLBACK or kicks off some application defined retry or rollback logic. This will typically "undo" the events of the transaction up to the failure to ensure that recoverable resources are not affected by the failure.

Figure 130 shows the savings and checking accounts scenario in two different systems. Both systems support a transactional environment, and both transactional environments know and communicate with each other. The transfer funds application is started as a transaction on system one in the Transactional Environment 1 (TE1), managed by the Resource Manager/Coordinator of TE1 (RMC1), and finished in TE2. RMC1 has the master or controller role, coordinating all resource managers of the resources involved in the transaction. The local RMs are controlled directly, and the remote RMs are controlled through the remote Resource Manager Coordinator of the remote transactional environments. Resource Manager Coordinators are also called *Sync Point Managers*.

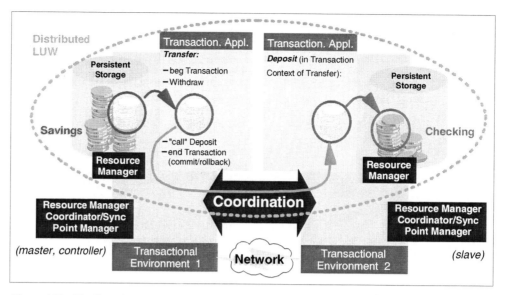

Figure 130. Distributed transactional environment (performing logical units of work)

A failure, ROLLBACK, or COMMIT in any of the transactional environments informs the controlling transactional environment, which in turn, coordinates a ROLLBACK or COMMIT in all the other transactional environments to keep the recoverable resources consistent. Transactional environments, which can participate in a distributed LUW, implement a two-phase commit.

You can also divide the application into parts with the transaction program located remotely to the RMC. You can separate the resource manager from the coordinator.

In summary, a transactional environment provides:

- Process management
- Starting server processes
- Monitoring process execution
- Dispatching work to processes
- Balancing process workloads
- Transaction management (including recovery)
- Secure client/server communications management

5.3.2 Requirements for the e-business solution

Transaction management extends the simple data access CRM solution. The business drivers, functional requirements, and non-functional requirements define the scope of a system that will have transaction management in its e-business solution design. This section extends the CRM data access scenario to include the design options for transaction management. For the purpose of illustration, we discuss a convenience banking application.

Business drivers

Business drivers for this CRM convenience banking example:

- Improve customer service:

  - Give end customers inquiry and update access to the information related to that customer, but that is maintained by the business.

- Provide customers with convenient access to services from home through the Internet. Extend the current Web-enabled publishing capability with a Web enabled transaction capability.

- Ensure that customer interaction is secure and confidential.

- Provide customization of the customer's experience.

• Reduce time and effort to deploy new enterprise applications:

- Reduce lead time to deploy new applications.

- Support and enable the branch channel by providing new capabilities and access to existing business systems and data.

- Provide broader leverage of existing centralized applications without having to rewrite or re-engineer these applications.

- Share and re-use business logic between different delivery systems.

- Provide a highly scalable and highly available Web-enablement of existing business transactions.

• Make prudent IT investments:

- Provide an enterprise architecture and infrastructure that scales to meet a broad range of business requirements.

- Ensure that corporate network and assets are secure from outside (Internet) attacks.

- Ensure a level of manageability for new systems equals existing systems.

- Ensure performance and response time for new systems equals existing systems for internal users and equals best-of-breed in the industry for customer Internet access.

Functional requirements
The functional requirements for this CRM convenience banking example are:

• View account balances
• View recent transactions
• Pay bills
• Transfer funds
• Stop payments

The example application follows this flow:

1. A user points their browser to the bank home page.
2. The user logs in and accesses their personalized page.
3. The user checks their account balances.
4. The user transfers funds between accounts.

Non-functional requirements
Non-functional requirements for this CRM convenience banking example are:

• *Security requirement*: User authentication, access only to customer information, secure transactions (high)

• *Operational requirement*: 24x7 (medium)

• *Performance requirement*: Response time for business transactions is 5 seconds for page to page (high)

- *Scalability*: Number of online users > (greater than) 50,000; number of concurrent online users is 200 to 300 (high)

- *Availability*: 98% of the time (high)

- *Extendibility*: Potential for the addition of new financial services, for example, stock trading (high)

- *Flexibility*: Should be able to work with all popular browsers (high)

- *Maintainability and manageability*: As in current systems (medium)

5.3.2.1 Component architectures that support transaction processing

CORBA is the standard distributed object architecture developed by the Object Management Group (OMG) consortium. Since the founding of the OMG, its mission has been to define open standards in software development so that objects written by different vendors in different languages, running on any platform, could interoperate in a distributed environment.

Even though CORBA, CORBA transaction services, and the available ORBs are mature, there is more focus on the Web application servers, containers, and Java runtime environments. These environments include Java-dedicated ORBs, which support distributed object technology with RMI and IIOP. CORBA ORBs and the Java ORB communicate with each other. Logical units of work can include resources managed in a legacy CORBA ORB and the new Java ORB. The Java ORB is built into the Enterprise JavaBean Server (EJS).

Enterprise JavaBean (EJB) technology can be viewed as CORBA restricted to Java, but extended for application services. This allows many shortcuts in the implementation of the EJS and makes it potentially faster than the general purpose ORBs. Figure 131 shows a logical architecture of a Web application server providing transaction management services using EJBs.

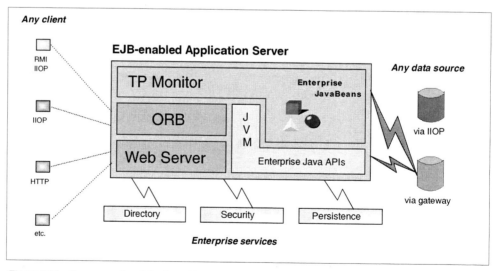

Figure 131. Component architecture: Enterprise JavaBeans/CORBA

The EJB architecture has the following characteristics:

- *Transactional*: EJB transactions use a subset of the Java Transaction Service (JTS) API for programmatically starting and stopping transactions. JTS supports distributed transactions that can span multiple databases on multiple systems.

- *Portable*: EJB components may run on any EJB server, on any operating system.

- *Multi-tier*: You can partition and deploy your application onto three or more interacting tiers, the client providing the presentation logic, the application server providing the business logic, and the data server providing the business data.

- *Distributed*: EJBs are intended to live on one machine and be invoked remotely from another machine.

- *Scalable*: A few product families that support or will support a container for EJBs include:

  - TP monitors such as IBM TX Series or BEA Tuxedo

  - Component Transaction servers such as IBM Component Broker Connectors (CB-Connector) or Microsoft Transaction Server

  - CORBA platform such as Inprise VisiBroker/ITS or IBM Component Broker Connector

  - Web platform such as IBM WebSphere Application Server

  - Database management systems such as IBM DB2 UDB, Oracle, or Sybase

- *Secure*: EJB architecture is built on the standard Java security services supported in the JDK. Java security supports authentication and authorization services to restrict access to secure objects and methods.

- *Protocol neutral*: EJBs are based on industry-standard protocols such as TCP/IP, IIOP, Java Remote Messaging Protocol (JRMP), HTTP, and even Distributed Component Object Model (DCOM).

Adding the EJB and Enterprise JavaBean Server technology to the Web server, the former business logic JavaBeans with connectors are replaced by EJBs. The major benefit over JavaBeans is that we can stay with distributed Java objects and have transaction and persistence support. Figure 132 shows the EJB programming model and walks through the EJBs manage transactions.

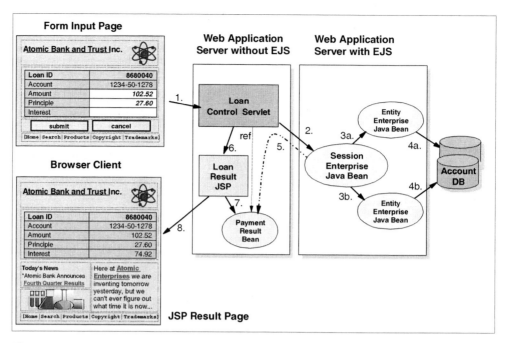

Figure 132. EJB programming model

The flow in the EJB and EJS programming model in Figure 132 for Web applications is outlined here:

1. From the browser, an HTML form with name-value pairs and an action is sent to the Web application server, which triggers a so-called *control servlet*.

2. The control servlet restores the state, parses the name-value pairs, connects to the transaction part of the application (which is a session EJB), and invokes the appropriate method.

3. The session EJB talks to the entity EJBs or other session EJBs.

4. The entity EJBs perform basic business logic and access the persistent storage.

5. The result is returned in the form of Java result beans tree and is kept alive by referencing the root bean by a temporary variable, which is valid through the later JSP call.

6. The control servlet calls the proper JSP to prepare the HTML reply, which usually is an HTML form.

7. The reply JSP references the result beans to display the attributes in constant text and fields.

8. The generated HTML is returned to the browser.

With the EJB and EJS technology, the complexity is moved out of the business code into the infrastructure. The infrastructure becomes more complex to setup, debug, run, and maintain. It is a single and one-time cost to provide a high-level platform.

EJB communication to CORBA/IIOP is provided as a standard. Non EJB and EJS environments, such as CORBA and RMI clients and servers can communicate with EJBs through EJSs.

Figure 133 illustrates the transactional capabilities of EJB/EJS. It indicates that:

- The EJB with a transaction server may be part of the Web application server.
- The Web application server and EJB server may be on different boxes.

The funds transfer demarcates explicitly the transaction boundaries. The transaction server, in turn, knows the "touched" resources – EJBs, DBMSs, and other LUW involved, new or legacy Transaction Servers (not shown). It performs a two-phase commit against the transactional environments of these resources.

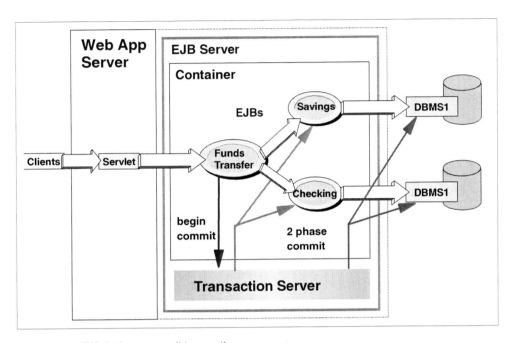

Figure 133. EJB 2-phase commit transaction

The advantages of the EJB technology are:

- A robust, distributed environment that provides all the necessary services for a good client/server middleware
- Provides a mapping to CORBA/IIOP
- 100% Java
- Development and deployment are separated
- Automation of many of the common programming tasks (object registration, location, activation, error-handling, etc.)

The disadvantages of the EJB technology are:

- It requires a highly skilled developers to create EJB applications.
- All EJSs may not yet work together.

5.3.2.2 Patterns that support solutions

Enterprise Solution Structure (ESS) architectural patterns are used to build solutions for CRM with transactions. Patterns are a way to describe situations and experiences so that similar applications can leverage the knowledge. When using patterns, you must:

1. Use business patterns to match CRM with transactions problem space.
2. Identify the best topologies that fit CRM with transactions e-business problems.
3. Understand applicable reference architectures.
4. Look at solution patterns that fit the reference architecture.

For more information on IBM Patterns for e-business, go to:
http://www.ibm.com/developerworks/patterns/

5.3.3 Decision blocks for CRM with transactions

The decision blocks for CRM with transactions describe the key decisions that need to be made. The tables discuss the impact of the decision on the solution and offer suggestions on how to make the decision. Figure 10 on page 30 illustrates the logical decision areas that require you to identify known options or products for each block. The decisions, impact, and suggestions discussed as part of the logical decision blocks provide a checklist for you to ensure that all aspects of the CRM problem domain have been explored and addressed in your solution.

5.3.3.1 Application server decisions and options

Table 39 describes the server decisions and options.

Table 39. Application server decision and options

Decisions	Impacts	Suggestions
Is this a logical two-, three- or n-tier solution?	The main impact is the placement of logic (presentation, business, and data access) on the tiers. In particular, is the application server in charge of managing transactions, security, and access to back-end applications.	A two-tier solution is only suitable for providing direct access to existing applications. Most likely, you will use an n-tier solution, with separation of the Web server from the application server to handle security, manage transactions, and access back-end applications.
Has it been determined whether to use component based development, traditional programming development, or integrated packages?	Existing packages, if they meet requirements, are usually faster to implement. Component-based development, with its built-in reuse capability, also offers implementation benefits in conjunction with appropriate development tools.	A component-based solution (such as EJB) provides the best choice if the application will change and needs to inter-operate with other systems. Procedural programming can be used to extend existing applications.
How will the application be split between client-side logic and server-side logic?	The key decision is who is in charge of the transactional context (for example, begin-commit in a two-phase commit). It can be the client, the server, or the back-end tier.	Use server-driven interaction, with a clear separation of interaction logic from business logic. Let the business logic handle transactions and access to back-end applications.

Table 40 describes the application development tool decisions and options.

Table 40. Application development tool decision and options

Decisions	Impacts	Suggestions
Will the application development tools facilitate different parts of the application to be built by personnel with appropriate skills?	Developing the presentation, business, and data access logic requires different skill sets. It is difficult to have one person or one team build the entire e-business application.	Make sure that the different tools (for example, for Web page creation, Web site management, UI building, application development, and connecting to the back-end systems) all work well together.
How much integration is provided by the application development tool set?	The degree to which the type of e-business application development is integrated into a single development environment can help provide productivity for the development team.	Ensure that all tools can inter operate, that is the parts produced in one tool are usable in another using round-trip engineering. Ensure that the parts that make up the entire project can be managed and controlled in a consistent manner.
How will a team development environment be supported?	The development tools should support a team environment providing integrity for application code.	The development environment should facilitate building an application from many parts developed by different teams. Also, debugging in such an integrated environment should allow all the parts in the application to be executed together.
Will the code be developed on one platform and deployed on another? How is the application deployed across n-tiers?	The development tools should allow development of code on the platform that is most productive for developers, and then assist in deployment to other platforms. The deployment must facilitate spreading the application appropriately across n-tiers.	The development tools should include the ability to package modules for deployment on different servers. This functionality can be provided by the development environment or by allowing development tools to inter operate with system management tools.
How does the tool assist the developer in ensuring all parts of complex components have been completed?	Components have very complex interfaces that need to be implemented correctly and completely to allow them to function correctly. For example, a server component may need to define a client side proxy, a copy helper, a key to find the component, an interface to store/restore the component, etc., to allow it to function properly in a n-tier solution.	Tools should provide smart guides that assist the developer in a step-by-step process to ensure that all the necessary parts of the components are properly defined.

5.3.3.2 Connectors decisions and options

Table 41 describes the connectivity decisions and options.

Table 41. Connector decisions and options

Decisions	Impacts	Suggestions
What enterprise systems, applications and data does the e-business application need to access?	The type of data, application, platform, and network may influence the technologies that may need to be considered in different architectural alternatives.	Use standard connectors (for example, JDBC or ODBC to access relational data) wherever possible. The only time that non-standard connectors should be used is when accessing existing applications without modification or when performance is a major issue.
How current does the information have to be?	If the information does not have to be updated in real-time, you may be able to use local extracts or caches to improve performance.	Use local extracts or caches for information, state, and personalization.
Will the application require synchronous or asynchronous access to the enterprise applications and data?	The use of asynchronous messaging with assured message delivery allows the application to continue operation even if the network connection or remote application is unavailable. Synchronous technology requires a connection to be available whenever the application is available.	Asynchronous messaging does not preclude using it in a synchronous mode. Resources involved in a two-phase commit transaction should be accessed in a synchronous mode.
Will you require access to different operating system, network protocols, application environments?	Although TCP/IP is the standard network protocol of the Web, your back-end systems may be using other protocols. Also, applications may be using standard or non-standard APIs. If protocol conversation is needed, you have to decide where is the best place to do the conversion.	Use protocol converters provided by the tool or product that is used for development. For example, most application servers provide connectors to communicate with CICS or IMS applications.
Is a new user interface (UI) required? If so, what kind?	If you are accessing enterprise data or application logic that currently has a defined user interface, a redesign of that interface allowing program access may be needed. Alternatively, the use of technologies allowing access to the logic and data may need to be employed.	Try not to change any of the enterprise application logic because there may be other interfaces to it already in place. Use wrappers and the appropriate call interface (for example, EPI versus ECI versus EXCI to access CICS applications). Performance may dictate the best call interface (for example, ECI over EPI for CICS.)

Decisions	Impacts	Suggestions
Will you require additional security policies?	Enterprise data and applications may have their own access security policies controlled and administered separately from those in place for the Internet environment. If access to enterprise data and applications is needed, how will security policies be enforced?	If the application server is a trusted node, it can act as a proxy to the enterprise data and applications. If not, the user IDs and passwords must be mapped from the application/Web server to the enterprise servers. Ensure that the connector technology that you are using can support the security needs.

5.3.3.3 Enterprise applications, data decisions, and options

Table 42 describes the enterprise applications, data decisions, and options.

Table 42. Enterprise applications and data disowns and options

Decisions	Impacts	Suggestions
Do the service hours for the enterprise data repository match the e-business application targets?	You may have to make some policy decisions about how to treat requests that cannot be handled immediately.	Options include asking the user to resubmit or placing the request on a queue for handling later, with possible confirmation by e-mail.
How will you map the access authorization rules for the corporate database to your e-business user identification?	This will be an important question if you intend to enable a controlled ability for certain Web users to update corporate database records.	Define authorization using access control lists to ensure that users can only modify their own data. You also need to map the user ID and password to role-based application or database user IDs. This mapping is many-to-one.
Is your e-business application using the corporate data for reference (that is, read-only access)?	There may be performance or other advantages to working with a local replica of the database if the requirement for data currency permits it.	Use local replicas or caches for read-only data that can be updated (for example, in batch mode) on a regular basis.
Is the data in a format that is easily accessed by distributed systems?	Implications that may (or may not) affect your design include different sorting sequences and number formats.	Enterprise data may be held in EBCDIC and require translation to ASCII for presentation on the browser.
If additional code is needed to gain access to data (for example, non-relational data), how will this code be developed?	You need to decide how this code will be developed and if there are resources available to develop this additional interface code.	If your enterprise data is located on a mainframe, you may need to develop additional CICS transactions or MQSeries triggered transactions to interface to existing data or application logic.

Decisions	Impacts	Suggestions
If access is to relational databases, can the SQL be structured to minimize network traffic?	When enterprise data can be accessed with SQL calls, you should review the number of calls needed to satisfy a request. Since issuing SQL calls can be simple, it is sometimes tempting to rely on this when designing the architectural alternatives. Be careful that your architecture does not force you into issuing too many SQL calls, therefore reducing performance because of network traffic.	Consolidate SQL calls with appropriate uses of joins to reduce network traffic. Use stored procedures to consolidate SQL calls to reduce network traffic. Use a transaction monitor to provide a way of reducing application-to-enterprise server interactions. Resist the temptation to design business logic into the stored procedure, because you will lose flexibility in your design.
What are the commit and rollback requirements of the application?	For Web applications, you need to pay particular attention to incomplete or canceled transactions. At times of slow network response, the user is likely to click the Stop button on the browser and immediately retry the transaction. Your application design must allow for this.	Use a transaction monitor in the application server to manage and coordinate transactions.

5.3.3.4 Security decisions and options

Table 43 describes the security decisions and options.

Table 43. Security decisions and options

Decisions	Impacts	Suggestions
Do transactions need to be encrypted?	Encryption is an expensive operation and will impact your end-to-end budget. Deciding such things as which transactions, or which parts of a message need encryption, and the levels of encryption needed inside the firewall versus outside the firewall may impact the design and certainly the technologies.	Where applicable, use proven standard technologies such as SSL.
How will users be identified?	Decide what information will be open to all visitors and at what point users need to be authenticated.	For transactions, user IDs and password are the minimum required for authentication. Use digital signatures if possible.

Decisions	Impacts	Suggestions
Does your customer need to restrict access to parts of the site? Does the company already have a secure DMZ into which the Web server could be placed?	The number and placement of firewalls is important to restrict unwarranted access to sensitive data and applications. Review existing IBM security guidelines and practice designing solutions that properly position components around firewalls for asset protection.	Always use a DMZ to separate the outside (untrusted) world from the internal trusted network. Separate informational Web serving from transactional Web serving, and use a firewall to route secure requests to the transactional Web server. Use a second firewall to access the internal trusted network.
What privacy rules should be applied to information provided by users?	Policies should be in place for the use of collected user data.	Ensure that the policies are consistent with the legislation of the countries in which the servers will reside governing the holding of personal data on computer files.

5.3.3.5 Performance decisions and options

Table 44 describes the performance issues in relation to the CRM solution with transactions.

Table 44. Performance issues

Performance unfriendly	Performance friendly
Client invokes a create method on a remote factory object, supplying the primary key attribute or attributes for a new object to be created. A reference to the newly created remote object is returned, and the client invokes multiple "setter" methods to initialize the remaining state oaf the new object.	Client invokes a create method on a remote factory object, supplying *all* of the attributes necessary to fully initialize the new object that is created. A reference to the newly created (and fully initialized) remote object is returned.
Client invokes a method on a remote object that changes the value of several attributes for that object. The client then invokes individual "getter methods" to obtain the state of each of those changed attributes	Client invokes a method on a remote object that changes the value of several attributes for that object. The result of the method call returns the new values of each affected attribute in a single stream.
Client calls several methods to queue up individual items of work for a remote object. Client then calls a "doIt" method that instructs the object to process the items.	Client invokes a "doIt" method on a remote object, passing in all of the work items as arguments of that single call.
Client repeatedly calls a remote object for distinct items of information. The information is locally manipulated and summarized by the client for presentation.	Client makes a single remote method call, and the remote object prepares, and then returns, only the summarized information as a result.
Client invokes a query on a remote object that returns a collection of references to other remote objects. The client then invokes multiple getter methods on each of the remote objects for local presentation.	Client invokes a query on a remote object that returns "rows" of attribute values from other objects local to itself. The client uses these remote object values without any additional network interactions.

Performance unfriendly	Performance friendly
Client invokes a method on a remote object that returns a large amount of data across the network.	Client invokes a method on a remote object that locally compresses result data and then returns it. The client decompresses this result data upon receipt.

5.3.4 Products supporting CRM with transactions

The choice of IBM product used to deliver your CRM application with transactions is driven by:

- The programming skills available today
- The programming skills available tomorrow
- Whether the browser is the primary user interface
- The robustness of the environment

  - TXSeries in conjunction with MQSeries is the most robust distributed choice.

  - OS/390 CICS or IMS with MQSeries is the most robust and scalable choice.

- Reuse potential

  - Component-based development may lead to greater reuse
  - EJB or Component Broker is designed for reuse

Figure 134 displays the WebSphere Application Server product suite and the roles each edition plays in delivering customer solutions. The illustration describes the product through its various editions: Standard Edition, Advanced Edition, and Enterprise Edition.

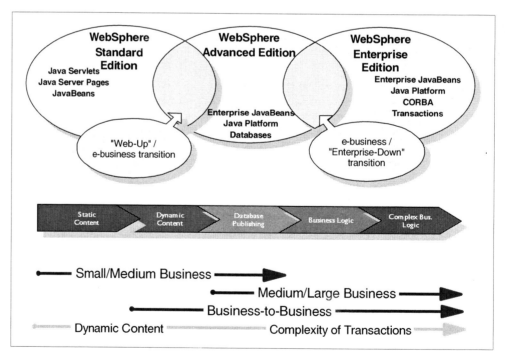

Figure 134. WebSphere Application Server product editions overview

5.3.4.1 WebSphere Advanced Edition

The key feature that WebSphere Advanced Edition carries over Standard Edition (compare Figure 119 to Figure 135) is the Enterprise JavaBean runtime environment. This provides container-managed persistence, bean-managed persistence, EJB/IIOP/CORBA support, a deployment manager, and JDBC connectors.

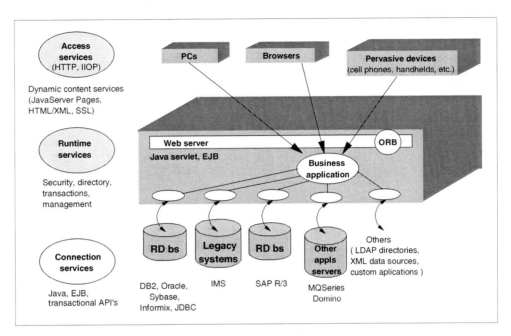

Figure 135. WebSphere Application Server Advanced Edition

5.3.4.2 WebSphere Enterprise Edition (TXSeries and CB)

WebSphere Enterprise Edition carries over Advanced Edition (compare Figure 135 to Figure 136) standard transaction management capabilities and the middleware for it to operate. This is provided in the TXSeries server, which includes IBM CICS transaction gateway and Encina. Enterprise Edition also has Component Broker (CB), which provides CB Connector and CBToolkit.

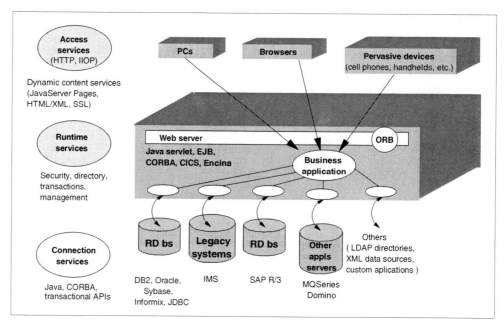

Figure 136. WebSphere Application Server enterprise edition

TXSeries is IBM's strategic transactional middleware product for Windows NT and UNIX. It offers a robust application server environment with the following capabilities:

- A range of programming models
- Inter-application communication (synchronous or asynchronous)
- High performance and availability (work load management)
- Security (authentication, authorization, and privacy)
- Host access
- Support of three-tier architecture
- Open tools support

CICS is the IBM TP Monitor for applications that:

- Use CICS for new client/server applications
- Front-end existing CICS applications
- Offer 3270 terminal based transactions support
- Rehost existing CICS applications

Encina is the IBM TP Monitor for applications using:

- C/C++/DCE RPC/UNIX style approach
- DCE Encina Lightweight Client (DE-Light) Gateway for Secure Web Transactions
- DE-Light Java client supports SSL to gateway

Component Broker is a CORBA-compliant middleware for new business applications. It enables the deployment and management of component-based applications that provide three-tier connectivity with enterprise systems. The CB Toolkit is a next generation development tool for component-based applications, supporting the lifecycle from design and analysis to code and test.

Component Broker does not stand alone, but rather cooperates with existing transaction and resource managers. It functions as an object server by providing an application environment that lets clients work with mature back-end systems through object-oriented middleware. It cooperates fully with IBM's industry-leading family of transaction servers.

CB Connector incorporates proven technology from other IBM middleware products such as CICS/ESA and Transaction Series (Distributed CICS and Encina). Over time, IBM intends to add Component Broker technology to Transaction Series so that these existing, proven platforms will also benefit from the new computing model.

Essentially, CB Connector is a platform for developing a new generation of flexible software, built using distributed objects technology. It is an ideal base for implementing thin-client topologies and cleanly separating the client-side concerns of ever changing user-interface technologies from the very different characteristics of the code needed to support business logic. The Internet is, of course, the most prominent example. CB Connector is very well-suited to that dynamic environment.

Choosing between CB and TXSeries

Component Broker is the preferred product selection if the customer:

- Wants objects across the enterprise leveraging a distributed object technology
- Needs tools
- Wants an integrated solution
- Wants CORBA standards

TXSeries is the preferred product selection if the customer:

- Has a transaction focus
- Needs high performance
- Will deploy a critical application
- Already has tools

5.3.5 Using Enterprise JavaBeans to manage transactions

IBM WebSphere Application Server is an e-business application deployment environment that is built on the open standards-based technology. It is the cornerstone of WebSphere application offerings and services. IBM WebSphere Application Server Advanced Edition is a high-performance EJB server, which implements EJB components that incorporate business logic. It supports multiple platforms, databases, and transaction systems to provide Java-based gateway and EJB connectivity.

For the sake of an example, the following sections discuss the typical steps in designing a banking solution with WebSphere Application Server.

5.3.5.1 Static view of the solution

The solution overview in Figure 137 introduces a candidate technology, WebSphere Application Server Advanced Edition, in the middle tier of the architecture. This component is responsible for the application business logic. It also manages the interface to the back-end database or application using EJB. Using JavaServer Pages, it creates the Web pages dynamically and serves them up to the Internet via the Web server.

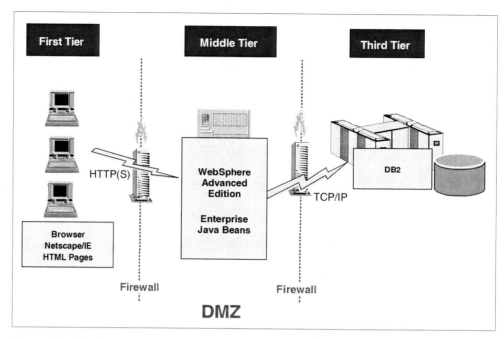

Figure 137. WebSphere Application Server Advanced Edition using EJBs: Static view

5.3.5.2 Dynamic view of the solution

Transaction management in WebSphere Advanced Edition is shown in Figure 138.

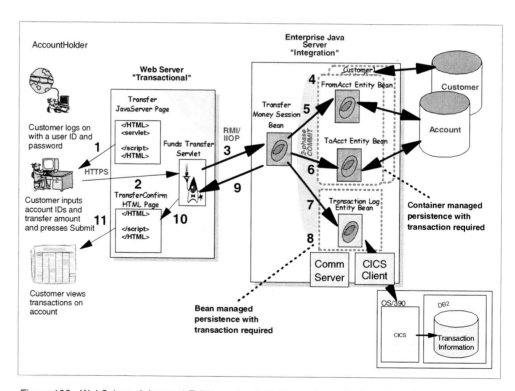

Figure 138. WebSphere Advanced Edition using EJB: Dynamic application view - Request

The following walkthrough describes the various components and interactions required to perform a transaction using the architecture shown in Figure 138:

1. The transfer JSP generates an HTML page that has a form to accept user requests for handling a transfer between accounts.

2. The user enters the transfer information (account from, account to, amount) and clicks the Submit button. A request is sent via HTTPS to the firewall that forwards the request to the Funds Transfer servlet on the Web server.

3. Funds Transfer servlet locates the `TransferMoney` session bean via JNDI. It sends a message with the transfer information and the CICS Web user ID to the TransferMoney Session Bean via RMI over IIOP through the firewall (which includes Tivoli FirstSecure to support IIOP).

4. After completing any necessary validation of the transfer information, the TransferMoney session bean begins a new transaction (using Java Transaction Services).

5. The TransferMoney session bean calls the `FromAccount` entity bean to set the balance (to withdraw funds), which in turn, changes the balance for the `FromAccount` in DB2 UDB. This entity bean uses container-managed persistence with a setting of Transaction-Required, so that this database activity occurs under the control of the TransferMoney transaction.

6. The TransferMoney session bean calls the `ToAccount` entity bean to set the balance (to deposit funds), which in turn, changes the balance for the `ToAccount` in DB2 UDB. This entity bean uses container-managed persistence with a setting of Transaction-Required, so that this database activity occurs under the control of the TransferMoney transaction.

7. The TransferMoney session bean calls the `TransactionLog` entity bean to log the information of the transfer, by interfacing with the CICS program. The session bean uses the CICS WebUser ID to access the CICS program through the CICS client using SNA. This entity bean uses bean-managed persistence with a setting of Transaction-Required, so that this CICS activity occurs under the control of the TransferMoney transaction.

8. The TransferMoney session bean commits the transaction causing all the entity beans to commit their changes.

9. The transfer money session bean returns a successful transfer along with user transaction information back to the servlet.

10. The servlet dynamically fills the transaction information into the HTML page

11. The HTML page is sent to the browser for display.

5.3.5.3 Security walkthrough
In Figure 139, the solution covers security architecture. It highlights the technologies and components used to provide security in the solution environment.

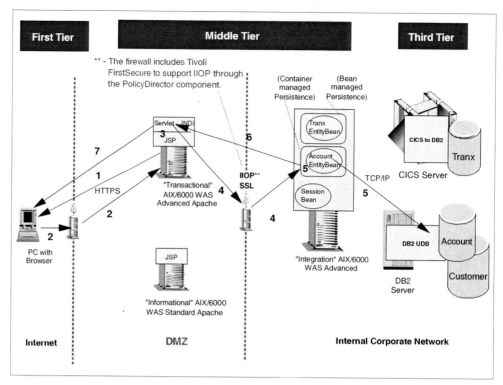

Figure 139. WebSphere Application Server using EJB: Dynamic application view - Security

The following walkthrough steps describe the interactions of the components in the architecture shown in Figure 139:

1. A user links to a secure logon URL for account access via the firewall. The integration server uses the logon JSP to send a login HTML page to the browser via SSL.

2. The user logs in through the login JSP by providing a user ID and password. The user ID and password are transmitted via HTTPS (using SSL) through the firewall, which routes it to the transactional Web server.

3. A login servlet in the transactional Web server authenticates the user ID and password and maps the user ID into a role-based CICS WebUser ID.

   Note: The mapping from User ID to CICS WebUser ID is many-to-one.

   This CICS WebUser ID is saved for the duration of the session.

4. The login servlet locates the Account Container via JNDI and sends a message to obtain the account information for the user via RMI over IIOP through the firewall (which includes Tivoli FirstSecure to support IIOP).

5. The account container finds the appropriate account entity beans and gets information from them. Each account entity bean may need to access the account information in DB2 UDB to obtain their information.

6. The account container returns account information to the servlet.

7. The servlet dynamically fills the account information into the HTML page, and returns the HTML page to the browser for display.

The following components are selected for the WebSphere Advanced Edition using an EJB solution:

- Web browser that is JavaScript capable

- Windows NT server (middle-tier transaction server and third-tier application server)

- WebSphere Application Server Advanced Edition (IBM HTTP Server, JDK)

- DB2 UDB (DB2 UDB client on the middle tier and DB2 UDB server on the third tier)

- CICS (client on the middle tier and CICS/ESA and DB2 UDB on the multiple virtual storage (MVS) third tier)

- IBM Communications Server

- IBM Firewall (Tivoli FirstSecure to support IIOP)

5.3.6 Using TXSeries to manage transactions

IBM WebSphere Application Server Enterprise Edition enables full e-business transactions over the Web. Using such open standards-based technologies as interoperable CORBA and EJBs, Enterprise Edition provides comprehensive, high quality middleware runtime services for distributed component applications. It also contains the industry's most complete support for integrating existing IT applications and resources for reuse on the Web.

IBM TXSeries is middleware used in high-performance distributed transaction processing environment. When sheer high-speed transaction processing is the goal, TXSeries provides the solution in distributed CICS, typically for COBOL applications, or IBM Encina, typically used for C and C++ applications. TXSeries supports the traditional, procedural programming model in the context of scalability, reliability, and security.

5.3.6.1 Static view of the solution

In Figure 140, the solution overview introduces a candidate technology, WebSphere Application Server Enterprise Edition, in the middle tier of the architecture. This component is responsible for the application business logic. It also manages the interface to the back-end database or application using servlets and TXSeries (CICS). Using JSP, it creates the Web pages dynamically and serves them up to the Internet via the Web server.

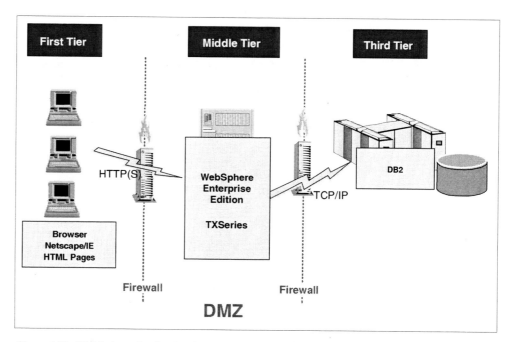

Figure 140. WebSphere Application Server Enterprise Edition using TXSeries: Static application view

5.3.6.2 Dynamic view of the solution

Transaction management in WebSphere Enterprise Edition using TX Series is shown in Figure 141.

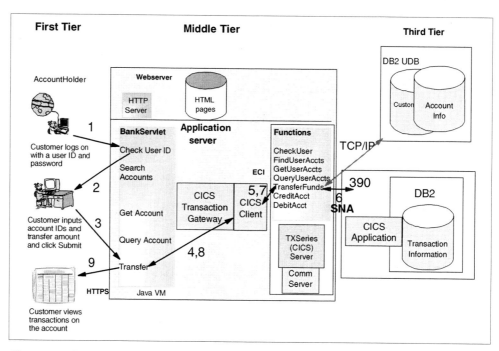

Figure 141. TXSeries: Dynamic application view - Request

The following walkthrough describes the various components and interactions required to perform a transaction using this architecture:

1. A user enters a user ID and password and clicks the Logon button. The login request is transmitted to the server using SSL through the firewall. The servlet check user ID is invoked to validate the user ID and password.

2. Upon successful login, the servlet queries the user's accounts and gathers information regarding the accounts. The servlet adds the summary account information to an HTML page and sends the HTML page via SSL to the browser for display to the user.

3. The user selects the accounts for the transfer, enters the amount to be transferred, and clicks the Submit button.

   Note: Each account selection may invoke an appropriate servlet to re-display the information pertinent to the account selected.

   The Submit button sends a request via SSL through the firewall, which activates the transfer servlet.

4. The transfer servlet composes a transfer ECI request from the user input, and sends the transfer ECI request to the CICS client through the CICS Transaction Gateway.

5. The CICS client unpacks the request, connects to the TXSeries (CICS) Server via the firewall and invokes the transfer application in the TXSeries Server as an ECI call using TCP/IP through the firewall.

6. The transfer application in the TXSeries Server starts a logical unit of work, validates the transfer of funds, sets the account balances on the accounts, creates a transaction log, and commits the results. The transfer application accesses the account databases using TCP/IP and the transaction log through the CICS server using SNA.

7. The transfer application returns the transfer results to the CICS client.

8. The CICS client returns the transfer results to the transfer servlet.

9. The servlet populates an HTML page with the successful transfer result and sends the page via SSL to the browser for display to the user.

5.3.6.3 Security walkthrough

The solution in Figure 142 covers the security architecture. It highlights the technologies and components used to provide security in the solution environment.

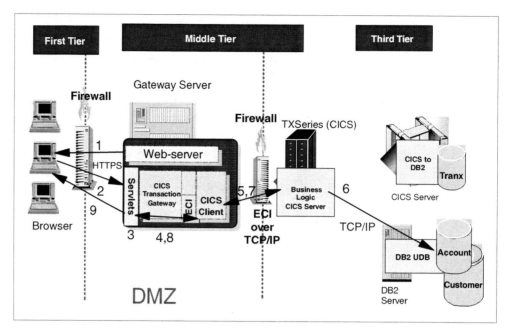

Figure 142. TXSeries: Dynamic application view (security)

The following walkthrough steps describe the interactions of the components in the architecture:

1. A user links to a secure logon URL for account access via the firewall. The server sends a login HTML page to the browser via SSL.

2. The HTTP request to login the user with a user ID and password is sent through the firewall using SSL, and invokes the check user ID servlet on the server.

3. The servlet authenticates the user ID and password, and maps the user ID into a role-based CICS WebUser ID.

   Note: The mapping from user ID to CICS WebUser ID is many-to-one.

   This CICS WebUser ID is saved for the duration of the session.

4. The servlet composes an ECI request to get the account information for the user, along with the CICS WebUser ID, and sends the request to the CICS client via the CICS transaction gateway.

5. The CICS client unpacks the request, connects to the TXSeries (CICS) Server via the firewall and invokes the GetUserAccts application in the TXSeries Server as an ECI call using TCP/IP through the firewall.

6. The GetUserAccts application in the TXSeries Server validates the CICS WebUser ID and gets the account information by accessing the customer and account databases using TCP/IP.

7. The GetUserAccts application returns the account information to the CICS client.

8. The CICS client returns the account information to the Check User ID servlet.

9. The servlet populates an HTML page with the account information and sends the page via SSL to the browser for display to the user.

The TXSeries components used include:

- TXSeries for AIX (CICS)
- DB2 UDB (the DB2 UDB server is installed on the second tier)
- CICS (CICS/ESA and DB2 UDB on the MVS third tier)
- IBM Communications Server for NT
- IBM Firewall

5.3.7 Using Component Broker to manage transactions

Component Broker is an object container capable of supporting CORBA and EJB objects that can leverage existing systems and coexist in a shared transactional environment. CORBA also provides customers with a choice of implementation language for clients and servers. CB can serve as an object transaction monitor to coordinate any combination of these resource managers, helping ensure data and transactional integrity for mission-critical applications. Like TXSeries, CB runtime is highly scalable, reliable, and secure.

5.3.7.1 Static view of the solution

In Figure 143, the solution overview introduces a candidate technology, WebSphere Application Server Enterprise Edition, in the middle tier of the architecture (it is identical to the WAS Enterprise Edition). This component is responsible for the application business logic. It also manages the interface to the back-end database or application using servlets and C++ objects in the CB container. Using JSP, it creates the Web pages dynamically and serves them up to the Internet via the Web server.

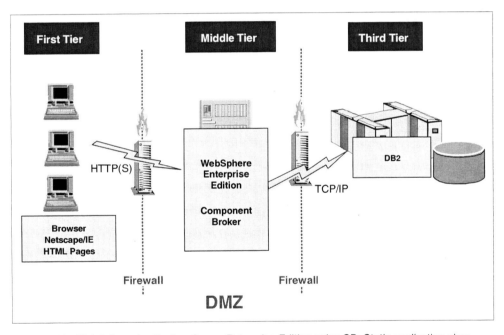

Figure 143. WebSphere Application Server Enterprise Edition using CB: Static application view

5.3.7.2 Dynamic view of the solution

Transaction management in WebSphere Enterprise Edition using Component Broker is illustrated in Figure 144.

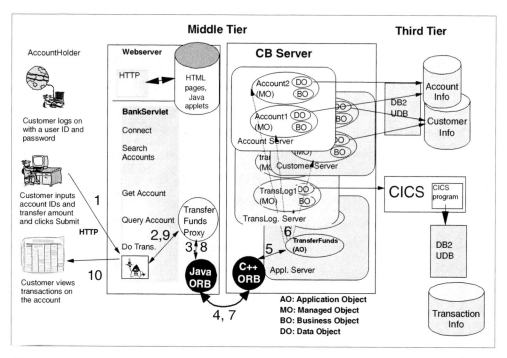

Figure 144. Component Broker: Dynamic application view (requests)

The following walkthrough describes the various components and interactions required to perform a transaction using this architecture:

1. A user enters transfer information (account from, account to, amount) and clicks the Submit button. The request is sent via SSL through the firewall to invoke the Do Trans. servlet in the Web server.

2. A servlet sends a message with transfer information to the transfer funds object. If this proxy object is not yet available, the servlet uses the standard CB programming model requests to gain access to it via the firewall (finds an appropriate Home using the factory-finder; and then uses the Home to find the transfer funds object).

3. The proxy object uses a client-side Java ORB to relay the message to the server.

4. Client-side ORB sends request (and security token) to the server-side ORB via IIOP through the firewall (which includes Tivoli FirstSecure to support IIOP).

5. Server-side ORB receives request, handles security issues (see next section for details), and invokes the method in the transfer funds application object.

6. The transfer funds application object gets the current transaction object and begins a transaction, performs the transfer of funds from account1 to account2, and then commits the transfer.

7. The transfer results are returned to the client via the ORB.

8. The client ORB returns the results to the transfer funds proxy.

9. The proxy returns the transfer results to the Do Trans. servlet.

10. The servlet generates an HTML page with the transfer results and sends it via SSL for display to the browser.

The details of performing transaction in step 6 are shown in Figure 145.

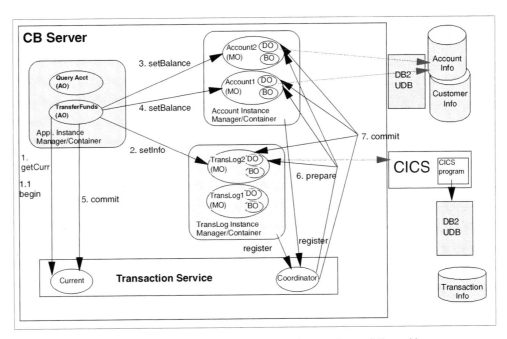

Figure 145. Component Broker: Dynamic application view (transaction walkthrough)

5.3.7.3 Security walkthrough

In Figure 146, the solution covers security architecture. It highlights the technologies and components used to provide security in the solution environment.

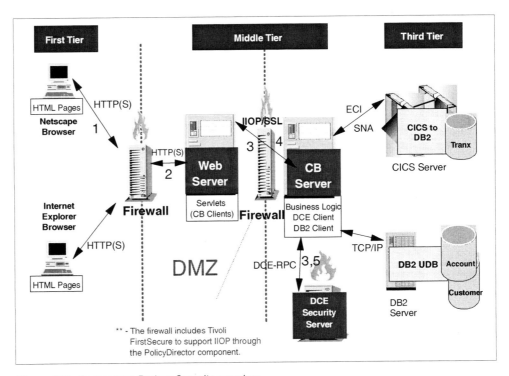

Figure 146. Component Broker: Security overview

The User authentication and message protection walkthrough steps describe the interactions of the components in the architecture:

1. A user links to a secure logon URL for account access via a firewall. A Web server presents a login page to the user. The user logins with a user ID and password.

2. The user ID and password are sent to the Web server via SSL through the firewall. The `checkUserID` servlet is activated in the Web server.

3. Servlet acquires access rights for user ID and password from the CB server via IIOP through the firewall (which includes Tivoli FirstSecure to support IIOP). The CB server delegates authentication to the DCE server and returns a security token (credential) to the servlet. The security credential can be stored for the duration of the session.

4. When a request is made from a servlet via IIOP through the firewall to the CB server to perform business logic, the client-side ORB sends the security credential along with the message to the server.

5. The CB server forwards the security token to the DCE security server, which verifies the user and sends a security token to the server. Then a security context is established. The security context includes a credential object that identifies the user and access rights (defined by mapping the user ID to a role-based CICS WebUser ID). It also defines a quality of protection that describes the protection (none, integrity, confidentiality) for messages between client and server ORBs.

The following Component Broker components were used:

- IBM DB2 UDB Software Developer's Kit (SDK)
- IBM Distributed Computing Environment
- IBM DB2 Universal Database (UDB) Personal Edition
- IBM VisualAge C++
- JavaSoft Java Development Kit (JDK)
- CBConnector
- CBToolkit (comes with CB)
- IBM Communication Server
- IBM Firewall (Tivoli FirstSecure to support IIOP)

5.3.8 Summary

Now we compare all three solutions for CRM with transactions according to the criteria defined on page 274.

Performance and capacity
An analysis of the response time budgets show that all solutions can handle the requirement (5 seconds turnaround time).

All solutions can handle ever increasing loads because of the use of transaction monitors in the middle tier. The TXSeries solution relies on CICS Transaction Monitor, which has been proven to have better performance as the load increases.

Security
All solutions provide reasonable security through the use of DMZ to isolate the core business applications and protect them from outside attacks. Also,

authentication of a user via a user ID and password provides authorization to use back-end applications.

The WebSphere Advanced Edition using EJB and WAS Enterprise Edition Component Broker solutions provide extra security measures. The EJB solution isolates the transactional Web server from the informational Web server. The Component Broker uses a separate DCE security server for authentication and authorization.

Availability
The WAS using EJB, TXSeries, and Component Broker solutions provides good availability because of the use of a transaction monitor in the middle tier, and the possibility of using WebSphere Edge Server to balance the load.

The TXSeries and Component Broker solutions are based on the WebSphere Enterprise Edition, which provides enterprise-level clustering that can be used to provide better availability.

Usability
The use of a transaction monitor in the middle tier for the WAS using EJB, TXSeries, and Component Broker solutions helps in ensuring that appropriate service providers are available to handle user requests in a timely fashion.

Maintainability and manageability
The WAS using EJB and Component Broker solutions is based on standards (EJB and CORBA) respectively and, therefore, should allow better interoperability and adaptability.

The WAS using EJB and Component Broker solutions is complex (due to the need to adhere to EJB/CORBA standards and their programming model), which will impact the ability to manage and maintain the solution.

The TXSeries could be easier to manage or maintain since it can directly relate to the 3270 applications in the backend.

Testability
The TXSeries solution would be the most straight forward to test, since there is a direct correspondence to back-end applications.

The WAS using EJB and Component Broker would be the most complex to test, because it would require all the parts of each component to be available and tested together and the complex programming model would require the various application development and deployment tools to work together during the test.

Extendibility and scalability
The WAS using EJB and Component Broker solutions is based on component architectures that facilitate incremental changes (extendibility) quickly and cost effectively via inheritance.

The TXSeries solution relies on CICS Transaction Monitors, which have proven to handle ever-increasing loads effectively (scalability).

Portability

The WAS using EJB and Component Broker solutions are based on EJB and CORBA component architecture standards and, therefore, will be portable to any other EJB/CORBA computing environment.

All solutions rely on Java servlets, which are portable across any computing environment with a compatible JVM.

Reusability

The WAS using EJB and Component Broker follows component architectures that facilitate reusability of the components developed.

Business quality

The TXSeries solution is the cheapest to build and may be able to take advantage of existing CICS skills and resources.

The WAS using EJB and Component Broker solutions is most expensive to build and requires new and updated skills and resources to handle the EJB/CORBA component architecture and programming model.

5.3.8.1 The advantages and disadvantages of using EJBs

The advantages of using EJBs include:

- All Java-based solution (write once, run anywhere)
- Follows the EJB standard
- Easy to interoperate with other EJB computing environments
- EJB component architecture facilitates the ease of adding or changing components and reuse of components in other EJB based applications
- ESS architecture provides added security by separating transactional from informational servers and a separate integration server
- The use of a transaction monitor in the middle tier helps manage performance, capacity, and availability

The disadvantages of using EJBs are:

- Handling high transaction volume could be a problem.
- EJB component architecture makes application development, maintenance, and management complex.
- It is expensive to build the required specialized skills and resources.

5.3.8.2 The advantages and disadvantages of using TXSeries

The advantages of using TXSeries include:

- Highly scalable in terms of numbers of transactions
- Very reliable
- Leverage existing CICS skills
- Interoperability between Encina and CICS allows for the mixing of two programming models, if required
- WebSphere Enterprise Edition allows for enterprise-level clustering, which helps in managing capacity and availability

- The use of a transaction monitor in the middle tier helps manage performance, capacity, and availability

The disadvantages of using TXSeries include that it is:

- Difficult to add new functionality

- Difficult to interoperate with other computing environments and reuse in other applications

- Difficult to find CICS skills

5.3.8.3 The advantages and disadvantages of using Component Broker

The advantages of using Component Broker include:

- It follows CORBA standards:
    - Easy to change
    - Components can be reused in other applications
    - Interoperability with any client and server component that follow CORBA standards
    - Bridges are available to other components using non-CORBA standards

- Can handle two-phase commits over heterogeneous resources

- Using DCE Security Server helps with authentication and authorization

- WebSphere Enterprise Edition allows for enterprise level clustering, which helps in managing capacity and availability

- The use of a transaction monitor in the middle tier helps manage performance, capacity, and availability

The disadvantages of using Component Broker include:

- Complexity in building solution
- Complexity in managing the solution
- May cause problems when scaling to large number of transactions

Chapter 6. E-commerce

This chapter discusses key design elements for e-commerce applications, focusing on the key technologies, products, design decisions, and a sample solution for online sales e-business problems.

The first part of the discussion is organized around the three areas necessary to support online sales (Figure 147):

- **Problem space**: Online sales describes situations where users will be interfacing with a business specifically for shopping or making purchases, and typically include the concepts of a shopping cart and an electronic wallet.

- **Technology and product space**: The technology should enable an online shopping process, with product catalogs, orders, and customer management. It describes the products WebSphere Commerce Suite (WCS) and IBM Payment Suites.

- **Design space**: Emphasis is on key design decisions regarding the client, network, server, application server, security, and performance.

We also present an online sales solution using WebSphere Commerce Suite and IBM Payment Suite and discusses competitive solutions.

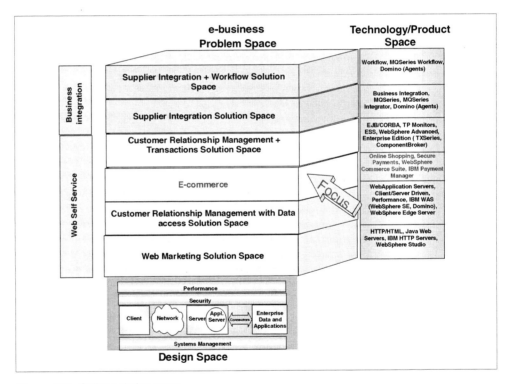

Figure 147. Online solution space

6.1 E-commerce overview

"E-commerce" is the act of doing business using electronic technology such as intranets, extranets, and the Internet. Commerce is the exchange of money for goods or services between companies or end consumers. Although there are many aspects to commerce and e-commerce, the most common image that the term conjures up is that of a Web-based catalog from which buyers can order products and the sellers can receive payments.

Whether you're running a promising start-up or an established enterprise, successful e-commerce means more than enabling customers to purchase your products and services online. It means meeting customers wherever they are. On another continent, from PDAs and mobile phones, around the clock with a level of service that keeps them coming back. You'll forge new customer relationships and grow existing ones. Relationships that will help generate new revenue and increase your profit margins.

E-commerce has evolved from consumers conducting basic transactions on the Web, to a complete retooling of the way partners, suppliers, and customers transact. Now you can link dealers and suppliers online as shown in Figure 148 and reap the following benefits:

- You can reduce both lag time and paperwork.

- You can move procurement online by setting up an extranet that links directly to vendors, cutting inventory carrying costs, and becoming more responsive to your customers.

- You can streamline your financial relationships with customers and suppliers by Web-enabling billing and payment systems.

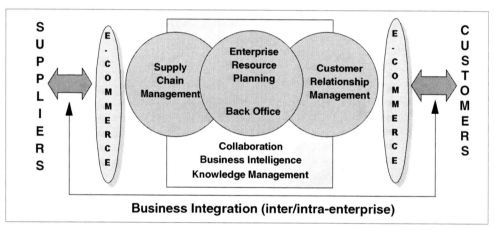

Figure 148. E-commerce business integration

Some objectives of e-commerce include:

- Extending the company reach to new customers

- Providing effective means of buying and selling over the Internet

- Managing payment transactions electronically

- Allowing consumers to purchase in confidence knowing their transactions are secure

- Generating higher revenues and lowering costs

- Enhancing companies competitive position

- Improving the efficiency of transactions and connections across the supply chain

- Strengthening the relationship between and among business partners, employees and employers, and individuals and institutions
- Connecting between and among suppliers, distributors, and consumers

6.1.1 E-commerce models

E-commerce evolved over recent years to include several models regarding the parties doing business, mainly:

- **Business-to-Business (B2B)**: B2B electronic commerce covers a range of business activities. For example, B2B systems exchange business documents, such as purchase orders and invoices, between pairs of partners in a supply chain. A B2B system can support trading between multiple buyers and suppliers. The B2B model also supports the implementation of virtual marketplaces for buyers and sellers who have trading partner agreements. Finally, B2B systems also automate the purchase of goods that support a business maintenance, repair, and operation (MRO).

- **Business-to-Consumer (B2C)**: B2C e-commerce is online retailing or e-tailing. It involves consumers who are shopping for, and buying, personal and household products. It also involves merchants using electronic marketing and merchandising techniques to attract and retain consumers as well as to promote products and services to consumers.

- **Consumer-to-Consumer (C2C)**: C2C e-commerce involves consumers using electronic tools to support transactions between individuals. Some of these are conventional in nature, for example, classified advertisements. Other C2C transactions include auctions of personal possessions or online bartering.

- **electronic Market places (eMP)**: e-marketplaces or exchanges, where a single large manufacturer can consolidate the purchase of the goods that are the input to its manufacturing process from many smaller companies.

  Such a marketplace may enable a large retailer to purchase the goods that it sells in its stores. Or, marketplaces can become trading marts or exchanges for commodity products or the range of products of a given type or associated with a particular industry segment.

  e-marketplaces employ a combination of technologies and services to enable buyers and sellers to interact in a dynamic environment and to establish and maintain relationships with supply chain partners.

  Buyers and sellers want to go where the action is. So you have to:

  - Create a bustling trading hub that really attracts the crowds.
  - Leverage dynamic pricing through real time exchanges and leading-edge content management.
  - Conduct rugged auctions that support the use of pervasive computing devices like PDAs and cell phones.
  - And let buyers and sellers facilitate the process through robust search capabilities and seamless workflow approvals.

- **Mobile commerce**: The explosive growth of mobile commerce (m-commerce) is a tremendous opportunity to generate new revenue. By extending your site to wireless users, using PDAs and mobile phones, you're poised to take advantage of what industry analysts say is the current trend in e-commerce solutions.

Mobile commerce is a fast growing market opportunity and analysts predict mobile devices will be the largest source of Internet and e-commerce transactions in the coming years.

Mobile protocols and device types that are available include:

– *Mobile phones with Short Message Service (SMS)*: Mobile phones equipped by a large screen could receive or exchange (send and receive) short text messages of about 160 characters.

– *Mobile phones with Wireless Access Protocol (WAP)*: Mobile phones equipped by small screens and limited keyboard support Wireless Access Protocol (WAP) and Wireless Markup Language (WML) to browse the Internet.

– *Wireless Personal Digital Assistant (PDA)*: Is equipped with a small screen and often no keyboard.

– *Laptops with wireless modems or connected to a mobile phone*: They provide standard browsing capability so no special application considerations are required.

6.1.2 E-commerce operations

E-commerce includes many types of operations and activities. Figure 149 shows the main electronic commerce business processes and the activities that integrate them.

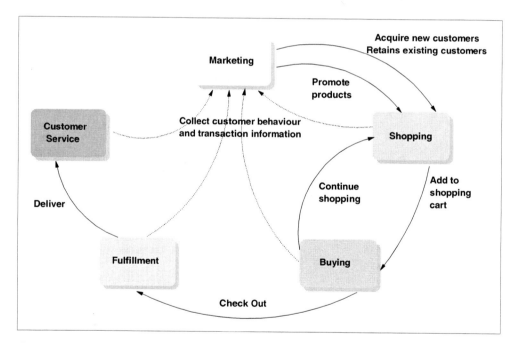

Figure 149. E-commerce business processes and the events that integrate them

The objectives for *e-commerce marketing* include acquiring new customers, retaining existing customers, promoting products, cross-selling products, and upselling products. Customer acquisition and retention are Customer Relationship Management activities. Promoting, cross-selling, and upselling are merchandising activities. An e-commerce system, especially a B2C system, should implement or integrate CRM capabilities.

The objective of the *shopping* process is to help the shopper find products to buy. Typically, this means browsing and searching a catalog. Catalogs should support flexible hierarchies of categories and subcategories. Both B2B and B2C applications should offer a range of methods for navigating catalogs and finding products. B2B applications support the ability to create catalogs for each customer account or customer contract. In addition, product information should be rich in structure and content.

In the course of the *ordering* process, shoppers or customers find the products they are interested in ordering. Ordering includes a collection of:

- Billing and shipping information
- Allocation of inventory
- Calculation of prices
- Calculation of taxes
- Calculation of shipping and handling charges
- Determination of payment method
- Authorization of payment
- Generation of orders
- Acknowledgement of orders

E-commerce systems should perform all these steps. B2C systems should support credit card and debit card payment. B2B systems must support purchase order payment.

The *fulfillment* process settles payment, takes the orders generated as output of the ordering process, and manages orders through the steps of picking, packing, shipping, and delivering the orders. E-commerce systems do not actually perform these steps. Typically, both B2B and B2C systems integrate external fulfillment systems to perform them while keeping track of order status.

The *customer service* process comprises the activities that occur after an order is generated. Within e-commerce systems, these activities include checking order status, inquiring about order histories, and returning goods. E-commerce should support these activities through customer self-service and integration with customer relationship management CRM.

6.2 Problem space for an e-commerce solution

As we apply the three-dimensional approach for building e-business applications, we start from the description of the problem space for e-commerce. Then, we discuss the technology, products, and decisions made during the process of building the e-commerce solutions.

Customers are striving for e-commerce solutions that provide the basic e-commerce operations discussed in 6.1.2, "E-commerce operations" on page 314. This includes advertising, marketing, shopping, purchasing, and paying. Moreover, the e-commerce solutions must support the following requirements:

- E-commerce functionality:
    - Web applications, to reach a broad range of users over the Internet.
    - Business systems to model the business system and enable e-commerce operations.

- Component-based tools to reuse components already developed, deployed, and tested.

- Management and administration
  - End-to-end management to customize the solution and fit the business needs.
  - Security to ensure confidence while performing the transaction.

- Architecture
  - Proven deployment architecture
  - Reliability, availability, serviceability
  - Connector technology
  - Scalability

Figure 150 shows additional key e-commerce functions that may or may not be supported.

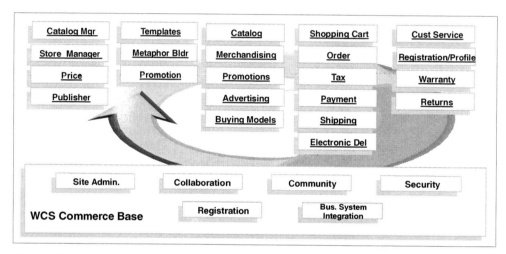

Figure 150. Typical electronic commerce function

6.3 Technology requirements for an e-commerce solution

In dealing with online sales e-business problems, you must understand the following key technology requirements:

- **Personalization**: To ensure that products and sales are customized to the buying habits of each consumer.

- **Secure payment transactions**: To ensure that payment information can be transmitted securely and the payment transaction can be completed quickly and securely.

- **Customer management**: To have customer information that is available throughout the sales cycle, from prospect to customer, sales to repeat sales, and orders to deliveries.

- **Order tracking**: To track an order in terms of location, availability, and timing. Also of concern in tracking orders is the integration with back end line of business (LOB) systems and the supply chain.

- **Catalog management**: To handle the creation, update, and maintenance of the product catalog, to ensure data integrity of products/price, and to provide flexibility in when price or product changes are reflected.

- **Scalability, availability, and performance**: To ensure that the solution can grow from a single machine serving a small local community to a large transaction engine serving a worldwide community.

- **Searching**: To allow a wide range of searches for products.

Now we explore each technology requirement in more detail.

6.3.1 Personalization

The underlying idea is to personalize the shopping experience for the customer by providing product information that is the most pertinent to their buying patterns.

In an e-commerce solution, personalization can be accomplished in an efficient manner. Because your system is constantly monitoring the products that customers place in their shopping carts, it can instantaneously offer related products or accessories for existing products. Personalization can also go beyond just the sale of products. Registered shoppers could also possibly change the look and feel of the virtual store to suit their preferences. The examples of recommended features are:

- Provide the ability to display a store catalog in multiple languages
- Provide the ability to display price in multiple currencies
- Provide a quick way for experienced customers, who know a product number, to move to the checkout screen, bypassing a long process of selecting a product

However, it is important that the personalization does not become too intrusive. For example, shoppers could become very annoyed if a related product is pushed onto the screen every time they access their shopping cart. An alternative is to offer one or two products during the checkout process. As always, it is important to ensure that the customer has a good shopping experience.

Figure 151 shows the personalization function by capturing the customer information:

- Static information previously entered by the customer during registration (like address book, payment, and demographic information)

- Dynamic information generated during the current e-commerce transaction like the product the customer is viewing, shopping cart content, and ordered product

Then the protected functions can make the shopper feel comfortable in a personalized environment by:

- Recognizing or identifying the shopper
- Retrieving shoppers' shipping and billing addresses
- Retrieving shoppers' payment methods and details
- Tracking old orders made by the shopper
- Finding preferred products for the shopper

Intelligent mining can help personalize the visit by:

- Analyzing and optimizing the site to fit the shopper
- Analyzing shopper behavior
- Placing advertisements that would be interesting to the shopper
- Making the Web site more interesting for the shopper

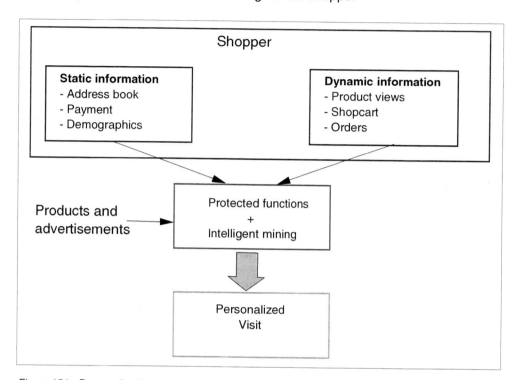

Figure 151. Personalization

6.3.2 Secure payment transactions

A key concern for customers in e-commerce operations is the secure payment for the products. They want to make sure that payment information can be transmitted securely and the payment transaction can be completed quickly.

Figure 152 shows key secure payment concerns of different parties involved in e-commerce transactions:

- Customer concerns include:

    - Is the merchant processing this transaction legitimate and trustful?

    - Will the credit card information or account number be misused or lost causing possible financial exposure or liability?

    - Will the payment for goods be collected by the actual merchant with the correct amount?

- Merchant concerns include:

    - Is the actual consumer performing the transaction? Or is it an imposter?

    - Will the consumer deny the payment for the goods already shipped, generating a loss of the shipping and handling costs?

- Bank concerns include financial losses generated by card fraud

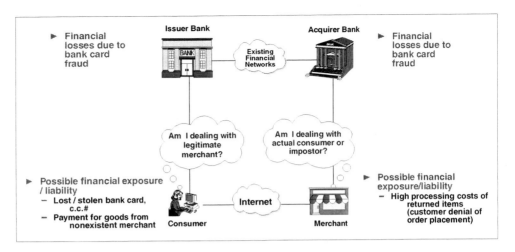

Figure 152. Secure payment concerns

The following technologies are used to overcome the key secure payment concerns:

- Secure Socket Layer (SSL):

    - Lowest level of security
    - SSL connection to customer and bank

- Merchant Originated Payments (MOP):

    - Manual entry of payment information each time
    - Treated as "card-not-present" transaction

- Full SET Secure Electronic Transaction:

    - Shopper has a wallet with a certificate
    - Strong SET encryption
    - Online transaction verification

- CyberCash:

    - Support of different Internet payment options including SET
    - Online transaction verification

Now we explore each of the secure payment methods in more detail.

6.3.2.1 Secure Sockets Layer (SSL)

Figure 153 shows the use of SSL in e-commerce transactions. SSL encrypts all data sent across a network connection. If someone intercepts the data packets over the network, it will be difficult for them to read the content.

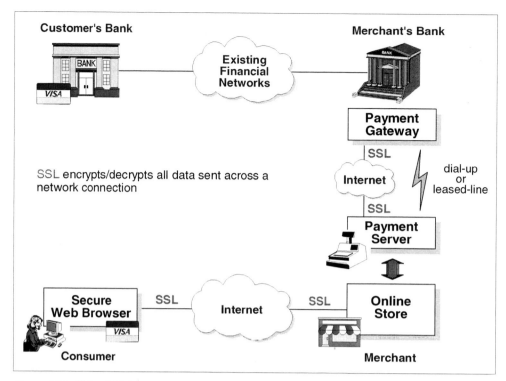

Figure 153. Using SSL in e-commerce transactions

The key advantages of SSL include:

- It's available through most Web browsers
- Using secure encrypted envelope
- Using encryption and decryption keys

The key limitations of SSL include:

- Not proving authenticity, because SSL will not detect an imposter using a consumer identity

- Card number must be manually entered every time

- Card providers VISA and Masters Card treat SSL transactions as "card-not-present"

You can find more details about SSL in Chapter 4, "Security" on page 205.

6.3.2.2 Merchant originated payment (MOP)

Figure 154 shows the use of MOP in the e-commerce transactions. In MOP, the customer purchase payment process is initiated by the merchant. This transaction is encrypted using SSL. Then the payment cycle is completed as a normal financial transaction using SET.

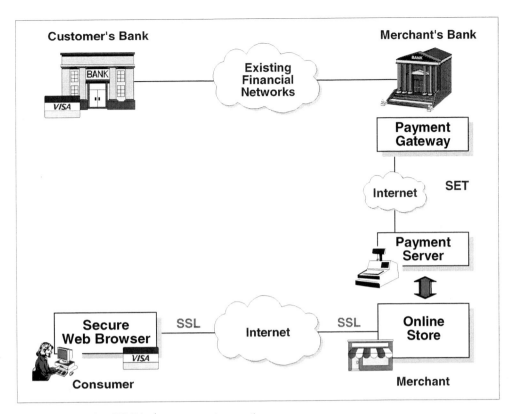

Figure 154. Using MOP in e-commerce transactions

The key advantages of MOP include:

- No consumer wallet needed, so the consumer does not worry about wallet creation and management
- No digital certificate required for the cardholder
- Using encryption and decryption keys
- Securing the merchant-to-processor flow with SET

The key limitations of MOP include:

- Does not prove authenticity of a consumer
- Requires manual entry of card number every time
- Treated as a "card-not-present" transaction

6.3.2.3 SET Secure Electronic Transaction

SET is an industry-standard protocol sponsored by MasterCard and VISA for secure (encrypted), "end-to-end" payment process. SET is a group of protocols designed for safe credit card payments over the World Wide Web. For more information about SET, refer to 4.4, "SET Secure Electronic Transaction protocol" on page 216.

6.3.2.4 CyberCash payment method

CashRegister provides businesses with the tools needed to accept multiple payment forms over the Web, including:

- Secure credit card transactions (including both SSL and SET)
- CyberCoin service, for cash payments from $0.25 to $10
- PayNow electronic check service, for interactive billing applications.

CyberCash involves the following parties:

- *Merchant*: Uses CashRegister to collect the payment over the Internet

- *Shopper*: Uses CyberCash Wallet *or* Microsoft Wallet to pay for the purchases over the Internet

- *Financial institutions*: Use Internet Payment Service to manage the payment services over the Internet

A typical credit card purchase cycle over the Internet using CyberCash involves the following steps:

1. *Shopping on the Internet*: The consumer selects an item to purchase on the Internet.

2. *Initiating the transaction*: After entering shipping and credit card information, the consumer is presented with a summary of the item, price, and billing information. The payment information is secured with industrial strength encryption and forwarded with the order form to the merchant's CyberCash CashRegister.

3. *CashRegister picks up merchant information*: The merchant's identification information is automatically added to the encrypted payment request.

4. *Through the CyberCash firewall to the bank*: Still encrypted, the payment request is forwarded over the Internet and is received through a secure firewall by the CyberCash CashRegister server. CyberCash instantaneously passes the payment request to the merchant's financial institution, which zips it on to the consumer's credit card bank to approve or decline payment authorization.

5. *Bank sends approval*: The consumer's credit card bank sends its response back through the merchant's financial institution to the merchant's CashRegister. The shopper also receives confirmation of credit card approval. The entire authorization process takes under 20 seconds.

6. *Transaction is completed and captured*: The merchant delivers the item to the shopper. The merchant requests financial settlement, or "capture", of the transaction through the CashRegister server. Funds are transferred to the merchant's account by its financial institution.

Secure payment recommendations

The following recommendations help in designing a secure payment solution:

- Use at least SSL encryption during transmission with a 128-bit certificate
- Protect order pages from staying in proxies or caches
- Request a user logon each time before entering the order process
- Use a thin client or a plug-in (electronic wallet)
- Establish certification authorities
- Authenticate the merchant with a certificate
- Authenticate the shoppers payment method (for example, each credit card) with a certificate
- Make online payment verifications using gateways to financial institutions
- Authenticate the financial institution with a certificate
- Store payment details in the protected database or better do not store them
- Establish low cost automatic processes

Provide different secure payment methods for different order sums (for example, micro payments).

6.3.3 Customer management

The customer management technology (Figure 155) issues that are related to e-commerce include:

- Make pertinent customer information available throughout the lifetime of the relationship with the customer.

- Place shoppers into groups to provide discounts and rebates.

- Determine what products the customer has previously purchased.

- Present products to the customer that are related to products already purchased in a simple, comprehensible tabular format.

- Maintain multiple address and credit card payment information for a customer.

- Determine what sales territory a customer is in.

- Group customers to facilitate marketing.

- Ensure that information about a customer can be accessed only by those authorized to do so.

- Track and graphically present customer revenue information.

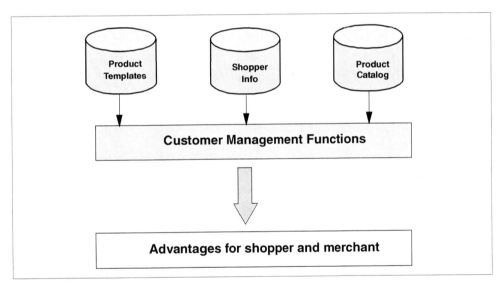

Figure 155. Customer management functions

6.3.4 Order tracking

Order tracking technology is necessary for both the customer and merchant. Figure 156 shows the parties that need to access the order information. Useful views for each party include:

- **Customer view**:
  - View orders that have been shipped and are pending
  - View items that are back ordered
  - View full or partial charges placed on the credit card
  - View the status of an order until it is received

    – View the scheduled delivery date for an order
    – View the shipping status of an order

- **Merchant view**: A merchant can do everything that a customer can, plus:

    – Schedule a delivery date for an order
    – Split an order as necessary
    – Charge the credit card for portions of the order completed
    – Track the status of an order until the order is fulfilled
    – Track the shipping status of an order

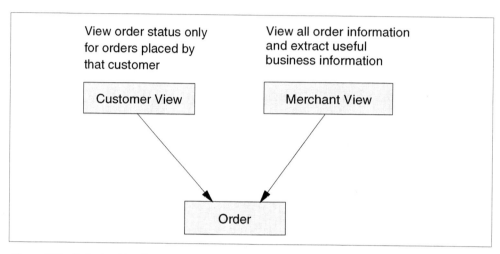

Figure 156. Order tracking from customer and merchant views

6.3.5 Catalog management

Catalog management technology issues include:

- Publishing the entire product catalog on the Web to existing and potential customers.

- Automatically updating the product catalog with items, prices, and pictures.

- Making the entire product catalog key word searchable and accessible with a mouse click on the Web.

- Locating products by product ID, descriptive key word or some other cross-reference.

- Making the prices in the product catalog viewable according to customer profile (a store can set different prices for special group(s) of customers).

- Showing images of products together with product text information consistently and accurately.

- Presenting product specifications as tables to facilitate the comparison of related products.

- Securing the product catalog from unauthorized access.

- Presenting the products, prices, descriptions, and tabular comparisons consistently.

- Making it easy to buy the product.

6.3.6 Scalability

The scalability requirements for e-commerce solutions include:

- Growing with your business by keeping the same data format, templates, and tools
- Selling a small number of products in a simple environment
- Going with your shop into a mall
- Getting your own site and URL at a provider
- Placing your own server at your business and connecting it to the legacy systems
- Moving from a single server to a multiple platform-distributed environment
- Selecting a merchant software that has connectors to legacy systems

6.3.7 Availability

Provide availability from different points of view:

- Use more than one Internet connection to protect your Web site from provider failure, or establish backup line.
- Use a firewall to protect against intruders or denial of service attacks.
- Use SSL to verify the server to the shopper.
- Establish redundant machines in case of server failure.
- Generate online data backup without maintenance windows.
- Use a staging server for online content maintenance.

6.3.8 Performance

Performance must take the following points into consideration:

- Estimate the user traffic regarding peak times for special hours and days.
- Estimate complexity of shopping process.
- Identify processes that consume excessive computing time like search engines or complex selects.
- Choose the right bandwidth to the Internet.
- Choose the right commerce software.
- Choose and scale the platform (type, memory, processors, discs).
- Arrange the software parameters.
- Maintain your software, logs, database.

6.3.9 Searching

The search capabilities of your e-commerce solution should let the customer find a product by using:

- A standardized expression for product groups, distinguished attributes, and attributes
- Different shopping metaphors

- The product search integrated within the other product metaphors as catalog browsing, branch shops, index lists, favorite products, or intelligent sales assistance

Special demands for search engines are:

- Let the user select between fuzzy and non-fuzzy search.

- Combine several keywords with "and/or".

- Tell the user the total number of results, but show them only the first 20, for example, and allow navigation through the results.

- Log all unsuccessful searches. The unsuccessful searches should be used by the editorial staff to assign unmatched keywords to products.

- Provide high performance technologies for searching.

- Provide product-specific pop-up lists to reduce the search area, for example, all red colored products, products cheaper than $5, products targeted for girls between 12 and 15, etc.

- Do not search on nonsense terms, for example, all products with an "e".

6.4 Products for the e-commerce solution

Regardless of the size of your business or your business model (B2C, B2B, e-marketplace, or mobile commerce), IBM WebSphere Commerce Suite (WCS) solutions help you compete on a level playing field. Based on open, industry-accepted standards, it delivers the speed you need for a fast return on your investment. WCS has the flexibility to integrate with your existing systems and those of your trading partners and suppliers. And the proven technologies to let you confidently engage in next-generation e-commerce.

6.4.1 WebSphere Commerce Suite

IBM WebSphere Commerce Suite (formerly IBM Net.Commerce) is a comprehensive set of integrated software components that help you build, maintain, and host stores and malls so you can sell your goods and services on the Web. It provides a total framework to conduct successful e-commerce that attracts customers and drives sales.

Figure 157 shows a high-level view of an e-commerce solution with WebSphere Commerce Suite at the core of the solution. It handles:

- Client requests initiated over the Internet
- Data interchange with database and existing systems
- Design, configuration, setup, and running new electronic stores
- Payment settlement and interface with payment options like SET, Merchant Originated Payment, and CyberCash

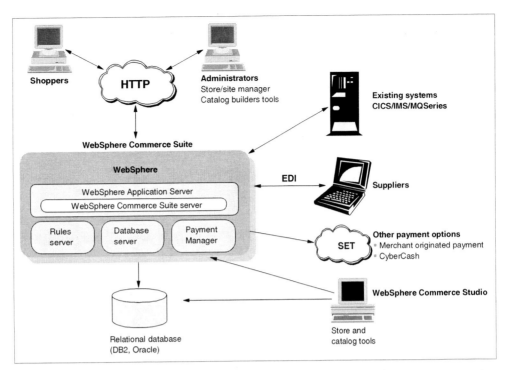

Figure 157. IBM WebSphere Commerce Suite provides a complete solution for e-commerce needs

WCS is a standards-based product to provide an open platform since customization is both a key requirement and strength for WCS. It has a Java programming model, with a complete set of robust tooling to support users in customizing and managing their environment. Figure 158 shows the main standards that are used and supported by WCS:

- The WCS Java environment provides support for EJBs, JSPs, servlets, JDBC, JTA/JTS, JNDI, JMS, and JavaBeans.

- Directory services provides support for LDAP directory (Tivoli security products and Domino). WCS supports single sign-on with WAS and Domino application servers.

- XML is used pervasively throughout the application (server configuration, store creation, messaging and mass load).

- Connector tools: WCS provides a direct connection to back-end systems using the emerging J2EE standard (Common Connection Framework).

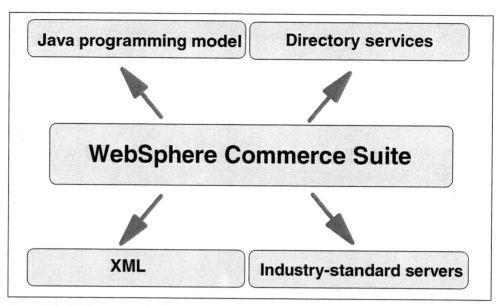

Figure 158. WCS open standards for an open solution

For more information about WebSphere Commerce Suite, refer to "WebSphere Commerce Suite" on page 153.

6.5 Decision blocks for an e-commerce solution

To develop an e-commerce solution, Framework for e-business highlights the design decision blocks shown in Figure 10 on page 30.

To achieve an optimal e-commerce solution, a designer should perform two fundamental tasks for each block:

- Describe the key decisions that need to be made, impact of the decision on the solution, and suggestions on how to make the decision.

- Identify the known options/products for each logical block.

This chapter discusses the key decisions in the following decision blocks:

- Application server
- Connectors
- Enterprise applications and data
- Security
- Performance

Now we discuss in more details the decision factors, for each decision block, to develop an e-commerce solution.

6.5.1 Application server

Table 45 shows the key decision factors, their impact on the application server design, and some suggestions.

Table 45. Application server logical block: Decisions, impact, and suggestions

Decisions	Impact	Suggestions
Should the e-commerce site be built from scratch or with pre-packaged merchant software?	WebSphere Commerce Suite software provides support for common functions such as shopping cart handling (insert, delete), address book, and total price calculation.	Make sure that pre-built functions are adaptable and that there are hooks for new functionality.
Does the merchant software allow the e-commerce site to be built rapidly and then incrementally customized?	The e-commerce Web site has to be changed continuously to meet the buying needs of customers, handle product changes, and remain interesting to visit.	The merchant software should allow a site to be built through a well-defined process using templates. It must allow any part to be customized easily and to incorporate changes to products, prices, and graphics.
Options for the application server: • WebSphere Application Server, this is preferred since it is bundled with the WebSphere Commerce Suite. • Lotus Domino Application Server		

6.5.2 Connectors

Table 46 shows the key decision factors, their impact on the connectors design, and some suggestions.

Table 46. Connectors logical block: Decisions, impact, and suggestions

Decisions	Impact	Suggestions
Will it be necessary to connect to host systems? If so, what systems are you to connect to?	WebSphere Commerce Suite includes connectors to CICS, IMS, and MQSeries. Consider any middleware that may be required. If Java servlets are used, what APIs can be used with the middleware?	Each access to a host system must be evaluated individually. Consider MQSeries or TXSeries for connecting to CICS-based host systems.
Will the connections be synchronous or asynchronous? Will it be necessary to maintain state in any connection? If so, where will the state be maintained?	Synchronous connections and those involving state are more complex to manage than asynchronous, stateless connections. Credit card validation involves a state and requires a synchronous connection.	Asynchronous connections can be used when online orders are processed in batch mode at a later time. Manage synchronous connections and state with middleware to reuse standard solutions such as the IBM Payment Server.

Decisions	Impact	Suggestions
Options for the connectors: • CICS • IMS • TXSeries • MQSeries • ODBC • JDBC		

6.5.3 Enterprise application and data

The enterprise application and data exist at the customer installation before the e-commerce solution is implemented. You need to carefully investigate the existing system to design the proper connectors to the existing system.

Table 45 shows the key decision factors, their impact on the enterprise application and data design, and some suggestions.

Table 47. Application server logical block: Decisions, impact, and suggestions

Decisions	Impact	Suggestions
Where does the data for online sales come from? Does it have to be manually entered?	In most cases, the company already uses an ERP system for basic product and price data and a marketing database for detailed product descriptions and pictures. It is important to leverage this existing data.	WebSphere Commerce Suite provides data import functions. When you write a preprocessor, which formats the data from the legacy system to the merchant software import format, you have to collect the data from these sources.
What method, if any, can you use to protect you product information from your competitors?	The Internet is open, so anything available to potential customers is available to competitors. Moreover, comparison agent software machines are searching continuously for products and prices.	Use business-to-business solutions that employ extranets and VPN to make special product information available to approved individuals.

6.5.4 Security

Table 48 shows the key decision factors, their impact on the security design, and some suggestions.

Table 48. Security logical block: Decisions, impact, and suggestions

Decisions	Impact	Suggestions
Does the whole shopping process need secure communication (usually via SSL)?	Secure communications will greatly impact performance, for example, SSL encryption needs a lot of computing power of your server. So reduce the use of secure communications to a minimum.	Viewing categories and products, and perhaps also handling the shop cart, does not need secure communications. However, the order process requires secure communications.

Decisions	Impact	Suggestions
How are the back-end applications and data that the online sales system connects to be protected?	Processing large volumes of orders requires synchronous connections from the online sales system to the back-end applications, thereby making the back-end applications and data open to attacks from the Internet.	Establish a DMZ to protect the back-end applications and data. The DMZ should allow only a trusted online sales system to communicate directly with the back-end applications and data.
How is the credit card used by the shopper verified?	Shoppers cannot be trusted to use authorized or valid credit cards. On the Internet, shoppers are anonymous and can be exploited to misuse the order process.	Use different kinds of online credit card verification to ensure validity.
Options for security • SET Secure Electronic Transaction • Secure Socket Layer (SSL) • Merchant Originated Payment (MOP) • CyberCash		

6.5.5 Performance

When tuning servers or technologies for performance, consider these points:

- Pay attention to all components of the solution.

- Understand, in detail, the interfaces and flows between the various components. For example, tuning your HTTP server may result in exposing a performance bottleneck in your commerce or database server.

- Plan for growth in the design.

- Use the latest levels of infrastructure and system software.

- Cache as much as possible.

6.6 E-commerce solution

Now we present a typical e-commerce solution for online sales. We split the process of creating a solution into the following logical blocks:

- Solution overview

- Static and dynamic application design view

- Discussion on the relative strengths and weaknesses of the WebSphere Commerce Suite solution

6.6.1 Solution overview

This example uses the case of building an online store.

A business needs to implement an e-commerce solution to support online sales. The new application is not built as a stand-alone solution, but instead needs to integrate with existing applications. The integration can be achieved on a functional basis or a data basis using a transaction interface or a data interface.

When trying to integrate with an existing application, it is important to research whether the application needs to be modified and determine if the changes are allowed. If the new application is going to use existing data, you must determine if the data can be used "as is" or if the structure needs to be changed, and if so, if this modification is possible. Note that in most cases, the objective is to leave the existing applications and data unchanged. Figure 159 illustrates an enterprise-out three-tier commerce application with online access to the third tier.

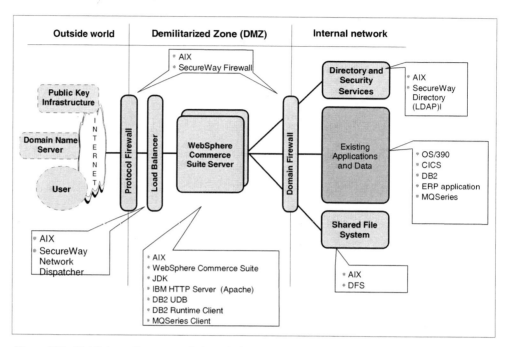

Figure 159. WebSphere Commerce Suite solution overview

6.6.2 Static and dynamic application design

Figure 160 shows the components used for the solution (static view) and the interaction between them (dynamic view).

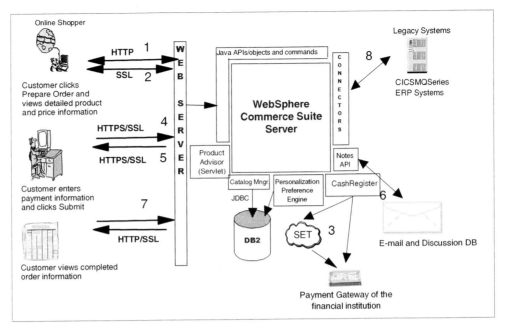

Figure 160. Dynamic solution design

Here is a step-by-step explanation of the e-commerce solution dynamic application design view:

1. The customer browses through the catalog, watches products, and puts them into the shopping cart. This may be assisted by the Product Advisor.

2. The customer prepares the order with information about product quantities.

3. The WebSphere Commerce Suite server switches to the CashRegister to get and verify the payment information, for example, a credit card number.

4. The customer enters the billing and shipping address.

5. The customer receives a completed order confirmation on an HTML page.

6. The customer receives a confirmation e-mail about the order and may discuss the product at a customer forum.

7. The customer views the order status.

8. WebSphere Commerce Suite transfers the order from the Internet database to the legacy system.

6.6.3 Dynamic application security

The security walkthrough is similar to the one described in 5.3.5.3, "Security walkthrough" on page 297. Refer to that chapter and section for more information.

6.6.4 WebSphere Commerce Suite solution strengths and weaknesses

The strengths of the solution using WCS are:

- Provides a wide range of tools to develop and modify the application.

- The applications can be extended and changed without interruption of the selling process.

- Supports several server and host platforms and multiple platform solutions.

- Is a proven, cost effective product that is already in version 5 with many product awards and a large user base installed.
- Has excellent documentation and online help.
- Each individual shopping process flow can be established.
- The database schema is documented and can be extended.
- Multiple platform support:

    - True choice to fit your IT environment
    - Windows NT, AIX, Sun, (S/390), AS/400
    - Unlimited growth path

- Many scalability options:

    - Server base options (PC, RS, S/390)
    - Architected design: Separate functions into separate servers; add more as needed
    - Dynamic Load balancing available

- Availability:

    - 24x7 operation possible
    - high availability cluster multi-processing (HACMP) software capability with AIX
    - Redundancy with Network Dispatcher

- Rich back-end integration options:

    - Large number of APIs provided
    - Tight linkage to order management, inventory control, payment system
    - MQSeries linkage available (13+ systems...)
    - EDI service available

- Business to business enhancements:

    - 'Shopping group' control and access
    - Support P.O. numbers
    - Account administration

- SET enabled:

    - SET enabled merchant server today
    - CommercePoint: Full SET implementation
    - eTill technology: Multiple payment protocols

- Flexible design and setup capabilities
- Advanced shopping experience:

    - "Virtual" sales assistant
    - Shopping metaphors cater to buyers' needs
    - Select and compare products based on features

- Advanced administration functions:

    - Stage content for approval, then load for production
    - Multiple sites/single server, with own DBs and URLs
    - Mass data import utility

The weaknesses of the solution are:

- Many objects and servers are involved.
- Testing is complicated and no tools are available.

Chapter 7. Business integration

IBM defines business integration as the integration of all the applications and processes that run a business to produce a unified, complete, and consistent view of the information needed to complete any business transaction. It means the creation of solutions that integrate diverse systems and applications to operate as one enterprise-wide business solution.

Business integration solutions are built upon the foundation of Enterprise Application Integration (EAI) technologies to provide a complete business-centric solution. EAI integrates internal applications, and business integration uses the same technology to extend the enterprise to the suppliers, distributors, and partners. Crucially, business integration solutions operate at the business process level, providing organizations with great business agility, allowing them to change business processes without changing their underlying technology. Business integration solutions are a key enabler for e-business operations, which need to have a set of integrated processes from the browser to the back-end systems and beyond.

Business integration usually covers not only application integration technologies but also workflow (Figure 161). The application integration component of Framework for e-business allows disparate applications, potentially written in different programming languages and built on different architectures, to communicate with each other. Workflow allows all business processes to be integrated across customers, suppliers, and core business applications and data.

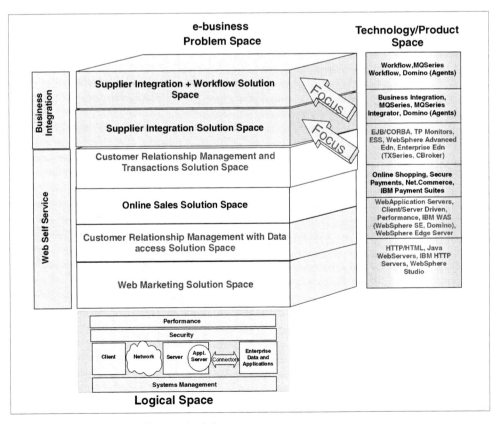

Figure 161. e-business problem and solution space

To introduce the subject one step at a time, we have broken it up into two parts:

- Supplier integration
- Supplier integration with workflow

Since the approaches in solving supplier integration and application integration problems are the similar, whenever we talk about supplier integration in this chapter, it is also true for application integration.

7.1 Supplier integration

Supplier integration solutions are required whenever there are mergers and aquisitions. This is when there are new requirements for applications to communicate with each other. Supplier integration solutions are also required when supply-chain integration requires applications to communicate with each other among the suppliers, the manufacturer, the distributor, and the retailer.

Some sample supplier integration opportunities include:

- Mergers and acquisitions
- Regulation and deregulation
- Packaged and new applications integration
- Supply-chain integration
- Value-chain integration
- e-business applications integration

This section discusses the key technologies, products, decisions, and experiences in building solutions for supplier integration problems. The discussion is organized around the three areas that are needed to support the supplier integration solution space:

- **e-business problem space**: Characteristics of B2B integration

- **Technology and product space**: Business integration technology, MQSeries, MQSeries Integrator, Domino (Agents)

- **Logical space**: Emphasis on key decisions in the client, network, application server, connectors, and security blocks.

We also present a case study and explain how the different products and technologies for this domain map into the solution.

7.1.1 Overview of the problem space

Supplier integration e-business problems describe situations where:

- Businesses need to integrate (facilitate communications) applications within the enterprise

- Businesses need to integrate their applications with other business applications

- Consumer access to enterprise applications

The main problem for this solution area is the integration of applications within the enterprise and between two or more enterprises.

7.1.2 Requirements for the new e-business solution

This section describes the various technological requirements that the supplier integration solution should fulfill. These technical requirements on a broad level are:

- Reliable messaging:
    - Information exchange independent of application programming model
    - Asynchronous information exchange, within or across enterprises
    - Guaranteed delivery of data
    - Support heterogeneous platforms/environments

- Integration:
    - Packaged/new and existing application integration
    - Intra- and inter-enterprise applications integration
    - Using existing business logic (no modification of programs when needed)
    - Lower cost of long term integration

- Transformation:
    - Heterogeneous platform, protocols, environment, standards support
    - Information exchange across disparate application domains

We discuss some of these requirements and see what they mean.

7.1.2.1 Reliable messaging

There are various messaging models that can be used. You can understand them in much more detail under basic communication patterns. As shown in Figure 162, there are different ways in which applications can communicate with each other. Some of these have overlapping functions.

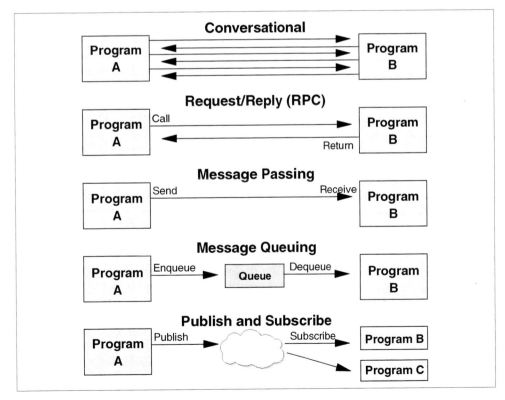

Figure 162. Communication patterns

Conversational is a communication model where two distributed appliactions exchange information by way of a conversation. Typically one application starts the conversation, sends some data and allows the second application to return some data. This is a synchronous form of communication. The conversational type is the same as either talk in UNIX or a chatroom on the Internet.

The *Remote Procedure Call (RPC)* model allows the execution of a program or a procedure on a remote system. The communication is done through the call to the remote procedure. The results of execution are sent back as a reply. This is also a synchronous form of communication.

In *message passing* model, one application sends a message, and the other recieves it. Message passing is about sending a message without worrying about any response or even that fact that it got there. This pattern is asynchronous.

The *message queuing* model allows applications to send messages to a queue and allow the other progream to dequeue those messages at will. This mode is asnchronous, that is the recieving program doesn't have to be available when the message is put in the queue. Message queuing is the same model as receiving physical mail from the post office, except that the physical mail is not assured delivery.

The last pattern, *Publish and subscribe*, is an example of a message bordering environment that allows the publication of messages and then the other programs can retrieve only those messages to which they have subscribed. An example of publish and subscribe would be if several recipients were interested in an activity they could subscribe and when the activity is published then, the subscribers would be automatically informed of the activity.

The advantages of this communication paradigm can be seen in the speed in which data changes are propagated, and the significantly reduced overhead compared to a polling model. In addition, the publish and subscribe model enables the development of loosely coupled and extremely flexible business systems, since the publisher (that is, the producer) and subscriber (that is, the consumer) applications do not have to know about each others existence, location, and state. This means that the overall system can be dynamically re-configured, new clients or services can be added without interruption to the operation, and all participating application components are completely shielded from any implementation aspects of other parts of the system.

Given that there are so many ways to communicate between applications, which one would be used more often? Well, given that the communications usually need to happen between applications and that there are no guarantees of the applications being up at all times, it would require some form of loosely coupled communication mechanism. In the worst case, it would be asynchronous communication, but it could be synchronous in the best case when everything is up and running.

The example in Figure 163 shows two enterprises that need to communicate with each other. Since there are no guarantees that the applications are available at all times, nor the network is guaranteed to be available at all times, asynchronous communication is a requirement. And since the communications need to take place between companies, there needs to be some form of security. Usually a VPN is used.

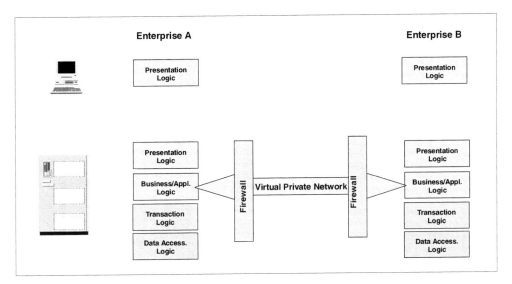

Figure 163. Business integration topology

7.1.2.2 Integration

Now, we know that we need to communicate in a loosely coupled manner, but what about the message format conversions required by different application? Another requirement is when a message needs to be delivered to more than one recipient. These problems are addressed by using a message broker.

Message brokering (MB) is an entity that takes information, or information requests, as messages from one or more applications and converting them seamlessly into the message formats that are acceptable to another program or set of programs. MB is gaining growing acceptance as the solution-of-choice in Enterprise Application Integration projects.

Let's look at two ways of doing this. One way is to recode the applications to explicitly make them talk to each other. Another way is to have a traffic cop in between the two applications (see Figure 164). In the latter case, the format conversion and the messsage routing would occur in the traffic cop.

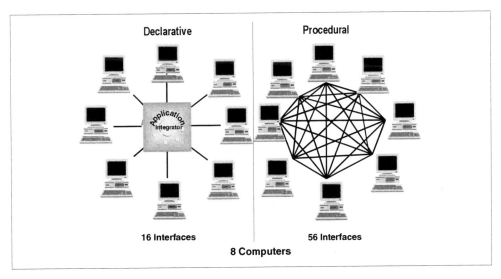

Figure 164. The effect of using a message broker

This traffic cop is the message broker, and its basic functions are:

- It defines data formats.
- It defines rules to:
  - Transform data formats
  - Route incoming messages to the right destination(s)

Table 49 shows some differences between a message broker and a point-to-point connectivity model.

Table 49. Declarative and procedural model

Declarative Enterprise Application Integration using a message broker	Procedural Data mapping using point to point connectivity
• Allows for any to any connectivity. • Data communication is abstracted from application logic. • Data elements are defined only once per application. • Publish and subscribe architecture is high performance and highly scalable across largest of enterprises. • High degree of methodology reuse.	• Point-to-point connectivity and data mapping required for every computer and application. • Programmers must define every input record and mapping of data for every interface. • Mapping model is too slow and hard to maintain behind a departmental scale. • Low level of methodology reuse.

7.1.2.3 Transformation

The solution should have the ability to support different types of data. XML is one technology that fits this requirement. By using XML, customers can standardize data, process integration, and application integration across the enterprise with both customers and partners.

What problem does it solve?

- A common syntax for data sharing
- A common syntax for data storage
- A common syntax for data transformation
- A common syntax for data search and query

XML provides a cross-platform portable mechanism for exchanging data. Like Java, XML refers to a family of specifications based on a tagged message format for "metadata". Unlike other tagged formats, it can contain any data, and be parsed by a generic piece of code in applications that has no prior knowledge of the content. This code, known as an XML parser or XML processor, can be written in most languages, with IBM, Sun, and Microsoft offering Java implementations to fast-start its developer community. Applications themselves can pre-load XML definitions of specific business data objects from flat files, RDBMS, OODBMS, or Message Queues. These are known as XML "schemas" or Data Type Definitions (DTDs).

XML can handle complex structures. It is hierarchical; for example, parent-child relationships can be expressed. It can be easily visualized as a Tree structure, and XML can be nested. For example, a sales order with multiple variable sized line items can be handled as one self-contained item.

XML is already in use in business application server and workflow solutions today.

For more information about XML, refer to 3.1.2.7, "Extensible Markup Language (XML)" on page 78.

7.1.3 Design block decisions

As shown in Figure 10 on page 30, the key decisions for designing a solution for this problem space are in the following decision blocks:

- Client
- Network
- Application server
- Connectors
- Security

For each decision block, you:

1. Describe the key decisions that need to be made, the impact of the decision on the solution, and the suggestions on how to make the decision.

2. Identify known options and products for each logical block.

7.1.3.1 Client

Table 50 shows the key decision factors, their impact on the client design, and some suggestions.

Table 50. Client logical block: Decisions, impact, and suggestions

Decision	Impact	Suggestion
Is there a need for assured message delivery from the client?	If you need a reliable connection, you may want to consider message-oriented clients. Otherwise standard HTTP may suffice.	If you use a messaging capable client, it is likely that you will use a messaging product. In this case, you have to consider any client licensing costs.

Table 51 shows known products and options and their features for the client logical block.

Table 51. Client logical block: Products and options

Products and options	Features
MQSeries for Java Client	- Works on many platforms - Simple API structure for quick development - Assured message delivery - Client licensing costs may be involved
Lotus Notes Client	- For existing Notes installations - Mobile client - Replication to the client assures message delivery

7.1.3.2 Network

Table 52 shows the key decision factors, their impact on the network design, and some suggestions.

Table 52. Network logical block: Decisions, impact, and suggestions

Decision	Impact	Suggestion
Is more than one protocol being used?	If yes, then the new application being developed has to handle communicating over different network protocols.	Think about a standard communications mechanism between applications that can hide the network protocols from the application being developed.
Is the network reliable?	If not, you may lose messages between applications across the network.	Use a reliable messaging software to avoid losing messages over an unreliable network. Alternatively, consider replication technologies.

Table 53 shows the known products and options and their features for the network logical block.

Table 53. Network logical block: Products and options

Products and options	Features
MQSeries	- Asynchronous communications desired - Works on many platforms - Simple API structure for quick development - Assured message delivery
Domino Replication	- Replication of databases (including messages) - Supports disconnected clients - For existing Notes installations

7.1.3.3 Application server

Table 54 shows the key decision factors, their impact on the application logic design, and some suggestions.

Table 54. Application logic logical block: Decisions, impact, and suggestions

Decision	Impact	Suggestion
Is the manufacturer big enough to dictate a single format for communicating messages between applications?	Is yes, the application does not have to handle format conversions. If not, the application needs to handle sending messages to required formats and converting them back to the required format upon receipt of messages.	If a single format is not an option, then try to separate the format conversion logic from the application logic and use a centralized format conversion mechanism.

Decision	Impact	Suggestion
Are there well established or understood rules? For example, is there a materials or supplier matrix that states who the supplier is for a given set of materials attributes?	As the number of rules increases, it will impact the maintenance, flexibility, and extendibility of the solution.	Separate the logic that handles rules from the application logic so that when they have to be updated or new ones added, the changes are limited to a small part of the application. You may want to consider using automated rules engine.
Has it been determined to use integrated packages?	The interoperability of the integrated package and the application being developed need to be understood. This will help influence which integrated package to use.	There are integrated packages that handle most of the requirements in business integration. Also there are standard formats used in a lot of cases, so you should do a good study of the format requirements.

Table 55 shows the known products and options and their features for the application logic logical block.

Table 55. Application logic logical block: Products and options

Products and options	Features
EDI	- Industry standard data interchange format - Vendors provide clearinghouse functions - Industry specific transactions (Health, Retail)
XML	- Data interchange format definition language - EDI/XML based standards body formed - Reusable components available to parse XML - Could be used with MQSeries Integrator in the future
MQSeries Integrator	- Converts formats using a GUI interface - Can implement rules using a GUI interface - Simple API structure for quick development - Integrated with MQSeries
Domino	- Domino Agents can be programmed - Leverage existing Domino programming skills - Integrated with MQSeries

Table 56 shows the key decision factors, their impact on the Application development tool selection, and some suggestions.

Table 56. Application Development tools logical block: Decisions, impact, and suggestions

Decision	Impact	Suggestion
If an integrated package is used, are there tools that will be used to customize it or integrate it into the overall solution?	The overall development time could be affected significantly by the amount of time it takes the developers to use the integrated package during development. Good tools can reduce this time.	The fewer the APIs there are, the easier it is to learn and use them. Try to balance this with the desire to choose a product with a very rich API set with a lot of feature functions.

Decision	Impact	Suggestion
What specific formats are handled by the tools? Are templates available?	Development time is reduced significantly if the required format templates are already available with the Integrated application development tools.	See if there are any format conversion adapters available that you can use in conjunction with the integrated application.

Table 57 shows the known products and options and their features for the application development tools selection logical block.

Table 57. Application development tools logical block: Products and options

Products and options	Features
MQSeries Integrator	- Converts formats using a GUI - Can implement rules using a GUI - Simple API structure for quick development - Integrated with MQSeries
VisualAge Tools	- Can generate MQSeries connector objects - Easy GUI-based development
Domino Designer	- Build agents to support application integration easily - Access to MQSeries via Lotus Script Extension (LSX) - Develops applications for Notes and Web client concurrently

7.1.3.4 Connectors

Table 58 shows the key decision factors, their impact on the connector design, and some suggestions.

Table 58. Connector logical block: Decisions, impact, and suggestions

Decision	Impact	Suggestion
How does the application server communicate with other applications within and outside the enterprise (for example, manufacturer to supplier applications communications)?	The type of data, applications, operating systems, and communications mechanism in use may influence the technology that may need to be used in different architectural alternatives.	Explore using a standard messaging software so that you don't have to maintain it and so it can reduce your solution development time.
Are all the involved applications available all the time?	If not, it may influence the communications mechanism you use.	Use a reliable asynchronous messaging (this does not preclude using synchronous communications) software to avoid losing messages over a unreliable network or when systems are down.
Do the existing applications need to be modified to integrate with a packaged messaging software?	The type of messaging technology used by existing applications may influence the amount of development time spent on integrating with a packaged messaging software.	Use a standards-based messaging software so that any changes in the future are minimal.

Table 59 shows the known products and options and their features for the connector logical block.

Table 59. Connectors logical block: Products and options

Products and options	Features
MQSeries	- Asynchronous communications desired - Works on many platforms - Simple API structure for quick development - Assured message delivery
MQSeries and CICS connector for Domino (MQ Enterprise Integrator)	- Provides MQ connectivity for Domino solutions - Integrated with Lotus Script

7.1.3.5 Security

Table 60 shows the key decision factors, their impact on the security design, and some suggestions

Table 60. logical block: Decisions, impact, and suggestions

Decision	Impact	Suggestion
Does the communications between the suppliers and the manufacturer need to be secure?	The type of security deployed will impact performance, firewall configurations, and application authentication.	Establish a VPN that sets up the appropriate firewalls to ensure encrypted messages between manufacture and suppliers applications.
How will the applications become authenticated?	This impacts the choice of certificate authority that is used.	Use a third-party certificate authority for business-to-business application authentication, and consider local certificate authorities for branch-to-branch.

Table 61 shows the known products and options and their features for the security logical block.

Table 61. Security logical block: Products and options

Products and options	Features
VPN	- Firewall to firewall communications - Difficult to break into - Firewalls are required at the manufacturer and the suppliers
MQSeries	- Use MQSeries exit APIs for encryption - Evaluate the Entrust/GSS kit for encryption

7.1.4 Products for the solution

So far we have looked at the e-business problem space and the technology requirements for supplier integration. This section introduces the products that can address these requirements.

The products provided within Framework for e-business that support business integration include:

- MQSeries Family of products:
  - MQSeries (MQ)
  - MQSeries Integrator (MQSI)
- Domino (Agents)

7.1.4.1 MQSeries family

These are the three components of the MQSeries family - MQSeries, MQSeries Integrator (MQSI), and MQSeries Workflow (MQSWF) (see Figure 165). This section looks at MQSeries and MQSI.

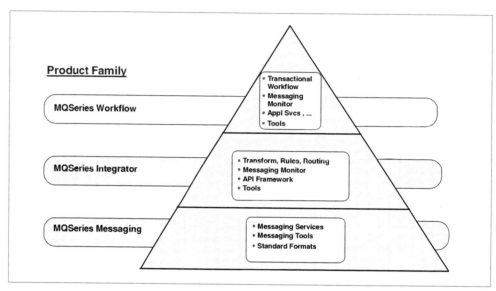

Figure 165. MQSeries: Cross-enterprise integration

MQSeries Messaging

The first component of the MQSeries family of products provides the base messaging functions, such as asynchronous communications, with assured message delivery. It also operates over multiple network protocols so that the programmer does not have to worry about it. And, it provides transactional message support. This means that all the messages can be successfully put or received in a single unit of work. Its features are:

- Assured, exactly-once delivery
- Single API across more than 35 platforms
- Network integration across SNA
- Support for TCP/IP, Sequenced Packet eXchange (SPX), NetBios
- Transactional control
- Content independence
- Single record support for more than 100 MB files

For more details on MQSeries Messaging, refer to "MQSeries" on page 162.

MQSeries Integrator

The value of an MQSeries Integrator solution is that it provides the core of enterprise intelligence. MQSeries Integrator has the following features:

- Heterogeneous platform support
- Layered design
- Database repository for rules and format definitions

- Assured delivery
- Transactional integrity maintained
- Message transformation and translation
- Intelligent routing

It maintains two types of knowledge:

- Knowledge of the business, including information and rules by which the business is run

- Knowledge of the applications in the enterprise systems

This knowledge allows the hub to take action, based on the type of messages that come in:

- Knowledge of the applications enables the transformation of message formats

- Knowledge of business rules and information requirements enables intelligent routing of information to where it's needed

- Knowledge of packaged application documents, held in application templates, enables a quick start to integrating these applications with the rest of the enterprise

Collectively, capabilities like these in the hub are usually known by the term *message broker*. MQSeries Integrator has all the capabilities to be a full message broker.

For more details on MQSeries Integrator, refer to "MQSeries Integrator" on page 166.

7.1.4.2 Domino (agents)

Agents are programs used for format conversions in Domino applications. They are programmed to execute:

- When a new work item (document) is created
- When a work item is updated
- On schedule to perform routine tasks
- When called by other agents

Tasks they usually perform are:

- Change field values in documents

- Send e-mail based on document contents (with an embedded link back to document)

- Archive documents that have completed the workflow process

Agents can be created in the Notes formula language, Lotus Script, or Java. Agents have access to the documents stored in the Domino database, including the capability to read, update, create, and delete. Agents are also used to programmatically access enterprise data and applications. Domino uses Object Store to store everything. Also, everything is done using documents. So, for this SI scenario, we looked at base MQSeries as a product for messaging and MQSeries Integrator as a message broker product that does formatting and rules.

Now, let's look at how we can do formatting and rules with Domino. If you did not have a tool like MQSI to help with format conversion and rules, you would have to write a program to convert formats and implement the rules. Well, that is exactly what you would do with Domino. Although, to do the programming in Domino, it is a little easier because of the availability of GUI tools. The program you would write in Domino to do format conversion and rules are called agents. When agents are written they are stored in the Object Store. There is an agent manager that monitors events and invokes the agents when required.

You can find more information on Domino agents in 3.2.2.1, "Lotus Domino" on page 143.

7.1.5 Solution

In this example, we consider a company that sells food products through various channels. They currently use a fax-based system as a communication link to their suppliers and business partners. Figure 166 shows how their business is integrated currently. A reorder is first recorded in the company's business system and then faxed to the supplier. A confirmation from the supplier is also entered in to the company's business system.

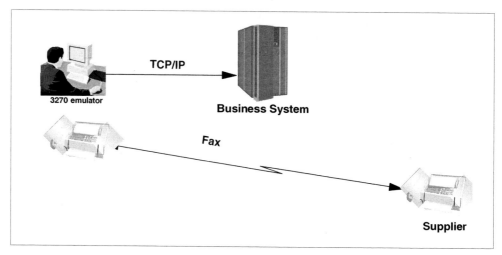

Figure 166. Existing customer environment

Due to their current model of business operation, they face the following problems:

- Paper-based management
- User transcription wastes productivity
- Typing errors
- Slower time to market

We now integrate this company's application with its suppliers and business partners. We also explain how the different products and technologies for supplier integration map into the solution.

For the solution, we discuss:

- **Solution overview**: Shows the runtime environment in each tier and the communication protocol between the tiers

- **Static application design view**: Shows the object, data, and function placement

- **Dynamic application view**:
  - To trace requests from clients through the tiers to satisfy the request
  - To trace security flow from the client through the tiers

- **Components selected**: Describes the set of products used to develop the solution

7.1.5.1 MQSeries Integrator-based solution

As you can see in Figure 167, the company is integrated with its suppliers and business partners using MQSeries Integrator. With this solution, when a new order is raised, it can be automatically communicated to various suppliers based on the properties of the order (using the rules engine in MQSeries Integrator). The formatter engine in MQSeries Integrator also helps convert the data to the format in which different suppliers understand. The suppliers can also communicate with Acme systems and update them with availability, shipment time, and so on. You see more details of the technology in this solution.

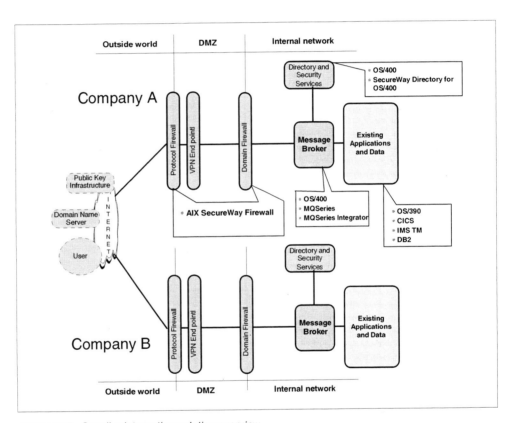

Figure 167. Supplier integration solution overview

Static and dynamic views of the solution

Figure 168 shows the static components and communications between them.

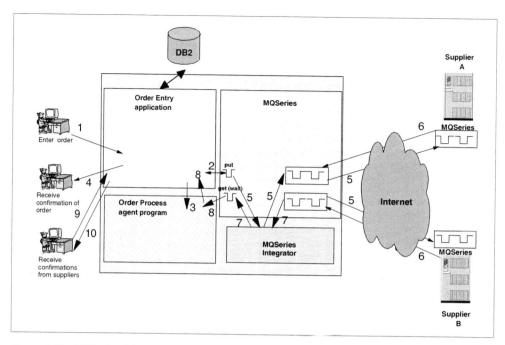

Figure 168. MQSeries Integrator: Dynamic application view (request)

The request walkthrough shown in Figure 168 follows this sequence:

1. A purchasing client enters the order using a CICS application (Order Entry application).

2. The Order Entry application puts a message on a queue for the supplier to MQSeries Integrator. MQSeries returns an acknowledgement to the Order Entry application that the message has been put on the queue.

3. The Order Entry application calls the Order Process agent program indicating that the message has been sent to the supplier. The Order Process agent program waits on incoming messages from the supplier.

4. The Order Entry application display a confirmation message to the user.

5. MQSeries Integrator gets the message from the queue, converts it into the proper format, and forwards the message to the appropriate suppliers.

6. The Supplier (A or B) gets the message from the appropriate queue, processes the order request, and puts a confirmation message on the output queue.

7. MQSeries Integrator gets the message from the supplier, converts the message from the supplier into a proper format, and puts into the queue.

8. The Order Process agent program, waiting on the message, wakes up, gets the message from the queue, and invokes an appropriate function in the Order Entry application to update the reorder information.

9. The user requests a order status check from the Order Entry application.

10. The Order Entry Application returns the confirmation from the supplier to the user.

Security walkthrough

The company uses a special user ID and password to communicate with its suppliers. VPN is used to encrypt the data sent between parties.

MQSeries Integrator: Pros and cons

The pros of using MQSeries include:

- Special purpose product targeted toward Enterprise Application Integration problems

- GUI-based tools for rules and formatting, including templates

- Can work across heterogeneous platforms and applications

- Highly scalable enterprise scale solution

The cons of using MQSeries include the high product cost.

7.1.5.2 Strength and weaknesses of the solution with IBM Framework

Lets look at a comparison of two products, MQSeries Integrator and Lotus Domino (not discussed as a complete solution in this chapter), in relation to the business integration problem space:

- *Performance* (response time targets): For business integration, sub-second response time may not be that critical given a lot of communications may be asynchronous.

- *Capacity* (total number of requests that can be handled): There is a potential that the MQSI solution may be able to handle higher work loads due to a design that has a well thought out format conversion algorithm.

- *Security*: Solutions using MQSI and Domino provide reasonable security through the use of firewalls to isolate the core business applications and protect them from outside attacks, authentication of user via user ID and password, and VPN.

- *Maintainability and manageability*: The MQSI solution may provide better maintainability and manageability due to GUI-based tools to modify rules and formats, as well as the addition of new ones. The Domino solution is only as good as the application design skills of the customer. Also, there is a good possibility that new agents would have to be written to add new function as well as format conversions.

- *Testability*: The MQSI solution would be easier to test due to the fact that such components as MQSI itself would have been well-tested already. Since, the Domino solution is mostly written from scratch, except for the forms capability, it is likely that the testing of this solution may take longer.

- *Extendibility*: The MQSI solution lends itself well to adding new rules and formats. The Domino solution would likely require more work to add new rules and formats.

- *Scalability*: The MQSI solution is likely to scale better than the Domino solution due to a better design. Albeit, the Domino solution does not lag behind too far because of it's replication capabilities that could be used to address scalability.

- *Business quality* (cost, schedule, staff, resources): The MQSI solution may be cheaper to build from a development work perspective, but the product cost is higher than Domino. The Domino solution is cheaper from a product cost perspective, but the development cost is higher due to programming requirements for the Agents.

- *Usability*: Both the solutions provide good usability from the purchasing and the supplier perspectives.

- *Portability*: Both solutions may be quite portable, but in the case of the Domino solution, using LotusScript may restrict portability to a certain extent.

- *Reusability*: The MQSI solution would have better reusability than the Domino solution.

- *Availability*: Due to asynchronous messaging availability of all systems in the solutions is not always required. Use of MQSeries in both the solutions also alleviates some of the problems caused due to unavailability of systems.

7.1.6 Summary

Table 62 shows a comparison between the MQSeries Integrator and Domino solutions.

Table 62. Comparison between the MQSeries Integrator and Domino solutions

MQSeries Integrator-based solution	Domino-based solution
More scalable due to separation of rules, routing, and formatting logic from application logic	Less scalable due to the need to write and modify agents
Enterprise-wide solution	Departmental solution
GUI-based comprehensive tools for rules and formatting	GUI-based limited function tool for setting up Workflow
High-priced solution	Low-priced solution
Less programming	Need to program Domino agents

On a broad level, for an enterprise-wide solution, the choice would be MQSeries Integrator. For a departmental solution, where scalability is not a major criteria, Domino would suit the requirements.

7.2 Supplier integration with workflow

Many business processes may be redundant or may even require manual intervention. e-business requires "adaptive enterprises". To be successful, companies are forced to deliver their services much faster and are looking for new ways to run their business. Interconnecting applications and business partners, making services accessible through new Web-based user interfaces, streamlining existing processes, and offering new ones, requires flexible and easy-to-change business processes.

You need consistent process execution across multiple customer access channels and back-end application systems. e-business needs workflow to define, execute, and control business processes. Besides the separation of business logic from its execution, workflow coordinates the integration of all applications needed to run the process – the key requirement to automate e-business scenarios.

There are several kinds of workflow. The simplest one is a completely automated flow that implements application to application automation. It is sometimes called *process flow*. Another kind of workflow connects not just applications, but people-related tasks. This is called *workflow automation*.

This section discusses the key technologies, products, decisions, and experiences in building solutions for supplier integration with Workflow e-business problems. The discussion is organized around the three areas that are needed to support the supplier integration with a workflow solution space:

- **e-business problem space**: Characteristics of workflow automation problems
- **Technology and product space**: Workflow technology, MQSeries, MQSeries Integrator, MQSeries Workflow, Domino Workflow
- **Logical space**: Emphasis on key decisions in the application server, connectors, and security blocks

7.2.1 Overview of the problem space

Supplier integration with workflow e-business problems describe situations where:

- Businesses need to automate their business processes to reduce overall cycle time.
- There is a need for a repeatable and consistent business process.
- There is a need for an auditable business process.

The process of providing a supplier integration solution, however, faces additional problems. These problems are related to:

- Business processes

  - Poorly understood
  - Poorly documented
  - Procedures not followed
  - Long cycle/response times
  - No constant improvements

- People

  - Missing information
  - Waiting for information
  - Not focusing on customer
  - Sleeping talents

- Applications

  - Unmanageably large ("monoliths")
  - Difficult and costly to maintain and adapt
  - Difficult to integrate
  - *Islands of automation*: Some pieces of a business process are automated, but there is no connection between them

Typically, only parts of the whole business process are automated today. They are known as "islands of automation" or "organization silos", because they are not yet integrated with each other. Programming these islands to exchange data is expensive and time consuming due to different computing platforms, different data formats, and the organizational boundaries the processes cross. To speed up cycle times – shorter time to market with new products or services – companies need to integrate these applications. Investing in application integration will allow automation of their business processes, for example, to gain fast and automated performance needed for straight-through processing.

7.2.2 Requirements for the new e-business solution

Understanding the problems in the supplier integration arena and the market forces pushing the companies to adopt a process automation, we can define the following requirements for a supplier integration solution:

- Flow control:
    - Message routing: Content, state, and rules based
    - Event driven routing
    - Workflow support: Across applications and people
    - Integrate application via a workflow model

- Configuration and management support
- Tools for development, debug/test, and administration
- Rapid deployment and ease of use
- Provide incremental levels of customization/integration services

The areas that need to be addressed as we look at integrating business processes are (Figure 169):

- The business rules that are to be used for workflow and process flow
- The people in the organization who are going to be involved
- The applications with which interaction must be done

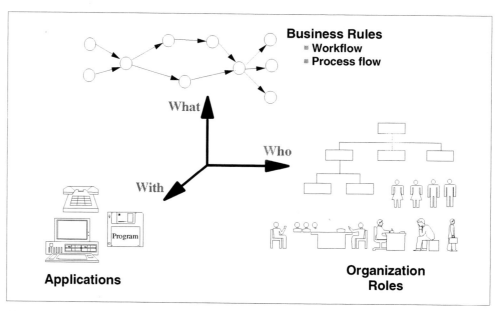

Figure 169. Business process integration dimensions

As discussed earlier, there are several kinds of workflow. The simplest one is a completely automated flow that implements application to application automation, sometimes called "process flow", which is shown in Figure 170.

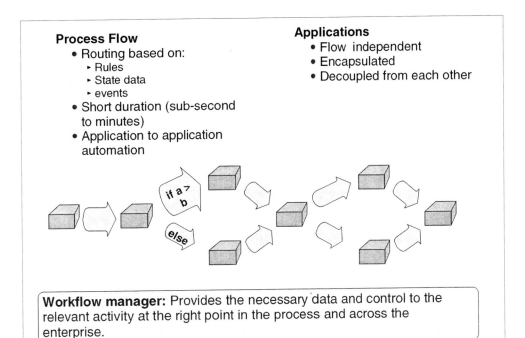

Process Flow
- Routing based on:
  - Rules
  - State data
  - events
- Short duration (sub-second to minutes)
- Application to application automation

Applications
- Flow independent
- Encapsulated
- Decoupled from each other

Workflow manager: Provides the necessary data and control to the relevant activity at the right point in the process and across the enterprise.

Figure 170. Process flow automation

A process flow consists of several flow independent applications, which are connected by the workflow manager. The workflow manager performs the routing between these applications based on predefined rules. The rules may refer to state data. State data is created and processed by the individual applications but mapped by the workflow manager between applications. The workflow management system allows for easy implementation of serial, parallel, and join processing. It creates audit data and allows the monitoring of the process status. Because process flows are completely automated, the typical duration of a request is rather short and ranges from milliseconds to minutes.

Another kind of workflow connects both applications and people-related tasks. This is called "workflow automation", which is shown in Figure 171.

Workflow automation consists of several flow independent applications, which are connected by the workflow manager. Some of these applications may be invoked directly by the workflow manager. Other steps in the workflow process show up in the work list of individual end users. If users pick a particular work item (step) from their list, the workflow manager will start the associated application at the users workstation and pass the according data to it. The work assignment to the people is based on complex rules. The rules depend on people's roles in the organization. As at least some of the activities are performed on behalf of people. The overall duration is longer and ranges from minutes to weeks.

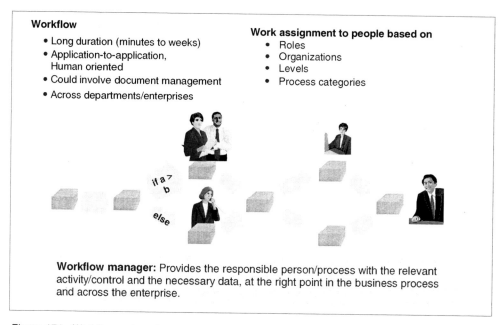

Workflow
- Long duration (minutes to weeks)
- Application-to-application, Human oriented
- Could involve document management
- Across departments/enterprises

Work assignment to people based on
- Roles
- Organizations
- Levels
- Process categories

if a > b else

Workflow manager: Provides the responsible person/process with the relevant activity/control and the necessary data, at the right point in the business process and across the enterprise.

Figure 171. Workflow automation

A process model is a powerful tool for structuring and formatting company information. One of the most valuable advantages of process models is the visibility of the business rules, showing what happens, when, and why. In addition, understanding a process flow makes it easier to adapt it to new requirements.

Business process models can be executed automatically by a workflow engine, making sure that the processes are executed the way they should be. It reduces work hand-off, and therefore, cycle time. This guarantees shortened cycle times and that all process instances follow the same rules and comply with the process definition. Changing business rules does not involve changes to application code anymore, so IT staff can focus on more technical matters. Business decision makers can change processes easily and fast, exploiting clear visibility of business rules and process models. Existing process models can be changed within minutes, or reused as templates for new processes. A workflow engine navigates business processes, routing data automatically between connected applications, and leveraging data from human intervention, when necessary. Processes automated like this will have much faster cycle times.

7.2.3 Design block decisions

The key areas for designing a solution for this problem space are:

- Client
- Application server
- Security

Note: The decisions for other key areas are similar to the ones discussed in 7.1.3, "Design block decisions" on page 341.

For each decision block, we:

- Describe the key decisions that need to be made, the impact of the decision on the solution, and suggest how to make the decision
- Identify known options and products for each logical block

7.2.3.1 Client

Lets begin with the client block and look at some key decision areas. Table 63 shows the key decision factors, their impact on the client design, and some suggestions.

Table 63. Client logical block: Decisions, impact, and suggestions

Decision	Impact	Suggestion
Is there a need for a workflow specific client?	A workflow specific client will impact the client hardware requirements.	Except for the case where the client is used for the sole purpose of a workflow client, it is better to choose a thin client.
Is there need for additional software (user applications) to be installed on clients to handle the automated workflow?	If yes then the client software and hardware requirements need to be evaluated.	Define the organization roles and policies first to asses this aspect. That will lead to a more knowledgeable estimate of hardware requirements.

Table 64 shows known products and options and their features for the client logical block.

Table 64. Client logical block: Products and options

Products and options	Features
Web browser	- Universal client - Easier to deploy for future growth - Not yet widely used as a workflow client - Some amount of programming required
Lotus Notes client	- Leverage existing Domino installations - Integrated with the mail system - Supported by MQSeries Workflow
MQSeries Workflow Client	- Designed to work with MQSeries Workflow - Workflow-specific GUI - No need for client-side programming

7.2.3.2 Application server

Table 65 shows the key decision factors, their impact on the network design, and some suggestions.

Table 65. Application logic logical block: Decisions, impact, and suggestions

Decision	Impact	Suggestion
How complex are my workflow requirements?	The complexity of the workflow requirements dictate the use of special purpose workflow package or a customized application.	If the workflow requirements indicate the need for a departmental-wide solution, consider a multi-purpose package, like Domino. For Enterprise-wide workflow requirements, explore special purpose packages, such as MQSeries Workflow.
Do you expect to scale this solution in the future?	Customized applications are usually difficult to scale.	Use an integrated package targeted specifically toward workflow and verify that it can scale. Try not to use a custom solution unless there are overriding reasons.
Are approvals required at one or more stages of the business process?	To avoid approval latencies, planning is required to institute approval chains which don't cause a bottleneck in the whole process.	Ability to define roles and policies up front will allow for a very flexible approval management structure.

Table 66 shows the known products and options and their features for the application logic logical block.

Table 66. Application logic logical block: Products and options

Products and options	Features
Domino (Workflow with Agents)	- Template/forms based solution - simple workflow functions - Quickstart solution - Not scalable
MQSeries Workflow	- GUI-based tools to help with development - Special purpose workflow package - Follows workflow management standards - Scalable solution

Table 67 shows the key decision factors, their impact on the application development tools selection, and some suggestions.

Table 67. Application development tools logical block: Decisions, impact, and suggestions

Decision	Impact	Suggestion
If an integrated package s used then, are there tools that will be used to customize it or integrate it into the overall solution?	The overall development time could be affected significantly by the amount of time it takes the developers to use the integrated package during development. Good tools can reduce this time.	The fewer APIs there are, the easier it is to learn and use them. Try to balance this with the desire to choose a product with a very rich API set with a lot of feature functions.

7.2.3.3 Security

Table 68 shows the key decision factors, their impact on the security design, and some suggestions.

Table 68. Security logical block: Decisions, impact, and suggestions

Decision	Impact	Suggestion
Are approvals required at one or more stages of the business process?	Approvals require authentication within the enterprise as well as across enterprises.	Use a third-party certificate authority for authentication across enterprises. For authentication within the enterprise, consider: - Local certificate authorities - User ID and password

7.2.4 Products overview for the solution

The products provided within Framework for e-business that support business process integration include:

- MQSeries Family of products:
    - MQSeries
    - MQSeries Integrator
    - MQSeries Workflow
- Domino (Workflow with Agents)

MQSeries Workflow

Integrating business applications into a workflow management system means that you remove the flow dependency from the application. The routing features of a workflow management system allow you to extract all information that is related to the process flow from an application program. Equally, process-relevant data is under control of the workflow system.

MQSeries Workflow is middleware and, therefore, similar to a database management system that allows you to extract standard data management functions from an application program. Whenever changes to the process flow need to be done, the applications that are part of the process model do not need to be changed. This also means that you can reuse your software components in other processes. Consequently, you can achieve significant cost savings.

The features of MQSeries Workflow include:

- Cycle-time reduction

  Improved time to market (for example, underwriting, loan approval)

- Improved corporate effectiveness

  - Cost savings (for example, increased productivity)
  - Timely activation of work

- Enabled consistent business process execution

  - End-to-end
  - Exceptions handling

- Improved customer satisfaction

  - End-to-end customer request management

- Business automation and integration

  - Integrate disparate systems and applications via business processes
  - Request coordination across multiple applications/processes

- Competitive advantage

  Enable rapid accommodation to change

You can find more details on MQSeries Workflow in "MQSeries Workflow" on page 170.

7.2.5 Dynamic view of the automated business process

In this example, we discuss the business process automated with MQSeries Workflow. The purpose of this exercise is to show the role, importance, and business advantages of workflow software.

We start from the existing environment where several departments of a manufacturing company have isolated islands of automation in the process of reordering parts from its business partners or suppliers (see Figure 172).

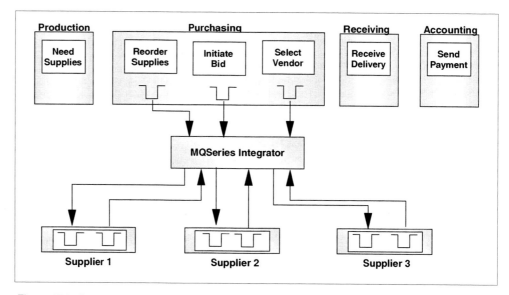

Figure 172. Business process before automation

Now we add MQSeries Workflow to logically connect all isolated pieces into a smooth business process. Figure 173 shows the steps involved in the automated process.

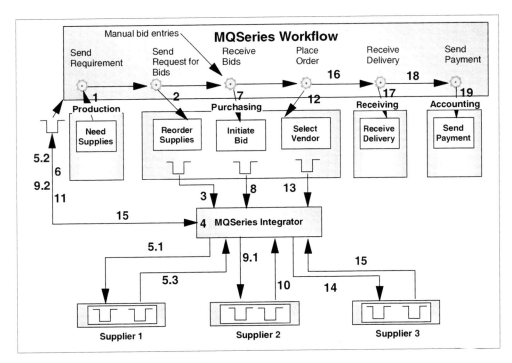

Figure 173. MQSeries Workflow solution

The steps in the MQSeries Workflow solution are explained here:

1. Production enters a request for raw materials. This starts the reorder process.

2. MQSeries Workflow prompts purchasing to approve and process the reorder.

3. Purchasing approves and enters the reorder. A message with the reorder data is sent to MQSeries Integrator.

4. The MQSeries Integrator rules engine looks up the rules database if a supplier exists for this material.

5. If a supplier has already been identified for this material, a reorder message (5.1) is sent to the given set of one or more suppliers. Then a message (5.2) is sent to MQSeries Workflow indicating that the reorder was sent. The supplier sends an acknowledgement of receiving the order (5.3). If a supplier has not been identified for this material, a Request for Price (RFP) exception is sent to purchasing to establish one (look RFP workflow steps 6-14).

6. MQSeries Integrator had queued a request to MQSeries Workflow indicating that an RFP needs to be started to establish a supplier for the requirement.

7. MQSeries Workflow prompts purchasing to enter an RFP.

8. RFP is queued to MQSeries Integrator.

9. MQSeries Integrator sends the RFP message (9.1) to a set of suppliers who are capable of supplying the material. MQSeries Integrator send a message (9.2) to MQSeries Workflow for each RFP sent to a supplier

10. RFPs are received by MQSeries Integrator.

11. RFPs are queued to MQSeries Workflow.

12. Upon receipt of all bids, MQSeries Workflow prompts purchasing to select a vendor or vendors.

13. Purchasing selects a vendor or vendors.

14. MQSeries Integrator sends the vendor selection message to the supplier along with a Purchase order.

15. Supplier sends confirmation of having received the reorder. MQSeries Workflow is also informed of this.

16. MQSeries Workflow prompts Receiving to acknowledge receipt of goods.

17. Receiving accepts the goods and enters the information into the receipt confirmation application. MQSeries Workflow is notified of this.

18. MQSeries Workflow proceeds to the next step. It prompts accounting to pay the bill.

19. Accounting pays the bill.

7.2.6 Strengths and weaknesses of the solution using IBM products

We perform this analysis based on the characteristics defined in 5.2.7, "Strengths and weaknesses of the solutions" on page 274:

- *Performance* (response time targets): Both Domino and MQSeries Workflow could have comparable response times for departmental level applications. For high workloads generated by enterprise-wide workflow applications, Domino workflow may not perform.

- *Capacity* (total number of requests that can be handled): MQSeries Workflow can handle high workloads as opposed to Domino workflow.

- *Security*: All solutions provide reasonable security through the use of:

  - Firewalls to isolate the core business applications and protect them from outside attacks

  - Authentication of user via a user ID and password

  - Virtual private networks

- *Availability*:

  - MQSeries Workflow provides better availability, because it provides for hot-pooling.

  - Also recoverability is better for MQSeries Workflow because, the Buildtime interface allows for recreation of the process very quickly.

- *Maintainability and manageability*:

  - The MQSeries Workflow solution may provide better maintainability and manageability due to GUI-based tools to modify definitions, as well as the addition of new ones.

  - The Domino solution will be only as good as the application design skills of the customer. There is a good possibility that if the process is complex the form-based design may not lend itself very well to it.

- *Extendibility*:

  The MQSeries Workflow solution is well-suited to adding new steps. The Domino solution may require more work to add a new function.

- *Scalability*: The MQSeries Workflow solution will scale better than the Domino solution.
- *Portability*:
  - The MQSeries Workflow can be ported to any system that supports MQSeries (which is available on many platforms.)
  - The Domino solution use of Lotus Script may restrict portability to other Domino systems.
- *Reusability*: The MQSeries Workflow solution would have better reusability than the Domino solution.
- *Business quality* (cost, schedule, staff, resources):
  - The MQSeries Workflow solution may be cheaper to build from a development work perspective but, the product cost is much higher than Domino.
  - The Domino solution will be cheaper from a product cost perspective but, the development cost will be higher due to programming requirements for the Agents. Also it may not be a long term solution.

Chapter 8. Business Intelligence

This chapter discusses the key design elements for Business Intelligence applications. The first part of the discussion is organized around the three areas that are necessary to support Business Intelligence (see Figure 174):

- **Problem space**: Business Intelligence refers to the ability to make better business decisions through the intelligent use of your data assets. It's about giving access to the right data, analyzing the data for insights, and using the insights to make better decisions.

- **Technology and product space**: The technology should enable Business Intelligence solutions namely data warehousing, data mining, and decision making. It describes the products Visual warehouse, OLAP Server, and Intelligent Miner for Data.

- **Design space**: Emphasis is on key design decisions regarding the client, network, server, application server, security, and performance.

We will also present a Business Intelligence solution using IBM Business Intelligence products offerings and discusses competitive solutions.

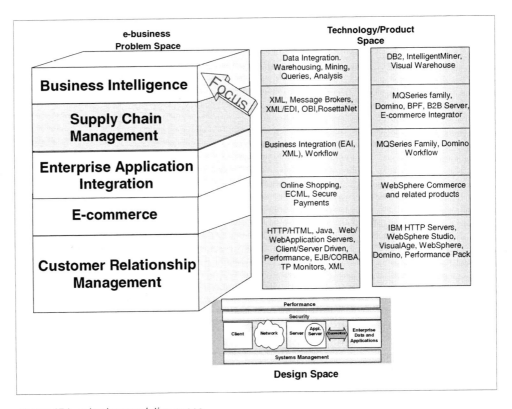

Figure 174. e-business solution space

8.1 Overview of Business Intelligence

Business Intelligence (BI) is the gathering, management, and analysis of vast amounts of data to gain insights to drive strategic business decisions and to support operational processes with new functions.

BI is about the development of information that is conclusive, fact-based, and actionable. It includes such technology practices as data warehouses, data marts, data mining, text mining, and OLAP. The objective of a BI solution is to transform data into useful information, such as customer profiles, buying habits, product profitability, and competitive analysis. It may involve analyzing volumes of data for unsuspected, but valuable, associations and insights. It includes streamlining data into useful reports and sharing that information with people inside and outside the organization who need that information.

Business Intelligence helps companies answer fundamental business questions about customers, such as:

- Who are my best customers and how do I attract more of them?
- How can I better predict buying behavior?
- How much should I spend marketing to a given customer and for how long?
- As customers mature and become more sophisticated, what are effective cross-selling tactics that we can use to sell to them?
- Which sales or service channels are most cost-effective for particular classes of customers?
- What's the right product to sell at the right time?
- How do I develop customized products on a mass scale?
- When am I about to cross that line of "over marketing" to a given customer (what's their "touch" threshold)?
- How do customers prefer to be contacted?

Most companies have the raw data to answer these questions from their operational systems (point of sale, reservations, customer service, accounts receivable, and the like). They also have data from external sources such as mailing lists, trade associations, government reports, and the Internet.

8.1.1 What Business Intelligence is

Business Intelligence (BI) is:

- Gathering, managing, and analyzing data
- Transforming that data into information to drive strategic business decisions
- Sharing that information across organizations to become information-driven e-businesses

BI takes all that disparate data, refines it, and shapes it into vital corporate knowledge. BI is fueled by technological advancements that include powerful parallel processing computer systems, inexpensive data storage, and the development of new algorithms for data mining, a process for discovering crucial information hidden in massive amounts of corporate data.

However, implementing a successful BI initiative is not as simple as installing the required technology. It is imperative that the business objectives for the project be clearly defined at the outset and that the project has upper management's complete support. At this point, the technological solution can be developed, and the expected benefits of undertaking the project quantified.

8.1.2 Main BI terms

Before we go into more details about BI, lets examine some of the terms related to Business Intelligence (Figure 175). The definitions we provide here are brief, since we explain the terms in more detail later in this chapter.

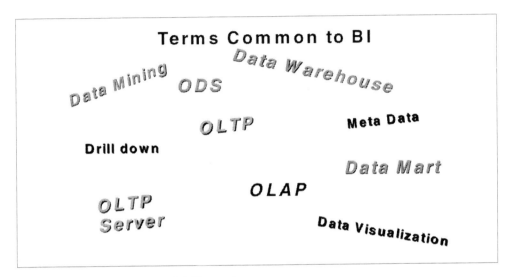

Figure 175. Common Business Intelligence terms

8.1.2.1 Operational databases
Operational databases are detail-oriented databases defined to meet the needs of sometimes very complex processes in a company. This detailed view is reflected in the data arrangement in the database. The data is highly normalized to avoid data redundancy and "double-maintenance".

8.1.2.2 Operational versus informational databases
The major difference between operational and informational databases is the update frequency:

- On operational databases, a high number of transactions take place every hour. The database is always "up to date", and it represents a snapshot of the current business situation, or more commonly referred to as *point in time*.

- Informational databases are usually stable over a period of time to represent a situation at a specific point in time in the past, which can be noted as historical data. For example, a data warehouse load is usually done overnight. This load process extracts all changes and new records from the operational database into the informational database. This process can be seen as one single transaction that starts when the first record is extracted from the operational database and ends when the last data mart in the data warehouse is refreshed.

8.1.2.3 Online transaction processing (OLTP)

OLTP describes the way data is processed by an end user or a computer system. It is detail oriented and highly repetitive with massive amounts of updates and changes of the data by the end user. It is also often described as the use of computers to run the on-going operation of a business.

8.1.2.4 Data warehouse

A data warehouse is a database where data is collected for the purpose of being analyzed. The defining characteristic of a data warehouse is its purpose. Most data is collected to handle a company's on-going business. This type of data can be called "operational data". The systems used to collect operational data are referred to as OLTP.

A data warehouse collects, organizes, and makes data available for the purpose of analysis. It gives management the ability to access and analyze information about its business. This type of data can be called "informational data". The systems used to work with informational data are referred to as *Online Analytical Processing (OLAP)*.

Data warehouse possesses the following characteristics:

- *Subject-oriented*: Data that gives information about a particular subject instead of about a company's on-going operations.

- *Integrated*: Data that is gathered into the data warehouse from a variety of sources and merged into a coherent whole.

- *Time-variant*: All data in the data warehouse is identified with a particular time period.

8.1.2.5 Data mart

A data mart contains a subset of corporate data that is of value to a specific business unit, department, or set of users. This subset consists of historical, summarized, and possibly detailed data captured from transaction processing systems, or from an enterprise data warehouse. It is important to realize that a data mart is defined by the functional scope of its users, and not by the size of the data mart database. Most data marts today involve less than 100 GB of data; some are larger. However, it is expected that as data mart usage increases, they will rapidly increase in size.

8.1.2.6 Data mining

Data mining is the process of extracting *valid, useful, previously unknown,* and *comprehensible* information from data and using it to make business decisions.

8.1.2.7 External data source

External data is data that cannot be found in the OLTP systems, but is required to enhance the information quality in the data warehouse. Figure 176 shows some of these sources.

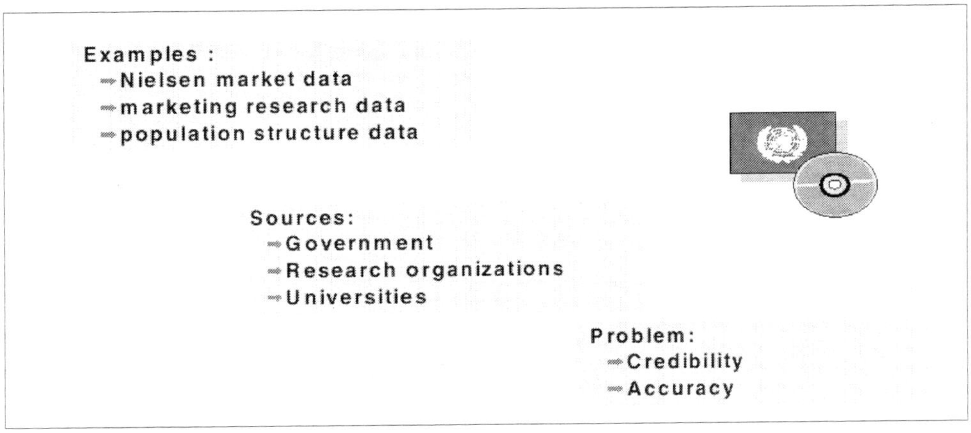

```
Examples :
  ⟶Nielsen market data
  ⟶marketing research data
  ⟶population structure data

      Sources:
        ⟶Government
        ⟶Research organizations
        ⟶Universities

              Problem:
                ⟶Credibility
                ⟶Accuracy
```

Figure 176. External data sources

8.1.2.8 Online Analytical Processing

OLAP is a category of software technology that enables analysts, managers, and executives to gain insight into data through fast, consistent, interactive access to a wide variety of possible views of information that has been transformed from raw data to reflect the real dimensionality of the enterprise as understood by the user.

OLAP functionality is characterized by dynamic multi-dimensional analysis of consolidated enterprise data supporting end-user analytical and navigational activities including:

- Calculations and modeling applied across dimensions, through hierarchies or across members
- Trend analysis over sequential time periods
- Slicing subsets for on-screen viewing
- Drill-down to deeper levels of consolidation
- Reach-through to underlying detail data
- Rotation to new dimensional comparisons in the viewing area

OLAP is implemented in a multi-user client/server mode and offers consistently rapid response to queries, regardless of database size and complexity. OLAP helps the user synthesize enterprise information through comparative, personalized viewing, and through analysis of historical and projected data in various "what-if" data model scenarios. This is achieved through use of an OLAP server.

8.1.2.9 OLAP server

An OLAP server is a high-capacity, multi-user data manipulation engine that is specifically designed to support and operate on multi-dimensional data structures. A multi-dimensional structure is arranged so that every data item is located and accessed, based on the intersection of the dimension members that define that item. The design of the server and the structure of the data are optimized for rapid ad hoc information retrieval in any orientation, as well as for fast, flexible calculation and transformation of raw data based on formulaic relationships. The OLAP server may either physically stage the processed multi-dimensional information to deliver consistent and rapid response times to end users, or it may populate its data structures in real-time from relational or other databases, or offer a choice of both. Given the current state of technology and the end user requirement for consistent and rapid response times, staging the multi-dimensional data in the OLAP server is often the preferred method.

8.1.2.10 Metadata

Metadata is the kind of information that describes the data stored in a database. It includes such information as:

- A description of tables and fields in the data warehouse, including data types and the range of acceptable values

- A similar description of tables and fields in the source databases, with a mapping of fields from the source to the warehouse

- A description of how the data has been transformed, including formulas, formatting, currency conversion, and time aggregation

- Any other information that is needed to support and manage the operation of the data warehouse

8.1.2.11 Drill-down

Drill-down can be defined as the capability to browse through information, following a hierarchical structure. A small sample is shown in Figure 177.

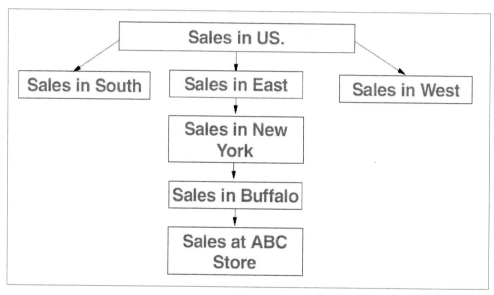

Figure 177. Drill-down

8.1.3 Business Intelligence implementations

Different approaches have been made in the past to find a suitable way to meet the requirements for OLAP. Figure 178 shows an overview of the four major models to implement a decision support system.

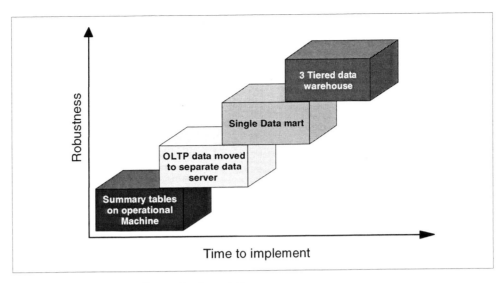

Figure 178. Business Intelligence implementations

The approaches that are shown are described in the following sections.

8.1.3.1 Summary table

A summary table on an OLTP system is the most common implementation that is already included in many standard software packages. Usually these summary tables cover only a certain set of requirements from business analysts.
Figure 179 shows the advantages and disadvantages of this approach.

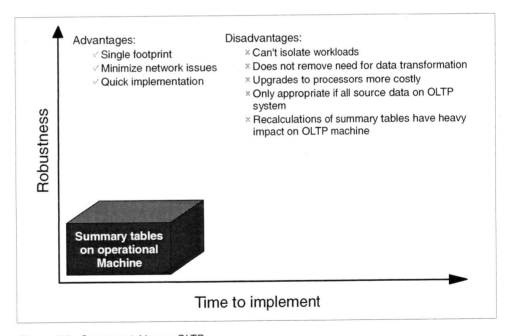

Figure 179. Summary tables on OLTP

8.1.3.2 OLTP data on a separate server

When OLTP data is moved to a separate server, no changes in the database structure are made. This mirroring is a first step to offload the workload from the OLTP system to a separate dedicated OLAP machine. As long as no restructuring of the database takes place, this solution is not able to track changes over time.

Changes in the past cannot be reflected in the database because the fields for versioning of slowly changing dimensions are missing. Figure 180 shows this approach, sometimes called "a poor man's data warehouse".

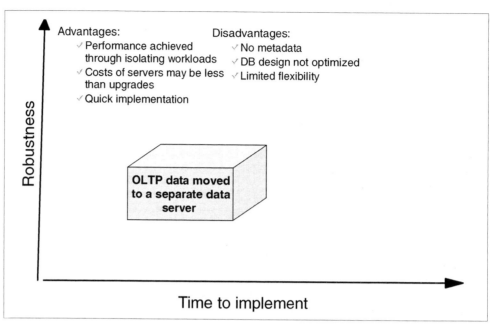

Figure 180. Poor man's data warehouse

The technique to move the original OLTP data regularly to a dedicated system for reporting purposes is a step that can be made to avoid the impact of long running queries on the operational system. In addition to the advantages in performance, security issues can be handled easily in this architecture.

Totally isolated machines eliminate any interdependence between analysis and operational workload. The major problem that will persist in this architecture is the fact that the database architecture has not changed or been optimized for query performance. The most detailed level of information is copied over to the dedicated analysis server.

The lack of summary tables or aggregations will result in long running queries with a high number of files and joins in every request. To build an architecture like this, file transfer or FTP can be sufficient for some situations.

8.1.3.3 Single data mart

A growing number of customers are implementing single data marts now to gain the experiences with data warehousing. These single data marts, which act as bricks, are usually implemented as a proof of concept and keep growing over time. The first brick in the data warehouse has to be kept under control, because too many single data marts would create an administration nightmare.

The *two-tiered* model of creating a single data mart on a dedicated machine includes more preparation, planning, and investment. Figure 181 shows this approach.

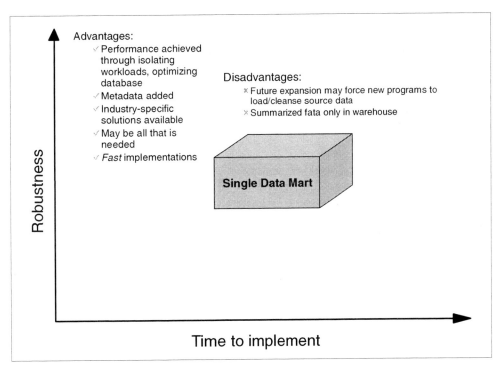

Figure 181. Two-tiered data mart

The major benefits of this solution compared to the other models are in performance, precalculated and aggregated values, higher flexibility to add additional data from multiple systems and OLTP applications, and better capabilities to store historical data.

Metadata can be added to the data mart to increase the ease-of-use and the navigation through the information in the informational database.

The implementation of a stand-alone data mart can be done very quickly as long as the scope of the information to be included in the data mart is precisely limited to an adequate number of data elements.

8.1.3.4 Three-tiered data warehouse

The *three-tiered* data warehouse model consists of three stages of data stored on the system or systems (Figure 182):

- OLTP data in operational databases

- Extracted, detailed, denormalized data organized in a Star-Join Schema to optimize query performance

- Multiple aggregated and precalculated data marts to present the data to the end user

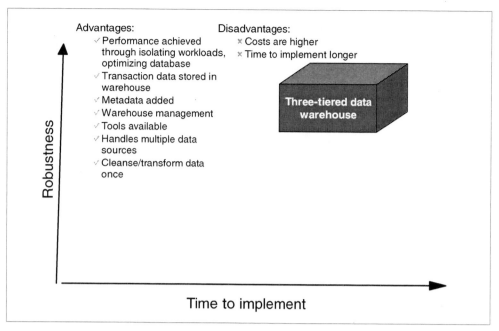

Figure 182. 3-tiered data model

The characteristics of this model are:

- Departmental data marts to hold data in an organizational form that is optimized for specific requests. New requirements usually require the creation of a new data mart, but have no further influence on already existing components of the data warehouse.

- Historical changes over time can be kept in the data warehouse.

- Metadata is the major component to guarantee success of this architecture, ease-of-use and navigation support for end users.

- Cleansing and transformation of data is implemented at a single point in the architecture.

- The three different stages in aggregating and transforming data offer the ability to perform data mining tasks in the extracted, detailed data without creating workload on the operational system.

- Workload created by analysis requests is totally off-loaded from the OLTP system.

8.2 Business Intelligence solution requirements

The key business requirements for a Business Intelligence solution include:

- *The need to increase revenues, reduce costs and compete more effectively*: Gone are the days when end users could manage and plan business operations using monthly batch reports, and IT organizations had months to implement new applications. Today companies need to deploy informational applications rapidly and provide business users with easy and fast access to business information that reflects the rapidly changing business environment. Business Intelligence systems are focused toward end-user information access and delivery and provide packaged business solutions in addition to supporting the sophisticated information technologies required for the processing of today's business information.

- *The need to manage and model the complexity of today's business environment*: The move toward the use of e-business, plus corporate mergers and deregulation means that companies today are providing and supporting a wider range of products and services to a broader and more diverse audience than ever before. Understanding and managing such a complex business environment and maximizing business investment is becoming increasingly more difficult. Business Intelligence systems provide more than just basic query and reporting mechanisms; they also offer sophisticated information analysis and information discovery tools that are designed to handle and process the complex business information associated with today's business environment.

- *The need to leverage existing corporate business information*: The investment in IT systems today is usually a significant percentage of corporate expenses. There is also a need to reduce this overhead and gain the maximum business benefits from the information managed by IT systems. New information technologies, such as corporate intranets and extranets, analytic applications, and enterprise information portals, help reduce the cost of deploying Business Intelligence systems to a wider user audience, especially such information consumers as executives and business managers. Business Intelligence systems also broaden the scope of the information that can be processed to include not only operational and data warehouse information, but also information managed by office systems and Web servers.

- *The need for fast, easy, and personalized access to an organization's business information*: This encompasses a wide range of business users, including both information providers and information consumers.

8.2.1 Business Intelligence solution architecture requirements

Figure 183 shows the entire data warehouse architecture in a single view.

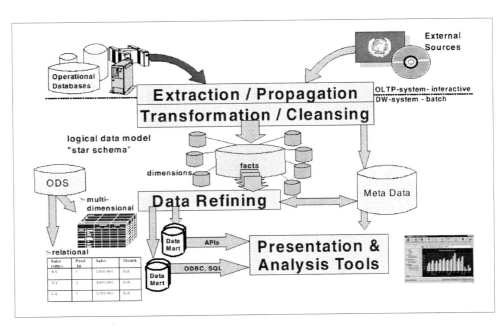

Figure 183. Data warehouse components

It presents the following ideas:

- The processes required to keep the data warehouse up to date as marked are extraction/propagation, transformation/cleansing, data refining, presentation, and analysis tools.

- The different stages of aggregation in the data are: OLTP data, Operational Data Source (ODS) Star-Join Schema, and data marts.

- Metadata and how it is involved in each process is shown with solid connectors.

The horizontal dotted line in the figure separates the different tasks into two groups:

- The tasks to be performed on the dedicated OLTP system are optimized for interactive performance and to handle the transaction oriented tasks in the day-to-day-business.

- The tasks to be performed on the dedicated data warehouse machine require high batch performance to handle the numerous aggregation, pre-calculation, and query tasks.

The following sections discuss each element shown in Figure 183.

8.2.1.1 Data sources

Data sources can be operational databases, historical data (usually archived on tapes), external data (for example, from market research companies or from the Internet), or information from the already existing data warehouse environment. The data sources can be relational databases from the line of business applications. They also can reside on many different platforms and can contain structured information, such as tables or spreadsheets, or unstructured information, such as plain text files or pictures and other multimedia information.

8.2.1.2 Extraction and propagation

Data extraction and data propagation is the process of collecting data from various sources and different platforms to move it into the data warehouse. Data extraction in a data warehouse environment is a selective process to import decision-relevant information into the data warehouse. Data extraction and data propagation is much more than mirroring or copying data from one database system to another.

8.2.1.3 Transformation and cleansing

Transformation of data usually involves code resolution with mapping tables (for example, changing *0* to *female* and *1* to *male* in the gender field) and the resolution of hidden business rules in data fields, such as account numbers. Also the structure and relationships of the data are adjusted to the analysis domain. Transformations occur throughout the population process, usually in more than one step. In the early stages of the process, the transformations are used more to consolidate the data from different sources, where in the later stages, the data is transformed to suit a specific analysis problem or tool.

Data warehousing turns data into information. On the other hand, *cleansing* ensures that the data warehouse will have valid, useful, and meaningful information. Data cleansing can also be described as the standardization of data. Through careful review of the data contents, the following criteria are matched:

- Correct business and customer names
- Correct and valid addresses
- Usable phone numbers and contact information
- Valid data codes and abbreviations
- Consistent and standard representation of the data
- Domestic and international addresses
- Data consolidation (one view), such as house holding and address correction

8.2.1.4 Data refining

Data refining is creating subsets of the enterprise data warehouse that have either a multidimensional or a relational organization format for optimized OLAP performance. Figure 183 shows where this process is located within the entire BI architecture. The atomic level of information from the star schema needs to be aggregated, summarized, and modified for specific requirements. This data refining process generates data marts that:

- Create a subset of the data in the star schema.
- Create calculated fields or virtual fields.
- Summarize the information.
- Aggregate the information.

This layer in the data warehouse architecture is needed to increase the query performance and minimize the amount of data that is transmitted over the network to the end-user query or analysis tool.

When talking about data transformation and cleansing, there are basically two different ways the result is achieved:

- **Data aggregation**: Change the level of granularity in the information. For example, the original data is stored on a daily basis; the data mart contains only weekly values. Therefore, data aggregation results in less records.

- **Data summarization**: Add up values in a certain group of information. For example, the data refining process generates records that contain the revenue of a specific product group, resulting in more records.

8.2.1.5 Physical database model

In BI, talking about the physical data model is talking about relational or multidimensional data models. Both database architectures can be selected to create departmental data marts, but the way to access the data in the databases is different:

- To access data from a *relational* database, common access methods, like SQL, or middleware products, like ODBC, can be used.

- *Multidimensional* databases require specialized APIs to access the usually proprietary database architecture.

8.2.1.6 Logical database model

In addition to the previously mentioned physical database model, there also is a certain logical database model. When talking about BI, the most commonly used logical database model is the *Star-Join Schema*. The Star-Join Schema is shown in Figure 184.

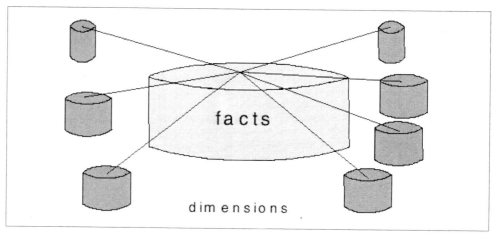

Figure 184. Logical data model

There are two components in the Star-Join Schema:

- **Fact tables**: "What are we measuring?"

  Contain the basic transaction-level information of the business that is of interest to a particular application. In marketing analysis, for example, this is the basic sales transaction data. Fact tables are large and often hold millions of rows, mainly numerical.

- **Dimension tables**: "By what are we measuring?"

  Contain descriptive information and are small in comparison to the fact tables. In a marketing analysis application, for example, typical dimension tables include time period, marketing region, product type, and so on.

8.2.1.7 Metadata information

Metadata structures the information in the data warehouse in categories, topics, groups, hierarchies, and so on. It is used to provide information about the data within a data warehouse, as given in the following list and shown in Figure 185:

- "Subject oriented", based on abstractions of real-world entities like 'project', 'customer', organization', etc.

- Defines the way in which the transformed data is to be interpreted, such as '5/9/99' = 5 September 1999 or 9 May 1999 — British or US?

- Gives information about related data in the data warehouse.

- Estimates response time by showing the number of records to be processed in a query.

- Holds calculated fields and pre-calculated formulas to avoid misinterpretation, and contains historical changes of a view.

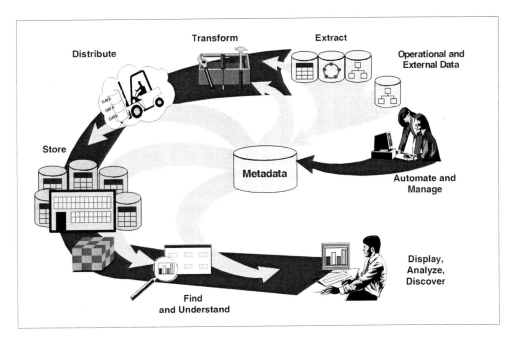

Figure 185. Metadata

The data warehouse administrator perspective of metadata is a full repository and documentation of all contents and all processes in the data warehouse. From an end user perspective, metadata is the roadmap through the information in the data warehouse.

8.2.1.8 Operational data source

The operational data source (see Figure 183 on page 375) can be defined as an updatable set of integrated data used for enterprise-wide tactical decision making. It contains live data, not snapshots, and has a minimal history that is retained.

Here are some features of an ODS:

- **Subject oriented**: It is designed and organized around the major data subjects of a corporation, such as "customer" or "product." They are not organized around specific applications or functions, such as "order entry" or "accounts receivable".

- **Integrated**: It represents a collectively integrated image of subject-oriented data which is pulled in from potentially any operational system. If the "customer" subject is included, then all of the "customer" information in the enterprise is considered as part of the ODS.

- **Current valued**: It reflects the "current" content of its legacy source systems. "Current" may be defined in different ways for different ODSs depending on the requirements of the implementation. An ODS should not contain multiple snapshots of whatever "current" is defined to be. That is, if "current" means one accounting period, then the ODS does not include more that one accounting period's data. The history is either archived or brought into the data warehouse for analysis.

- **Volatile**: Since an ODS is current valued, it is subject to change on a frequency that supports the definition of "current." That is, it is updated to reflect the systems that feed it in the true OLTP sense. Therefore, identical queries made at different times may likely yield different results because the data has changed.

- **Detailed**: The definition of "detailed" also depends on the business problem that is being solved by the ODS. The granularity of data in the ODS may or may not be the same as that of its source operational systems.

8.2.1.9 Data mart

Figure 183 on page 375 shows where data marts are located logically within the BI architecture. The main purposes of a data mart are listed here:

- Store pre-aggregated information
- Control end-user access to the information
- Provide fast access to information for specific analytical needs or user group
- Represents the end users view and data interface of the data warehouse
- Creates the multidimensional/relational view of the data
- Offers multiple "slice-and-dice" capabilities

The database format can either be multidimensional or relational.

8.2.1.10 Presentation and analysis tools

From the end user's perspective, the presentation layer is the most important component in the BI architecture shown in Figure 183 on page 375.

To find the adequate tools for the end users with information requirements, the assumption can be made that there are at least four user categories. Any combination of these categories may be used.

- **Power user**

  Users that are willing and able to handle a more or less complex analysis tool to create their own reports and analysis. These users have an understanding of the data warehouse structure and interdependencies of the organization form of data in the data warehouse.

- **Non-frequent user**

  This user group consists of people that are not interested in the details of the data warehouse but have a requirement to access the information from time to time. These users are usually involved in the day-to-day business and don't have the time or the requirement to work extensively with the information in the data warehouse. Their virtuosity in handling reporting and analysis tools is limited.

- **Users requiring static information**

  This user group has a specific interest in retrieving precisely defined numbers in a given time interval, such as:

  > "I have to get this quality-summary report every Friday at 10:00 AM as preparation to our weekly meeting and for documentation purposes."

- **Users requiring dynamic or ad hoc query and analysis capabilities**

  Typically, this is a business analyst. All the information in the data warehouse might be of importance to those users, at some point in time. Their focus is related to availability, performance, and drill-down capabilities to "slice and dice" through the data from different perspectives at any time.

Different user-types need different front-end tools, but all can access the same data warehouse architecture. Also, the different skill levels require different visualization of the result, such as graphics for a high-level presentation or tables for further analysis.

8.2.1.11 Data mining

Data mining is the process of extracting previously unknown, comprehensible, and actionable information from large databases (see Figure 186).

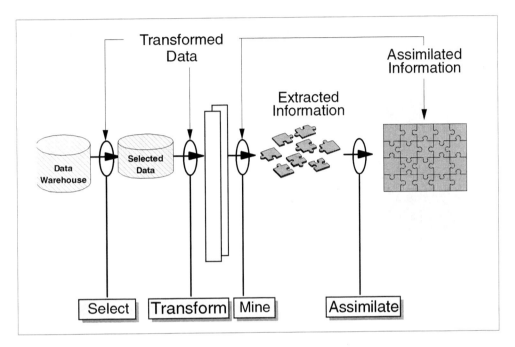

Figure 186. Data mining processing

Examples of data mining include:

- Discover customer buying patterns
- Perform credit analysis and approval

Data mining techniques include:

- **Clustering**: This technique is demographic and neural. For example, group a set of individuals, based on demographics, and determine who is product brand loyal, store brand loyal, and so on.

- **Classification**: This technique includes tree induction and neural induction. Data from these classifications is defined by how the graphed data looks:

    - Tree induction is represented in a hierarchical "tree" of related items.
    - Neural induction represents an affinity group with center values having a greater affinity to other nearby data points. For example, buyers of expensive sport cars are typically young suburban professionals, where luxury sedans are bought by elderly wealthy persons.

- **Predicting values**: This technique predicts the likelihood of a product purchase for a particular group of customers.

- **Similar time series**: This technique states, given product sales for a particular promotion, find other products with similar behavior.

- **Discovering associations**: This technique is demonstrated in the following two examples:

  – Of the shoppers who purchased milk, 55% also purchased some other type of dairy product, and 42% also purchased bread.

  – When a customer buys orange juice, they also buys brandy in 60.0% of the cases; this pattern is present in 3.371% of transactions.

- **Discovering sequential patterns**: This technique is demonstrated in the example where 42% of new pharmacy account customers who use Plan X will also return for a second prescription within 21 days.

- **Statistical functions**: Descriptive measurements, such as univariate, which are measurements based on only one variable per observation, and bivariate, which are measurements based on two variables per observation.

8.3 Product overview for Business Intelligence solutions

Now we look at the products and tools provided by IBM (and its key partners) for supporting a Business Intelligence software environment. These products are listed in Figure 187. We use the IBM Business Intelligence structure to categorize and describe these products.

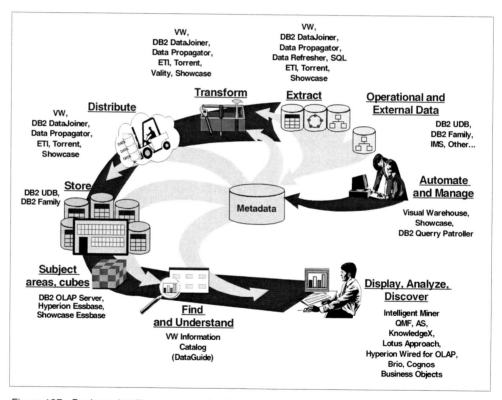

Figure 187. Business Intelligence product set

8.3.1 Business Intelligence applications

IBM Business Intelligence applications are marketed under the DecisionEdge brand name. DecisionEdge is a CRM solution that allows organizations to analyze consumer behavior with the objective of increasing market share and customer profitability. To date, IBM has announced DecisionEdge packages for the finance, insurance, telecommunications, utilities industries, and Fraud and Abuse Management. Each DecisionEdge offering provides integrated hardware, software, consulting services, and business applications centered on an industry-specific data model.

DecisionEdge for telecommunications, for example, analyzes customer information measuring profitability, predicting customer behavior, analyzing attrition, and assists in the creation of tailored customer marketing programs.

DecisionEdge for Finance, Banking, and Securities offers pre-defined solutions in the areas of marketing and sales, and risk and profitability analysis. All DecisionEdge packages support the OS/390, OS/400, UNIX, and Windows NT operating environments. They include the VALEX marketing automation and campaign management software developed by Exchange Applications.

DecisionEdge also capitalizes on IBM's heavy investment in information mining research. By using the Intelligent Miner development environment, DecisionEdge provides the optional *Intelligent Miner for Relationship Marketing* application to help the business user obtain a better understanding of key business issues such as customer segmentation, potential buying, and loyalty behavior. IBM is placing increasing emphasis on the use of Business Intelligence applications. They are bringing applications to market in several industry areas including student administration, retail banking, local and state human services, and e-commerce. Business Intelligence applications are also available for the DB2 OLAP Server. This product (which was developed by IBM and Hyperion Solutions) employs the same API as Hyperion Essbase. Therefore, it can be used with the many industry-specific third-party application packages available for Essbase.

8.3.2 Business Intelligence tools

Business Intelligence tools can be broken down into three categories:

- Query and reporting
- OLAP
- Information mining

8.3.2.1 Query and reporting

The main IBM query and reporting offering is the *Query Management Facility* (QMF) family of tools. Recently, IBM introduced QMF for Windows, a native Windows version of QMF that supports access to DB2 databases and any relational and non-relational data source supported by its DB2 Data Joiner middleware product (see description below). QMF host objects are compatible with QMF for Windows. They extend the enterprise query environment to Windows and the Web. Output from QMF can be published to the Web and passed to other Windows applications such as Lotus 1-2-3, Microsoft Excel, and other desktop products via Windows OLE.

To increase the scope of its query and reporting offerings, IBM has forged relationships with Brio Technology, Business Objects, and Cognos. IBM intends the relationships with these tool vendors to be more than mere joint marketing deals. They also involve agreements to integrate the products from these companies with IBM's Business Intelligence offerings, for example, in the area of metadata interchange.

8.3.2.2 Online Analytical Processing

IBM's key product in the OLAP marketplace is the *DB2 OLAP Server*, which implements a three-tier architecture for performing complex multidimensional data analysis. The middle tier of this architecture consists of an OLAP analytical server developed in conjunction with Hyperion Solutions. This server is responsible for handling interactive analytical processing and automatically generating an optimal relational star schema based on the dimensional design the user specifies. This analytical server runs on Windows NT or UNIX and can be used to analyze data managed by a DB2 Universal Database server. Support for Oracle servers is planned for a future release. The DB2 OLAP Server supports the same client API and calculation engine as Hyperion Essbase, and any of the many third-party GUI- or Web-based tools that support Essbase can act as clients to the DB2 OLAP server.

The value of the DB2 OLAP server lies in its ability to generate and manage relational tables that contain multidimensional data, in the available Essbase applications. These applications support the product and features within Visual Warehouse for automating the loading of the relational star schema with information from external data sources such as DB2, Oracle, Informix, IMS, and VSAM.

8.3.2.3 Information mining

IBM has put significant research effort into its *Intelligent Miner for Data* product, which runs on OS/390, OS/400, UNIX and Windows NT, and can process data stored in DB2 databases, any relational database supported by DB2 Data Joiner, and flat files.

The Intelligent Miner for Data provides a single framework for database mining using proven, parallel mining techniques. Business applications for this technology vary widely, and a variety of mining algorithms is provided. Here are some typical examples of how mining algorithms available in the Intelligent Miner for Data are applied:

- You can use clustering for market segmentation, store profiling, and to reveal buying behavior.

- Associations enable you to discover product associations in a market basket analysis, site visit patterns for an e-commerce site, and combinations of financial offerings purchased in different geographical areas.

- Sequential patterns reveal buying patterns in a series of purchases made or multiple Web site visits over time.

- Classification algorithms enable you to profile customers based on a desired outcome, such as propensity, to buy high-end electronics.

- You can use predictive algorithms to score customers by factors such as the likelihood of fraud, credit risk, or propensity to buy.

- Similar time sequences can reveal examples of similar stock price fluctuations over a period of time.

IBM also offers its *Intelligent Miner for Text* product, which provides the ability to extract, index, and analyze information from text sources such as documents, Web pages, survey forms, and so on.

8.3.3 Access enablers

Client access to warehouse and operational data from Business Intelligence tools requires a client database API. IBM and third-party Business Intelligence tools support the native DB2 SQL API (provided by IBM's Client Application Enablers) or industry APIs like ODBC, X/Open CLI, and the Hyperion Essbase and ESRI APIs.

Often, business information may be managed by more than one database server, and IBM's strategic product for providing access to this data is its *DB2 Data Joiner* middleware server, which allows one or more clients to transparently access data managed by multiple back-end database servers.

This *federated* database server capability runs on Windows NT, OS/400, and UNIX. It can handle back-end servers running IBM or non-IBM data products, for example, IBM DB2, Informix, Microsoft SQL Server, Oracle, Sybase, VSAM, IMS, plus any ODBC, IBI EDA/SQL, or Cross Access supported data source. Features of this product that are worthy of noting include:

- Transparent and heterogeneous database access using a single dialect of SQL.

- Global optimization of distributed queries with query rewrite capability for poorly coded queries.

- Stored procedure feature that allows a global DB2 Data Joiner procedure to transparently access data or invoke a local procedure on any DB2 Data Joiner-supported database. This feature includes support for Java and Java Database Connectivity (JDBC).

- Heterogeneous data replication (using IBM Data Propagator, which is now integrated with DB2 Data Joiner) between DB2, Informix, Oracle, Sybase, and Microsoft relational database products.

- Support for Web-based clients. The benefits of heterogeneous data access are magnified by the efficiencies of Internet and Java technologies. DB2 DataJoiner enables you to extend a wide range of data sources to Web applications. Using DB2 DataJoiner, you can:

  - Access DB2 Universal Database, IMS, VSAM, Oracle, Microsoft SQL Server, Informix, Sybase, NCR Teradata, and others from your favorite Web browser

  - Integrate DB2 DataJoiner with Web gateways and Web application development tools for transparent database access over a network

  - Write DB2 DataJoiner stored procedures in Java for transparent access to remote data

  - Access all JDBC-compliant data sources, as well as legacy data sources such as VSAM and IMS

8.3.4 Data warehouse modeling and construction

IBM supports the design and construction of a data warehouse using its Visual Warehouse product family and data replication tools, and via third-party relationships with Evolutionary Technologies International (for its ETI-EXTRACT Tool Suite) and Vality Technology (for its Integrity Data Reengineering tool).

The *Visual Warehouse* product family is a set of integrated tools for building a data warehouse. It includes components for defining the relationships between the source data and warehouse information, transforming and cleansing, acquired source data, automating the warehouse load process, and managing warehouse maintenance. Built on a DB2 core platform, Visual Warehouse can acquire source data from DB2, Informix, Microsoft, Oracle, Sybase, IMS databases, VSAM and flat files, and DB2 Data Joiner-supported sources. With the release of DB2 UDB v7.1 in the Summer of 2000, the functionality of Visual Warehouse was included in a new product, DB2 Warehouse Manager.

Organizations have the choice of two Visual Warehouse packages, both of which are available with Brio Technology, Business Objects, or Cognos add-ins for information access. The base package, Visual Warehouse, includes:

- DB2 Universal Database for metadata storage.

- A Visual Warehouse Manager for defining, scheduling, and monitoring source data acquisition and warehouse loading operations.

- A Visual Warehouse agent for performing the data capture, transformation, and load tasks.

- The Visual Warehouse Information Catalog (formerly known as DataGuide) for exchanging metadata between administrators and business users.

The second package, *Visual Warehouse OLAP*, adds the DB2 OLAP Server to the mix. It allows users to define and load a star-schema relational database and perform automatic pre-calculation and aggregation of information as a part of the load process.

Visual Warehouse provides several features that make the implementation and management of a data warehouse more efficient:

- Its use of agent technology
- Its management capabilities
- Its handling of metadata
- Its ability to invoke user-written and third-party tools to perform additional processing outside the scope of the product

The first of these, its use of agent technology, is intended to satisfy the performance requirements for loading large warehouse information stores. Data is acquired and loaded into an information store by warehouse agents whose job is to move information directly from one or more data sources to one or more warehouse information stores. Unlike many competing products, information does not have to pass through a central intermediate server that may otherwise become a performance bottleneck as data volumes grow.

Visual Warehouse agents run on OS/400, OS/2, UNIX, and Windows NT. Depending on the volumes of data being moved, any given implementation may have one or many agents running concurrently. The source data to be captured, transformed, and loaded into the warehouse information store by one or more agents is defined in a business view. The definition, scheduling, and monitoring of business view operations is handled by the Visual Warehouse Manager, which runs under Windows NT.

In addition to initiating agent activities, the Visual Warehouse Manager can also be used to schedule user-written data capture and transformation applications, as well as applications available from IBM Business Partners. This facility is employed by Visual Warehouse to enable the loading of Hyperion Essbase multidimensional data. It also integrates other non-agent-driven processing such as ETI-EXTRACT programs, IBM data replication jobs, and Vality data cleansing processes.

Visual Warehouse also plays a key role in managing the metadata associated with the IBM Business Intelligence environment. In such an environment, there are two types of metadata to be managed:

- **Technical metadata**: Associated with the design, building, and operation of a data warehouse.
- **Business metadata**: Used in conjunction with the Business Intelligence tools used to access and analyze warehouse data.

The Visual Warehouse Manager employs its own DB2-based metadata store for managing the technical metadata associated with the building and managing of a data warehouse. As mentioned earlier, IBM has developed interfaces to products from Hyperion Solutions, Evolutionary Technologies International, and Vality Technology for metadata interchange with Visual Warehouse. Metadata can also be exchanged with Business Intelligence tools from Brio Technology, Business Objects, and Cognos.

Included with Visual Warehouse is the *Visual Warehouse Information Catalog* (formerly known as DataGuide). The objective of this information catalog is to document and manage the business and underlying technical metadata that helps business users access and exploit the Business Intelligence environment. Business users can browse this metadata using both graphical-and Web-based interfaces.

Metadata in the Visual Warehouse Information Catalog is stored in a DB2 database and can be accessed and maintained using supplied SQL and application APIs. It can be imported and exported using files formatted in a documented tag language. IBM supplies a variety of sample applications that use these interfaces to exchange metadata with third-party products (Hyperion Essbase, Bachman DBA, Microsoft Excel, for example). Visual Warehouse Manager's technical metadata can also be imported into the information catalog. With Visual Warehouse, IBM supports the Metadata Coalition's Metadata Interchange Specification (MDIS) for moving metadata into and out of the Visual Warehouse Information Catalog.

IBM's data replication capabilities are based on its *Data Propagator Relational* product, which has now been integrated into DB2 Universal Database (for homogeneous data replication) and DB2 Data Joiner (for heterogeneous data replication). The replication facility captures data changes from DB2 source databases, and applies those changes to a DB2-managed data warehouse. Data changes are transported from the source to the target warehouse via staging tables. SQL is used to retrieve and transform data from the staging tables and apply it to the DB2-based warehouse at user-defined intervals. DB2 Data Joiner can also act as a data source or target for the replication facility. This means it can be used to replicate data from a third-party relational DBMS to a DB2-based data warehouse, or to replicate data from a DB2 data source to a data warehouse managed by a non-IBM relational DBMS.

Other IBM products for data warehouse construction include *Data Propagator NonRelational*, for capturing data changes from IMS databases, and *Data Refresher* for capturing and transforming data stored in non-relational databases and files such as IMS and VSAM.

IBM partner Evolutionary Technologies International markets the *EXTRACT ToolSuite* for generating warehouse data capture and transformation applications. This consists of:

- **Data Conversion Tool**: For defining data cleanup and transformation rules and generating data acquisition programs.

- **Pre-built Data System Libraries (DSLs)**: For key operating and database environments including SAP, IDMS, IMS, VSAM, and leading relational database products. A DSL defines the native access method to be used for processing data, the grammar for generating application programs, and the business rules available to the Data Conversion Tool.

- **Master ToolSet**: For extending, creating, and maintaining DSLs.

IBM has been working with ETI to optimize the DB2 DSL (to support parallel loading, for example), and to integrate EXTRACT with Visual Warehouse in the areas of metadata interchange and EXTRACT program scheduling. One of the key benefits that EXTRACT adds to Visual Warehouse is support for additional data sources and application packages such as SAP.

Vality's *Integrity Data Reengineering* tool complements both Visual Warehouse and ETI–EXTRACT by adding a capability to analyze the *content* of data extracted from operational systems and enhance the quality of data before it is loaded into a data warehouse. During the data re-engineering process, unique data entities are identified in data from multiple systems. This allows the data to be merged, reconciled and consolidated, even when there is no common key to support the merge. Important metadata that is discovered in this process can be used to validate and adjust the data model for the data warehouse information store. As with ETI, IBM has worked with Vality to integrate Integrity with Visual Warehouse in the areas of metadata interchange and program scheduling.

8.3.5 Products provided by other companies

The following sections provide a brief description of the products referred to earlier.

8.3.5.1 MicroStrategy

MicroStrategy drives emerging e-business applications such as narrow cast networks and electronic Customer Relationship Management (eCRM). It is a scalable, high-performance, and open platform that provides insight into business operations and empowering businesses to build lasting, profitable customer relationships.

To achieve competitive advantages, insight must be sifted from mountains of information. This insight must be timely and relevant, and reach out to individual employees, partners, and often millions of customers. MicroStrategy 7 offers a set of tools to derive this information from the data, including:

- **MicroStrategy Agent**: A Windows-based interface for power analysts and application developers, with a full range of analytical functionality, a rich function library, workflow, and data mining integration.

- **MicroStrategy Intelligence Server**: Collaborates with the relational database manager to perform complex analysis with maximum efficiency, scalability, and high availability.

- **MicroStrategy Web's easy-to-use all-HTML interface**: For deployment to a diverse user community, can be accessed through any Web browser, providing interactive analysis and ad hoc querying.

- **MicroStrategy applications**: Accessible through an enterprise portal using MicroStrategy InfoCenter, a platform for self-subscription to personalized information delivery.

MicroStrategy has a three-tier architecture. End users access the application server where the MicroStrategy code runs. The server connects, through DB2 Connect, to the data server, where the actual DB2 data is stored. The database can also house the metadata for the MicroStrategy code.

For more information about MicroStrategy, see: http://www.microstrategy.com/

8.3.5.2 Business Objects

Business Objects give business users the ability to access, analyze, and share information in intranet, extranet, and e-business environments, while providing the IT department with the necessary tools to control and manage enterprise-wide and inter-enterprise user access. Business Objects is a powerful, easy-to-use tool that lets users combine, compare, and report on data from a wide range of sources, including the Internet. Users can then perform sophisticated OLAP analysis on the data, even when working offline. Business Objects offers a wide array of products that address different end user needs for accessing and querying a database. These include Web tools such as WebIntelligence, BI Portals, and query reporting tools. For more information, refer to: http://www.businessobjects.com/

8.3.5.3 Cognos

The Cognos platform provides end-to-end coverage of all end users needs, both inside and outside the organization, while delivering a unified data infrastructure critical to running a business today. With the Cognos platform, you gain sophisticated visualization and score carding, reporting, analysis, and ad hoc query capabilities, as well as prepackaged e-applications. It gives suppliers, partners, and customers a single point of personalized access to information through the portal interface. It also leverages existing infrastructure and IT investment with the Cognos robust, secure solution. For more information, refer to: http://www.cognos.com/

8.3.5.4 Brio

Brio Technology offers a complete, integrated intelligence infrastructure that addresses the unique decision-making needs of today's e-enabled world. The Brio ONE solution, which includes Brio.Enterprise, Brio.Report, Brio.Portal, and Brio.Applications, is specifically designed to empower everyone in the extended enterprise by delivering dynamic, reliable, easy access to real-time business information, regardless of where that information is stored, and regardless of the user's location. The Brio ONE solution enables the organization to build and deliver Business Intelligence, enterprise reporting, self-service information exchange, and analytic applications to the broadest possible range of users in client/server, Web-based, and hosted application environments, all with

unmatched ease of experience and scalability. Brio ONE allows customers to derive higher business value from all current information sources, including Enterprise Resource Planning (ERP), sales force automation (SFA), and Customer Relationship Management (CRM) applications, production systems, analytic applications and business spreadsheets, data marts, data warehouses, intranets, extranets, and others. For more information, refer to:
http://www.brio.com/

8.3.5.5 SAP Business Warehouse

The SAP Business Warehouse is a proprietary warehouse structure that gathers information from the SAP operational systems, making it available for analysis by the end user community. SAP BW offers an all-in-one package including:

- Data extractors
- Administrator workbench
- OLAP engine
- Graphical user interface for reporting and analysis
- Prefabricated reports

Applications include:

- Infocubes
- OLAP processor

For more information, see: http://sap.com/

8.3.5.6 PeopleSoft Enterprise Performance Management

PeopleSoft Enterprise Performance Management (EPM) is a new product offering that includes four business solutions:

- Customer Relationship Manager (CRM)
- Workforce Analytics
- Strategy/Finance
- Industry Analytics

These solutions are targeted to specific industries such as Merchandise and Supply Chain Management. Each is composed of the following base components:

- Analytic applications
- Enterprise warehouse
- Workbenches
- A balanced scorecard

For more information, see: http://peoplesoft.com/

8.3.5.7 Siebel CRM

Siebel offers a business Customer Relationship Management software solution that has a three-tier architecture. The custom Siebel client software accesses the application server software on Windows NT, AIX, or OS/400. The application server can access data within DB2 in the OS/390 environment. Recognition Systems runs natively on the S/390 platform, in a single tier architecture. The company offers Campaign Management (CM) software that automates the process of implementing and tracking sales and marketing activities. It attaches to a relational database to analyze and manage the customer contact across all touch points, as well as managing the sales activities associated with a customer. It also allows access to a marketing database used to plan for campaigns, query the database to get counts, set up and execute campaign designs, and track customer responses. For more information, see: `http://siebel.com/`

8.3.5.8 ETI Extract

ETI Extract is a GUI-based data movement, transformation, and manipulation tool. The access system is based on templates and covers many operating systems, databases, and filing systems. The template approach in its architecture lets you effectively customize ETI to suit virtually any circumstance, whether it is for a data migration, data warehouse, or any other special data movement requirement. It maintains its own repository of metadata and has tight metadata and scheduling coupling using the IBM Visual Warehouse. There is a strong case for ETI when:

- You have different types of sources on different platforms.
- The complexity of the manipulations needed is complex or unknown.
- Performance is key.
- There is a reasonable likelihood of rework later.

For more details on ETI Extract, go to: `http://www.eti.com/home/home.htm`

8.4 BI solution

Now we present a typical multi-tier Business Intelligence solution that describes:

- **Solution overview**: Shows runtime environment in each tier and the communication protocol between tiers

- **Static application design view**: Shows object, data, and function placement

- **Components selected**: Describes the set of products used to develop the solution

8.4.1 Solution overview

Building a BI application requires the consideration of two separate, but linked, design topics:

- Creating the information access involves designing and creating the necessary data structures, user interfaces, and processes used to access and productively use information relevant to the user's Business Intelligence (BI) needs.

- Populating the data warehouse involves designing and creating the processes to extract, cleanse, restructure, and move data into or between the appropriate data stores in the warehouse. It is needed if the required data does not already exist in the warehouse, or if the data is not in an optimal form to satisfy the user's needs.

As the data warehouse environment matures, the design and development focus shifts increasingly from the population topic to the user application.

8.4.1.1 Populating the data warehouse

The population topology defines the processes used to extract, cleanse, restructure, and move data into or between the various data stores in the warehouse. The basic topology repeats in a series of steps within the full process. Current "good practice" implements the process in batch mode, but a more real-time approach can be implemented if needed.

Few, if any, data warehouse population processes are simple enough to be performed in a single step. The basic "building block," which works on the (read dataset - process - write dataset) model, is then applied to the problem in as many steps as the designer thinks is appropriate for the problem.

Figure 188 shows a common three-step process.

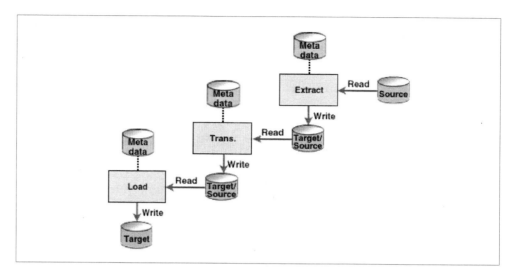

Figure 188. Three-step process to populate the data warehouse

Each of the three steps is explained here:

1. **Extract**: The extract application extracts data from the source data set. This data set is typically owned by another application and used in a read/write fashion by that application.

   The extraction rules may be as simple as including all data, to a more complex process involving extracting only certain fields from certain records under varying conditions. One key condition is if this record is new or changed. When only new or changed records are extracted, the process is often called "change capture".

2. **Transform**: The transform application transforms data from an input to an output structure according to the supplied rules. Transformation covers a wide variety of activities, including:

   - Joining together data from many inputs
   - Validating and cleansing data of errors
   - Transforming data in individual fields based on predefined rules or based on the content of other fields and so on

   When two or more inputs are involved, there is generally no guarantee that all inputs will be present when required. Transform must be able to handle this situation.

3. **Load**: The load application loads the input data into the target data set. As with extract, load can range from a simple process of overwriting the target data set to a complex process of inserting new records and updating existing records.

Figure 189 shows the runtime topology of the internal population process (all data population processes occur in the internal environment).

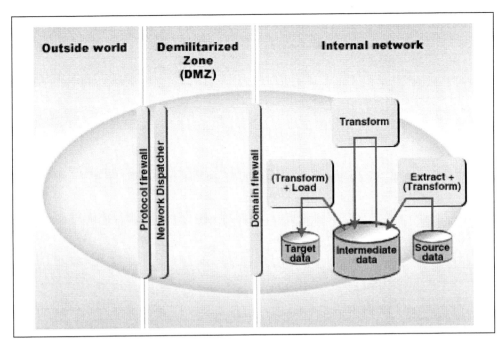

Figure 189. Internal population runtime topology

The process flow in Figure 189 follows this sequence:

1. A population application extracts and optionally transforms the source data into intermediate data.

2. Optionally, a population application then transforms the intermediate data into further intermediate data.

3. A population application takes intermediate data (produced by either of the two previous steps) and optionally transforms and loads it into target data.

The diagram explicitly shows that the process can be performed in two or three steps. The process can also be reduced to one step, where extract, transform, and load all occur in one process that directly produces target data. Furthermore, the mid-section of the diagram can be repeated as often as necessary to produce a multi-step process.

8.4.1.2 Creating the information access

The information access topology describes the most common BI applications. The user has read-only access to the data. Read-only data provides maximum consistency in a multi-user analysis or reporting environment.

Figure 190 shows a typical information access runtime topology with a BI application in the internal network.

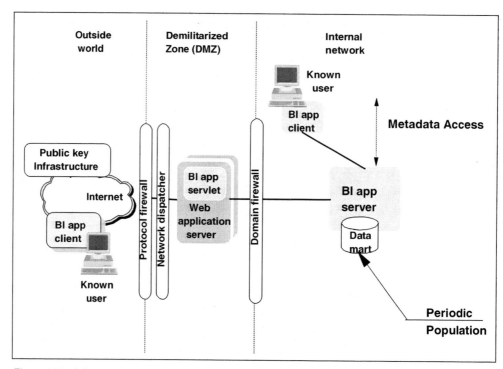

Figure 190. Information access runtime topology with a BI application in the internal network

The most common and simplest configuration places the BI application in the internal network and provides the broadest range of possible functions to known users of the system. This configuration represents a number of the most common BI implementations.

First is the case where a trusted user, such as an employee or agent, accesses the BI application server using a LAN or other traditional connection. Many traditional BI applications are constructed using a fat client approach, with substantial BI functions on the client.

The second case shows access by a known, trusted user, such as a customer or supplier, to a BI application in the internal environment. In this scenario, the data is up-to-date. However, there may be security concerns about giving external users access to the internal network. Given this concern, this approach is more likely where an extranet has been established, rather than for broader access from the Internet. In addition, an internal user can access identical data on the intranet. A thin client approach reduces remote application maintenance issues.

8.4.2 Static application design

A multi-tier solution places the major server components on two or more platforms. We focus largely on cases where there are two platforms bearing major functionality, but the basic principles and product choices shown in the two-tier examples can be readily extended. Figure 191 shows the static application design.

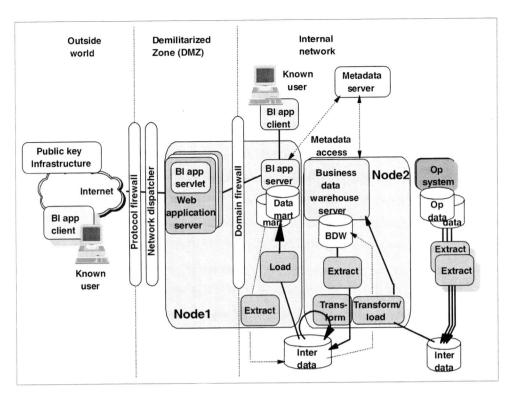

Figure 191. BI solution: Static application design view

Figure 191 represents a fairly typical tiered data warehouse configuration. All BI server functionality and data are stored internally, providing maximum security. This topology is likely where a data warehouse is required for internal use, with a design focus on reconciling data from numerous sources. Suitable for internal users attached locally, this topology also allows identified and verified user access from the Internet.

Two largely independent population systems are illustrated. The first is responsible for the population of the Business Data Warehouse (BDW). The data comes from many source systems, principally the operational systems (Op system in the figure, through intermediate data store) but can also be fed back from the data mart as represented by the dotted line. Because of the multiple sources involved, the transformation function is rather complex. The second population system is responsible for data mart population. Transformations are somewhat simpler in this system, but managing the distribution to multiple data marts (only one is shown) is a more significant issue.

Metadata access is provided from the BI application server and from the BDW server. In this case, both are required because of the drill-through from the BI application to the BDW server. Where drill-through is not supported, metadata access is required only from the BI App.

Providing separate nodes for the BDW and data marts, as shown here, overcomes many of the problematic issues. In particular, it optimizes platform choice for the different processing needs of the BDW and BI applications. Although not shown explicitly here, this configuration also allows multiple nodes at the data mart level, supporting disparate BI application platform requirements and distribution of data and function in the internal network.

8.4.3 Selected components

The following products have been chosen for the solution presented in Figure 191:

- Node1 is running on OS/390.

- BI application server can run various BI products listed in 8.3, "Product overview for Business Intelligence solutions" on page 382 (DB2 OLAP Server, for example), plus DB2 for OS/390, and DB2 utilities.

- Business data warehouse server runs on DB2 for OS/390 using DB2 utilities.

- Load block is running Visual Warehouse (VW) agent, DB2 utilities, and IBM Data Propagator (DPROP)

- Extract block is using ETI-EXTRACT and DPROP.

- Transform/load block is based on running DB2 utilities, VW agent, and DPROP.

- Metadata server is running on Windows NT with Visual Warehouse and Warehouse Manager installed.

Chapter 9. Performance

The performance metric of an e-business solution is typically defined as the response time for the end user for any given request. This request may be for information or to have the application store or analyze information on their behalf or any other interaction with the applications. The user, quite rightly, has no concept of how much work and how many systems are actually involved or what technology is being used or what transactions need to be performed. A simple transaction may turn out to be a very complex series of data flows involving multiple systems in multiple locations. It may cause events to cascade through multiple systems before the summarized result is presented to the user.

Designing e-business applications with acceptable performance characteristics is one of the most challenging aspects of the development process. This is particularly true when building applications that are aimed primarily at an external audience (for example, customers, suppliers, etc.). In these kinds of environments, user demand may be difficult to predict, and navigational patterns are not always known in advance or necessarily controllable. Although data in this area is currently limited, experience has shown that there are several viable options that companies can use either individually or in combination to address performance-related issues:

- Partitioning and distributing application logic based on tasks or roles
- Replicating some or all content across multiple servers and using routing mechanisms to balance workloads
- Using higher capacity, higher performing server platforms

One example of partitioning workloads is to have all static content served up by standard or commodity Web server platforms, while all dynamic page generation and computation is handled by a separate server. The Framework's second-tier (Web-enabled application servers), in essence, becomes a collection of "specialty" servers, each assigned a specific task or role.

This chapter discusses the problem areas or bottlenecks that hinder the performance of an application, the technologies that are used to make performance friendly applications, and the products that are provided by the Framework that are used to enhance performance.

9.1 Bottlenecks

Lets first understand where the bottlenecks exists in this environment. Figure 192 shows the basic flow of information over a network. In this figure, you can see the three key areas where bottlenecks exist:

- Client
- Network
- Server

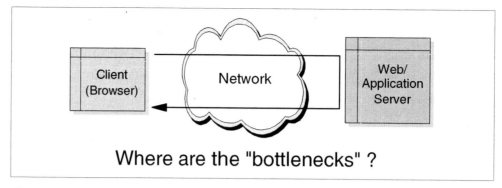

Figure 192. Basic flow

9.1.1 Client and network

One side of the performance issues is network performance. We generally associate client issues with this because it is the client perspective that is where performance is judged.

Issues that cause performance problems in this area are:

- Slow client response times
- Limited network bandwidth
- Long network path lengths

There can be performance problems at the client, slower processors, lower versions of the JDK, and other processes using the system resources. There can also be performance problems in the network such as long disjointed routes or many users.

9.1.2 Server

The server could be a Web server or an application server. Issues that cause performance problems are:

- Slow server response times
- Servers unable to keep up with the workload
- Bigger boxes are too expensive
- No planned redundacy in the design

We discuss more later on the technologies that are implemented on the servers to solve the bottlenecks that exists on them.

9.2 Technologies

This section discusses the technologies that help maximize the performance for applications. It examines these technologies with respect to servers, security, network, and load balancing.

9.2.1 Network

Network latency is always a big factor for performance. Latency can be defined as the round trip time between two systems due to the sum of the delays in the network components traversed. Latency is bounded on the low end by the sum of the following components:

- Minimum times to transmit the electronic components in the path
- The time required to serialize the data onto media in the path
- The propagation time required to cross the media

When processing and buffering are added to components in the network path, you sources of variance are added to the latency. As the utilization of the media increases, queuing for access to the media grows, generating additional variance in latency as well. Variances in latency are measured by changes in response time for end users. It is not as important to understand the absolute value for latency, as it is to know how the application flows interact with latency.

Starting with the initial client request, most application flows are serialized, they make a request and get a response. A user enters or selects a uniform resource locator (URL) and waits for the resulting page to appear. More advanced pages will solicit some form of user input and then return a page of information or results, but this model still resembles a request/response serialized flow.

Figure 193 shows the latency points along the path of the Web application.

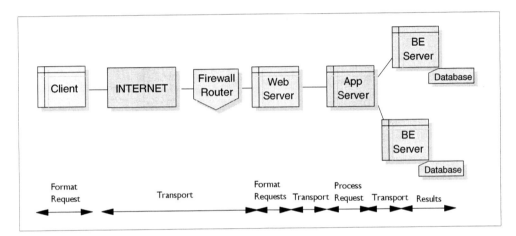

Figure 193. The latency picture

You may have control over some of the latency points. However, there may most likely be some latency points that you will have no control over like the Internet.

A common performance metric is interactive response time as perceived by the end user. As you are developing Web applications, build a response time budget. This should be a realistic budget. The numbers in Figure 194 are not actual, but could be representative of a real application.

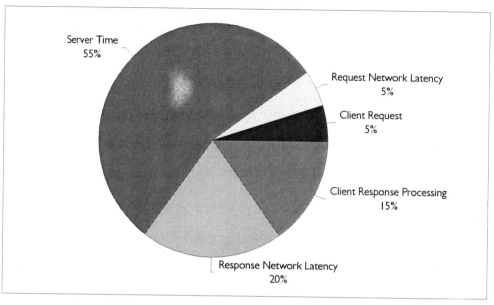

Figure 194. Success tip: Response time budget

If you want a total response time of three seconds, and you know that the network latency can be as much a two seconds and the server side processing can be as much as two seconds, you know that the overall response time budget is unrealistic.

9.2.2 Servers

This section begins with a discussion on Web Servers and then database servers. The following section looks at issues related to threads, server-side includes (SSI), logging, and caching. Then, Section 9.2.2.2, "Database server" on page 402, discusses connection management, locking, and SQL.

9.2.2.1 Web servers

A Web server functions as the hub of e-business solutions. The role of the Web server has changed quickly and dramatically. The Web publishing era, where an HTTP server was only responsible for serving up static information, is over. The Web server has become the mid-tier, middleware application server connecting a Web client to back-tier databases, transaction systems, and applications.

A Web application server can perform a wide variety of tasks, from serving up static Web pages to coordinating distributed units of work involving multiple back-end systems. The first guideline for achieving good performance is to define and understand your workload.

While you can run all types of workloads together on a Web server, each type of workload has its own performance and scaling "signature" (use of resources, bottlenecks, etc.) Your e-business application architecture and design should take this into account. Certainly you may have determined that you will need more than a single Web server and perhaps even if your initial assessment has determined that one Web server is sufficient. Usually there are two logical nodes for Web servers:

- **Informational Web node**: Serves static and dynamic Web pages to the users
- **Transactional Web node**: Can access back-end systems in the trusted network for transaction processing activities

This is a valuable segmentation for the physical implementation as well. We have found that server specialization is very common, that is, to segregate Web servers by tasks and tune for each task differently. For example, you can segregate servers for banner advertising or database serving from the servers handling static page content. By segregating servers into task oriented groups, and monitoring the performance of each group (therefore, each task) separately, site response can be tuned more effectively.

After you segment the tasks and assign one type of work per Web server, you can evaluate the performance and scaling issues for the chosen task and select the platform and infrastructure with the "best fit". The static Web pages and the transaction processing can be served by two different types of hardware server, characterized as expensive "thoroughbreds" and commodity "pack mules":

- **Thoroughbreds**: Handle computation-intensive loads with high-end machines
- **Pack mules**: Handle static Web serving by spraying static requests across as many cheap commodity Web servers as necessary

There are many ways to make an Internet e-business solution a success. However, even with good historical data and the best planning, the Web can be unpredictable. Unplanned events can occur that dramatically drive up Web activity in an unpredictable way. For these reasons, the following recommendations are important:

- Plan for alternate content with reduced complexity.
- Modularize content to allow selective "abandonment".
- If you are using "pack mules", you must be able to add or delete individual servers at will.

Threads
Some Web servers allow the configuration of both a minimum and maximum number of threads. Pick a reasonable, but large enough, number of threads to handle your peak workloads. Then set the maximum number of threads equal to the minimum number. This avoids the overhead of creating and destroying threads during peak processing hours.

Limit the use of server-side includes
SSI allow you to insert information into CGI programs and HTML documents that the server sends to the client. When server-side include processing is enabled, the Web server parses each byte of every HTML file and CGI program searching for the existence of an SSI directive and, if found, processes it. This is a great feature for processing dynamic content, but it requires a large amount of CPU processing. SSI processing can be controlled by the use of the embeds directive. If you do not use SSIs, set embeds off.

Caching
The addition of memory to a system almost always improves performance. This is because physical input/output is a relatively expensive operation in terms of latency. It makes intuitive sense then that by dedicating memory in a Web server to store frequently accessed HTML pages and images, you will improve performance. As a rule of thumb, your Web server should have enough random

access memory (RAM) to accommodate all network buffers, frequently used applications, images, and HTML, including those mounted via distributed file system (DFS). This is especially important for dynamically generated pages, which can be reused.

Logging

The Web server logs, in particular the access log, record important information about the use of the Web server. However, these logs can become very large and should be pruned or archived regularly. Logging can have a surprisingly large impact on response time and throughput. For this reason, you will often find that vendors turn logging off for bench-marking purposes.

Of course few, if any, production sites would turn logging off. Because high-use Web sites have correspondingly high logging activity, logs should be placed on the fastest devices available. Striping and mirroring of logs can also help to improve performance by streamlining I/O operations. Turning off unnecessary directives, such as identity check, or other log files, such as the referer log, can minimize logging overhead.

Log analysis tools can help you to understand the way the pages in your system are used. They allow you additional insight into the proper layout of your site as well as helping you to identify opportunities to cache the most frequently used pages on your site to improve performance. Use the logs to identify your peak processing periods. Then collect information from your peak periods to use for trend analysis. You may particularly want to look for statistics like the number of connections per second and the number of hits per second to understand your workload. This will help you to anticipate the need to add additional servers or to upgrade existing server resources. By actively monitoring your workload, you can become proactive in managing the workload to minimize response time and maximize throughput.

CGI and server-side Java

IBM Framework for e-business defines the infrastructure for developing e-business solutions. This includes the relationship between the Web server and server-side Java elements. IBM's analysis of the performance characteristics of this environment provides some useful guidelines for e-business solution designers, including:

- Any of the techniques used to connect a Web server to application logic (CGI, in-process API, Java servlets, etc.) should be insignificant when compared to the time required to execute the application logic.

- Most existing Web applications have been implemented using CGI. Java servlets provide 4 times to 10 times better throughput compared to CGI.

- Java servlets run faster if they are instantiated and preloaded in `servlet.properties`. Servlet invocation by class name rather than instance name is slower.

9.2.2.2 Database server

There are performance and throughput considerations relating to the use of databases in this environment. The following topics deserve special attention and are covered in detail:

- Connection Manager
- Locking
- SQL

Connection management

Every request to a database requires the use of a database connection. A Web application server makes data requests on behalf of the Web client by either directly accessing the data system or by using a data access gateway to perform that service. In either case, building database connections dynamically to serve single requests can add significant time to a Web "transaction".

In a high throughput environment where many concurrent requests are being serviced, the resources spent in building and tearing down database connections can be detrimental to performance and scalability. A much less resource-intensive way to handle these requests is to create a pool of pre-established database connections. For example, in a recent performance test, response times for simple transactions were reduced from 0.27 seconds to 0.09 seconds simply by making use of pre-existing database connections, rather than closing and allocating new ones.

Associated with a database connection is the concept of a user and user authority on one or more data objects. System resources spent in ascertaining a user's data rights can significantly add to response time and resource utilization. Servicing data requests in an un-trusted Internet environment typically requires much more extensive authentication checking than servicing data requests in a secure, intranet environment where clients are "trusted".

Locking

Locking mechanisms are used by database managers to handle resource allocation among many users without compromising data integrity. While necessary and valuable, locking tends to impact the ability to handle multiple requests for the same data resource concurrently.

Until the introduction of distributed databases in the 1980s, many database vendors lived with their customer's complaints that page-level locking was too restrictive. Many customers wanted the enhanced data availability where data could be locked at the row, instead of the page, level. But with the addition of network latencies that accompanied distributed access came a heightened need for finer granularity in data and index locking mechanisms.

Today, most large database vendors support row-level locking. The way in which the Web application server maintains a state can add to lock contention issues for the database. Because in Web applications every request is a separate entity, applications that need to maintain information between requests must decide the method in which they will preserve the state.

Assuming a Web application performs remote updates, as in the case of electronic commerce, which options are available for maintaining state, while minimizing lock contention? The first, and least exclusive alternative is *optimistic locking*. With optimistic locking, the ability to apply updates is verified incrementally as the business logic progresses. Updates are not actually attempted until all business conditions are met. The side affect of this approach is that the original data values must be revalidated before updates are actually applied. For example, if the customer is browsing an online catalog and places an item into their shopping cart, then at checkout time they may find that the desired item is out of stock. A second option is to logically flag data fields as updated to reserve them until the end of the unit of work, at which time they will be permanently changed. While in this case the shopper can buy exactly what they want, at checkout time the "flags" must be removed.

Finally, updates can be incrementally applied as the business logic progresses. As in the previous case, the shopper is assured of the items they put into their basket. However, if the shopper changes their mind, this approach can restrict other users from acquiring a desired resource while requiring application programmers to include compensating transaction logic into their code. Each option introduces performance benefits and business and application trade-offs. Choose the alternative that best fits your application update needs.

SQL

The efficiency of the SQL access strategy to a relational database is the most important factor in determining the elapsed time of SQL execution. Of course, the access path selected is as much a function of database design as SQL coding. But in general, given a good database design, 95% of a SQL statement response time is a function of the selected access path.

If we assume that the SQL has been coded in the most efficient manner, what can we do to reduce resource usage and elapsed time? First, like any SQL-based application, object checking, authorization checking, and access path selection must be performed before SQL can be executed. In static SQL, these tasks are done only once at bind time. With dynamic SQL, all three tasks are performed at first request. Depending on the database management system and server configuration, they may be required for each request. The key to reducing response time is to limit the number of pre-execution tasks that must be accomplished and to limit the number of SQL requests necessary to satisfy the business request.

9.2.3 Load balancing

Simply stated, if you begin with one server platform and approach maximum capacity, there are three alternatives to increase throughput:

- **Change out processor**: Move from the current processor to a faster processor
- **Add processors or nodes**: If your current processor supports SMP
- **Cluster processors**: Load balance among a group of processors

These options are not mutually exclusive of course, and each has its advantages and disadvantages. You can *even* implement a combination of all three. It is beyond the scope of this book to explore the performance characteristics of e-business solutions among all possible permutations, but we discuss one of them, clustering, in some detail.

Load balancing designs range from the relatively simple "round robin" Domain Name Systems (DNS) approaches to more sophisticated dispatchers, such as the IBM Network Dispatcher, that include server side monitors. The relatively simple round-robin type approaches for load balancing usually dispatch server requests to members in an active server group in an alternating pattern or to a specific server for a window of time. This type of load balancing system often works by using the calls made to the Domain Name System to resolve site names into IP addresses.

Round-robin type designs return alternating IP addresses for the servers that make up the common server pool. This type of load balancing system usually lacks a feedback loop from the servers and tends to dispatch work to servers regardless of their current workload. The systems making the requests of the servers also tend to remember which server they were initially told to use and direct all future requests for that name to the same server. Unless the workload is very consistent across all the clients in terms of the server load required and the volumes requested, and the servers are identical in capacity, the round robin approach can cause some servers to bear more load than others. If some users generate requests for relatively more CPU-intensive CGI calls or other types of dynamic pages versus some users requesting static pages that may be in cache, the round-robin approach usually does not balance the workloads.

Because the round-robin approach usually is not aware of current server workloads or the impact of the request being assigned, it just assigns the first request from a user to the next server in the rotation. This approach is more of a user allocation approach versus a true load-balancing approach.

A more sophisticated approach of load balancing is provided by Web server clustering. Most Web publishing applications (for example, those that do not do transactions that require several interactions between a browser and Web server) will benefit from a load balancing configuration. An e-business solution (for example, that include transactions) can take advantage of clustering by implementing specific session data techniques ranging from:

- **Low cluster synergy with no direct cluster support**: This implementation takes advantage of the "sticky ports" feature of Network Dispatcher to ensure that all transactional interactions (sessions) are run on the same Web server.

- **Medium cluster synergy**: Is achieved by keeping session data in a cookie and passing it along with each interaction. This helps ensure load balancing, but incurs significant overhead for processing the cookie each time.

- **High cluster synergy for e-business solutions**: Is implemented by storing the session data in a distributed data store available to all Web servers in the cluster. Both the medium and high cluster synergy options require modifications to the e-business application.

9.2.4 Security

This section looks at how such security applications SSL, firewall, authentication, and directory servers affect performance. It also examines the best practices to follow while developing or deploying these applications.

9.2.4.1 SSL

As mentioned earlier, there are two major encryption methods: symmetric (single key) and asymmetric (two keys). Symmetric encryption is much faster than asymmetric, but performance is not the only reason for choosing an encryption method.

The major challenge with symmetric key encryption is key distribution. Since there is only one key, all parties involved in communication must have a copy of this key. Asymmetric encryption uses two keys, a public key and a private key.

The public key is freely distributed while the private key is safe. There are two major phases of SSL session encryption:

1. Exchange of the key
2. Secure data communications

There are several different key exchange algorithms (RSA, Diffie-Hellman, and so on), as well as data communications encryption algorithms (DES, IDEA, Triple DES, and so on). Each of these algorithms has performance attributes. For example, Diffie-Hellman key exchange is "faster" than RSA key exchange. Although this is true, Diffie-Hellman does *not* offer one important "security" provision. It does not guarantee identity. Unlike RSA, in which you are sure to whom you are speaking, Diffie-Hellman can make no such promise. So, choosing one algorithm based strictly on performance may be unwise.

The process of using SSL is split into two basic phases (see 4.3, "Secure Sockets Layer (SSL) protocol" on page 214):

1. Establishing a session and exchanging a secret key
2. Exchanging data

The duration of the second phase is limited by "keep alive" timer. This value is set in the HTTP header. If the "keep alive" timer (typically 60 second, but this value is configurable) has not expired, the client and server can use the existing session ID and secret key to communicate. This is a key performance issue, since most of the time "running" an SSL session is spent in secret negotiations (phase one). Figure 195 illustrates the time required for session establishment and session resumption.

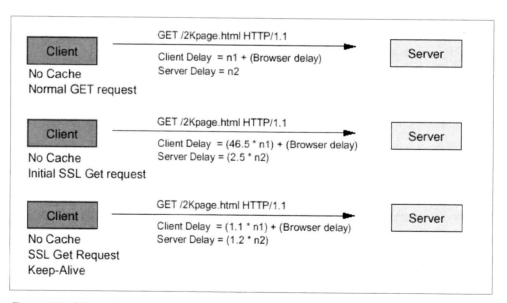

Figure 195. SSL performance

There are several interesting points to observe in Figure 195:

- The greatest amount of time in SSL session establishment is spent on the client. The client has a lot of work to do.

- Session establishment delay is measurable and effect the end-to-end budget. The time it takes to set up a SSL connection should be taken seriously in the design.

- When a session is already established, the delay in an SSL session is "reasonable". Once the SSL connection is established, the dialog between the server and client go on with minimal impact (assuming no other system or network constraint).

- Hardware encryption can greatly reduce the response time and CPU time required for the SSL handshake.

In conclusion, use SSL only when it is required. That is, use it when confidentiality, authentication and integrity are required and not provided by some other means.

9.2.4.2 Authentication and access control lists (ACL)

Authentication also has an effect on the end-to-end budget. The good thing is, the first time a user is prompted for their username and password, performance is the not the primary consideration. As long as it appears that the system is working to grant access, the user is usually happy. But once the user is authenticated, they have little patience for additional delay. The basic authorization technique used in a Web server is to control access to part or all of the contents of a Web server and is implemented via access control lists.

ACL information is stored in password files. The size of these files plays a significant role in performance. Tests indicate that password files should be relatively small (less that 10,000 users). Files with 100,000 users can become a performance bottleneck. If a solution must support large numbers of users that must be authenticated, password files may be divided into multiple subset files (for example, to support 100,000 users, divide the files into 10 files each containing 10,000 users). This is supported in many Web servers. In this example, 10,000 users will consume about 700K of memory on a Windows NT server. The first time a named ACL is called, the server loads that ACL file into memory. Subsequent calls will access the information in memory.

9.2.4.3 Directory server

Basic authorization is not always sufficient for enterprise access. There are two important mechanisms to extend this authentication. The first is to extend or replace the Web server ACL function by mapping to a common backing store or directory server. The benefits of using a system or enterprise directory service include consolidating duplicate information into a single repository to make the network and applications easier to manage, and using an industry standard API such as the Lightweight Directory Access Protocol (LDAP) for all interactions with sensitive data.

Most directory server products, such as the IBM SecureWay LDAP Directory, provide several options to increase scalability and to provide load balancing. These features include replication (for example, the ability to create and run many instances of a complete directory to ensure there is a copy "close" to all users in the network) and split name space (such as to ensure that "local" data is available where it is needed without replicating it across the network where it is seldom / never used).

The quantity of directory servers and their contents should be included in the architecture design of the e-business solution. The internal organization of data within the directory server itself can also have a major impact on the performance of your application. The namespace definition of an LDAP or X.500 directory server determines how each object and attribute are stored within the tree structure (directory/subdirectory). If, for example, your application needs to read five data "fields" (name value pairs) related to a person, you may be able to find the entry using its distinguished name (DN) and access all five fields, all with one LDAP call. Or, you may require six LDAP calls; one to find the starting entry and the reference pointers (relative distinguished names (RDN)) to five other entries where the required information is stored.

In some cases, the directory server is completely defined by a software vendor or by the customer and can not be modified to ease transversal by your solution. In other cases, where your e-business solution is part of a major re-engineering effort you can, and should, have a major say on namespace definition to ensure that the information you need is accessible by as few LDAP calls as possible. In either case, the number and complexity of the interfaces to a directory server must be considered in your overall design budget.

A second alternative to basic authentication using a directory server is to use SSL certificates for authentication. This technique has the same impact as the first method, with the added benefit and cost of SSL.

9.2.4.4 Firewall

The two primary functions of a firewall are packet filtering and application proxy. Packet filtering is just that: filtering packets. Decisions to discard packets are made based on protocol, service port, IP addresses, etc.

Packet filters are generally very good performers when there are just a few defined. As the number of packet filter rules grows, so does the decision path length.

Proxies, on the other hand, offer more robust security options. Simply stated, a proxy is a "middleman". A client accesses the proxy and then the proxy accesses the server on behalf of the client. There are two types of proxies: transport/circuit and application. *Transport proxies* (such as SOCKS) work at the transport layer and require a "socksified" client. *Application proxies* require no modification to the client, but require a proxy for each application (for example, HTTP, FTP, Telnet, etc.).

Think of a proxy as a translator. If you want to have a conversation with a French speaking person and needed a translator, it would impact the speed in which you communicated. Proxy servers, in the same fashion, have a major impact on performance and response time. As mentioned several times, firewalls are implemented for security reasons. If firewalls exist in the deployment network, they must be included in your budget calculations.

One important conclusion is, compared to normal packet forwarding, firewalls with logging and proxy enabled can reduce throughput by as much as 50%. Today's firewall systems employ more than just proxy and packet filtering. A comprehensive firewall will do Stateful filtering/inspection, network address translation (NAT), extensive logging, IP spoofing detection, SYN attack detection, and anti-virus scanning. Each of these elements have a cost in the budget and must be considered in the overall performance budget.

9.3 Products

IBM offers two primary products for performance:

- WebSphere Edge Server
- Andrew File System (AFS)

The third product is the WebSphere Application Server. It has built-in features for performance improvements:

- Cloning
- Remote Open Servlet Engine (OSE)
- Servlet Redirector
- Workload Management with EJB

9.3.1 WebSphere Edge Server

IBM WebSphere Edge Server is a complete product approach to today's challenges of Web site response time, scalability, and reliability. The Edge Server provides an integrated solution for local and wide-area load balancing, content-based quality of service routing, and Web content filtering and caching for multi-vendor Web server environments. The name "Edge Server" indicates that the software usually runs on machines that are close (in a network configuration sense) to the boundary between an enterprise's intranet and the Internet.

IBM WebSphere Edge Server includes:

- Intelligent load balancing that directs user requests to the best server
- Reverse proxy caching, which improves Web server response time
- Forward proxy caching, to reduce network bandwidth requirements
- Streaming media redirection for RealNetworks proxies
- The ability to monitor applications for better load balancing decisions
- Powerful rules engine and content-based routing for differentiated quality of service
- Support for Web content filtering and blocking
- A streamlined installation and configuration process
- Tivoli Ready for system management with Tivoli management software

The Edge Server includes two main components that provide complementary functionality:

- Caching Proxy
- Network Dispatcher

9.3.1.1 The Caching Proxy

The Caching Proxy was previously called WebSphere Traffic Express. This component intercepts data requests from end users, retrieves the requested information from content-hosting machines, and delivers it back to the end users. Most commonly, the requests are for documents stored on Web server machines (also called *origin servers* or *content hosts*) and delivered via HTTP. However, you can configure the Caching Proxy to handle other protocols, such as FTP.

When retrieving certain types of content, the Caching Proxy stores it in a local cache before delivering it to the requester. The most prominent example of cacheable content is static Web pages (those without portions that are dynamically generated at access time). Caching enables the Caching Proxy to satisfy subsequent requests for the same content directly from the cache, which is much quicker than retrieving it again from the content host. The Caching Proxy can be useful both when hosting Web-accessible content and when providing Internet access:

- When used by content hosts, the Caching Proxy is installed as a *reverse proxy* between the Internet and the enterprise's content hosts. It intercepts user requests arriving from the Internet, forwards them to the appropriate content host, caches the returned data, and delivers it to the users across the Internet.

- When used by Internet access providers, the Caching Proxy is installed as a *forward proxy* between an enterprise's end users and the Internet. It forwards users' requests to content hosts located across the Internet, caching and delivering the retrieved data to users.

9.3.1.2 The Network Dispatcher

WebSphere Edge Server includes a load balancing component, Network Dispatcher, which improves the scalability and availability of Web, FTP, or other TCP-based server clusters. It consist of three components:

- Dispatcher
- Interactive Session Support (ISS)
- Content Based Routing (CBR)

The Network Dispatcher intercepts data requests from end users, but rather than actually retrieving data, it forwards the request to the server machine that is currently best able to fill the request. In other words, it load balances incoming requests among a defined set of machines that service the same type of requests. A load balancer is sometimes termed a *sprayer* because it divides an incoming stream of requests and distributes them to the machines that service them.

The Network Dispatcher can distribute requests to many types of servers, including both HTTP origin servers and Caching Proxy machines. If desired, you can write rules that specify the criteria used by the Network Dispatcher when determining which server can best handle a request. Like the Caching Proxy, the Network Dispatcher can be useful both when hosting Web-accessible content and when providing Internet access.

- When used by *content hosts*, the Network Dispatcher is installed between the Internet and the enterprise's back-end servers, which can be content hosts, Caching Proxy machines, or mail server machines that service the POP3 or IMAP protocols. The Network Dispatcher acts as the enterprise's single point-of-presence on the Internet, even if the enterprise uses multiple back-end servers because of high demand or a large amount of content. If the Network Dispatcher's Content Based Routing (CBR) module is installed together with the Caching Proxy, HTTP requests can even be distributed based on URL or other administrator-determined characteristics. This eliminates the need to store identical content on all back-end servers.

- When used by *Internet access providers*, the Network Dispatcher is installed between an enterprise's end users and two or more Caching Proxy machines in the enterprise's intranet, to balance the load between them. Load balancing multiple Caching Proxy machines provides highly reliable access to the Internet even in the face of high demand. You can also guarantee high availability by installing a backup Network Dispatcher to take over if the primary one fails temporarily.

Dispatcher

Three key functions perform the work of the Dispatcher component: the executor, the advisors, and the manager. These functions interact to balance and route the incoming requests between servers:

- **Executor function**: Supports port-based routing of TCP connections. It monitors the number of new connections, the active connections, and connections in a finished state; does garbage collection of completed or reset connections; and supplies this information to the manager. It can route connections to servers based on the type of request received (for example, HTTP, FTP, and SSL).

- **Advisors function**: Queries the servers and analyzes the results by protocol before calling the manager to set weights as appropriate. Currently there are advisors available for HTTP, FTP, SSL, NNTP, Telnet, SMTP, IMAP, and POP3. The Dispatcher also permits you to write your own custom advisors. Using advisors is optional but recommended because they give Dispatcher more information on the health of the servers and the applications they are running.

- **Manager function**: Collects information from the executor, the advisors, and from a system-monitoring program, such as ISS. Based on the information the manager receives, it adjusts how the TCP server machines are weighted on each port and gives the executor the new weighting for use in its routing of new connections.

There are many ways that you can configure Dispatcher to support your site. As shown in Figure 196, the IBM Network Dispatcher (IND) is defined as the primary address, www.ibm.com. When a request for a file is received, the Dispatcher:

1. Determines which Web server is best suited to service the request.
2. Changes the destination Medium Access Control (MAC) address.
3. Forwards the request.

Each of the Web servers has the loopback adapter address set to the same address as the dispatcher, so when they respond, the client's machine thinks it gets a response from: http://www.ibm.com

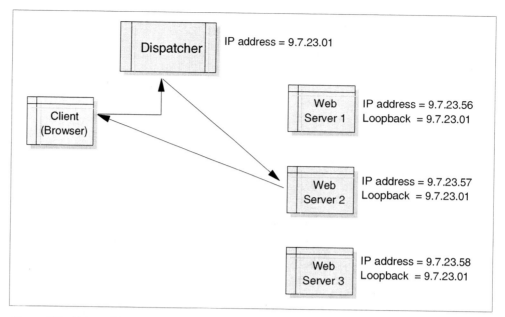

Figure 196. Using a Dispatcher

There are many ways that you can configure Dispatcher to support your site.

If you have only one host name for your site to which all of your customers will connect, you can define a single cluster of servers, and any ports to which you want to receive connections. For each of these servers, you configure a port through which the Dispatcher communicates.

Another way to configure the Dispatcher is appropriate if you have a very large site with many servers dedicated to each protocol supported. In this case, you may want to define a cluster for each protocol with a single port but with many servers, as shown in Figure 197.

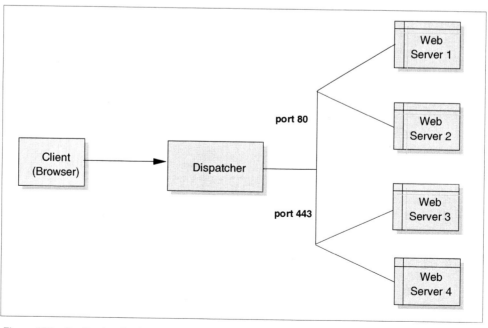

Figure 197. Configuring the Dispatcher

A third way to configure the Dispatcher is necessary if your site does content hosting for several companies or departments, each coming into your site with a different URL. In this case, you may want to define a cluster for each company or department and any ports to which you want to receive connections at that URL.

The issue with this configuration is that, here, its not possible to use the same server for a request from the same client. The issue can be resolved if you can define the Dispatcher with affinities. The solution lies in sticky ports, meaning all requests to that port remain with a particular physical server for a short period of time. When a client connects to a sticky port, an entry for that client's IP address is made in the affinity table, and a timestamp is set. If a new connection from the same client arrives, and the timestamp has not expired, then the new connection is sent to the same server as before (Figure 198).

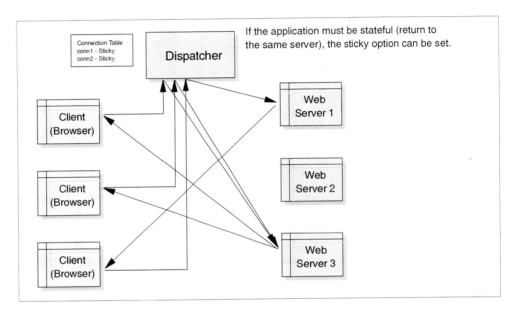

Figure 198. Dispatching with the sticky option

You can turn on the "port stickytime" by setting the numbers of seconds to a value more than zero. Over time, the client will finish sending transactions, and the affinity record will go away. Hence, you have the meaning of "stickytime". Each affinity record lives for the "stickytime" in seconds. When subsequent connections are received within the stickytime, the affinity record is still valid and the request goes to the same server. If a subsequent connection is not received within stickytime, the record is purged; a connection that is received after that time will have a new server selected for it.

The Dispatcher component offers a built-in high availability feature. There are two ways to provide this feature:

- Simple high availability configuration
- Mutual high availability configuration

Both configurations involve the use of a second Dispatcher machine. In case of *simple high availability configuration*, the second dispatcher monitors the main, or primary, machine and stands by to take over the task of load balancing should the primary machine fail at any time. In the *mutual high availability configuration*, both machines actively perform load balancing of client traffic, and both machines provide backup for each other. In a simple high availability configuration, only one machine performs load balancing. In a mutual high availability configuration, both machines load balance a portion of the client traffic. For mutual high availability, client traffic is assigned to each Dispatcher machine on a cluster address basis. Each cluster can be configured with the non-forwarding address (NFA) of its primary Dispatcher. The primary Dispatcher machine normally performs load balancing for that cluster. In the event of a failure, the other machine performs load balancing for both its own cluster and for the failed Dispatcher's cluster.

Interactive Session Support

Interactive Session Support (ISS) is the domain name system (DNS) based component of Network Dispatcher that can be used for wide-area load balancing. ISS balances the load on servers by communicating with agents (ISS load-monitoring daemons) installed on each server machine, and then it alters the IP address returned to the client via DNS. ISS can also detect a failed server and forward traffic around it. Once every monitoring period, ISS ensures that the information used by the DNS or the Dispatcher component accurately reflects the load on the servers. ISS daemons can also provide the same server load information to the Dispatcher component.

The ISS system administrator controls both the type of measurement used to measure the load and the length of the load monitoring period. The load on a node can be determined by measuring various resources such as a CPU usage, disk availability, or process count. You can configure ISS to suit your environment, taking into account such factors as frequency of access, the total number of users, and types of access (for example, short queries, long-running queries, or CPU-intensive loads).

If you are using ISS on its own for load balancing, a domain name server is required. This may be either an actual DNS name server or — if you set up a small, separate subdomain for a new nameserver — a replacement name server provided by ISS. Using this approach, ISS runs on a name server machine. A client submits a request for resolution of the DNS name of an ISS service, which has been set up by an administrator. ISS then resolves the name to the IP address of a server in the cell, and forwards this IP address to the client.

Example of a site using Dispatcher and ISS to manage servers

Figure 199 illustrates a site in which all servers are on a local network. The Dispatcher component is used to forward requests, and the ISS component is used to provide system load information to the Dispatcher machine. A domain name server is not needed.

In this example, the ISS daemon is installed on each server. The administrator can configure which machine is used as the monitor. There is a priority ordering so that a lower-priority machine will take over as monitor only if the primary monitor has failed.

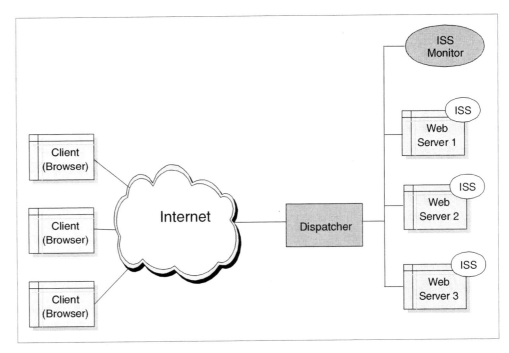

Figure 199. Using Dispatcher and ISS together

Content Based Routing

Content Based Routing (CBR) gives you the ability to specify a set of servers that should handle incoming requests based on the content of the request. This powerful feature can be used to send specific requests to more powerful servers for better quality of service. CBR also eliminates the requirement to have identical content on all servers that are being load balanced. However, because CBR allows you to specify multiple servers for each type of request, the requests can still be load balanced across a subset of servers for optimal client response. CBR also detects when one server in a set has failed, and stop routing requests to that server. The load balancing algorithm used by the CBR component is identical to the proven algorithm used by the Dispatcher component. Now we take a closer look at the two most popular protocols for use with CBR:

- **CBR for HTTP requests**: Using CBR with the caching proxy component of WebSphere Edge Server gives you the ability to specify a set of servers that will handle an HTTP request based on regular expression matching the content of the request. CBR allows you to partition your site so that different content or application services can be served by different sets of servers. This partitioning will be transparent to clients accessing your site. By allowing multiple servers to be assigned to each type of content, you are protected if one server fails. CBR recognizes the failure and continue to load balance client requests to the other servers in the set.

  When a request is received by the caching proxy, it is checked against the rules that have been defined in the CBR component. If a match is found, then one of the servers associated with that rule is chosen to handle the request.

  For example, one way to divide your site is to assign a set of servers to handle only CGI requests, and assign another set of servers to handle all other requests. This stops compute-intensive CGI scripts from slowing down the servers for routine HTML traffic, allowing clients to get better overall response time. Using this scheme, you can also assign more powerful workstations for routine requests — giving clients better response time without the expense of upgrading all your servers.

Another possibility for partitioning your site is to direct clients who are accessing pages requiring registration to one set of servers, and all other requests to a second set of servers. This would keep casual browsers of your site from tying up resources that could be used by clients who have committed to your registration.

- **CBR proxy for IMAP or POP3**: CBR proxy can provide a single point of presence for many IMAP or POP3 servers. Each server can have a subset of all mailboxes serviced by the point of presence. For IMAP and POP3, CBR is a proxy that chooses an appropriate server based on the user ID and password provided by the client (the CBR proxy does not support rules-based load balancing).

An example of a method for distributing requests based on client user ID is the following. If you have two (or more) POP3 servers, you can choose to divide the mailboxes alphabetically by user ID. Client requests with user IDs that begin with the letters "A" through "I" can be distributed to server 1. Client requests with user IDs beginning with the letters "J" through "R" can be distributed on server 2 and so on. You can also choose to have each mailbox represented on more than one server. In that case, the content of each mailbox must be available to all servers with that mailbox. In the event of a server failure, another server can access the mailbox.

To have only one address represent multiple POP3 mail servers, the CBR proxy can be configured with a single cluster address that becomes the POP3 mail server address for all clients. When a POP3 request arrives at the proxy, the proxy attempts to contact all the configured servers for the port using the client's user ID and password. The client's request is directed to the first server that responds. Use the sticky/affinity feature in conjunction with the CBR proxy for IMAP or POP3 servers. The affinity feature allows subsequent requests from the same client's user ID to be directed to the same server.

9.3.2 Andrew File System (AFS)

The file-sharing component, known as IBM Andrew File System (AFS), is an enterprise file system that enables cooperating hosts (clients and servers) to efficiently share file system resources across both LANs and WANs. It provides non-disruptive real-time replication of information across multiple servers, which guarantees data consistency, availability, global stability, and administrative efficiency, necessary by large distributed Web sites or by Web sites with volatile content requiring considerable administrative effort to maintain content links and URLs to file I/O mapping. As shown in Figure 200, an AFS cell can solve the content management problem by forming a single source from where the multiple servers access files.

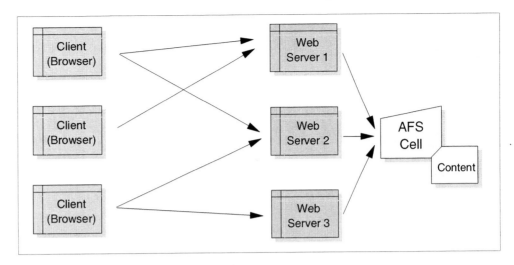

Figure 200. Multiple servers (single content)

AFS has provided scalable file administration and file sharing for large enterprises for many years, based on its use of a virtual name space to make naming and logical directory structures of files independent of their physical location. AFS clients and AFS servers are used to establish this virtual name space capability. In typical LAN file systems, this is achieved by installing AFS clients on user workstations and communicating with an AFS server that manages the I/O operations associated with the actual files. In a Web site, the AFS clients can be installed on HTTP servers to reduce the administrative effort associated with maintaining URL to file I/O mapping relationships. In addition, HTTP servers that are simultaneously AFS clients can significantly increase the connectivity capacity to Web server content and can provide local and geographically distributed access efficiency. AFS is a central and scalable file system:

- It is central because AFS brings together all of the files within the file system into a single name space. Every AFS user shares the same name space, making all AFS files easily available from any AFS machines. With AFS, the name of a file is independent of both the file's and the user's physical location, contributing to ease of file sharing and resource management.

- It is scalable because AFS can to manage a very large number of files, spread across many geographical locations. When remote files residing on AFS servers are accessed by remote AFS clients, they are cached on the client machines to improve performance. This makes remote working across global distances feasible, since it is possible to access your own files from sites many thousands of miles away as if they were local.

Both small and large-scale distributed environments benefit from AFS mechanisms to reduce the server and network load:

- AFS caches data on client machines to reduce subsequent data requests directed at file servers, substantially reducing network and server loads. Servers keep track of data given to clients through *callbacks*, guaranteeing cache consistency without constant queries to the server to see if the file has changed. It is important to underline that AFS also allows disk cache, not just memory cache. This is a key advantage of AFS over other shared file systems.

- The AFS remote procedure call (RPC) reads and writes data to an RPC stream, further improving the efficiency of data transfer across a local or wide area network.

Extended security is guaranteed through Kerberos authentication and ACLs. AFS Kerberos-based authentication requires that users prove their identities before accessing network services. Once authenticated, AFS ACLs give individual users or groups of users varying levels of permission to perform operations on the files in a directory.

The AFS component also offers replication techniques for file system reliability. Multiple copies of frequently accessed (but infrequently changed) data are replicated on multiple file servers within a cell. When accessing this information, a client chooses among the available servers that house replicas. If one server is unavailable or unreachable, the client goes to another server. Replication also reduces the load on any particular server by placing frequently accessed information on multiple servers. Moreover, management utilities are provided to ease the load of system administrators in growing environments. Backup, reconfiguration and routine maintenance are all done without any system down time. Files remain available to users during these operations. This is done by creating online clones of volumes.

AFS commands are RPC-based. Administrative commands can be issued by any authenticated administrator from any client workstation. System databases track data location information, authentication information, and protection groups. These databases are replicated on multiple servers, and are dynamically updated as information changes. Server processes accomplish many tasks automatically, such as restarting servers, tracking file locations, and updating file servers with new binaries and configuration files.

9.3.3 Workload management in WebSphere Application Server

WebSphere provides a number of tools and techniques that come into play when implementing configurations that provide scalability, load-balancing, and failover.

9.3.3.1 Cloning

Cloning is a mechanism build into the WAS Advanced and Enterprise Editions that allows for the creation of multiple copies of an object such as an application server. Cloning is the process of taking a server that you've set up, and creating a model based on that setup. Once you a model is made, you can create clones of that server.

The model is a logical representation of the application server, that exists only as information managed by the WAS. It has the same structure and attributes as a real application server. It may contain servlet engines, EJB containers, servlets, EJB's, etc. and allow the administrator to view and modify any properties of these logical objects. But it is not associated with any node, and does not correspond to any real server process running on any node.

The clones created from this model, on the other hand, represent real application server processes running on real nodes. They are identical in every way to the model from which they were created, except for some clone-specific attributes, which must be set on a per-clone basis. Furthermore, if the system administrator makes changes to the model, these changes are automatically reflected to all the clones. Several clones from the same model may be instantiated on multiple nodes, and it is also possible to instantiate multiple clones on the same node.

With extra clones running, you can improve the performance of your server. However, there is a point of diminishing returns. That is, a point where the more clones that you add actually slow you down with the extra maintenance and traffic generated by the clones and the management of them.

The set of all the clones of one model of an application server constitutes a logical group called a *server group* or *cluster*. The various workload distribution mechanisms use this abstraction of a server group to define the set of application servers among which they are to distribute the client requests. Since by definition all the clones are identical, the workload distribution mechanisms can safely assume that any one of the clones is equally capable of servicing any request. We now discuss the two types of cloning:

- **Vertical cloning**: Refers to the practice of defining multiple clones of an application server on the same physical machine. Experience has shown that a single application server, which is implemented by a single JVM process, cannot always fully utilize the CPU power of a large machine and drive the load up to 100%. This is particularly true on large multiprocessor machines, because of inherent concurrency limitations within a single JVM. Vertical cloning provides a straightforward mechanism to create multiple JVM processes, that together can fully utilize all the processing power available.

- **Horizontal cloning**: Refers to the more traditional practice of defining clones of an application server on multiple physical machines. It allows a single WebSphere application to span several machines while presenting a single system image. Horizontal cloning can provide both increased throughput and failover.

9.3.3.2 Workload Management (WLM)

Workload Management is the primary mechanism for load-distribution of requests directed at EJBs. In a simple, non-load-balanced EJB in WebSphere, each client of the bean holds a stub that contains a CORBA reference to the corresponding bean on the server. Whenever the client invokes an operation on that bean, the request is simply forwarded to the server object associated with that CORBA reference. Note that the client can be a stand-alone Java program using RMI/IIOP, a servlet operating within a WebSphere servlet engine or another EJB.

When using the WLM facility, the simple client stub above is augmented by a smart stub, that contains a collection of CORBA references to multiple instances of the same bean in different servers. Whenever the client invokes an operation on the bean, the smart stub automatically and transparently forwards the request to any one of the available server objects, thereby achieving both load-balancing and failover when appropriate. The smart stubs transparently communicate with the WebSphere EJB server (EJS) runtime to keep track of which servers and EJB instances are available at any given time. The WLM facility is enabled through one of three alternatives:

- EJBs developed and deployed from VisualAge for Java are automatically processed through WLM.

- EJBs developed and deployed outside of VisualAge for Java must first be deployed inside the WebSphere run-time, then the WLMjar processor (a.bat file on Windows NT, a .sh file on UNIX) must be run against the deployed EJB with WebSphere.

- With WebSphere, when you deploy a bean inside the WebSphere run-time, you can specify that the bean is WLM enabled.

The only type of EJB references, not subject to load-distribution through WLM, are the instances of a given stateful session bean. This is because stateful session beans cannot be replicated or shared between multiple servers.

Appendix A. Test tips

This section gives you some insight to IBM Tests 811 and 812. The section is designed to give you an idea of what to expect before you enter the examination to remove as many elements of surprise as possible.

The Designing e-business Solutions certification (Test 811) covers the material described in this book in some detail. The certification is designed to prepare you to design e-business solutions with minimal supervision. You must be competent enough to gather requirements, design the solution, and support the it through development. In performing this role, it is expected that a solution designer will be able to call on the services of technology specialists to assist in the design or articulate specific areas of the e-business solution. It is not expected that a successful e-business solutions designer will know everything about every area of the IBM Framework for e-business.

The e-business Core Knowledge Technologist test (Test 812) is designed for technology specialists looking to broaden their knowledge on e-business as a whole. The test is not as in-depth as the solution designer Test 811, because you already expected to be performing a specialist role. The certification is deigned to broaden the field of knowledge, to cover the breadth of IBM Framework for e-business. The pre-requisite for the e-business technologist certification requires you to hold a professional certificate in at least one technology (for example, IBM Certified Advanced Technical Expert - DB2 - DRDA). You can find a complete list of approved technical certifications for the IBM Certified for e-business Solution Technologist at:

http://www.ibm.com/certify/certs/eb_tcert.shtml

You can also find more information on e-business certification at:

http://www.ibm.com/certify/certs/eb_index.shtml

A.1 The test format

The certification examination is a multiple choice test. There are 60 questions to be completed in 75 minutes (the format of the test can be changed at any time). Before you begin the test, you are given an opportunity to complete a couple of sample questions (unrelated to the certification) to become familiar with the electronic test format and process.

Once the test begins, a timer appears in the corner of the screen, which counts down the time remaining. Multiple choice answers can be selected using your mouse and you select to advance to the next question. You may advance to the next question without entering an answer.

Marks are awarded for each correct answer. For questions with more than one response required, no marks are awarded for partially correct answers. Questions that require more than one response must be clearly marked. The test will be marked out of a possible 800. A passing mark is 600.

After the last question, there is a summary page that lists all the questions and your answers. Therefore, if you did not answer any questions, they will be clearly marked on this summary page. If you have time remaining, you can review any or all of the questions on the test. Once the clock runs out of time, the test automatically stops.

The testing center should give you the results of your test upon completion. The test result will have your score and indicate whether you passed of failed the certification. These results are automatically sent to IBM, and the official certificate will be posted within a few weeks.

A.2 The test questions

Tests 811 and 812 are composed of three types of questions:

- Simple questions requiring only one correct answer
- Multiple response questions requiring more than one correct answer to be selected
- Extended questions that usually require you to either read a passage of text or refer to a diagram (these are usually the harder or more complex questions)

The test is well balanced between the type of questions to give you a good chance of passing.

The single response questions usually have one option that is very obvious. For example, question 8 from sample Test 811 is:

8. Which is *not* a multi-platform standard used in the IBM Framework for e-business?

   a. Java
   b. HTTPS
   c. Microsoft Back Office
   d. Object Management Group (OMG)

This question is looking for a technology standard that is not used in the IBM Framework for e-business. Microsoft Back Office is not an IBM product and does not feature in the course material as a solution technology for collaboration under the IBM Framework for e-business. The trap in this question is to consider OMG, which is not a standard but a standards group.

Another way to dissect the options is to first eliminate the obviously incorrect entry. From the available options, there is often one option that does not exist or is completely irrelevant to the question. You should identify this one and eliminate it immediately. Then there will be an option that is part of the IBM Application Framework but that does not apply to the question. This option is often a bit harder to eliminate because you will recognize the term and want to include it in your reasoning. After eliminating the non-existent option and the incorrect option, there will be two remaining options that may be right. The correct answer will always be the most correct answer that is specified in the IBM Application Framework for e-business.

For example, question 13 from sample Test 811 is:

13. Which IBM Framework for e-business component is responsible for tying together the core logic encapsulated in tags and the JavaBean components used by JavaServer Pages?

a. Applets
  b. Scriptlets
  c. Servlets
  d. Beanlets

This question is looking for a valid component. There is no such thing as a Beanlet so this option is immediately eliminated. Options A, B, and C are all valid components. The applet is a client side component that manages processing at the client. This option is eliminated because it is probably not involved in tying together core logic and the JavaBeans in JSPs. The final two options are scriptlets and servlets. Servlets can be used in JSP tags to retrieve data for presentation. Scriptlets can contain any code fragments that are valid for the scripting language specified in the *language* directive. But the question ask for "tying together" element, we can safely eliminate servlets and choose scriptlets as the most appropriate answer.

A.3 Sample Test 811: Designing IBM e-business solutions

This test is copied from the Web page at:

`http://www.ibm.com/certify/tests/sam811.shtml`

The following sample questions are taken from the pool of questions for Test 811.

1. An IBM Framework for e-business Web application must invoke legacy business logic. Which programming patterns are good methods for maintaining good separation between Web application logic and business logic?

   a. Domain firewall (facade) pattern
   b. Singleton pattern
   c. Factory method pattern
   d. Command pattern

2. The business logic for the funds transfer function of the home banking e-business application runs as a CICS transaction. Which IBM Framework for e-business connector product would you use to connect the e-business application to CICS?

   a. CICS Web server
   b. CICS Client for Java
   c. CICS Transaction Gateway
   d. CICS Transaction Monitor

3. You have just upgraded your site to a dispatcher model with multiple servers. What is the role of a distributed file system such as DFS in this model?

   a. It provides a single logical location for Web content.
   b. It allows information developers to deploy content directly to servers.
   c. It provides automatic fail-over support.
   d. It reduces space requirements.

4. What can be used by the Web server to identify the browser that made the current request?

   a. The session object
   b. The cookie data
   c. The request header
   d. The browser object

5. Given an IBM Framework for e-business environment where EJBs are not local to the HTTP server, where would they be found?

   a. Tier 0
   b. Tier 1
   c. Tier 2
   d. Tier 3
   e. Tier 4

6. What is an Internet firewall?

   a. A computer located between two networks which acts as a message router
   b. A computer located between two networks which acts as a protocol router
   c. A computer located between two networks which acts as a security service provider
   d. A computer located between two networks which acts as a packet filter

7. In an environment consisting of an Internet firewall, a demilitarized zone and an intranet firewall, which protocol(s) are typically allowed to pass through the Internet firewall?

   a. IIOP
   b. FTP
   c. HTTP/HTTPS
   d. JAVA

8. Which is NOT a multi-platform standard used in the IBM Framework for e-business?

   a. Java
   b. HTTPS
   c. Microsoft Back Office
   d. Object Management Group (OMG)

9. For every minute your e-business Web site is down, you loose $5000 in sales to your competitor. Which operating system should you choose to host your Web site to minimize down time?

   a. Linux
   b. Windows 98
   c. AS/400
   d. Windows NT 4.0

10. Which statement does NOT describe how transactions are used by e-business applications to ensure that data in a database is correctly created or updated?

   a. The transaction context is associated with a particular program.
   b. Rollback is done when an error has occurred and the effects should be discarded.
   c. Multi-phase commit ensures that all changes occur or none occur.
   d. Commit makes the changes permanent.

11. Which widely used technology is NOT an industry wide common standard?

   a. CGI
   b. JSP
   c. SSI
   d. CSS
   e. SSL

12. An e-business application is being developed to enable two companies to exchange information contained in a DB2 database and Lotus Domino over the Internet. Which standard is recommended by the IBM Framework for e-business to be used to represent the data?

    a. EDI
    b. IIOP
    c. HTML
    d. XML

13. Which IBM Framework for e-business component is responsible for tying together the core logic encapsulated in tags and the JavaBean components used by JavaServer Pages?

    a. Applets
    b. Scriptlets
    c. Servlets
    d. Beanlets

14. An expression in a JavaServer Page is represented with the following syntax:

    a. <! Expression >
    b. <%= Expression %>
    c. <JSP:Expression>
    d. <@ Expression @>

15. Which type of information would be least likely to be saved in an e-business application LDAP directory?

    a. URLs
    b. Object references
    c. Compressed multimedia video data
    d. Database names

16. What types of security mechanisms are utilized by AFS?

    a. SSL
    b. Kerberos
    c. ACL
    d. x509

17. A Java applet running in a Web browser cannot normally write a file to the client's file system. How can the applet request write access in a Netscape 4.0 browser?

    a. Write a custom SecurityManager that enables file access.
    b. Use the PrivilegeManager object to request UniversalFileAccess
    c. The Web server must send the request in HTTP header.
    d. An applet property in the HTML page must be set to enable access.

A.4 Sample Test 811: Answers

The answers to the questions posed in the previous section are listed here:

1. AD
2. C
3. A
4. C
5. D
6. BD

7. C
8. C
9. C
10. A
11. C
12. D
13. B
14. B
15. C
16. BC
17. B

A.5 Sample Test 812: e-business Core Knowledge

This sample test was copied from the Web site at:

`http://www.ibm.com/certify/tests/sam812.shtml`

1. A distributor would like to minimize its reprogramming and maintenance requirements, and avoid proprietary solutions. To do this, the distributor's e-business applications should have which of the following characteristics?

   a. HTML-based, quick to deploy, leverages core systems
   b. Java-based, quick to deploy, leverages core systems
   c. Standards-based, quick to deploy, leverages core systems
   d. Enterprise JavaBeans based, quick to deploy, leverages core systems

2. An electronic components manufacturing company would like to convert to an Internet-based B2B system. Which of the following is a key consideration?

   a. Will the firm's customers use an updated browser?
   b. Is the B2B solution compatible with Windows 2000?
   c. Is the company equipped with Message Oriented Middleware and integrated with EDI?
   d. Will Java technology be used to access legacy systems? If so, will the legacy database integrate with Java Server Pages?

3. A sportswear chain plans to use e-business to revitalize its company by offering merchandise on the Web, and accepting orders from its existing catalog sales. Which of the following major customer relationship management (CRM) problems will this company need to solve?

   a. Ensuring accessibility to legacy systems
   b. Personalizing products and services so that customers will have 24x7 access
   c. Ensuring that all back-end applications and systems communicate with each other
   d. Ensuring e-business software and systems will be compatible with the existing ones

4. Which of the following best describes valid file types for text, graphics, color photos, audio files and video files that might be called up by a Web application?

   a. Text with *.html, graphics with *.jpg, color photos with *.gif, audio files with *.wav, video files with *.mpg
   b. Text with *.http, graphics with *.jpg, color photos with *.gif, audio files with *.wav, video files with *.mpg

c. Text with *.http, graphics with *.jpg, color photos with *.gaf, audio files with *.wav, video files with *.mpg

d. Text with *.html, graphics with *.jpg, color photos with *.gaf, audio files with *.wav, video files with *.mpg

5. Which of the following best describes the processing of a Java servlet?

a. Most of the processing occurs in the server.

1. Server requests/receives HTML file.
2. Server interprets HTML file contents, encounters servlet tag.
3. Server starts Java VM as Sandbox and passes servlet info.
4. Java VM requests/receives through server files (Java class files)
5. Java VM invokes servlet constructor(), init(), start(),... methods.

b. Most of the processing occurs in the browser.

1. Browser requests/receives HTML file.
2. Browser interprets HTML file contents, encounters servlet tag.
3. Browser starts Java VM as Sandbox and passes in info.
4. Java VM requests/receives through browser files (Java class files)
5. Java VM invokes servlet constructor(), init(), start(),... methods.

c. Most of the processing occurs in the server.

1. The servlet can be invoked from an HTML form using the ACTION attribute of the "FORM" tag.
2. Then the init() method is called when the servlet engine first loads the servlet.
3. It executes once for every client request.
4. After the servlet runs, the destroy() method is called when the engine is getting ready to unload a servlet.

d. Most of the processing occurs in the server.

1. The servlet can be invoked from an HTML form using the ACTION attribute of the "FORM" tag.
2. Then the init() method is called when the servlet engine first loads the servlet. It only executes once.
3. The HTTPservlet service() method is called for every client request.
4. After the servlet runs, the destroy() method is called when the engine is getting ready to unload a servlet.

6. Which of the following best describes the processing steps for a Java applet?

a.

1. Servlet receives HTML request.
2. Browser interprets HTML file contents, encounters applet tag.
3. Browser starts Java VM as Sandbox and passes applet info.
4. Java VM requests/receives through browser applet files (Java class files)
5. Java BM invokes applet constructor(), init(), start(),... methods.

b.

1. Browser requests/receives HTML file.
2. Browser interprets HTML file contents, encounters applet tag.
3. Browser starts Java VM as Sandbox and passes applet info.
4. Java VM requests/receives through browser applet files (Java class files)

> 5. Java BM invokes applet constructor(), init(), start(),... methods.

  c.

> 1. Java Server page makes request to database access bean.
> 2. Browser interprets HTML file contents, encounters applet tag.
> 3. Browser starts Java VM as Sandbox and passes applet info.
> 4. Java VM requests/receives through browser applet files (Java class files)
> 5. Java BM invokes applet constructor(), init(), start(),... methods.

  d.

> 1. The Enterprise JavaBean sends the HTML request to the applet.
> 2. Browser interprets HTML file contents, encounters applet tag.
> 3. Browser starts Java VM as Sandbox and passes applet info.
> 4. Java VM requests/receives through browser applet files (Java class files)
> 5. Java BM invokes applet constructor(), init(), start(),... methods.

7. Which of the following describes a characteristic of XML?

   a. XML data can be saved within a servlet on the application server.
   b. XML's ability to extend tags is based on its XHTML tag perimeters.
   c. XML provides users the ability to create new tags to write their own markup language.
   d. XML tags are limited to 50 Document Type Definitions. XML is extensible as long as you create tags within the 50 DTDs.

8. Which of the following best describes a Java servlet?

   a. It is Java code that runs in the client, is invoked in an HTML file and runs inside the Java Virtual Machine (JVM). It can invoke JavaBeans for business logic or connection to back-end systems and can invoke JSPs to create view in the client.
   b. It is Java code that runs in the server, is invoked in an HTML file, and runs inside the Java Virtual Machine (JVM). It can invoke JavaBeans for business logic or connection to back-end systems and can invoke JSPs to create view in the client.
   c. It is Java code that runs in the client, is invoked in an HTML file, and runs inside the Java Virtual Machine (JVM). It can invoke JavaBeans for business logic or connection to back-end systems and can invoke JSPs to create view in the client.
   d. It is Java code that runs in the server, is invoked in an HTML file, and runs inside the Java Virtual Machine (JVM). It can invoke JavaBeans for business logic or connection to back-end systems, and can invoke JSPs to create view in the client.

9. All of the following are benefits of solutions based on the IBM Framework for e-business EXCEPT:

   a. They leverage existing systems
   b. They leverage traditional skills
   c. They integrate information and business processes
   d. They improve time to market for enterprise solutions

10. An insurance company has an environment of mixed systems including Solaris, HP-UX, OS/390, OS/400, AIX and NT. Why is the IBM Framework for e-business important to them?

a. Java helps to ensure that all server operating systems are supported.
b. The IBM Framework for e-business allows server centric applications.
c. The support of multi-platform standards increases the flexibility of deployment.
d. The IBM Framework for e-business allows customers to easily run non-IBM operating systems and applications on IBM hardware.

11. Rough Cut Lumber has a client/server environment with multiple systems including Apple Macintosh, IBM OS/2, IBM Network Stations and network computers, and Microsoft Windows 9X. Why would the IBM Framework for e-business be considered a critical factor for Rough Cut?

a. It supports any client.
b. It leverages core systems.
c. It supports Microsoft deployments on both the client and the server.
d. It is open and standards based, and supports all key operating systems.

A.6 Sample Test 812: Answers

The answers to the questions in the previous section are listed here:

1. C
2. C
3. B
4. A
5. D
6. B
7. C
8. B
9. B
10. C
11. A

Appendix B. Competitive information

This appendix discusses competitive e-business solutions. Where applicable, either the IBM Framework for e-business or components of the framework are compared to what IBM competitors have or intend to have in the marketplace.

B.1 Microsoft .NET architecture overview

The Microsoft .NET platform and architecture announced by Microsoft are a much extended set of software functions, products, components, and services designed to facilitate the development and deployment to the Internet of highly interactive, Web-based applications, embracing the wide range of devices expected to be in use. .NET builds upon Microsoft's previous architecture Windows 2000 DNA, which was mainly concerned with the "middleware plumbing". .NET goes further, adding new approaches for how applications are built and deployed in the Internet environment. It also introduces a radical new business model of software as a service.

The overall structure of Microsoft .NET is shown in Figure 201, alongside the current Windows 2000 DNA architecture. Both are centered around the Microsoft COM+ programming model, a Microsoft alternative to the popular open Java/CORBA distributed object programming model.

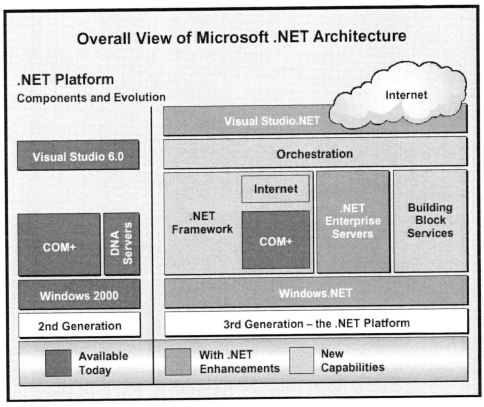

Figure 201. Overview of Microsoft .NET architecture

The main components of .NET are:

- **Microsoft .NET User Experience**: New capabilities of .NET's "next-generation user experience", including a new Universal Canvas, an XML-based compound information architecture, a natural user interface, integral digital media support, privacy-enabling controls on personal information, and new Dynamic Delivery for secure, seamless installation, updates, roaming, and off-line operation.

- **Microsoft .NET Infrastructure and Tools**: A new XML-based programming model will help developers build, deliver, integrate, operate, and federate Web services. A new Visual Studio .NET toolset will provide support for XML-based Web service development. Also new is a workflow and process modelling tool, BizTalk Orchestration, aimed to simplify business process integration over the Internet. The .NET Infrastructure and Tools exploit and use the services and support of the new, all XML-enabled family of Windows DNA 2000 servers, which are now renamed the .NET Enterprise Servers.

- **Microsoft .NET Building Block Services**: These are a new set of distributed, programmable services to run across multiple machines, in data centers and over the Internet, to aid applications development by providing core, common functions and services accessible everywhere. These services include identity, notification and messaging, personalization, schematized storage, calendar, directory, search, and software delivery. They include Web services such as Passport, the MSN Hotmail Web-based e-mail service, MSN Messenger, and MSN Communities. In the future, developers may call these in their applications. Different instances of these services can cooperate and exchange information via a "federation" process.

- **Microsoft .NET Enterprise Servers**: These are the new Windows 2000 DNA servers (SQL Server 2000, BizTalk Server 2000, Commerce Server 2000, Exchange Server 2000, Application Center Server 2000, Host Integration Server 2000, and ISA Server 2000), which are proposed as a key infrastructure foundation for .NET. The servers support XML, which is used as the enabling open standard underneath .NET.

- **Microsoft .NET Device Software and Windows .NET**: This is software to power most types of intelligent Internet-connected devices. Microsoft has promised to deliver new versions of the Windows operating systems supporting the .NET platform in late 2001 and 2002. It says that the software will XML-enable any device, support intelligent interaction with the network and .NET services, and its new user experience to non-PC devices, such as pocket PCs, set-top boxes, cellular phones, and game consoles.

- **Microsoft .NET Framework**: These enabling technologies provide core support services to the architecture, including normal alphanumeric data and XML structured data support, base-classes, and a common run-time environment for applications in any of the .NET-supported languages, plus support for the new user interface. These are the main elements of the new architecture, which will be delivered in a set of new or enhanced products and services over the next two years.

B.1.1 Microsoft .NET products and services

The .NET vision is supported by a plan to provide new products and services to implement the .NET architecture. Today's business model of licensed software sales is expected to move toward the .NET concept of software and Web services, where software is a service sold on a time or usage basis. The new offerings will include:

- **Windows .NET**: The next versions of today's Windows family will include the new .NET user experience technologies, be closely integrated with .NET Building Block services, and provide integrated support for digital media. Windows .NET will be self-supporting, with Web services delivering support and updates automatically. The first release of Windows .NET (Whistler) will be available in late 2001, with the full version (Blackcomb) expected in 2002. Microsoft will also continue to support non-.NET Windows versions.

- **MSN .NET**: MSN .NET will link MSN content services and the .NET platform. MSN .NET will support a single "digital personality" for users, and enable easy, safe access to information, entertainment, and people at any time, any place, and on any device. A new, integrated client, will combine MSN dynamic Web services, content, and other .NET services, for an integrated consumer UI.

- **Consumer Subscription Services**: Microsoft will also offer premium services in traditional Microsoft consumer areas, like entertainment, games, education, and productivity, exploiting the new .NET facilities.

- **Office .NET**: Office .NET adds four innovations to the popular Office suite. A natural UI will streamline user-service interaction. A new client and services architecture will add functionality, performance, and automatic deployments. Universal collaboration services will support collaborative working inside and outside the firm. The services will extend "any time, any place, and on any device", and will add personalization features.

- **bCentral for Microsoft .NET**: Microsoft said it will also boost its bCentral small business portal with new .NET-based services, including:

  - *Outlook Web services*: To bring browser-based messaging, calendaring, and Personal Information Manager (PIM) features via an Outlook interface, and a Web folder for file storage and remote access.

  - *Enhanced commerce and Customer Relationship Management (CRM) services*: To let small business customers serve their customers online, with hosted catalogs, and customer interaction tracking and personalization. It said that these expanded bCentral services will be made available in late 2000.

- **Visual Studio .NET**: An XML-based programming and Rapid Application Development (RAD) product, supported by the MSDN developer service and .NET Enterprise Servers. It is claimed that Visual Studio .NET will allow delivery of highly distributed, programmable services.

B.1.2 .NET benefits

Microsoft has articulated four main benefits that it believes .NET will bring, when the vision is released:

- *Improved user experience*: More productive services will be built into the new operating system, via new user interfaces and new intelligent Internet devices. By enabling multiple devices and services to be more easily linked together, these are claimed to improve privacy and control, based on the Platform for Privacy Preference Project (P3P) specification.

- *Ease-of-use/simplicity*: .NET will support continuous delivery of software to customers via a distributed computing model on the Internet, which is a major advantage for ease of maintenance and speed of upgrade distribution, for both users and suppliers.

- *Internet standards*: .NET is based on Internet protocols and standards for interactions between devices and services, and in particular relies on XML and the Simple Object Access Protocol (SOAP), among others, which will improve interoperability with other systems environments.

- *Business integration and opportunity*: The .NET vision may open opportunities for ISVs and developers to build Internet services and businesses more easily, and to integrate those offerings directly with business partners and customers.

B.1.3 Architecture comparison

Table 69 describes the comparison between the Microsoft .NET architecture and IBM Framework for e-business.

Table 69. Architecture comparison between Microsoft .NET and IBM Framework for e-business

Architectural feature	IBM Framework for e-business	Microsoft .NET
Availability and deployability	Available since 1999; fully deployable now	Staged availability through 2000 and 2002
Architecture maturity	Mature, fully articulated, and proven architecture	New vision
Field deployment experience	Successfully deployed in several thousand enterprise customers	New vision
Target marketplace and audience	Enterprise and SME businesses; individual business users	Enterprise and SME businesses; individual business users; individual consumer users
Broad architecture categorization	Multiple hardware-platform, open standards-based, middleware, software centric architecture, Java based	Single Intel platform and Windows operating system-centric, supports fat and thin client, based around Microsoft COM+
Extent of architecture	Very extensive, commencing above the operating system layer, and extending well into the applications enablement, and applications component assembly space in the applications layer	Extensive, rooted in core Microsoft operating systems, with strong inclusive software services, through layered middleware software, extending to the lower edge of the applications layer with proposed future Web services.

Architectural feature	IBM Framework for e-business	Microsoft .NET
Core architectural model	n-tier, highly distributed, Internet-based, server-centric, thin-client, architecture for the Web and corporate networks, with strong component-based software development support, and rich component and e-business patterns support for e-business applications development	n-tier, distributed, Internet exploitative, Windows 2000 centric, Microsoft core and open standards-based architecture for the Web and corporate networks, supporting Microsoft software component models and a vision of reusable Web services
Core programming model	Based primarily around the Java, EJB, and CORBA programming model, with support for COM+ integration	Based primarily around the Microsoft COM+ programming model, with some interoperability support for other models
Programming languages supported	Java, C++, and others	C, C++, and C# focused
Primary open standards supported	XML, LDAP, CORBA, SQL, SOAP, and Java	XML, LDAP, COM+, SOAP, and SQL
Hardware and software support	Intrinsically multi-platform orientated	Primarily single platform focused
Native runtime environment	OS/390, OS/400, AIX, Windows 2000, Solaris, HP–UX, Linux, OS/2, and others	Windows 2000 family systems
Integrates capabilities	Integrates well with most other enterprise platforms via integration middleware, 39 in all	Quite good integration with other selected enterprise platforms
Interoperability and existing system integration approach	Supports data integration, transaction integration, message-based integration, XML-based integration, software component-based integration, and applications integration, all via open standards mechanisms	Is planned to support data integration, transaction integration, message-based integration, XML-based integration, software component-based integration and applications integration, via a mixture of open and proprietary standards
Openess of architecture	Fully open architecture entirely built upon open industry standards, and highly extensible	Semi-proprietary architecture rooted in Microsoft standards, but with quite extensive open standards support

Architectural feature	IBM Framework for e-business	Microsoft .NET
Scalability of architecture	Very highly scalable to highest levels (clustered OS/390 or UNIX platforms) with highly proven main software-enabling components, for example, OS/390, DB2 UDB, MQSeries, CICS, and IMS/DC	Scalable to quite high levels (clustered Windows 2000 systems), supported by certain key subsystems, for example, SQL Server 2000, IIS 5.0, some parts unproven
Support for Linux	Full, primary platform support, some out now	Limited integration support only as another UNIX
Inclusivity of other platforms and architectures	Architecture inclusive of Windows 2000 as a prime platform	Architecture essentially exclusive, but supports integration with other platforms
Support for pervasive and mobile computing	Very strong and available now	Strong support planned over roll-out period
Support for e-business and Internet commerce	Powerful WebSphere Commerce Server available now, Security, Hosted Services, Payment Services, and e-marketplace services already offered with key partners	Commerce server software, small business portal being extended, enhanced Web services planned for 2001, 2002; many third-party ASP offerings
Approach to applications solution assembly	Extensive 1000+ business software component collection of EJB components for RAD assembly; prototypical e-business applications, use architecture patterns	Fairly wide availability of COM+ software components; BizTalk Orchestration approach to build workflows; intent to make own and third-party Web Services widely available in the future
Product comprehensiveness	Extensive support of IBM product sets	Full product support planned
Product availability and timescale	Large majority of architecture enabling product available now	Windows 2000 available now
Product strength and robustness	Many major components with track-record in large enterprise use, for example, DB2, MQSeries, CICS, WAS, etc.	Operating system platform gaining acceptance and some core sub-systems well proven, for example, SQL server, exchange
Integration of product components	Reasonable, but less tight and cohesive than Microsoft	Very good for those components available, and expected in additional new items

Architectural feature	IBM Framework for e-business	Microsoft .NET
Enabling product pricing and packaging	Enterprise-level pricing and packaging, but adjusted sharply down to market competitive levels, and increasingly better packaged	Volume-commodity market pricing background, enterprise components now reaching enterprise pricing levels, clear packaging strategy
Vendor services and support	Provides fullest range of services and support with own large service force, plus partners	Most services and support provided by channel partners, trained and supported by vendor
Range and scope of vendor support	Extensive, support covers all aspects	Product hot-line, some consulting and architectural help
Scale of vendor support	Largest in the industry	Direct resources are limited, but indirect resources are large
Third-party vendor support	Strong support form major ISVs, business partners, and system integrators	Basic Windows 2000 is widely supported
Market channels and business partners	IBM direct sales and extensive business partner channels including ISVs plus SIs and resellers	All channels delivery, Microsoft evangelism, extensive set of partner channels, OEMs, ISVs, and MSPs
Compliant Independent Software Vendor (ISV) applications software available	Supports many leading enterprise applications; SAP, Seibel systems, Ariba, I2; has many applications running on the platform	Basic Microsoft 2000 is widely supported, with many certified and available applications

B.1.4 Summary

Lets us summarize two offerings from IBM and Microsoft.

B.1.4.1 IBM Framework for e-business

IBM Framework for e-business is the strongest solution for enterprises with heterogeneous environments. It is required for environments where e-business solutions, a proven architecture, and product set with a real track record of customer deployment are needed. Deep, across-the-board commitment to open standards and full support for all major platforms, including the emerging Linux, provides the greatest future flexibility and avoidance of lock-in. An advanced e-business applications enabling capability, through server software, the WebSphere Software Components, and IBM Patterns for e-business, promises the fastest development of new e-business applications with the least "new build" required. Extensive global vendor services and support, from the largest and most experienced qualified resource in the industry, stands behind the architecture. It has gained great experience of its deployment in thousands of customers over the past two years.

B.1.4.2 Microsoft .NET

Microsoft's software platform has scaled-up to enterprise level, exploiting the growing power and low cost of Intel-based hardware platforms. In .NET, Microsoft has articulated a strong advance over its Windows 2000 DNA architecture of 1999. At its heart, the Windows 2000 operating system has proved much more capable, scalable, and reliable in its different versions than many critics predicted. It also stands as a strong underpinning for the new .NET architecture.

Indeed, many of the architecture's core software services are actually included within the operating system at no extra cost. Most of the products of .NET will be rolled out over the following two years, so a detailed evaluation today is more difficult. The vision may become compelling for those enterprises already committed heavily, or exclusively, to the Microsoft platform, and whose e-business initiatives are not time-critical. In particular, the approach to reducing development time and effort, through reusable Web services, will become attractive only when large numbers, and a rich diversity of such services, are available, which is not the case today. While more use of open standards, notably XML, is seen in .NET than in prior Microsoft proprietary approaches, the vision is still one that commends building most new applications on the Microsoft platform, while integrating with other, seen as legacy, platforms.

B.2 Sun Microsystems e-business overview

Sun Microsystems has emerged with an increasingly complete "enterprise middleware" software-stack, now covering similar ground to the Microsoft Windows 2000 DNA architecture. The company faces very stiff competition for its UNIX servers from the new high-end-capable Windows 2000/Intel platform players, who will seek to undercut Sun's prices significantly. Sun, however, remains the most active and aggressive "single vendor, complete hardware and software vendor" in the market, and still has many supporters and excellent business results to its credit.

Sun has made some important acquisitions in:

- **Forte Corp**: Adds application development tools and enterprise application development software. These include:

    - Forte Fusion (also known as EAI Suite)
    - Forte for Java Enterprise Edition (formerly SynerJ)
    - Forte for Java Internet Edition (formerly NetBeans)
    - Forte for Java Community Edition (formerly NetBeans)
    - Visual Workshop C++ (formerly Forte C++)
    - Performance Workshop for Fortran (formerly Forte Fortran)
    - Forte 4GL (formerly Application Environment)

- **NetBeans**: Offers development of cross-platform Java-based IDE

- **StarDivision**: A cross-platform office productivity suite, competing with Lotus and Microsoft Office

- **StarOffice**: A leader in Linux with over 4 million users

- **StarPortal**: A Web-enabled follow-on to StarOffice; a Java-based solution

Figure 202 illustrates the positioning of the above mentioned products in the Sun e-business model.

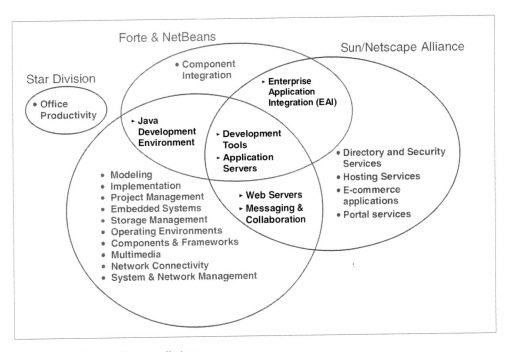

Figure 202. Sun middleware offering

iPlanet E-Commerce Solutions, a Sun-Netscape Alliance, was established in March 1999 by America Online, Inc. and Sun Microsystems, Inc. to power the next wave of the net economy through thought leadership, technical innovation, expert services, and the creation of exceptional customer satisfaction. The iPlanet Platform is the software environment designed to enable rapid assembly and deployment of scalable Internet services.

iPlanet forms the basis of Suns e-business run environment, providing:

- Internet bill presentation and payment:

    - For banks and ISPs
    - "Out-of-the-box" billing application with industry specific templates
    - BillerXpert Consolidator

- Internet selling:

    - Packaged applications to create a Web-based sales channel
    - SellerXpert, MerchantXpert, PublishingXpert

- Internet trading communities:

    - Foundation for Internet selling, billing, payment, and procurement
    - Management of membership, trading relationships, and security

- Strategic Internet procurement:

    - End-to-end automation and management of purchasing process
    - BuyerXpert
    - Integration through Commerce Integration Suite

- e-Market maker platform

    - Packaged applications to create B2B markets
    - Uses all iPlanet applications and infrastructure servers

B.3 Oracle e-business overview

Oracle Corporation continues to do well in e-business, with its database-centric, software-only, offering for multiple hardware platforms, and a strong position in e-business applications and professional services. Oracle is a natural and close partner with Sun Microsystems for these reasons, and the two work closely together.

The Oracle9i Application Server provides an integrated environment for development, deployment, and management of Internet applications you need to run your e-business. Oracle 9i Application Server is available in three editions: Standard, Enterprise, and Wireless. Rather than patching together point solutions from diverse vendors, customers that embrace the Oracle Internet Platform gain faster time to market and overall lower cost of ownership through reduced complexity.

The key features of Oracle 9i Application Server are (as illustrated in Figure 203):

- **Caching Services**: Web cache and database cache

- **Communication Services**: Oracle HTTP powered by Apache, Multiple Listener support including stored procedures, Java servlets, and JSPs, and Oracle Wireless

- **Presentation Services**: Oracle Portal, Oracle Internet File System, Apache jServ and Perl Interpreter, Oracle JavaServer Pages, Oracle PL/SQL Server Pages (PSP), Forms Services, Reports Services, Discoverer Viewer

- **Business Logic Services**: Oracle JVM, Oracle PL/SQL, and Business Components for Java

- **System Services**: Oracle Enterprise Manager, Oracle Advanced Security, Developer Kits for Oracle Database Client, XML, and LDAP

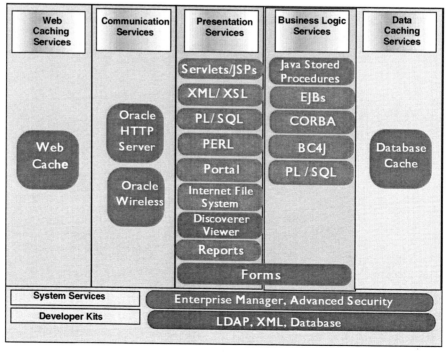

Figure 203. Oracle 9i Application Server

The key benefits of Oracle 9i Application Server (Oracle 9i AS) are:

- *Simple*: To buy, to install, to manage; all core middle-tier services have been integrated enabling customers to build and deploy portals, transactional applications, and Business Intelligence facilities with a single product.

- *Complete*: Together, the database server and the application server offer a complete solution for building and deploying any type of application to the Web including portals, transactional, Business Intelligence, and enterprise integration applications.

- *Integrated*: The database server and the application server share a common set of technology components that allow developers to build applications once and deploy them in a variety of architectural configurations. By sharing these common technology components with the database, Oracle 9i AS provides the reliability, availability, and scalability features necessary for deploying e-business applications.

Table 70 compares IBM and Oracle e-business offerings.

Table 70. Comparison of IBM and Oracle e-business solutions

IBM	Function	Oracle
IBM DB2	DataBase	Oracle 9i Database
IBM WebSphere Application Server	Java Server	Oracle 9i internet Application Server
IBM WebSphere Portal Server	Enterprise Portal	Oracle 9i internet Application Server includes Portal Server formerly WebDB)
IBM WebSphere Everyplace IBM WebSphere Transcoding Publisher IBM WebSphere Voice Server	Wireless	Oracle 9i internet Application Server Wireless Edition
IBM MQSeries Workflow IBM MQSeries Integrator IBM WebSphere Host Integration IBM WebSphere B2B Integrator	Integration & WorkFlow	Oracle 9i internet Application Server (formerly Oracle Message Broker, Oracle Workflow Cartridge, Oracle Integration Server)
IBM WebSphere Commerce Suite (buying pattern analysis) AND 3rd party offering Annuncio (dynamic use of clickstream)	Clickstream	Oracle 9i internet Application Server
IBM WebSphere Edge Server	Web Cache	Oracle 9i internet Application Server
IBM WebSphere Application Server	Data Cache	Oracle 9i internet Application Server
IBM Secureway Policy Director	Security	Oracle 9i internet Application Server
IBM Secureway LDAP IBM WebSphere Application Server (Apache)	Directory	Oracle 9i internet Application Server (Apache)
IBM Tivoli Policy Director IBM WebSphere Site Analyzer IBM WebSPhere Edge Server	Systems Management	Oracle Enterprise Manager Oracle 9i Internet Application Server (management features)
IBM WebSphere HomePage Builder IBM WebSphere Studio	Web Design	Oracle internet Developer Suite* (includes Forms Developer & Designer) Oracle 9i Application Server (includes Forms Server)
IBM Visual Age for Java	Java Tools	Oracle internet Developer Suite* (includes JDeveloper & Oracle Portal)

The strengths of the Oracle e-business solution are:

- Strong brand name in the database market, creating leverage into large install base of DB customers (20,000) to cross-sell Oracle 9i Application Server

- According to IDC, holds the #3 ranked market share in the Application Server Software Platform market

- Has strong packaged enterprise solutions (CRM, ERP, etc.)

- Sizable, aggressive service, and direct sales organization

- Sales representatives have strong industry-specific skills

- Increasing strength in partner relationships

- First-to-market advantage in announcing simplified packaging of 70+ products into Oracle 9i Internet Application Server and Oracle 9i Database

- Good performance with both data and Web caching
- Good offering for "Oracle-only" solutions

The weaknesses of the Oracle e-business solution are:

- Interoperability is limited only to Oracle applications/products
- Limited platform support for enterprise customers (iAS doesn't run on S/390 and has weak connections to legacy systems)
- Increased pricing pressures; Oracle solution is more expensive than IBM
- Post sales and support hidden costs
- Upgrade patches costly to implement
- No object/relational mapping tools and weak development tools for J2EE
- Proprietary CORBA implementation (JCORBA)
- Limited support for J2EE specifications and lack of deployed J2EE references on iAS
- Lack of new features in iAS 9i (mostly packaging and marketing)
- Poor systems management

B.4 BEA WebLogic and IBM WebSphere software comparison

BEA competes with IBM in four products: WebLogic, TUXEDO, eLink, and MessageQ. All other BEA products compliment the features of these four products.

If you compare BEA and IBM product by product, feature to feature, and not consider the whole picture, the comparison would be quite even. The core products, WebSphere Advanced Edition and WebLogic Server, have very similar functionality. Where one product is better in some details, the other product is better in others. Products develop rapidly so it doesn't matter if today they do not have some feature, because it may be included tomorrow.

The important factor is the overall e-business solution. BEA does not have a strong overall solution for e-business, where IBM does. BEA has to partner with many other vendors, but it doesn't give them the same solution as from a single vendor. IBM products also work with third-party tools. However, the level of integration, quality, lower risk, and faster time to market is the main IBM competitive differentiator.

B.4.1 BEA and IBM e-business product and technology comparison

Table 71 shows a detailed feature comparison with the products BEA and IBM have to offer for delivering e-business solutions.

Table 71. IBM WebSphere versus BEA WebLogic software platform comparison

Feature	BEA software	IBM software
Web application server	WebLogic Express WebLogic Server	WebSphere Application Server, Standard Edition; WebSphere Application Server, Advanced Edition

Feature	BEA software	IBM software
Teleprocessing monitor (high-end transaction server)	WebLogic Enterprise TUXEDO	WebSphere Application Server, Enterprise Edition (TXSeries)
Message queuing	TUXEDO/Q	MQSeries
Web server	HTTP embedded in WebLogic	Apache HTTP server embedded in WebSphere
Directory (LDAP)	*No apparent BEA offering available*	SecureWay Directory
Relational database	*No apparent BEA offering available*	DB2 Universal Database
Tivoli ready	BEA Manager for WebLogic	Included with most IBM products
Technology bridging	Nokia and/or Capslock (BEA third party partner)	WebSphere Everyplace Suite
Data bridging	*No apparent BEA offering available*	WebSphere Transcoding Publisher
Portal	*No apparent BEA offering available*	WebSphere Portal Server
Personalization	WebLogic Personalization Server	WebSphere Personalization
Voice understanding	*No apparent BEA offering available*	WebSphere Voice Server
Language translation	*No apparent BEA offering available*	WebSphere Translation Server
Site analysis	*No apparent BEA offering available*	WebSphere Site Analyzer
Scalability and performance	*No apparent BEA offering available*	WebSphere Edge Server (Network Dispatcher and Caching Proxy)
Distributed file system	*No apparent BEA offering available*	AFS (IBM open-source)
Application integration	eLink Integration Server	MQSeries Integrator Common Connector Framework
Web-host connectivity	Java adapter for M/F-JAM	Host integration solution
Security administration	*No apparent BEA offering available*	SecureWay Policy Director
e-commerce server	WebLogic Commerce Server	WebSphere Commerce Suite
Collaboration	*No apparent BEA offering available*	IBM and Lotus products
Business process workflow	WebLogic Process Integrator	MQSeries Workflow

Feature	BEA software	IBM software
XML business integration tools	*No apparent BEA offering available (XML parser only)*	WebSphere B2B Integrator
UDDI	*No apparent BEA offering available*	UDDI services
Integrated development tools	WebGain Studio (BEA third-party partner)	WebSphere Studio; WebSphere Homepage Builder; VisualAge for Java; VisualAge Generator
Component solutions	WebLogic Commerce Server	WebSphere Business Components

B.4.2 WebSphere software platform summary

The WebSphere software platform includes comprehensive applications and integrated development tools. This means you can build, test, and deploy Web applications faster, making your business more agile and responsive. BEA WebLogic does not compare well to the WebSphere software platform end-to-end family of e-business infrastructure products. The technical advantages of the WebSphere software platform yield many business benefits, such as a lower total cost of ownership and an enhanced return on your investments. The bottom line is you can create a more competitive e-business with WebSphere software.

B.4.2.1 Lower total cost of ownership

With the WebSphere software platform, you can get a lower total cost of ownership. Consider your own requirements and obtain acquisition costs from IBM and BEA. Then add up the additional costs required to use and support the products from multiple vendors that a WebLogic-based e-business typically requires. You'll see that the IBM WebSphere software platform offers:

- Immediate and sustained business value
- Lower overall licensing fees for the collection of distinct products
- Lower development costs (per project) because integration is simpler and development productivity is higher
- Lower integration and support costs

B.4.2.2 Higher business competitiveness

With the WebSphere software platform, a CIO can lead an IT department as it helps an e-business to be more competitive because:

- Higher IT productivity and pace of development enable you to build, test and deploy e-business solutions faster in response to evolving customer needs.
- Comprehensive offerings provide you with more innovative options for your e-business to capture and maintain a competitive edge.
- With a lower total cost of ownership resulting from greater productivity and comprehensiveness, your e-business can invest the savings according to management judgment—in greater profit, lower prices, and faster growth.

Appendix C. Special notices

This publication is intended to help I/T specialists to learn the fundamentals of IBM Framework for e-business. The information in this publication is not intended as the specification of any programming interfaces that are provided by IBM, or other companies, products. See the PUBLICATIONS section of the IBM Programming Announcement for more information about what publications are considered to be product documentation.

References in this publication to IBM products, programs or services do not imply that IBM intends to make these available in all countries in which IBM operates. Any reference to an IBM product, program, or service is not intended to state or imply that only IBM's product, program, or service may be used. Any functionally equivalent program that does not infringe any of IBM's intellectual property rights may be used instead of the IBM product, program or service.

Information in this book was developed in conjunction with use of the equipment specified, and is limited in application to those specific hardware and software products and levels.

IBM may have patents or pending patent applications covering subject matter in this document. The furnishing of this document does not give you any license to these patents. You can send license inquiries, in writing, to the IBM Director of Licensing, IBM Corporation, North Castle Drive, Armonk, NY 10504-1785.

Licensees of this program who wish to have information about it for the purpose of enabling: (i) the exchange of information between independently created programs and other programs (including this one) and (ii) the mutual use of the information which has been exchanged, should contact IBM Corporation, Dept. 600A, Mail Drop 1329, Somers, NY 10589 USA.

Such information may be available, subject to appropriate terms and conditions, including in some cases, payment of a fee.

The information contained in this document has not been submitted to any formal IBM test and is distributed AS IS. The use of this information or the implementation of any of these techniques is a customer responsibility and depends on the customer's ability to evaluate and integrate them into the customer's operational environment. While each item may have been reviewed by IBM for accuracy in a specific situation, there is no guarantee that the same or similar results will be obtained elsewhere. Customers attempting to adapt these techniques to their own environments do so at their own risk.

Any pointers in this publication to external Web sites are provided for convenience only and do not in any manner serve as an endorsement of these Web sites.

The following terms are trademarks of the International Business Machines Corporation in the United States and/or other countries:

e (logo)® @
IBM ®
AIX
AS/400
AT
CICS
CICS/ESA
CT
Current
DataGuide
DataJoiner
DB2
DB2 OLAP Server
DB2 Universal Database
DRDA
Extended Services
HotMedia
IBM Payment Server
Intelligent Miner
Mobile Connect
MQSeries
Net.Data
Netfinity
OS/2
OS/390
OS/400
Presentation Manager
QMF

Redbooks
Redbooks Logo
RACF
RS/6000
S/390
SanFrancisco
SecureWay
SP
System/390
TXSeries
VisualAge
Visual Warehouse
WebSphere
WorkPad
XT
400
Lotus
1-2-3
Approach
cc:Mail
Lotus Notes
Domino
eSuite
Lotus eSuite
Notes
Sametime
Tivoli
Tivoli Ready

The following terms are trademarks of other companies:

Tivoli, Manage. Anything. Anywhere., The Power To Manage., Anything. Anywhere.,TME, NetView, Cross-Site, Tivoli Ready, Tivoli Certified, Planet Tivoli, and Tivoli Enterprise are trademarks or registered trademarks of Tivoli Systems Inc., an IBM company, in the United States, other countries, or both. In Denmark, Tivoli is a trademark licensed from Kjøbenhavns Sommer - Tivoli A/S.

C-bus is a trademark of Corollary, Inc. in the United States and/or other countries.

Java and all Java-based trademarks and logos are trademarks or registered trademarks of Sun Microsystems, Inc. in the United States and/or other countries.

Microsoft, Windows, Windows NT, and the Windows logo are trademarks of Microsoft Corporation in the United States and/or other countries.

PC Direct is a trademark of Ziff Communications Company in the United States and/or other countries and is used by IBM Corporation under license.

ActionMedia, LANDesk, MMX, Pentium and ProShare are trademarks of Intel Corporation in the United States and/or other countries.

UNIX is a registered trademark in the United States and other countries licensed exclusively through The Open Group.

SET, SET Secure Electronic Transaction, and the SET Logo are trademarks owned by SET Secure Electronic Transaction LLC.

Other company, product, and service names may be trademarks or service marks of others.

Appendix D. Related publications

The publications listed in this section are considered particularly suitable for a more detailed discussion of the topics covered in this redbook.

D.1 IBM Redbooks

For information on ordering these publications, see "How to get IBM Redbooks" on page 451.

- *Getting started with Data Warehouse and Business Intelligence*, SG24-5415
- *Design Considerations: From Client/server applications to e-business Applications*, SG24-5503
- *Business Intelligence Certification Guide*, SG24-5747
- *Patterns for e-business: User-to-Business Patterns for Topology 1 and 2 using WebSphere Advanced Edition*, SG24-5864
- *e-Commerce Patterns Using WebSphere Commerce Suite Patterns for e-business Series*, SG24-6156

D.2 Referenced Web sites

These Web sites are also relevant as further information sources:

- http://www.ibm.com/certify/tests/sam811.shtml
- http://www.ibm.com/certify/tests/sam812.shtml
- http://www.ibm.com/ebusiness
- http://www.tivoli.com
- http://www.ibm.com/software/ad/vajava
- http://www.lotus.com/home.nsf/welcome/dominodesigner
- http://www.ibm.com/software/webservers/components
- http://www.ibm.com/software/webservers/appserv
- http://www-4.ibm.com/software/ts/mqseries
- http://www.ibm.com/developerworks/patterns
- http://www.ibm.com/services/partners/SPfaq2a.html
- http://www.ibm.com/security
- http://www.specbench.org
- http://www.ibm.com/software/data/db2/udb
- http://www.w3c.org
- http://www.ibm.com/index.htm
- http://www.java.sun.com/products/jsp
- http://www.w3.org/Protocols/HTTP/1.1/rfc2616.pdf
- http://www.ecma.ch/stand/ECMA-262.htm
- http://java.sun.com/j2ee

- `http://java.sun.com/j2ee/connector`
- `http://www.ibm.com/software/webservers/appserv/library.html`
- `http://www.ibm.com/software/webservers/appserv/security_v35.pdf`
- `http://www.netobjects.com/products/html/nfmx.html`
- `http://www.ibm.com/software/webservers/studio/index.html`
- `http://www.ibm.com/software/webservers/httpservers`
- `http://www.ibm.com/software/webservers/dgw/index.htm`
- `http://www.microstrategy.com`
- `http://www.eti.com/home/home.htm`
- `http://www.businessobjects.com`
- `http://www.cognos.com`
- `http://www.brio.com`
- `http://sap.com`
- `http://peoplesoft.com`
- `http://siebel.com`

D.3 How to get IBM Redbooks

Search for additional Redbooks or redpieces, view, download, or order hardcopy from the Redbooks Web Site

    ibm.com/redbooks

Also download additional materials (code samples or diskette/CD-ROM images) from this Redbooks site.

Redpieces are Redbooks in progress; not all Redbooks become redpieces and sometimes just a few chapters will be published this way. The intent is to get the information out much quicker than the formal publishing process allows.

D.4 IBM Redbooks collections

Redbooks are also available on CD-ROMs. Click the CD-ROMs button on the Redbooks Web Site for information about all the CD-ROMs offered, updates and formats.

How to get IBM Redbooks

This section explains how both customers and IBM employees can find out about IBM Redbooks, redpieces, and CD-ROMs. A form for ordering books and CD-ROMs by fax or e-mail is also provided.

- **Redbooks Web Site** ibm.com/redbooks

  Search for, view, download, or order hardcopy/CD-ROM Redbooks from the Redbooks Web site. Also read redpieces and download additional materials (code samples or diskette/CD-ROM images) from this Redbooks site.

  Redpieces are Redbooks in progress; not all Redbooks become redpieces and sometimes just a few chapters will be published this way. The intent is to get the information out much quicker than the formal publishing process allows.

- **E-mail Orders**

  Send orders by e-mail including information from the IBM Redbooks fax order form to:

	e-mail address
In United States or Canada	pubscan@us.ibm.com
Outside North America	Contact information is in the "How to Order" section at this site: http://www.elink.ibmlink.ibm.com/pbl/pbl

- **Telephone Orders**

United States (toll free)	1-800-879-2755
Canada (toll free)	1-800-IBM-4YOU
Outside North America	Country coordinator phone number is in the "How to Order" section at this site: http://www.elink.ibmlink.ibm.com/pbl/pbl

- **Fax Orders**

United States (toll free)	1-800-445-9269
Canada	1-403-267-4455
Outside North America	Fax phone number is in the "How to Order" section at this site: http://www.elink.ibmlink.ibm.com/pbl/pbl

This information was current at the time of publication, but is continually subject to change. The latest information may be found at the Redbooks Web site.

IBM Intranet for Employees

IBM employees may register for information on workshops, residencies, and Redbooks by accessing the IBM Intranet Web site at http://w3.itso.ibm.com/ and clicking the ITSO Mailing List button. Look in the Materials repository for workshops, presentations, papers, and Web pages developed and written by the ITSO technical professionals; click the Additional Materials button. Employees may access MyNews at http://w3.ibm.com/ for redbook, residency, and workshop announcements.

IBM Redbooks fax order form

Please send me the following:

Title	Order Number	Quantity

First name _____ Last name _____

Company _____

Address _____

City _____ Postal code _____ Country _____

Telephone number _____ Telefax number _____ VAT number _____

☐ Invoice to customer number _____

☐ Credit card number _____

Credit card expiration date _____ Card issued to _____ Signature _____

We accept American Express, Diners, Eurocard, Master Card, and Visa. Payment by credit card not available in all countries. Signature mandatory for credit card payment.

Index

Numerics

3-tier application architecture   13

A

access beans   159
Access Builder for SAP R/3   133
access control lists (ACL)   407
Access Integration pattern   27
Account Access pattern   29
accountability   47, 207
ACID   109, 110
ACL (access control lists)   407
acquirer   218
acquirer payment gateway   218
add processors or nodes   404
administration   47
administrative relationships   218
Advanced Edition   150, 153
affordability   176
AFS (Andrew File System)   416
agents   145
Alert protocol   215
Andrew File System (AFS)   416
APPLET tag   83
applets   83
application components   126
application firewall   232
application integration   27
application patterns   100
application program   112
application programming model   16
Application protocol   215
application proxy   222, 408
application server   358
application-level protocol   66
application-level proxy   222
asset protection   47
assurance   47
asymmetric key cryptography   205, 208
Atomic commit   112
atomicity (ACID)   109, 279
authentication   407
authentication services   231
authenticity   207
authorization   46
authorization services   231
automated business process   360
availability   47, 60, 274, 275, 307, 352, 362

B

B2B (Business-to-Business)   313
B2C (Business-to-Consumer)   313
Bank Teller Business Components   142
bastion   227
bCentral   433
BEA WebLogic   442

bean-managed persistence (BMP)   91
BI (Business Intelligence)   24, 366
BMP (bean-managed persistence)   91
bottlenecks   397
brand   217
Brio   389
build   129
building new applications   11
business component   156
business drivers   52, 245, 280
business integration   335
Business Intelligence (BI)   24, 50, 366
business logic   100, 103
business metadata   387
business object   156
Business Objects tool   389
business process   156
business quality   61, 274, 308, 351, 363
Business-to-Business (B2B)   313
Business-to-Consumer (B2C)   313

C

C++ Access Builder   133
C2C (Consumer-to-Consumer)   313
CA (Certificate Authority)   211
caching   401
Caching Proxy   161, 409
capacity   60, 274, 306, 351, 362
cardholder   217
CashRegister   321
catalog management   317, 324
CB (Component Broker)   293, 303, 309
CBR (Content Based Routing)   415
CCF (Common Connector Framework)   121, 122, 127
CCI (Common Client Interface)   127
Certificate Authority (CA)   211
Certification Authority   218
Certified for e-business
    Solution Designer   3
    Solution Technologist   5
CGI (Common Gateway Interface)   82, 402
chained transactions   116
Change Cipher Specification protocol   215
change out processor   404
child   116
CICS Java gateway   181
CICS transaction   176
CICS Web Support   178
circuit-level gateway   222, 233
classification   381
client   31, 341, 398
client-driven processing application model   248
cloning   418
    horizontal   419
    vertical   419
cluster   419
cluster processors   404

clustering 381
CMP (container-managed persistence) 91
Cognos 389
collaboration 19
Collaboration Application Service Provider 29
Collaboration pattern 27
command bean 104
command interface 104
command target 103
commercial messaging 162
Common Client Interface (CCI) 127
Common Connector Framework (CCF) 121, 122, 127
common directory schema 226
Common Gateway Interface (CGI) 82, 402
Common Object Request Broker Architecture (CORBA) 70, 105, 282
communication protocol 215
competitive e-business solutions 431
Component Broker (CB) 293, 303, 309
Components Composer 141
confidentiality 207
connection management 403
connection pooling 265
connections 132
connectivity 176
connectors 16, 41, 121, 126, 145, 253, 344
consistency (ACID) 109, 279
Consumer Subscription Services 433
Consumer-to-Consumer (C2C) 313
container 124, 126
container-managed persistence (CMP) 91
Content Based Routing (CBR) 415
content host 409
contractual relationship 218
controller command 158
controls and views 156
convenience banking 54
conversational model 338
cookies 77
CORBA (Common Object Request Broker Architecture) 70, 105, 282
CORBA security 231
CORBA Stack 107
CRM (Customer Relationship Management) 23, 237
CRM solution 54
cryptography principles 207
Customer Information Control System 175
customer management 316
Customer Relationship Management (CRM) 23, 237
CyberCash 321

D

data aggregation 377
data mart 368, 380
data mining 368, 381
Data Propagator Relational 387
data refining 377
data sources 376
data summarization 377
Data System Libraries (DSL) 388

data warehouse 368
    construction 385
    modeling 385
database 156
database server 402
databean command 159
databean manager 159
DataGuide 387
DB2 20
DB2 OLAP Server 384
DB2 Universal Database 171
DCE (Distributed Computing Environment) 183
decision block 286
decision blocks for CRM 255
declarative programming 90
DECS (Domino Enterprise Connection Services) 145, 147
demilitarized zone (DMZ) 221
deployment descriptor 126
design block 356
design space 22, 30, 311
Designing IBM e-business solution 423
DHTML (Dynamic HTML) 78
digital certificates 211
digital signature algorithm (DSA) 210
DII (Dynamic Invocation Interface) 108
directory 70, 144
directory server 407
directory services 224
    standards 225
discovering associations 382
discovering sequential patterns 382
Dispatcher 411, 414
distributed 283
Distributed Computing Environment (DCE) 183
Distributed Debugger 134
distributed object model 186
Distributed Program Link (DPL) 177
distributed transaction processing (DTP) 110
distributed transaction standards 110
DMZ (demilitarized zone) 221
Document Object Model (DOM) 80
Document Type Definition (DTD) 78
DOM (Document Object Model) 80
Domino 244, 347
Domino (agents) 347
Domino Access Builder 133
Domino AgentRunner 134
Domino Application Server 144
    CRM with data access 270
Domino Designer 18, 135, 242
Domino Enterprise Connection Services (DECS) 145, 147
Domino Enterprise Server 144
Domino Everyplace Quick Start 201
Domino Global WorkBench 137
Domino Mail Server 143
Domino object model 145
Domino Objects 136
Domino solution 276

Domino UI Java Applets   136
Domino Web server   242
DPL (Distributed Program Link)   177
drill-down   370
DSA (digital signature algorithm)   210
DSI (Dynamic Skeleton Interface)   108
DSL (Data System Libraries)   388
DTD (Document Type Definition)   78
DTP (distributed transaction processing)   110
dual-homed gateway   228
durability (ACID)   109, 279
Dynamic HTML (DHTML)   78
Dynamic Invocation Interface (DII)   108
Dynamic Skeleton Interface (DSI)   108

E

EAB (Enterprise Access Builder)   132
EAI (Enterprise Application Integration)   24
e-business   7, 10
   application requirements   8
   cycle   10
   functional requirements   54
   life cycle   10
   nonfunctional requirements   55
   Oracle   440
   patterns   9
   security   205
   solution design   51
   solution requirements   245, 280, 354
   solution space   22, 238
   Sun Microsystems   438
   VPN   234
e-business Core Knowledge   426
e-business problem space   353
ECI (External Call Interface)   177
ECMA (European Computer Manufacturers Association)
81
ECMAScript   81
e-commerce   23, 311
   marketing   314
   models   313
eCRM (electronic Customer Relationship Management)
388
EIS resource adapter   127
EJB (Enterprise JavaBeans)   89, 105, 282, 308
EJB components   91
EJB container   92
EJB Development Environment   134
EJB framework   90
EJB Home   93
EJB Home interface   93
EJB Home interface object   92
EJB object   93
EJB programming model   93
EJB Remote interface object   92
EJB security   232
EJB Server   91
EJB transaction service   120
Electronic Commerce pattern   25
electronic Customer Relationship Management (eCRM)

388
electronic Market places (eMP)   313
e-Marketplace pattern   27
e-marketplaces   313
eMP (electronic Market places)   313
Encina   183
   factory   186
   status server object   186
Encina Monitor   185
Encina PPC Executive   185
Encina PPC Gateway/SNA   185
Encina Recoverable Queuing Service (RQS)   185
Encina Structured File Server (SFS)   185
Encina++   186
   distributed object model   186
end-to-end model   220
eNetwork Emulator Express   202
eNetwork Web Express   202
Enterprise Access Builder (EAB)   132
Enterprise Application Integration (EAI)   24, 335
enterprise data and application   39
Enterprise Edition   150, 153
Enterprise Information System (EIS) tier   15
Enterprise Intranet Portal   29
Enterprise Java logical interface block   94
Enterprise JavaBeans (EJB)   89, 105, 282, 308
   Java Transaction Services   110
   managing transactions   295
Enterprise JavaBeans container   94
Enterprise Solution Structure (ESS)   285
Enterprise Toolkit for AS/400   134
Enterprise Toolkit for OS/390   134
Enterprise Toolkit for Workstations   134
entity beans   159
entity EJB   90
EPI (External Presentation Interface)   177
ESS (Enterprise Solution Structure)   285
ETI Extract   391
European Computer Manufacturers Association (ECMA)
81
EXCI (External CICS Interface)   177
EXCI User Interface   180
existing customer environment   55
Extended Enterprise   26
extendibility   274, 275, 307, 351, 362
eXtensible Stylesheet Language (XSL)   78
External Call Interface (ECI)   177
External CICS Interface (EXCI)   177
external data source   368
External Presentation Interface (EPI)   177
EXTRACT ToolSuite   388
extraction and propagation   376

F

factory   186
file transfer protocol (FTP)   66, 70
firewall   221, 408
   objectives, rules   224
first tier   14
FirstSecure   195

flat transactions 115
Forms Designer 136
Forte Corp 438
forward proxy 410
Frameset Designer 136
framework 98
Framework for e-business 7, 437
   Certification for e-business 3
   elements 13
   overview 8
   products 65, 129
   products supporting CRM 264
   system model 13
   technology 65
FTP (file transfer protocol) 70

G

Global Sign-On 195
grading symbols 61

H

Handshake protocol 215
Hashed Message Authentication Code (HMAC) 210
high cluster synergy 405
HMAC (Hashed Message Authentication Code) 210
horizontal cloning 419
HotMedia 19
HTML (Hypertext Markup Language) 78
HTTP (Hypertext Transfer Protocol) 70, 74
HTTPS 76
HttpServlet 85
HttpServletRequest 86
HttpServletResponse 86
HttpSession 86
Hypertext Markup Language (HTML) 78
Hypertext Transfer Protocol (HTTP) 70, 74

I

IBM Boundary Server 195
IBM Caching Proxy 161
IBM Certified for e-business 3
IBM HTTP Server 240, 242
IBM Mobile Connect 203
IBM Network Dispatcher 161
IBM Patterns for e-business 24
IBM SanFrancisco 139
IBM WebSphere software 442
IDE (integrated development environment) 131, 132
IDL stubs and skeletons 108
IIOP (Internet Inter-ORB Protocol) 70
IMAP4 71
IMS (Information Management System) 173
Information Aggregation pattern 26
Information Management System (IMS) 173
informational data 368
informational environment 26
informational Web node 401
Instant Feedback 137

integrated development environment (IDE) 131, 132
integration 339
integration requirements 57
integrity 175, 207
Integrity Data Reengineering 388
Intelligent Miner for Data 384
Intelligent Miner for Text 384
interaction controller 100, 101
Interactive Session Support (ISS) 414
International Standards Organization (ISO) 70
Internet Inter-ORB Protocol (IIOP) 70
Internet Message Access Protocol (IMAP) 71
Internet Protocol (IP) 66
Internet topology 68
IP (Internet Protocol) 66
IP address 68
iPlanet 439
islands of automation 353
ISO (International Standards Organization) 70
isolation (ACID) 109, 279
ISS (Interactive Session Support) 414
issuer 217

J

J2C 152
J2EE 124
J2EE application model 124
J2EE Connector architecture 126
J2EE specification 124
J2EE standards 151
J2SE 125
Java 2 Connectivity 152
Java 2 Platform, Enterprise Edition 124
Java 2 Platform, Standard Edition 125
Java applet 83
Java components 81
Java Message Service (JMS) 96
Java Naming and Directory Interface (JNDI) 96
Java servlet API 85
Java servlets 85
Java standard extensions 125
Java Transaction API (JTA) 96
Java Transaction Service (JTS) 111
Java Virtual Machine (JVM) 231
JavaMail 1.1 125
JavaScript 81
JavaServer Pages (JSP) 87
JDBC 94
JDBC 2.0 Extension 125
JDBC-ODBC bridge driver 95
JMS (Java Message Service) 96
JNDI (Java Naming and Directory Interface) 96
JScript 78
JSP (JavaServer Pages) 87
JSP expression 88
JSP JavaBean tag 88
JSP processor 87
JSP scriptlet 88
JTA (Java Transaction API) 96
JTS (Java Transaction Service) 111

JVM (Java Virtual Machine)   231

K
Kerberos authentication   418

L
latency   398
LDAP (Lightweight Directory Access Protocol)   70, 225
leveraging knowledge, information   12
Lightweight Directory Access Protocol (LDAP)   70, 225
LINK   177
load balancing   404
loan business logic   251
loan JSP   251
local queue manager   163
locking   403
logging   402
logical database model   377
logical space   353
logical unit of work (LUW)   109
Lotus Domino   143
Lotus Domino Application Server   266
Lotus Enterprise Integrator   147
low cluster synergy   405
LUW (logical unit of work)   109

M
maintainability   61, 274, 275, 307, 351, 362
manage   189
manageability   274, 275, 307, 351, 362
Management Information Base (MIB-II)   73
Master ToolSet   388
MDIS (Metadata Interchange Specification)   387
medium cluster synergy   405
merchant   216
merchant originated payment (MOP)   320
message brokering   339
message header   75
message passing model   338
Message Queue Interface (MQI)   162
message queuing   338
message types   75
messaging   144
meta directory   226
metadata   370
    business   387
    information   378
    technical   387
Metadata Interchange Specification (MDIS)   387
methodologies   96
MIB-II (Management Information Base)   73
Microsoft .NET   431, 438
    Building Block Services   432
    Device Software and Windows .NET   432
    Enterprise Servers   432
    Framework   432
    Infrastructure and Tools   432
    products, services   432

User Experience   432
MicroStrategy   388
MicroStrategy Agent   388
MicroStrategy applications   389
MicroStrategy Intelligence Server   389
MicroStrategy Web's easy-to-use all-HTML interface   389
middle tier   15
MIME (Multipurpose Internet Mail Extensions)   72
mobile commerce   160, 313
Mobile Connect   203
model   157
Model-View-Controller (MVC)   89
MOP (merchant originated payment)   320
MQI (Message Queue Interface)   162
MQSeries   20, 161, 162, 346
MQSeries Adapter   164
MQSeries Adapter Offering   162
MQSeries Everyplace   162, 165
MQSeries Integrator   162, 346, 351
MQSeries Integrator-based solution   349
MQSeries Messaging   346
MQSeries Workflow   162, 359
MSN .NET   433
Multipurpose Internet Mail Extensions (MIME)   72
multi-tier   283
MVC (Model-View-Controller)   89

N
Native API partly Java driver   95
Native-protocol all Java driver   95
nested transactions   115
Net.Commerce   326
NetBeans   438
NetGens   8
NetObjects Fusion   240
Net-protocol all Java driver   95
network   34, 342, 398
    infrastructure   16, 56
    latency   398
Network Dispatcher   161, 410
Network News Transfer Protocol (NNTP)   71
network-level protocol   66
NNTP (Network News Transfer Protocol)   71
non-repudiation   207
NotesPump   145
n-tier distributed environment   13

O
object adapter   108
Object Management Group (OMG)   282
    Object Transaction Services   110
Object Request Broker (ORB)   108
object store   144
Object Transaction Monitor   115
Object Transaction Service (OTS)   111
object-oriented concepts   98
objects   96
octet   69
Office .NET   433

OLAP (Online Analytical Processing)   172, 368, 369
OLAP server   369
OLTP (online transaction processing)   368
OLTP data on separate server   371
OMG (Object Management Group)   282
one-phase (1PC) commit protocol   113
one-way function   205
Online Analytical Processing (OLAP)   172, 368, 369
online transaction processing (OLTP)   368
Open Transaction Monitor Access (OTMA)   175
operating system security   231
operational data source   379
operational databases   367
operational relationship   218
optimistic locking   403
Oracle   440
Oracle 9i Application Server   440
ORB (Object Request Broker)   108
ORB interface   108
Order Capture   140
order tracking   316, 323
organization silos   353
origin server   409
OTMA (Open Transaction Monitor Access)   175
OTS (Object Transaction Service)   111
Outline Designer   136

P

pack mule   401
packet filtering   221, 232
Page Designer   136
parent   116
Patterns for e-business   24
payment gateway   218
payment result bean   251
PDA (personal digital assistant)   14
PeopleSoft Enterprise Performance Management   390
performance   50, 60, 254, 274, 306, 351, 362, 397
    Andrew File System (AFS)   416
    bottlenecks   397
    client   398
    load balancing   404
    network   398
    products   409
    security   405
    server   398, 400
    technologies   398
    WebSphere Edge Server   409
personal digital assistant (PDA)   14
personalization   316, 317
pervasive computing   198
physical database model   377
Policy Director   191
Policy Director for MQSeries   191
policy services   231
POP3 (Post Office Protocol)   71
port   67
port stickytime   413
portability   61, 176, 274, 275, 308, 352, 363
portable   283

Portals pattern   29
Post Office Protocol (POP3)   71
predicting values   381
Privacy Manager   193
problem space   22, 238, 244, 277, 311, 353
process flow   352, 354
products   65, 409
products for Framework for e-business   129
Programmer's Pane   136
protocol neutral   283
protocols   65
public key   208
public key cryptography   205, 208
Public Key Infrastructure   195
publish and subscribe   338

Q

QMF (Query Management Facility)   383
Query Management Facility (QMF)   383
queue managers   163

R

RAD (Rapid Application Development)   97
Rapid Application Development (RAD)   97
RDBMS (relational database management system)   94
RDN (relative distinguished names)   408
record layer protocol   215
records   215
recoverability   176
Recoverable Queuing Service (RQS)   185
recoverable resource   279
relational database management system (RDBMS)   94
relative distinguished names (RDN)   408
reliable messaging   337
Remote Method Invocation (RMI)   96
Remote Procedure Call (RPC) model   338
replication   144
resource manager   112, 279
response time budget   399
reusability   61, 274, 276, 308, 352, 363
reverse proxy   410
Risk Manager   192
RMI (Remote Method Invocation)   96
RMI Access Builder   133
RMI/IIOP 1.0   125
round robin   404
RPC (Remote Procedure Call) model   338
RQS (Recoverable Queuing Service)   185
run   142
running applications   12

S

SAP Business Warehouse   390
SASL (Simple Authentication and Security Layer)   225
SAX (Simple API for XML)   79, 80
scability issues   254
scalability   61, 176, 254, 274, 275, 307, 351, 363
scalable   283

SCM (Supply Chain Management) 24
screen scraping 58
screening filter 227
screening router 221, 227
secret key cryptography 205, 208
secure 283
secure delegation services 231
Secure Electronic Transaction 216, 321
secure payment recommendations 322
secure payment transaction 316, 318
Secure Sockets Layer (SSL) 72, 76, 214, 319, 405
SecureWay Wireless Gateway 202
security 46, 60, 144, 175, 205, 274, 306, 345, 351, 362, 405
    architecture 226
    collaborator 230
    plug-in 230
    server 229
    WebSphere Application Server 228
Security Manager 193
server 398
Server API program 82
server group 419
server-driven processing application model 248
servers 400
server-side includes (SSI) 401
Server-Side Java 402
Servlet 2.2 125
ServletContext 86
servlets 85
session EJB 90
session state management 253
SET Secure Electronic Transaction 216, 321
SGML (Standard Generalized Markup Language) 79
Short Message Service (SMS) 314
SI (supplier integration) 54
Siebel CRM software 390
similar time series 381
Simple API for XML (SAX) 79, 80
Simple Authentication and Security Layer (SASL) 225
Simple Mail Transfer Protocol (SMTP) 72
Simple Network Management Protocol (SNMP) 73
simple object access protocol (SOAP) 152
single data mart 372
SMI (Structure and Identification of Management Information) 73
SMS (Short Message Service) 314
SMTP (Simple Mail Transfer Protocol) 72
SNMP (Simple Network Management Protocol) 73
SOAP (simple object access protocol) 152
socket secure proxy 222
SOCKS 222
Solution Designer 3
solution strengths, weaknesses 274
Solution Technologist 5
SQL (Structured Query Language) 404
SQLJ 94, 133
SSI (server-side includes) 401
SSL (Secure Sockets Layer) 72, 76, 214, 319, 405
SSL handshake 76

SSL Handshake Protocol 76
SSL Record Protocol 76
Standard Edition 149, 264
Standard Generalized Markup Language (SGML) 79
standards-based LDAP client and server 225
StarDivision 438
Star-Join Schema 377
StarOffice 438
StarPortal 438
static server object 186
statistical functions 382
sticky port 405, 413
Storage Management Solutions 196
Structure and Identification of Management Information (SMI) 73
Structured Query Language (SQL) 404
Studio 140
subscribe, publish 338
sub-transaction 116
Sun Microsystems 438
supplier integration (SI) 54, 336
    with workflow 352
Supply Chain Management (SCM) 24, 50
symmetric key cryptography 205, 208
Sync Point Managers 279
system level contracts 127
system management 16, 44

T

TargetableCommand interface 104
task command 159
TCP (Transmission Control Protocol) 66
TCP/IP 66
TCP/IP suite 66
technical metadata 387
technology 65, 398
    behind Framework for e-business 65
technology and product space 22, 50, 311, 353
Telnet 72
test
    format 421
    questions 422
    tips 421
Test 811 3, 421
    answers 425
    sample questions 423
Test 812 5, 421
    answers 429
    sample questions 426
testability 61, 274, 275, 307, 351
Text Analyzer 141
The business patterns 25
The composite patterns 25
The integration patterns 25
thin client 14
third tier 15
thoroughbred 401
threads 401
three-tiered data warehouse 373
TIDL++ 187

tips for Tests 811, 812   421
Tivoli Disaster Recovery Manager   196
Tivoli FirstSecure   195
Tivoli Global Sign-On   195
Tivoli Policy Director   191, 195
Tivoli Policy Director for MQSeries   191
Tivoli Privacy Manager   193
Tivoli products   21
Tivoli Public Key Infrastructure   195
Tivoli Risk Manager   192
Tivoli SANergy   198
Tivoli Security Manager   193
Tivoli security products   21, 190, 205
Tivoli Space Manager   196
Tivoli Storage Area Network Solution   197
Tivoli Storage Management Solutions   196
Tivoli Storage Manager   196
Tivoli Storage Network Manager   197
Tivoli User Administration   191
top-level transaction   116
TP Monitor   115, 116
TP Monitor (Transaction Processing Monitor)   116
traffic cop   340
transaction   20
transaction manager   111
transaction monitor   176
transaction processing   110
Transaction Processing Monitor (TP Monitor)   116
transaction products   173
transaction systems   173
transactional   282
transactional Web node   401
Transactional-C   187
Transactional-C++   187
transactions   108, 150, 277
transcoding   79
transformation   340
transformation and cleansing   376
transforming business processes   10
transforming core business processes   10
Transmission Control Protocol (TCP)   66
transport mode   224
transport proxy   408
tunnel mode   223
two-phase commit (TPC) protocol   113
TXSeries   175, 188, 293, 299, 308

U

UDDI (Universal Description, Discovery and Integration)
152
UI logic   100, 103
Uniform Resource Locator (URL)   69
Universal Description, Discovery and Integration (UDDI)
152
URL (Uniform Resource Locator)   69
usability   61, 274, 275, 307
User Administration   191
user interface (UI) elements   78

V

VBScript   78
VCE (Visual Composition Editor)   132
vertical cloning   419
view command   159
virtual private network (VPN)   223
Visual Composition Editor (VCE)   132
visual programming   132
Visual Studio .NET   433
Visual Warehouse   386
Visual Warehouse Information Catalog   387
Visual Warehouse OLAP   386
VisualAge for Java   18, 131
VPN (virtual private network)   223

W

WAP (Wireless Access Protocol)   314
Web application   100
Web application server   35, 247
Web browser   73
Web enabling Encina   187
Web marketing   237, 238
Web server   238, 400
Web Services Description Language (WSDL)   152
Web technology   73
WebSphere Advanced Edition   293
WebSphere Application Server   20, 205, 418
    Advanced Edition   150, 153
    Advanced Single Server Edition   153
    CRM with data access   267
    Enterprise Edition   150, 153
    security   228
    security architecture   230
    Standard Edition   149, 264
Websphere Application Server   149
WebSphere Business Components   139
WebSphere Business Components (WSBC)   18
WebSphere Commerce Suite   153, 326
WebSphere Edge Server   161, 266, 409
WebSphere Enterprise Edition   293
WebSphere Everyplace Suite   200
WebSphere security   232
WebSphere software platform   444
WebSphere solution   276
WebSphere Studio   18, 137, 240
WebSphere Test Environment (WTE)   132
well-known ports   68
WfMC (Workflow Management Coalition)   171
Windows .NET   433
Wireless Access Protocol (WAP)   314
WLM (Workload Management)   419
workflow   145, 170, 354
    automation   352, 355
Workflow Management Coalition (WfMC)   171
workload management   150, 418
Workload Management (WLM)   419
WSBC (WebSphere Business Components)   18
WSDL (Web Services Description Language)   152
WTE (WebSphere Test Environment)   132

X

X.500   70
X/Open Distributed Transaction Processing Standard   110
X/Open XA protocol   110
XML   78
    applications   80
    processor   80
XML Metadata Interchange   135
XML parser   135
XSL (eXtensible Stylesheet Language)   78

IBM Redbooks review

Your feedback is valued by the Redbook authors. In particular we are interested in situations where a Redbook "made the difference" in a task or problem you encountered. Using one of the following methods, **please review the Redbook, addressing value, subject matter, structure, depth and quality as appropriate.**

- Use the online **Contact us** review redbook form found at ibm.com/redbooks
- Fax this form to: USA International Access Code + 1 845 432 8264
- Send your comments in an Internet note to redbook@us.ibm.com

Document Number **Redbook Title**	SG24-6248-00 IBM Framework for e-business: Technology, Solution, and Design Overview
Review	

What other subjects would you like to see IBM Redbooks address?

Please rate your overall satisfaction: O Very Good   O Good   O Average   O Poor

Please identify yourself as belonging to one of the following groups:
O Customer
O Business Partner
O Solution Developer
O IBM, Lotus or Tivoli Employee
O None of the above

Your email address:
The data you provide here may be used to provide you with information from IBM or our business partners about our products, services or activities.

O Please do not use the information collected here for future marketing or promotional contacts or other communications beyond the scope of this transaction.

Questions about IBM's privacy policy?
The following link explains how we protect your personal information.
ibm.com/privacy/yourprivacy/